The Films of John Cassavetes tells the inside story of the making of six of Cassavetes' most important works: *Shadows, Faces, Minnie and Moskowitz, A Woman Under the Influence, The Killing of a Chinese Bookie,* and *Love Streams.* With the help of almost fifty previously unpublished photographs from the private collections of Sam Shaw and Larry Shaw, and excerpts from interviews with the filmmaker and many of his closest friends, the reader is taken behind the scenes to watch the maverick independent at work: writing his scripts, rehearsing his actors, blocking their movements, shooting his scenes, and editing them. Through words and pictures, Cassavetes is shown to have been a deeply thoughtful and self-aware artist and a profound commentator on the American experience.

This iconoclastic, interdisciplinary study challenges many accepted notions in film history and aesthetics. Ray Carney argues that Cassavetes' films participate in a previously unrecognized form of pragmatic American modernism that, in its ebullient affirmation of life, not only goes against the world-weariness and despair of many twentieth-century works of art, but also places his work at odds with the assumptions and methods of most contemporary film criticism. Cassavetes' films are provocatively linked to the philosophical writing of Ralph Waldo Emerson, William James, and John Dewey, both as an illustration of the artistic consequences of a pragmatic aesthetic and as an example of the challenges and rewards of a life lived pragmatically. Cassavetes' work is shown to reveal stimulating new ways of knowing, feeling, and being in the world.

"Film is an art, a beautiful art. It's a madness that overcomes us. The artist is really a magical figure. The idea of making a movie is to pack a lifetime of ideas and emotions into a two-hour form – two hours where some images flash across the screen. And the hope is that the audience will forget everything and that celluloid will change lives. That's a preposterously presumptuous assumption, yet that's the hope of every filmmaker."

The Films of John Cassavetes

CAMBRIDGE FILM CLASSICS

General Editor: Ray Carney, Boston University

Other books in the series:

Peter Bondanella, *The Films of Roberto Rossellini*
Sam B. Girgus, *The Films of Woody Allen*
Robert Phillip Kolker and Peter Beicken, *The Films of Wim Wenders*
Scott MacDonald, *Avant-Garde Film*
James Naremore, *The Films of Vincente Minnelli*
James Palmer and Michael Riley, *The Films of Joseph Losey*
Scott Simmon, *The Films of D. W. Griffith*
David Sterritt, *The Films of Alfred Hitchcock*
Maurice Yacowar, *The Films of Paul Morrissey*

The Films of John Cassavetes

Pragmatism, Modernism, and the Movies

RAY CARNEY
Boston University

Photographs by
Sam Shaw and Larry Shaw

CAMBRIDGE
UNIVERSITY PRESS

Published by the Press Syndicate of the University of Cambridge
The Pitt Building, Trumpington Street, Cambridge CB2 1RP
40 West 20th Street, New York, NY 10011-4211, USA
10 Stamford Road, Oakleigh, Melbourne 3166, Australia

First published 1994
Reprinted 1994

Printed in the United States of America

Library of Congress Cataloging-in-Publication Data is available.

A catalogue record for this book is available from the British Library.

ISBN 0-521-38119-3 hardback
ISBN 0-521-38815-5 paperback

For Diane

Dream dreams, and write them,
Aye, but live them first.

Contents

Acknowledgments   *page* ix

Introduction: Thinking in Space, Time, and the Body   1

1 Selves in the Making (*Shadows*)   27

2 Noncontemplative Art (*Faces*)   74

3 Beating the System (*Minnie and Moskowitz*)   114

4 An Artist of the Ordinary (*A Woman Under the Influence*)   143

5 The Path of Greatest Resistance (*The Killing of a Chinese Bookie*) 184

6 Compositions and Decompositions (*Love Streams*)   235

Epilogue: The Religion of Doing   271

Notes   283

Bibliography   308

Filmography   313

Index   317

Acknowledgments

This book takes its origin from two events with which I was involved: the fifteen-city American tour of the complete films of John Cassavetes, sponsored by the Walker Art Center and the Pacific Film Archive and curated by Bruce Jenkins, that took place during 1989 and 1990; and the comprehensive retrospective of the filmmaker's work presented in Avignon, France, in July 1989, at Jerome Rudes's French–American Film Workshop. In the course of organizing a series of lectures, panel discussions, and other special events to support the screenings in both countries, I had the unique opportunity to meet and get to know many of John Cassavetes' closest friends and artistic collaborators. They kindly came forward to share personal anecdotes and information about the making of the films, generously gave of their time (in scores of telephone conversations, numerous letters and written recollections, and more than two hundred hours of taped interviews), and provided me with access to previously unpublished plays, screenplays, and other writings by the filmmaker. Those individuals include: Peter Falk, Ben Gazzara, Elaine May, Seymour Cassel, Robert Fieldsteel, Larry Shaw, Sam Shaw, Al Ruban, Ted Allan, Jo Lustig, Jay Cocks, Jonas Mekas, Leola Harlow, Meta Shaw, Susan Shaw, Nancy Bishop, Lelia Goldoni, and Tim Ferris. This book could not have been written without their help. The photographs by my dear friends, Sam Shaw and Larry Shaw, which illustrate this volume and are being published in America for the first time, speak for themselves. They truly take us behind the scenes to watch this great artist at work. I am deeply grateful for their permission to use them.

Among my own circle of friends and colleagues, I would single out three individuals who helped substantially, often through their loyal opposition to some of the ideas presented here. Ara Corbett, one of the most thoughtful students of Cassavetes' work, shared many suggestive observations about the films, a few of which found their way into my argument. George Blue-stone, a friend and colleague at Boston University, helped me to refine many of my ideas, which were first presented to him in conversation. Scott Simmon of San Francisco State University kindly read the manuscript and commented copiously on it. At Cambridge University Press, Beatrice Rehl, Michael Gnat, and Cary Groner made many useful suggestions.

Since Cassavetes' films have been largely ignored by academic film schol-arship, most writing on his work still unfortunately takes place in a critical vacuum; however, I want to acknowledge how much I have learned from five scholars who have broken away from the pack: Maria Viera, Carole Zucker, George Kouvaros, Janet Zwierzynski, and my former student, Lucio Benedetto, all of whom contributed to a special "John Cassavetes" issue of *Post Script* magazine, which Gerald Duchovnay of East Texas State Uni-versity had the vision to commission. When it comes to the writings of William James and Ralph Waldo Emerson, which figure prominently in my text, I am, as always, deeply indebted to the pioneering work of Richard Poirier, a friend and former teacher. My final, and most profound, debt of gratitude is expressed in my dedication.

Introduction

Thinking in Space, Time, and the Body

The minds of some of you, I know, will absolutely . . . refuse to think in non-conceptualized terms. I myself absolutely refused to do so for years altogether. . . . I went thus through the "inner catastrophe" of which I spoke in the last lecture. I had literally come to the end of my conceptual stock in trade. I was bankrupt intellectualistically, and had to change my base. No words of mine will probably convert you, for words can be the names only of concepts. But if any of you try sincerely and pertinaciously on your own separate accounts to intellectualize reality, you may be similarly driven to a change of front.
– William James[1]

Truth is something which occurs when actions take place; not when phrases are contrived. . . . Truth is not a right word which can be printed. It is a right deed which can be done. . . . [When this is not the case, feeling] not only postpones, but *replaces* behavior in an exercise of calculated substitution.
– Jonathan Kozol[2]

The contention of the following pages is not only that John Cassavetes was one of the most important artists of the twentieth century, but that the originality of his work was precisely what doomed it to critical misunderstanding and neglect. It is a truism in the fine arts that the most profoundly original art may look ugly at first, and it would be hard to find a better illustration of the point than the initial popular and critical response to Cassavetes' *Husbands*, *The Killing of a Chinese Bookie*, *Opening Night*, or *Three Plays of Love and Hate*. Reviewers heaved brickbats at his work throughout his career. The gentler ones called it "unpolished," "meandering," "diffuse," or "undisciplined"; the less charitable labeled it "pointless," "self-indulgent," or "out of control"; the outright dismissive wrote it off as simply "dreadful" and "utterly without interest or merit" (these last two

I

appraisals are from John Simon and Stanley Kauffmann, respectively).[3] Though it seems a near miracle to be able to keep one's sense of humor in the face of such a critical pounding, Cassavetes frequently joked about the resistance to his movies. On one occasion in particular, I remember him imitating an imaginary viewer watching one of his films. He slouched down in his chair and flailed his arms wildly in front of his face, as if shielding his eyes from the fury of an atomic blast, while chortling: "A new experience? Oh, no! Save me! Anything but that!"[4]

The formulation is a telling one. Cassavetes understood that his films offered new forms of experience. When we watch them, we are asked to participate in new intellectual and emotional structures of understanding. At least for the time of the viewing experience (and to the extent we yield ourselves to it rather than defending ourselves against it), our consciousnesses are altered. Our nervous systems are reprogrammed. Our range of sensitivities is subtly (and sometimes not so subtly) shifted. We are made to notice and feel things we wouldn't otherwise. But one doesn't get to a new place without leaving old positions behind, and, as the anecdote takes for granted, the process of being exposed to new ways of knowing can present a bit of a shock to the system. The films can only teach us new understandings by forcibly denying us old ones, and that can be bewildering. They can only freshen and quicken our responses by altering our habitual modes of perception, and that can be disorienting. Their stylistic defamiliarizations and assaults are their way of doing this, and it is only to be expected that they should make us more than a little uncomfortable at moments. That, of course, is where any artist of sufficiently large ambitions risks getting into trouble with his public.

It really is an old story in the history of artistic appreciation. Marshall McLuhan pointed out that "when they are initially proposed, new systems of knowledge do not look like improvements and innovations. They look like chaos."[5] The genius of Cassavetes' work, as well as the special challenge it presents for criticism, is that it makes meanings in fundamentally different ways from most other American film. In fact, it seems clear to me that the ways of knowing that mainstream American movies accustom us to can actually get in the way of appreciating what Cassavetes is offering, which is why during his lifetime it paradoxically seemed the more "cinematically literate" the viewer or critic, the more likely it was that he would miss the point of his work.

Thus, by way of introduction to what I would argue is the most brilliant yet still most misunderstood body of work in American feature filmmaking, I want to attempt what is probably an impossible task: to characterize the reigning systems of knowledge within American film. In very brief compass (and with a certain degree of enforced simplification), I will describe what seems to me to be a pervasive system of cinematic understandings embodied by a dominant stylistic system of expression, as a prelude to indicating a few of the most important respects in which Cassavetes' work departs from it.[6] In order to facilitate the most concise yet accessible presentation of such an enormous subject, I am going to use illustrations deliberately chosen from a small number of the most familiar films by canonical directors, but I would emphasize that the stylistic syndrome I am describing is not in the least limited to these works and filmmakers, but applies to the overwhelming body of serious American dramatic filmmaking in the studio tradition from around 1940 to the present. The only additional difficulty the analysis presents is that, as is the case with any dominant system of understanding, what I am going to be describing may not seem to be a set of artistic and intellectual conventions. It may seem more like the way life is, or the way movies simply have to be. When something is everywhere, it is always a little hard to see; and it usually takes work as different as Cassavetes' to make us aware of it at all.

The dominant style embodies what might be called a visionary/symbolic aesthetic, marked by a number of interrelated stylistic proclivities which, for lack of better terms, I am going to call its essentializing, metaphorizing, subjectivizing, visionary, and contemplative tendencies. In the limited space available, I will take them up in order and deal with each as briefly as possible.

The essentializing convention manifests itself in several different stylistic tendencies, all of which are premised on a surface–depth model of expression involving a systematic redirection of attention away from what are generally considered to be relatively unimportant expressive surfaces to crucially important depths of motivation, feeling, or belief. One moves from superficial, confusing, or accidental social expressions to enduring, explanatory essences.[7] The movement inward and downward has become so much a part of the visual language of film and television that it is taken for granted by, and therefore seldom questioned by, most viewers. When "60 Minutes" intercuts a shot of an interviewee's twitching hands to convince us that he is lying; when a climactic scene in a movie or television drama uses a mood-music orchestration or an expressive close-up or lighting effect to tell us what the characters are feeling even if they aren't saying anything; when a narrative relies on "deep psychology" to account for why a character said or did something – in all of these cases, the effect is what I am calling an essentializing one. The viewer is encouraged to translate from superficial

3

public expressions to more important emotions or ideas; from fluxional or unreliable expressive surfaces to stable, constant, trustworthy underlying states of feeling and belief. (We bring this convention into our lives when we search for simplifying motives or purposes in people's otherwise puzzling or provocative behavior, when we tell ourselves that if we could only understand someone's intentions or feelings, their words or behavior would make sense.)

There are a number of ways the essentializing agenda manifests itself in film. In many movies the act of moving from surfaces to depths is facilitated by having the character simply tell us what his or her essential attitudes and feelings are. In Hitchcock's *Vertigo*, Scotty Ferguson's acrophobia and its essential effect on all of his future behavior is made the explicit subject of several of his early conversations with other characters. In *Psycho*, Norman Bates himself describes his mother complex to Marion Crane in his first major conversation with her (though without using that term, of course). However, the presentation of intentional depths or motivational essences need not be so verbal. Characters frequently "perform" their essential states of being without directly talking about them at all. Roger Thornhill's tones of voice and physical mannerisms "tell us" that he is harried, frustrated, and put-upon, yet resourceful, urbane, and dashing in virtually every scene of *North by Northwest*. In *Strangers on a Train*, Bruno's simpering tones and narcissistic behavior "declare" his willful, warped dangerousness every time he is on camera.

In slightly more complicated cases, where the characters don't directly speak or act out their essential impulses, their films do the speaking for them, through the deployment of specific stylistic effects. Just as words or actions do in the other cases, the lighting, music, framing, editing rhythms, presence of significant props, or other aspects of the film's style translate the characters' essential feelings and beliefs into clearly visible or audible events. In *Casablanca*, a key-lighting effect on Bergman's hair and face tells us that she feels things for the Bogart character long before she says anything about it or dares to act on her feelings. In *Psycho*, the lighting on Norman Bates's face, the presence of the stuffed birds, the kick-lighting of them, and the looming angles at which they are photographed when Norman and Marion are in his office, all warn us about Norman independently of anything he says or does. Even if these characters don't know their essential feelings or states of being, their film knows; even if they can't or won't tell us how they feel or what they are, the style tells us. The mutable surfaces of life are anchored in stable, deep meanings.

The stuffed birds in *Psycho* suggest the second stylistic aspect of visionary/

4

symbolic film. It is insistently metaphoric in its thrust. *Citizen Kane* is only the most extreme illustration of the tendency. At virtually every point in the film, the viewer is encouraged to make a quasi-allegorical move – to translate from the physical to the metaphysical, from worldly objects to imaginative significances, from external actions and events to indications of psychological and emotional states. The lowliest freshman in Film 101 knows to do this with *Citizen Kane* without even having to think about it. Even in the first few seconds of the film, she knows to turn mere, mundane experiences into grand, imaginative symbols of something else: From the scratched "No Trespassing" sign, to the languorous movements of the camera along the layers of fences, walls, and cages, to the desolation of the grounds around the mansion, to the snow-globe and the dying word of the lonely old man (all underpinned by lugubrious music and linked together by meditative lap dissolves), virtually every prop, piece of scenery, camera angle, lighting effect, and musical strain functions metaphorically. In this world, even the most pedestrian objects – a fence, a sign, a snow-globe – clearly don't just mean themselves, they mean something imaginative. The fence is more than a fence; it speaks of the barriers to intimacy Kane erected during his life. The "No Trespassing" sign is more than a sign; it summarizes Kane's state of self-imposed imaginative exile and its scratches tell us about his state of emotional dilapidation. The snow-globe is more than a snow-globe; it figures a youthful paradise lost. Welles locates us in a dreamscape, a world of imaginatively resonant metaphor and symbol, a realm of the imagination in which the most prosaic facts and events of ordinary life are transformed into emblems of profound spiritual realities.

Metaphors so abound in *Citizen Kane* that it is hard to find a scene, an event, or a prop that doesn't function, at least partially, in a metaphoric way. In the Christmas scene involving Thatcher and the young Kane early in the movie, the match cut of the sled left behind in the snow and the sled being opened as a present is metaphoric. The way Thatcher towers over Kane is metaphoric. The depressed camera angle is metaphoric. In the scene at Mrs. Kane's Boardinghouse, both the visual aspects of the scene (the overall background–foreground juxtaposition of the figure of the boy frolicking in the snow outside the window as the three adults whispering inside discuss his fate, and the detailed blocking of the various figures), as well as the verbal aspects of the scene (like the boy's shout of "union forever") are clearly and obviously metaphoric. In the Xanadu/jigsaw puzzle scenes, even the most naive viewer knows to read the cavernous architectural spaces, the small size of the figures, their distance from each other, and the echoic sound effects less for their manifest content than for their latent, symbolic significance. They signify Kane's emotional estrangement from Susan, and the loneliness and emptiness of their lives.

Citizen Kane may be the most thoroughgoing demonstration of this form of expression, but the metaphorization of experience is pervasive throughout most of what are regarded as being the major artworks produced within the studio system. In movies otherwise as different from one another as *The Saga of Anatahan, Psycho, The Trial, 2001, Apocalypse Now, Days of Heaven, Heaven's Gate, Blade Runner, Blue Velvet,* and *Blood Simple* (and even in mass entertainment like *Edward Scissorhands* and *Batman Returns*), events, objects, and interactions are relentlessly shifted one notch to the side to signify something more abstract and general than the mere fact. Virtually nothing is simply itself.

The metaphoric turn is actually only an instance of a more general phenomenon that might be called the subjectivizing of experience in these works. The Hollywood studio tradition, especially when it is functioning at its most "artistic," is devoted to using external actions, objects, events, and sounds to figure internal states of feeling or awareness. Objects and events become outward and visible signs of inward and spiritual conditions. The contents of the world are systematically translated into the contents of consciousness. Scene after scene in Hitchcock's major American work (*North by Northwest, Vertigo, Rear Window, Psycho*) functions in this way. When Hitchcock backprojects waves crashing on the shore behind Scotty and Madeline as they kiss in *Vertigo*, and edits their sound into the film, it's obvious that he is not interested in the ocean but in a visible and acoustic representation of Scotty's surging feelings. In *Psycho*, when Marion Crane drives to the Bates motel, the time of night, the rainstorm, the glare of the headlights in her eyes all function principally as expressions of her consciousness. She is in a storm at night but it is clearly not outer, but inner weather that we are seeing. The rainstorm is an external and, as a literal event, a relatively unimportant indication of her storm of emotion (which is why all signs of the rain can suddenly disappear as soon as her mood shifts or another character steps to the center of the narrative).

Although solitary or silent scenes favor it, the subjectivizing project is operant even in many scenes when more than one character is present. Consider the bravura concluding sequence in *Casablanca*, the final parting of Rick, Ilsa, and Lazlo on the airport runway (with Renault and another minor character looking on). Every bit as much as Hitchcock does during Marion Crane's drive and Welles does at the start of *Kane*, but with five characters present at once, Curtiz moves the moment out of the realm of worldly events and into a realm of interior imaginative eventfulness. In a standard stylistic pattern that is repeated at climactic moments in hundreds of films, four things take place: the characters are immobilized; the action of the scene is put on pause; the dialogue is more or less stopped; and the photography switches to a series of intercut tight closeups.[8] In this particular instance, in more than thirty eyeline-matched shot–reverse shots, Curtiz has Humphrey Bogart, Ingrid Bergman, and Paul Henreid exchange emotionally freighted glances with only the minimum number of lines of dialogue as a pretext to motivate them: Rick looks at Ilsa; Ilsa looks at Rick; Ilsa looks at Lazlo; Lazlo looks at Ilsa; Lazlo looks at Rick; Rick looks at Lazlo; all three look at the plane revving up; Rick looks at Ilsa again; Ilsa looks at Rick; Ilsa looks at Lazlo; Ilsa looks at Rick, and so on. The "action" of the scene is almost entirely interior. For two or three minutes, the expressive mode of the film shifts from worldly action to imaginative reaction, from halting, fumbling speech to richly eloquent, emotionally charged silences. Even the revving of the airplane's propellers that punctuates the sequence at one moment really only functions as a kind of objective correlative for the revving up of the character's and viewers' emotions. To paraphrase a line Bergman speaks earlier in the movie, this is a world in which the sound of cannon fire *is* the sound of one's heart pounding.

As the scene with Rick, Ilsa, and Lazlo illustrates, Hollywood's subjectivizing stylistic project accomplishes a subtle but profound redefinition of the relationship of the self to the world. To the maximum extent possible within the formal constraints of a dramatic work of art, the "I" is turned into an "eye," and life is made visionary (in both the optical and the imaginative sense of the word). Hitchcock's works are virtually machines for creating narrative situations in which visual and visionary relationships take the place of physical, social, or verbal ones. That is to say, what *Casablanca* does only intermittently, Hitchcock does almost continuously. Throughout many of the major scenes in *North by Northwest*, *Rear Window*, *Vertigo*, and *Psycho*, the main characters are placed in situations in which only a visual/visionary relationship with their surroundings is available. As much as possible, they are silenced, physically immobilized, moved to a certain distance from the objects of their attention, and confined to visual relationships with them: L. B. Jeffries sits in one place and looks through his telephoto lens at his neighbors across the courtyard; Roger Thornhill flees a crop duster in a cornfield or stands outside a house on top of Mount Rushmore staring through the windows, but unable to communicate directly with the people in the plane or the house; Scotty Ferguson rides around in his car watching Madeline travel from place to place and speculating about what it all means, but unable to interact with her; Arbogast and Lila Crane wander through the Bates mansion turning it into a series of strictly visual experiences. In being socially or physically marginalized and denied possibilities of closer contact with or more direct involvement and interaction with what they see, these characters are prevented from doing anything other than looking, seeing, thinking, and feeling. They turn themselves into transparent eyeballs, living intensely through their eyes and in their minds and emotions, but relinquishing virtually every other way of being in the world.

The agenda is obviously a visionary one. These characters sacrifice possibilities of social relationship or physical interaction with the persons and objects in front of them to be freer to speculate, wonder, and think about them. They keep down their social involvements and expressions in order to enlarge their imaginative functions. In slightly contracting the character's physical presence (keeping him immobile), easing the requirements of social expressiveness (keeping him silent), and disencumbering him from physical involvements and social responsibilities (having him look at people he doesn't know or can't directly interact with), possibilities of purely imaginative relationship are enriched. In systematically substituting forms of vision (both optical and imaginative) for forms of action and practical social expression, the range of emotional associations and sympathies is enormously enlarged.

This expansion of imaginative possibilities is supported by the point-of-view shooting and editing convention. Point-of-view shooting and editing (which is almost universal throughout Hollywood filmmaking) is premised on the belief in truth expressible through seeing, and on the possibility of "looking" relationships and knowledge into existence. Seeing, feeling, knowing, and being are equated, so that to "see" something is to feel or know it; to feel or know it is to "be" it. Once this equation is made, characters are able to leave the complexities of physical involvement and practical expression behind. To "know" in this way is not to have to say or do anything. To "be" in this way is to liberate oneself from having to express one's being in a more practical way.

What is more important than a character's imaginative stance, however, is the viewer's. The viewer is placed in almost exactly the same imaginative position as one of the characters in these films. He is moved to a slight distance from what he sees in order to enter into a specially liberated and imaginatively enriched relationship with it. Like the character, he is encouraged to hold the world at an imaginative arm's length, as it were, the better to be free to speculate, wonder, and think about the objects of his attention. He takes one step backward, imaginatively speaking, from phenomenal events, and enters into a fundamentally conceptual or intellectual relationship with them. In a word, he assumes an essentially contemplative relationship with experience.

There are several ways this is accomplished. Hitchcock's work, and other films that rigorously employ point-of-view shooting and editing, make the viewer collaborate with the character simply by compelling him to see things through the character's eyes and therefore to some extent to see them in a way similar to how the character does. The viewer of *North by Northwest* or *Psycho* enters into the same intense, speculative, yet slightly intellectual relationship with what Roger Thornhill sees in the house on Mount Rushmore and what Lila Crane sees in the Bates mansion as do the characters. The viewer of *Vertigo*, held at the same visual and imaginative distance from Madeline that Scotty is, and therefore denied the possibility of entering into a more intimate or emotional involvement with her, wonders along with Scotty as he follows her across northern California. The viewer of *Rear Window*, kept at the same physical and emotional distance from what he sees as is L. B. Jeffries, is consequently compelled to assume virtually the same intellectual relationship with it that Jeffries has. In being held at a certain, crucial distance, the viewer's relationship with what is seen becomes somewhat detached and abstracted.

This point-of-view editing convention is only one way in which works in this tradition cultivate a fundamentally contemplative relationship with what is seen, however, and filmmakers entirely less devoted to point-of-view shooting and editing than Hitchcock create the same effect in many other ways. The visual sublimities of Kubrick's work, the metaphoric insistence of Welles's, the mythopoetic freightings of Coppola's, the photographic preciousness of Lynch's or De Palma's, the narrative mannerism of Joel Coen's, are all ways of moving the viewer to a slightly distanced imaginative position from the experiences presented. In fact, the entire narrative project of the visionary/symbolic mode of filmmaking, as I have been describing it, is a way of placing the world at a certain imaginative distance. Insofar as experience is aestheticized or generalized, the essentializing, metaphorizing, and subjectivizing tendencies each, ever so slightly, relax the claims of the visible and audible world and induce a moderate state of abstraction in the viewer. In being allowed to contemplate the abstract imaginative or psychological significance of events, props, and stylistic effects, the viewer is released from responding more intimately. He is moved to a slight meditative distance from experience. (I would note that in many films, *Citizen Kane* being only the most blatant example, even the characters themselves play the distancing game, repeatedly offering abstract or intellectual interpretations of their own and other characters' actions. After so many sermons about Kane's "need for love," it is hard not to have a fairly abstract stance toward specific scenes.)

The result, however achieved, is to change the nature of experience. In moving the world into the mind, reality is ever so slightly derealized. When concepts replace percepts, the world is subtly drained of some of its sensory content, its idiosyncrasy, its prickly particularity, its unpredictability, its mutability. In being made to illustrate abstract points, the edges of perceptual experience are rounded and its roughness smoothed.

Now it is of the essence of Cassavetes' oeuvre (and undoubtedly the source of many of his problems with audiences and critics) that it declines to understand experience in these ways. His films simply reject essentializing, metaphorizing, subjectivizing, abstracting, and contemplative forms of knowledge and relationship. Sensorily concrete ways of knowing replace metaphorical or abstract ones. Perceptions replace conceptions. A sweaty, assaultive, in-your-face intensity of involvement with experience takes the place of the contemplative distance that the other sort of film cultivates.

The essentializing and metaphorizing tendencies of films within the visionary/symbolic tradition inevitably clarify, tame, and stabilize the potential confusions of perceptual experience in certain respects: The complexity of surface events is able to be traced back to simplifying "deep" meanings. A character's fluxional expressions of himself are anchored in enduring intentions and qualities. Behavioral quirks are traced back to an essential, unchanging core of being. Cassavetes simply rejects that understanding of experience. Viewers are denied access to intentional depths, and asked to navigate shifting (and potentially bewildering) expressive surfaces. As an illustration, consider the scene near the beginning of *Faces*, in which two men, Freddie and Richard, vie for the affection of a girl named Jeannie. Rather than allowing the viewer to redirect his attention from surface events to clarifying imaginative depths, Cassavetes forces him to grapple with unanalyzed and unexplained expressive surfaces. The viewer is put in the position of not knowing quite who the characters are, why they are behaving in the way they are, or exactly how to interpret their specific expressions. Furthermore, the characters keep changing: They are nice one moment and nasty the next, considerate at one point, self-centered at another. The consequence is to force the viewer to abandon the attempt to trace expressive behavior back to a reductive set of "essential" intentions, feelings, and attitudes (that is, if it doesn't send him scurrying out of the theater in bewilderment). The viewing process is changed completely. While the other kind of film encourages us to tunnel under perceptual instabilities and expressive vagaries, Cassavetes holds us on the phenomenal surfaces of life

10

almost to the point of sensory overload. We surf on a wave of shifting sensory experience: anxiously, uncertainly, carefully reading unanalyzed bodily movements, voice tones, gestures, and facial expressions.

This is a world in which experience is not transparent (allowing us to look through a turbulent, changeable surface to a stable resolving depth), but opaque. There is nothing but surface. There are no clarifying essences, explanatory metaphors, or private depths of subjectivity by means of which we can get inside characters and events to simplify them. Cassavetes rejects the Romantic convention of the redeeming or explaining "interior." There is no explanatory secret, no revelatory clue, no deep explanation. What we see and hear is, in the most profound sense, all that "is." To borrow a phrase from William James's "Pragmatism and Humanism" (with James's own emphasis), "behind the bare, phenomenal facts...there is *nothing*."[9]

An important ramification of the shift from conceptions to perceptions is that the experience of time is brought back for both characters and viewers. Essential or metaphorical truth is freed not only from perceptual complexity, but from perceptual changeability. Cassavetes' truth is temporal. It is created by characters and received by viewers in time. Because all film relies on time for its effects, one might naturally enough assume that all cinematic experience is equally temporal in nature, but the crucial difference is that the events in visionary/symbolic works conceptually and spatially pattern themselves in ways that let the viewer largely disregard their temporal unfolding, while those in Cassavetes' force him to mount the stream of time, picking his way, moment by moment, through a sequence of changing events – continuously revising his understanding of the previous moment in the light of the subsequent one.

Juxtapose any conversation in *Citizen Kane* or *The Trial* with one in Cassavetes' *Shadows* or *Faces* and the chasm that looms between the two forms of presentation is apparent. Welles employs a variety of methods – interpretive framing, tendentious camera angles and lighting, special lenses, symbolic props, editorializing blockings, mood-music orchestrations – to facilitate the reading of a series of atemporal patterns out of the interactions between his characters. The meanings of his scenes, almost without exception, are summarized by a static visual pattern (e.g., the blocking of characters' relative positions or a lighting effect on their faces), a dominant metaphor or symbolic object (the "No Trespassing" sign or snow-globe), or a mood-establishing musical strain on the sound track. In contrast, characters, events, and interactions in *Shadows* and *Faces* almost never abstractly declare their meanings in these ways. They don't pattern themselves out of time – visually, metaphorically, or acoustically.[10] Cassavetes suspends his characters and viewers in a present-tense universe in which one small thing after another must be patiently observed and pieced together without being able to predict where anything is headed. In the scene with Richard, Freddie, and Jeannie in *Faces*, the bodies of the three figures clumsily approach and withdraw from each other. Their voice tones hesitantly suggest, then anxiously retract, possibilities. Their faces ripple with shifting expressions. The viewer is never able to rise above the perceptual tumble to organize what is happening in terms of a concept. The experiences Cassavetes presents keep moving out from under any scheme of understanding within which we would contain them. (As I will demonstrate in the following chapters, to the extent that patterns of expression do emerge even in Cassavetes' work, they are moved against by his own deliberate pattern-breaking countermovements.)

The nature of knowledge changes from what it is in a conceptually organized work. Knowledge does not loft us above the uncertainty of perceptual experience, but involves coming to grips with its temporality, tentativeness, uncertainty, and partiality. It is not accidental that most of the directors in the visionary/symbolic tradition (including Welles) favor generally static blockings to communicate characters' relative imaginative and social positions, while Cassavetes (like Jean Renoir or Vittorio De Sica) presents bodies and expressions almost continuously in motion. For the one kind of filmmaking truth can be schematically summarized because it stands still; for the other it will never stop moving long enough to be storyboarded, lighted, or summarized in a static image. Welles's scenes are the equivalent of dramatic tableaus. His emphasis on visual and spatial forms of organization (the way paintings are organized, rather than the way works of music are) means that his scenes and shots usually telegraph their meanings more or less instantaneously. We can almost always "get" the meaning of a scene in *Kane* or *The Trial* at a glance. It is of the essence of the experience of *Shadows* and *Faces* that their truths are created by characters (and understood by viewers) only gradually. Cassavetes' figures are everything in our process of discovering them, and nothing outside of that process. They are everything at one particular moment, shot, and scene, and something else the next.

Essentializing and metaphorical modes of presentation can even take the time out of an explicitly temporal series of events. Consider the montage of conversations between Kane and his new bride, Emily, depicting the disintegration of their marriage. Months of married life are condensed into a few telling gestures, looks, and snippets of conversation amounting to no more than two or three minutes of running time. At that ratio of compression, the conceptual packaging is more or less all there is. There are plenty of ideas *about* experience and metaphors *for* experience, but very little actual perceptual experience. Welles's relative indifference to the detailed presentation of facts and events (a depiction of what Kane and Emily actually said and did over the course of many months) is compensated for by the enormity of the truckload of abstract meanings about their situation he dumps in our laps. In effect, conceptual knowledge is the only kind permitted. We are clued into Kane and his wife's increasing estrangement from one another through: changes in the musical accompaniment; the increasingly chilly tones of their voices; the increasing severity of Emily's clothing, makeup, and hairdos; changes in the lighting on her face; Kane's progressively more businesslike costuming and increasing preoccupation with reading the newspaper at the table; and, in the final shot, the space that looms between them at the breakfast table. The sequence is virtually allegorical: It reads loud and clear as "the disintegration of a marriage," which is to say that phenomenal events are not allowed to complicate its transmission of intellectual meanings.

In starkest possible contrast, in *Faces*, the depiction of Richard and his wife's mutual discontent, their failures of communication, their large and small emotional betrayals takes place in time and space, and with sensory particularity – slowly and excruciatingly. Rather than giving us intellectual outlines of experience, metaphoric or symbolic summaries, conceptual shorthand sketches about marital decline, Cassavetes forces the viewer to live through a confusing welter of ungeneralizable perceptual events. He presents knowledge that cannot be disentangled from space and time.

Another way of putting this difference is to say that while the visionary/symbolic tradition takes us up into our heads, Cassavetes calls us to the reality of our bodies. His truth is embodied, enacted, performed. Performed truth is different from metaphorical, essential, or subjective truth because it is anchored in the body. In Cassavetes' work, meaning is not brought into existence intellectually or abstractly. It is not located in the heart or the mind (and thereby able to be communicated by a lighting effect or a musical strain on the sound track). It is not visionary (in either the optical or the imaginative sense). It is enacted in a practical expressive transaction between two or more characters. Jimmy Stewart and Cary Grant can "look" truths into existence in a Hitchcock movie, but Cassavetes' actors must "do" them. Bogart and Bergman can commune imaginatively at the end of *Casablanca* without saying or doing anything at all. Meaning is abstract in

13

those films. It can be the product of an act of looking, thinking, or feeling; but in order for Cassavetes' characters to "mean" anything, they must talk, gesture, move, and physically interact.

The difference points to a fundamental difference in the function of the actor in the two kinds of films. In mainstream American filmmaking (and especially the work of virtuoso practitioners of the symbolic/visionary mode of expression like Hitchcock, Lang, Welles, Sternberg, Kubrick, Malick, Spielberg, Lynch, and the Coens), the actor is *not* the fundamental generator and controller of meaning; the filmmaker is. Following in the footsteps of Kuleshov and Eisenstein, the most important meanings in these works are created separate from the actor's body and are stylistically imposed upon it (with a mood-music orchestration, an expressive lighting effect, an editing effect, or in some other way). The actor is the more or less passive recipient of meanings created and manipulated by the nonactors in the production: the director, cameraman, editor, set designer, musical orchestrator, and scriptwriter. In Cassavetes' work, the movements, gestures, postures, facial expressions, and voice tones of the actor are the fundamental source of meaning. Of course, it is not that there are *no* extrapersonal visual or acoustic meanings in Cassavetes' work, but the meanings made by the pro-duction's nonactors are always secondary to, and supportive of, the mean-ings made by its actors. Even the most benighted reviewers of Cassavetes' work noticed this when they called it an "actors' cinema." What they were responding to was that meaning was generated and controlled by the expres-sions of the actors' faces, bodies, and voices. It was performed, rather than, as in mainstream American filmmaking, being created in what is usually called more "purely cinematic" ways.

It would be hard to overstate the unusualness of Cassavetes' decision to let the actors bear the expressive burden in his work. It is extremely rare for a director to use the acting – the faces, bodies, and movements of individuals – and not the impetus of the narrative, the abstract meaning of characters' speeches, or the visual and acoustic style, to carry the meaning. It is to embrace an expressive challenge that virtually all other films choose to avoid. In works as different from one another as *Rear Window*, *2001*, *Apocalypse Now*, *Blood Simple*, and *Bob Roberts*, the acting is almost entirely what accomplished stage actors call "indication," meaning it does not actually use the face, body, and voice to create the meaning, but rather involves the pantomiming of an expression that the nonacted aspects of the film (the dialogue, lighting, music, narrative events, etc.) then persuade the viewer to interpret in a particular way.

To know what Kane means in the political convention, we primarily consult the visual and acoustic style (and secondarily, the meaning of his spoken words). Neither involves any acting in Cassavetes' sense of the concept. Kane "is" the effects of the mise-en-scène, the lighting, the focal length of the lenses used, the framing, the camera angles, the distances at which he is photographed, the acoustic processing of his voice. When Welles dwarfs his figure in this scene or in later scenes at Xanadu; when Kubrick accompanies a shot of a space station with the music of Strauss in *2001;* when Hitchcock uses Bernard Herrmann's music on the sound track, and kick-lights Janet Leigh's face during the driving in the rain scene in *Psycho,* the viewer is given an expression of the meaning of the moment or the characters independent of the actual, practical, personal, bodily expressions of the actors. In contrast, to know what Richard and Freddie "are" in *Faces* we have to watch John Marley's and Fred Draper's faces and bodily expressions, and listen to their voices with extraordinary care and sensitivity. Nothing else tells us what they mean.

The difference between performed and stylistically indicated meanings makes an enormous difference in the nature of interpersonal expression and interaction in the two kinds of films. Visionary stylistics makes unmediated expression possible, both between characters and between characters and viewers. Communication becomes a form of mind reading. It is not only clear, automatic, and nearly instantaneous, but is stunningly untrammeled by linguistic entailments. That's what happens in the scene on the tarmac in *Casablanca.* Visionary stylistics make possible virtual transfusions of consciousness between Rick, Ilsa, and Lazlo, as if the contents of consciousness could simply be poured through the eyes from one character to another, as well as from the characters' eyes into those of the viewers. Eyes speak to eyes. Mind communes with mind. Heart responds to heart. Rick, Ilsa, Lazlo, and the viewer participate in a visionary community of complete and absolute understanding. In these nearly telepathic exchanges of feeling and knowledge, neither the inherent resistance of spoken words nor the clumsy mediations of bodily and gestural language impede the frictionless, perfect communion of spirits.

Insofar as point-of-view shooting and editing presents experience in terms of glances and visions, it reinforces this narrative project by offering an almost purely disembodied, nonsensory, derealized model of experience. These works take truth out of our bodies or actions and relocate it in our minds. In the most extreme cinematic examples (like the scene on the tarmac), the world is turned into glances – a series of intellectually freighted looks and emotionally charged stares, usually presented in close-up. But whether in close-up (*Casablanca* or *Twin Peaks*) or in long-shot (*Rear*

Window and *Vertigo*), life is made visionary. Characters might as well be brains in vats. Bodies cease to matter and speech is silenced. Presentations of pure states of vision and feeling are systematically substituted for practical, worldly expressions of the self. Seeing or feeling something substitutes for doing something.[11] Meaning is moved out of the world of action and event and relocated in the mind and emotions. Intentions replace actions. Truth migrates inward, away from practical, social expression. (The verbal correlative to this migration of meaning away from the body and senses and into the mind and feelings is that the bald statement of something is allowed to take the place of the complex enactment of it. Abstract declarations of ideas, beliefs, or intentions are allowed to substitute for intricate bodily expressions and mediated social presentations of one's meanings.)

In short, we are in the realm of what I previously called the contemplative turn out of bodily and expressive life. The contemplative turn clearly speaks to a deep cultural need, or these films would not have been so widely viewed and accepted. The desire to disengage from the arena of action and expand into the realm of vision obviously appeals to many viewers; but, however pervasive and appealing, Cassavetes utterly rejects this entire form of knowing and being. The contemplative turn was, for him, a turn out of life. To look but not touch, to feel but not act, to see but not speak, was to deny everything that mattered in experience. It was to renounce the world of action. It was to flee from the life of the senses. It was to do nothing less than to forsake the world. His works tell us in all but words that in moving from perceptions to conceptions, from involvements to visions, from expressions to feelings, we lose part of life, and not the least part. In taking the world up into our minds, the world of actions is ever so slightly drained of importance. In allowing sensibility to substitute for behavior, we repudiate the world of the senses and the body. For truth to leak out of the realm of events and migrate into the intellect and unexpressed states of emotion, was to lose virtually everything that he regarded as being true.[12]

For Cassavetes, as for William James, truth is not an intellectual relation, but a course of action. It is not a state of consciousnesses, but a form of practice. Meaning is not a conceptual, intellectual, or visionary clarification of the clutter of experience, but a way of living and moving within that clutter. Meaning is not a mental phenomenon, but is anchored in, and cannot be abstracted from, our actual tones, gestures, and social expressions of ourselves. In Cassavetes' antivisionary cinema, "deep" feelings, beliefs, visions, intentions, or goals count for nothing except insofar as they are translated into practical expressive acts. Cassavetes delivers us into a world in which not the abstract knowing or the being, but the expressive doing is what counts. He would have agreed with Emerson when he wrote (in section five of the first "Nature" essay) that the function of life is "all to form the Hand of the mind – to instruct us that good thoughts are no better than good dreams, unless they be executed!"[3] Cassavetes' works refuse to allow their characters to entertain an intellectual or visionary relationship with the events in their lives, and refuse to allow their viewers to entertain an intellectual or visionary relationship with the characters or events on screen. Both are held in the realm of the visible and tangible. Both are asked to embrace the world, not rise above it. Characters are required to live in and to express themselves in space, time, and the body, and the viewer is required to learn how to feel and know in those same ways.

The consequence of Cassavetes' commitment to anchoring his films in bodily expressions and sensory reality is that personal expression becomes much more complex than it is in the other kind of work. Where consciousness cannot be weightlessly expressed or frictionlessly exchanged between characters, it must be relayed from one character to another (and from the characters to the viewer) in a series of frictional, error-prone, inherently imperfect acts of translation. Expression becomes inherently problematic. One of the recurring subjects of Cassavetes' work is, in fact, the difficulty of self-expression. The subject can't really arise at all in a film like *Psycho* or *Casablanca*. Marion Crane, Rick, or Ilsa don't have problems expressing themselves within their works since they simply "are" whatever their glances and the stylistic effects of their films tell us they are. They don't have the problems that Cassavetes' characters do of translating their consciousnesses into forms of performed behavior, because they can simply "glance" their feelings into expression.

The audience has to work less hard in those films, too. Conceptions are easier to deal with than perceptions. Statements of intention are easier to understand than presentations of behavior. Performed meanings inherently defy conceptual appropriation (just as they do in a work of dance). Embodied meanings are more multivalent and temporally evanescent than disembodied meanings. While the visual metaphors and symbolic stylistics in the visionary/symbolic tradition figure knowledge that has been cleaned up, cut up, and boiled down to conceptual essences, Cassavetes forces the viewer to wade through something much closer to dirty, unanalyzed, raw data. He leaves the imperfections and noise and mistakes of an expressive interaction in, while Sternberg, Hitchcock, and Welles take them out. The result is that their stylistic effects will always speak more eloquently and clearly about their characters and situations than Cassavetes' and his characters' nonconceptual, nonvisionary, nonmetaphoric forms of expression.

Visionary action at a distance allows interactions to be smooth and disembodied; experience in Cassavetes' work is jagged, lumpy, and prickly. Visionary action at a distance allows you to keep your hands clean expressively; Cassavetes asks his characters to roll up their sleeves and get them dirty. Lynch's, Kubrick's, and the Coens' scenes will be clear to a degree Cassavetes' never approach. The beauty of Rick and Ilsa's acts of imaginative communion is replaced by a jittery melee of bodies in motion and collision in *Faces*. The visual sublimities of *2001* are replaced by the confusion of flawed verbal and physical expressions in *Minnie and Moskowitz*.

Cassavetes presents something much harder to read than pantomime glances and visionary stylistics: sly tones, changing facial expressions, unpredictable bodily movements, and ambiguous gestures, compromised by deviousness and deceit, muddled by conflicting emotional agendas, and confused by the characters' own expressive clumsiness.[14] In the scene with Richard, Freddie, and Jeannie, it is not at all clear during their dance of mutual attraction and repulsion what is going on at each moment. The scene is hard to understand, and even when momentarily understood is hard to keep up with, since wherever it is at one moment it is sure to be somewhere else the next. Cassavetes employs a language of the body and the face that is far more complex and fluid than the language of visionary/symbolic works.

Cassavetes' method, then, changes the way we watch a movie, changes what counts as knowledge in it, and changes how we feel about it and use it. Truths created in time and space and embedded in the body are necessarily different from essential truths. Meaning is received (both by viewers and by characters) with interruptions and delays, and requires continuous updating and correction. Sensorily concrete truth has none of the generality and authority of abstract truth. While these other filmmakers put their mastery on display, and make meanings that are masterful, enduring, and richly resonant, Cassavetes reminds us that errors (and activities of error correction) are in the nature of all experience, and that making and decoding meanings are fallible, imperfect processes.

He reminds us that we live life thick, before it has been thinned down into essences, metaphors, or patterns, and that we can't rise above the thickness without fundamentally betraying the truths of felt experience. That is why he declines to provide shorthand stylistic understandings or a guided tour through the experiences he presents in the form of mood music, expressive lighting, tendentious framing, or visual metaphors. His favorite shot at a climactic moment is not an expressive close-up, nor a close-up at all, but a medium-distance shot that includes more than one character, in which we don't quite know where to look, what we are supposed to see, or what conclusions we are meant to draw. Cassavetes doesn't make points, direct our understanding, or editorialize about what we see and hear. His world is not cut into bite-sized pieces for ready intellectual consumption. He wants to restore the perceptual density and cognitive complexity that the visionary/symbolic aesthetic elides, the emotional multivalence and fragmentation it unifies. He wants to compel his viewers to come to grips with temporal realities that it omits. In the service of doing that, he is willing to put the viewer through an experience in which the learning curve may be quite steep for a long while. Of course, he knows that that may drive out of the theater a few viewers who want their experiences easier than those he offers. They want to be told what to notice, think, and feel, so as not to be asked to work so hard, to live so intensely, for themselves.

Unlike *Citizen Kane*, the opening minutes of *The Killing of a Chinese Bookie* offer absolutely nothing in the way of a summarizing metaphor about the meaning of the main character's life and work. In fact, they do the opposite, pushing the viewer through a series of fragmented, partial views that don't add up. *Bookie* calls us to a world very different from the pellucidness of *Kane*: a world where objects and events don't have "significant" written all over them, a world of mystery, complexity, and uncertainty, a world that defies imaginative possession at a distance. The principal character, Cosmo Vitelli, makes no "Rosebud" pronouncements, nor does his creator. Rather than ushering us into a magic kingdom of luscious symbolic resonances, directing our attention, and controlling our interpretive process, as Welles does, Cassavetes asks us to pick our way slowly and uncertainly through unanalyzed perceptual events for which conceptual understandings are unavailable. While filmmakers in the visionary/symbolic tradition use metaphors and essential understandings to clarify and resolve meanings, Cassavetes plunges us into the middle of a muddle of nonmeanings, conflicting meanings, incomplete meanings, and unresolved possibilities. The stylistic parsings and highlightings of experience in the visionary/symbolic tradition speed up and facilitate reading, while Cassavetes slows it down and troubles it. He works to delay understanding as long as possible, because in his view understanding is a form of closure to experience. In a word, at any moment, it's almost impossible to know exactly what we are seeing, why it matters, or what it signifies – if anything. This is not merely an initial condition. Even after *The Killing of a Chinese Bookie* is over, we are still probably at least a little uncertain what we have lived through. Even after we have seen *Faces* or *Opening Night* four or five times, their meanings haven't attained the clarity and definitiveness with which meaning in the other kind of film starts off.

There is no question that the very originality of Cassavetes' work was one of the principal reasons it met with such widespread resistance. Critics and viewers went in looking for essentializing presentations of experience and left frustrated when they couldn't find them. They searched for metaphors to guide their interpretive process and were bewildered when none were forthcoming. They craved visual elegance and verbal eloquence, and Cassavetes gave them expressive sprawl and perceptual clutter. (Not having a clue as to how to explain this, most of Cassavetes' critics misattributed it to the scripts being improvised and the camerawork and editing being careless.) What critics like Kael, Canby, Kauffmann, and Simon failed to realize was that Cassavetes' goal was not to play the same expressive game as Lynch, the Coens, or Kubrick, but to drop out of it altogether.

I want to conclude by focusing on two specific aspects of Cassavetes' work that are important to understanding his first film, *Shadows*. Cassavetes had a fundamentally different notion of selfhood from filmmakers working in the mainstream American tradition, as well as a fundamentally different conception of the self's relationship with others. To take up the first issue, in Cassavetes' work, the self is opened up to a degree that is simply not encountered in most other films. It is fluid and changeable. This is different from the situation in any of the mainstream films I have mentioned. Given their simplifying and essentializing tendencies, it is in the nature of these works that they endow their characters with more or less established, resolved identities, identities that are stable and closed off from change.

Consider Hitchcock's work as an example one more time. In *Strangers on a Train*, it's obvious that, no matter what is said or done to them, diabolical Bruno will be Bruno and genial Guy will be Guy. They're never going to be any different; and for either of them to change even a little would, in fact, violate everything the film stands for. Similarly, no matter what indignities Roger Thornhill is subjected to, he will always be the same charming, slightly harried character he is in the first minutes of *North by Northwest*. These characters will be themselves, because they have selves – definite, defined, formulated selves – to be.

Contrast that with the genuine unpredictability of the identities Cassavetes creates. Cassavetes was often criticized for the vagueness or imprecision of his characters, but that is only another way of saying that in his work the self is less a bundle of fixed attributes and attitudes, a set of qualities to be presented to the world and maintained against change, than a capacity of continuously adjusted awareness and responsiveness. To adapt one of William James's formulations, for Cassavetes the self is less something made than something forever in the making. All of Cassavetes' major figures powerfully communicate the impression of selfhood in process. Lelia, Jeannie, Chet, Moskowitz, Mabel, Cosmo, Myrtle, Gloria, and Sarah Lawson just won't sit still for a psychological portrait. Their identities are flexible, fluxional, and, at least partially, unformulated. They keep revising themselves, often, it seems, for no particular reason. They change merely to find out what the change will feel like. Much of Lelia's mugging, vamping, and general "carrying on" in *Shadows* (and much of Gus's, Mabel's, or Gloria's similar behavior in later films) seems completely self-generated, spontaneous, and impulsive, done sheerly for the fun of fooling around with different possible tones, styles, stances, and identities.

The consequence is not only to make a character's moment-to-moment expressions much less predictable than they are in the other sort of film (we never know what Lelia or Mabel is going to say or do next), but to make his or her relationships with other characters much more volatile. When the identities of the individuals in a social or emotional relationship are so fluxional, scenes become open to possibility. Scenes and interactions don't follow a linear path of development. Expressive tangents and diversions, sudden arguments, surprising jokes, crazy switches of tone keep intruding. Interactions between characters become genuinely open-ended, unmechanical, unpredictable. Where characters are so ready to change themselves, seemingly anything can happen, and does: There is almost no telling where a scene or human relationship is headed from one minute to the next in Cassavetes' work.

But the openness of Cassavetes' characters is much more radical than their merely being open to change or defying prediction, and that leads to the second difference between Cassavetes' characters and those in virtually all other American feature film. The Cassavetean self is open in the sense of pulling down the walls that normally separate one character from another. Like onstage performers, characters like Lelia, Mabel, and Gloria make themselves up and revise themselves in a continuous process of dramatic improvisation in response to the different audiences before which they appear. Their identities are relational; they are, at least in part, negotiated with others. Cassavetes' leading characters figure an extreme degree of awareness of, sensitivity to, and responsiveness to others; yet that is not to put it strongly enough. Cassavetes' characters are so open to external influences and so willing to make adjustments in their positions that it would be better to say that it is as if their identities are not theirs alone, but are shared with others. They are not in complete control of their selves, but turn over part of the control to others. Their selves are not solid and bounded, but soft and permeable; others reach into them, affect them, change them, and at times even inhabit them. They allow themselves to be possessed by others. Their identities are supremely vulnerable – continuously susceptible to violation or deformation.

This figures an entirely different imaginative situation from the one in Hitchcock's work, in which the characters are not only closed off from change, but equally closed off from each other. The major figures in Hitchcock's work (including Bruno, Guy, Roger Thornhill, L. B. Jeffries, Scotty Ferguson, Marion Crane, and Norman Bates) embody a sense of the self as an almost completely self-sufficient, self-contained, walled fortress of consciousness – a consciousness so private, inward, isolated, and shielded from contact with other consciousnesses that it might as well be surrounded by a moat. Our consciousnesses estrange us; they make us islands unto ourselves. Notice how in *Psycho*, for example, every experience, every encounter, every object Marion Crane, Norman Bates, Arbogast, Lila Crane, and Sam come into contact with is instantly dropped into their own well of private and incommunicable interests, obsessions, and feelings. There is no attempt at communication, no desire for communication, and no communication possible even if there were either.

The Hitchcock character is so encased in the armor of his autonomous, unitary, insulated subjectivity that, far from having a relational identity, he can be said hardly even to come into contact with anyone else, let alone to open himself to being psychologically reached by them, emotionally wounded by them, or changed by them. The Hitchcockian self is so finished, stable, and consistent that there is no room left for anyone else to get inside it. In all of Hitchcock's work, no matter how many characters may be present in a scene at once, the individual figures never deeply reach each other spiritually, emotionally, or imaginatively. In a word, interactions are not genuinely interactional. As Arbogast's or Sam's conversation with Norman Bates in *Psycho* (or Lila's and Sam's earlier conversation with the county sheriff) illustrate, Hitchcock's characters are walled into established positions which, in the course of a conversation or other interaction, they merely maintain and defend. Conversation between two characters consists of the comparison or collision (depending on whether the encounter is friendly or hostile) of one fixed, closed-off position with another. The participants are billiard balls who bounce off each other without ever touching more deeply or allowing themselves to be touched.

Even characters in the most putatively "intimate" relationships in Hitchcock's works never really open up to each other. There is a line in *North by Northwest* about Roger Thornhill getting under Eve Kendall's skin, but that is precisely what Hitchcock's maintenance of states of inviolable subjectivity prevents from happening. In the unintentionally ironic metaphor of the film, the obvious fact is that they never touch each other more deeply than fingertip to fingertip. In *Vertigo*, there are numerous references to Scotty and Madeline/Judy being in love with each other, but even at the height of their passion, they are utterly estranged by the chasm of their incommunicable consciousnesses, their completely different understandings of all of the events they have lived through. (I would note parenthetically that the *body* of the Hitchcock character is made susceptible to control and entrapment precisely because the mind and emotions are so unreachable. Norman Bates must attack Marion Crane's body, Scotty must track Madeline's physical movements, and Roger Thornhill's adversaries must entice him to move from one location to another in order for the one set of characters to have any significant relationship at all to the other. The body must be tracked, moved, manipulated, and penetrated, because the soul is so utterly inaccessible.)

Citizen Kane may seem to present more genuine social interaction, yet its characters are just as closed as those in *Psycho*. Their identities are as hermetically sealed and preserved, and their relationships are as noninteracting and unresponsive as those in Hitchcock. Welles's figures hardly ever reach each other intellectually (you have the distinct impression they're not even listening to each other, but only to themselves), let alone touch each other emotionally. The moral is pointed twice, once by the narrative and again by the style. In terms of the narrative, there's no delicate opening of one soul to another; there are no mercurial imaginative movements, no emotional slipping and sliding, but only the butting up against each other of completely closed-off, worked-out selves. In terms of the aspects of the style I have described, the same thing is communicated in an even deeper way. The metaphoric freightings, essentializing character psychology, static blockings, tendentious framings, and editorializing lighting demonstrate that what is being presented in shot after shot is the comparison and contrast of a small number of previously established and completely static symbolic positions.

In the boardinghouse scene, for example, the blocking tells us the same thing the plot does: that Thatcher and Mary are imaginatively together "here," that Jim is imaginatively apart from them "there," and that the child is imaginatively "somewhere else." They are completely isolated in their own worlds, and the deep-focus photography and tendentious blocking do not tolerate anyone intruding into anyone else's psychological space. In the love-nest confrontation, Jim Gettys's, Susan's, Emily's, and Kane's respective imaginative positions have been completely established by the start of the scene, are unalterably maintained during it, and haven't changed by its end. The scene doesn't represent a real interaction, but rather the playing out of a series of schematic differences. The breakfast table montage sequence may seem to be different insofar as it traces a nominal shift in the characters' imaginative positions, but the entire premise of the sequence is that the disintegration of Kane and Emily's marriage follows a completely predictable and foreordained trajectory. The sequence can read as movement, but the movement is as predetermined and mechanical as the movement of planets in Newtonian physics. Emily and Kane don't really make themselves vulnerable to being wounded by each other; they aren't affected emotionally by each other. There is no openness in their identities and no openness in their interaction. Welles presents two formulated, finished selves who are so far from being open to change and possibility that they can't even hurt each other.

I don't mean to seem to be picking on Hitchcock and Welles; I mention them only for the advantage of being able to cite works with which everyone is familiar. The syndrome of the isolated, atomic self and the noninteracting interaction is general throughout American film (though it may have taken Cassavetes to make us fully aware of how prevalent it is). In the overwhelming majority of studio films, even when characters are most passionately talking together, they almost never actually allow themselves to be influenced by each other. They do not genuinely hear each other. They do not make themselves vulnerable to the other's point of view. They do not truly open themselves to perspectives that would disrupt their states of confident self-composure. Rather, in film after film they take one of two tacks: either, on the one hand, talking for victory (in Dr. Johnson's phrase), staking out, maintaining, and defending a position; or, on the other, withdrawing inward, more or less ignoring the other characters' positions and feelings, and going their own ways emotionally.[15]

Either interactional strategy is equally a form of closure, a way of walling the self off from disruption and change. When Richard Gere and Julia Roberts jockey for control of their relationship in Pretty Woman, when Michael Douglas and Charlie Sheen collude in Wall Street, just as when (to descend somewhat further down the evolutionary tree) Stallone, Schwarzenegger, Eastwood, or Norris go on their rampages, no matter how robust the social interaction may seem to be, the characters might as well be alone, talking to themselves. No number of soliloquies make a dialogue. The identities and paths of relationship of these figures with others are fundamentally closed off, finished, walled in. When Travis Bickle cruises in his cab in *Taxi Driver*, he is not genuinely open to anyone or anything. He is locked within a state of silent, insulated subjectivity. Even when he is supposedly interacting with his cronies in the coffee shop, notice how each character actually talks not with the others, but to and from himself, to and from his own independent center of being. In none of these films do characters actually listen to and respond to each other. They give out, but never really take in. They do not open themselves to each other's feelings or ideas. The self becomes a position to be defined, maintained, and (if possible) expanded; but never to be opened up, never to be allowed to be invaded or inhabited by another.

There are powerful cultural reasons why so many American movies should imagine characters and their relationships in this way. The individualism and competitiveness of American society apparently predispose most audiences (and filmmakers) to imagine themselves as maintainers of independent positions and defenders of nonnegotiable identities. Viewers obviously prefer to see themselves in this way, no matter how much emotional and psychological damage the fiction causes.[16] Cassavetes leaves the capitalistic model of self-contained and competitively protected identity behind. To the extent that some of his characters do attempt to take refuge in fixed, formulated identities, his narratives are wrecking balls designed to batter down the walls they would erect around themselves. Even lovers hardly touch in the other sort of film; but virtual strangers like Tony and Lelia, or Davey and Lelia (in *Shadows*), Chet and Louise, or Richard and Jeannie (in *Faces*), make themselves profoundly vulnerable to each other. Cassavetes' characters let others get to them. They let others into their hearts.

Needless to say, this is not an easy world in which to live. In fact, it is the hardest of all possible worlds. In opening oneself to being moved and enlightened by interactions with others, one opens oneself equally to grief and suffering. The unwalled self is a vulnerable self. The unfinished self is continuously in danger of coming apart at the seams. Interactions that are as open-ended as Cassavetes imagines them to be become frighteningly unstable. Cassavetes' universe is a risky one. Life becomes perilous in a way it is not in the other sort of film. It also becomes extremely stimulating and exciting for anyone brave enough to rise to its challenges.

The individual's power is exerted in an extremely complex and demanding situation. Characters have enormous expressive burdens placed on them. However, the great inspiration of Cassavetes' work is its conception that the apparent constraints on our expressions and limitations on our freedom need not be constraints at all, but can be supreme stimulations to creative performance. He tells us that we can find our finest freedom in these very conditions. We find it not by turning out of action into a state of meditation or vision, not by leaving bodily realities behind, not by rising above the clutter of perceptions or fleeing from the imperfections of temporal knowledge, but by diving into the world of practical actions and expressions and functioning within its complex entailments. That leaves all of the important questions still unanswered, of course. How can we actually express ourselves within time and space? How can we shape our destinies in the realm of the senses and in the body? How can we have a nonconceptual, noncontemplative relation to experience? How can we radically open up the self and its relationships with others without destroying both? To understand these things, we must turn to the films. We must allow Cassavetes to become our teacher.

Note: The chapter that follows deals with Cassavetes' first film, *Shadows*, but since there is widespread misunderstanding about how much of it was improvised, a clarification is in order. In fact, almost all of the important scenes in the film as it now stands (and all of the scenes I am going to be discussing) were *not* improvised, but scripted. The confusion arose because *Shadows* was shot twice and released in two different versions. The first version (shot in 1957 and screened in the fall of 1958) was indeed based on a series of guided improvisations in which Cassavetes outlined the basic characters and scenes and let the actors make up their dialogue. However, what is less well known is that Cassavetes was deeply dissatisfied with the result and reshot the film in 1959, changing the events, emphases, and interactions thoughout, this time with the actors working from a script of his own creation. That print (which retained only a small number of scenes from the earlier shoot) was screened in November 1959 and is the one that comes down to us. The title card that ends it, describing the film as an "improvisation," was retained from the discarded version as Cassavetes' continuing expression of gratitude to his actors, even though it no longer accurately characterized the work and served to mislead critics.

I

Selves in the Making

Shadows

How different they are, mental feelings and real feelings. Today, many people live and die without having had any real feelings – though they have had a "rich emotional life" apparently, having showed strong mental feelings. But it is all counterfeit. . . . People allow themselves to feel a certain number of finished feelings. . . . This feeling at last kills the capacity for real feeling, and in the higher emotional range you feel nothing at all. . . . All emotions, including love and hate, go to the adjusting of the oscillating, unestablished balance between two people who amount to anything. If the novelist puts his thumb in the pan, for love, tenderness, sweetness, peace, then he commits an immoral act. He prevents the possibility of a pure relationship. . . . Life is so made that opposites sway about a trembling center of balance. . . . We must balance as we go.
                                                              – D. H. Lawrence[1]

I don't know whether I succeed in expressing myself, but I know that nothing else expresses me. Nothing that belongs to me is any measure of me; on the contrary, it's a limit, a barrier, and a perfectly arbitrary one. Certainly, the clothes which, as you say, I choose to wear, don't express me; and heaven forbid they should!
                                                              – Henry James[2]

When John Cassavetes died in 1989, it was not entirely surprising that most of the news pieces devoted more time to his career as an actor than as a filmmaker. To the general public, Cassavetes was far better known for his character roles in movies like *The Dirty Dozen, Rosemary's Baby, The Fury, Whose Life Is It, Anyway?*, and *Tempest*, than as the writer-director of his own independent movies. His own films never entered the cinematic vernacular critically or commercially. They were just too far off the beaten path for most viewers or critics to become aware of them. Because he free-lanced on the fringes of the studio system, without the support of the massive publicity and distribution budgets of the majors, most of his films received extremely limited and brief releases – in most cases, playing in only a few cities for a week or two. During his lifetime, only his three weakest works were available on video (*Gloria, Too Late Blues*, and *A Child Is Waiting*).

The reason those three films were ported over to video is the same reason they are Cassavetes' least interesting films: They were coproductions with major studios. That guaranteed that they would be widely advertised, distributed, and viewed (and ultimately tied into videocassette deals), but it also meant that they could not be as daring or original as the eight films in which Cassavetes controlled every aspect of the production – *Shadows, Faces, Husbands, Minnie and Moskowitz, A Woman Under the Influence, The Killing of a Chinese Bookie, Opening Night*, and *Love Streams*. Even today, three of those films – *Husbands, Minnie and Moskowitz*, and *Love Streams* – are not currently available on videotape or disc.

In his best work, Cassavetes defined one extreme version of what it means to be truly independent of the commercial calculations and committee-based decision making of corporate studio practice: not only writing and directing his own scripts, but overseeing and participating in every aspect of the production process – making casting decisions, shooting scenes (when he wasn't acting in them), editing (in his house in his earliest work), composing music (with the help of longtime collaborator, Bo Harwood), even writing his own press packs and doing the layouts for many of the posters and newspaper ads (using the photographs and artwork of another of his most devoted creative collaborators, Sam Shaw).

He was a perennial outsider, sparring with the system throughout his career and energized by the battle. Even as he was just starting out as a young television and film actor in the mid-1950s, when anyone else would have been busy building his résumé by ingratiating himself with the powers-that-be, he repeatedly expressed his dissatisfaction with the films in which he appeared. He had three basic objections:

The roles he was asked to play were false and melodramatic.
The methods of studio filmmaking worked against an actor giving an emotionally complex performance. Actors were treated not as one of the most important aspects of a film, but as small cogs in a gigantic machine organized more to suit the requirements of the crew and the studio bureaucracy than to facilitate emotional expression. First, to keep the budget down, scenes were shot out of the actual order in which they occurred, preventing the actors from developing an emotional "line" through the film. Second, even within one scene, dialogue and actions

were not played straight through, but in short bits and pieces (master shots, close-ups, over-the-shoulder shots, reaction shots, and more) in order to accommodate the cameraman. Third, an actor spent most of his time on the set waiting for complex light and camera setups, which then were used as a reason to constrain his movements by forcing him to hit "marks" (where the lighting and focus had been preestablished).

His most general objection was that Hollywood made films the way Detroit manufactured cars or Madison Avenue wrote ads: It mass-produced a product designed to maximize profits. It attempted to sell it to the largest possible audience by telling them what they wanted to hear or by confirming what they already knew, and it made the whole experience as easy and as close to mindless as possible. As he once put it, "the only art America appreciated was the art of making money."

It was appropriate that even at the very start of his career, many of the parts the young actor played were outsiders or misfits. Even more telling was the edgy intensity he brought to them. The tightening of his jaw, the darting of his eyes, the nervous movements of his mouth made him seem slightly dangerous and more than slightly unpredictable even in routine roles. Otherwise pedestrian movies like *Edge of the City, Crime in the Streets*, and *The Killers* were redeemed by his quirky inwardness.

As in the contemporaneous performances of Dean, Brando, and Clift (all of whose acting influenced him), it was bizarrely as if Cassavetes' energies were pitted *against* the works in which he appeared. He seemed a ticking time bomb, at any moment ready to explode out of the film he was in. You had the sense that he was not quite contained by the role, not quite expressed by the actions and words of the script. He pushed the envelope of representation. He was always, at least potentially, somewhere else – which was, of course, why he was worth watching.

One never quite knew what Cassavetes would say or do next, in a role or his life. It was typical of his brashness that, appearing on Jean Shepherd's "Night People" radio show to publicize *Edge of the City*, the 27-year-old actor stunned his host by proclaiming that the Martin Ritt melodrama wasn't that hot, and that he could make a better movie. He concluded with a rhetorical flourish: If each of the listeners sent in a dollar or two, he'd make "a movie about *people*." It was more an act of bravado than a thought-out fund-raising strategy, but when approximately $2,000 in dollar bills and change trickled into the station over the next few days, Cassavetes' career as a producer, writer, and director was unexpectedly launched – as much to his own surprise as that of anyone else.

Free-lancing on the fringes and doing it all: (*left*) making up Meade Roberts (Mr. Sophistication) for *The Killing of a Chinese Bookie*; blocking an action scene in *Opening Night* – one in which Cassavetes does not act – by "running through it" with the actors; (*right*) visualizing a shot just before acting in it in the dentist's office scene in *Husbands* (note that Cassavetes is wearing Gus's

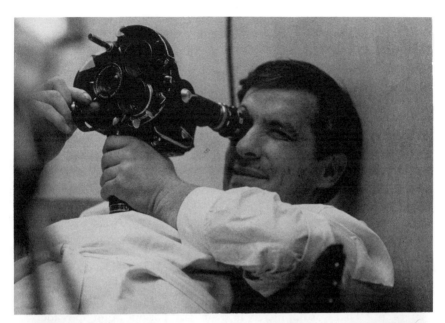

gown); checking the sound and sharing a joke in *A Woman Under the Influence* (*clockwise, from lower left:* Nick Spaulding; Eddie Shaw, who plays Dr. Zepp; the filmmaker's mother, Katherine Cassavetes, who appears in four of his films; Mitch Breit; Cassavetes, listening to the Nagra; Elizabeth Deering; and Bo Harwood, who did the music for many of the films).

As even his closest friends would admit, there was a con-man, "rug-merchant" side to Cassavetes' personality that frequently led him to say something without fully considering the consequences. This was one of those times. (There would be many others throughout his career, when Cassavetes would cook up half-baked schemes on the spur of the moment that, to his utter amazement, someone would then take him up on.) The filmmaker later admitted that never in his wildest dreams did he actually expect anyone to send a nickel, and had no idea what to do with the money once he got it; but the other side of his personality was a Boy Scout sense of keeping his word and living up to his promises, no matter how impulsively made. Once Shepherd turned the money over to him, Cassavetes felt absolutely honor bound to make a movie with it. Anyway, he thought it would be fun, something he could never resist.

Shadows was begun with a group of actor friends in New York that very week in 1957 – without a script or a professional crew, using rented lights and a 16mm camera. No one, including the filmmaker, had the faintest idea what they were doing. "We made every mistake you could," Cassavetes later said.[3] That was not merely false modesty; at one point lip-readers had to be brought in to allow new dialogue to be dubbed onto the sound track. Not only was the original sound completely inaudible, but no one had thought to keep a record of what the actors had said. Not surprisingly, it took almost three years until he had a print with which he was satisfied.

As that anecdote illustrates, it's impossible to draw a line between the marginality that Cassavetes cultivated and the marginality he had thrust upon him. If he worked outside of the system, with little or no institutional support, it was to a large extent because he chose to. He deliberately marginalized himself, so it should not be surprising that he was unusually sensitive to the situation of figures who themselves were on the margins of mainstream society in one way or another. Notwithstanding his reputation as the chronicler of the American middle class, all of Cassavetes' films reserve a special tenderness for powerless or vulnerable or fringe figures – the waitresses, car parkers, and taxi drivers of life – who are only let onto the edges of middle-class consciousness briefly if at all. Even when he chose to deal with characters who solidly embodied middle-class backgrounds and values (Maria Forst, Minnie Moore, Mabel Longhetti, Cosmo Vitelli, Gloria Swenson, and Sarah Lawson), it is significant that the moments in their lives on which Cassavetes chose to focus were those in which they were precipitated into states of crisis and were suddenly forced to reexamine themselves. If the one group is socially marginalized, the other, more like Cassavetes himself, is situated imaginatively on the margins.

Even more than being interested in figures in marginal positions, Cassavetes was interested in marginal feelings. To use his own phrase, he was determined to give voice to the "small feelings" that he believed American corporate values (in life and filmmaking) ignored or suppressed. His entire oeuvre is an effort to honor the lost or forgotten impulses in life, the tiny pulsings of emotional confusion or discovery that most other films simply omit. In his opinion, to bring them to consciousness, in a film or a life, is to begin to resist the vast forces of homogenization deployed throughout American culture, which is why the plots of his films almost always involve forcing characters to confront their lost or forgotten feelings. There is no filmmaker more willing to make cinematic time and space for the registration of the tiny, unspoken impulses and emotions in our lives, or who more resoundingly demonstrates that film can honor minority imaginative positions in its style without dealing with minority groups in its plot.[4]

Shadows's bittersweet comedy focuses on the minority position in both the sociological and the imaginative sense of the term. It not only centers around three figures who are outsiders to mainstream society, but, even more important, it labors to give voice to the little feelings that most other films leave out. The three main characters are two jazz musician brothers and their younger sister, who room together in Greenwich Village–like digs. Cassavetes locates them on the margins of mainstream American society in two respects: In the first place, they are part of the late-1950s "lost generation." Second, not only are all three African American, but while the oldest brother, Hugh, is dark-skinned, the two younger siblings, Lelia and Ben, are light enough to pass for white, which makes them full members of neither white society nor black.

The narrative has an anecdotal sprawl. Cassavetes presents a week or so in their lives as they make their way on the shaggy fringes of the beat milieu. He follows the three siblings through a series of independent episodes, intermittently bringing two or three of them together in their apartment or a coffee shop to maintain the sense that their destinies are related.

Hugh, the oldest brother, is struggling to make a career as a jazz singer, but not doing very well. He gets a low-paying gig in Philadelphia working with a girlie line, but is humiliated on stage when his act flops and the girls are brought on to replace him. He travels with and appears in most of his scenes with his friend and manager, Rupert, and many of their episodes involve their mutual attempts to get his career going.

Ben, slightly younger, is another jazz musician, a trumpeter, but it marks his difference from Hugh that he never actually attempts to perform. While Hugh at least measures his artistic dreams against the resistance of com-

Cassavetes on the importance of remaining true to the small feelings in his own life: "There is a compromise made if you work on a commercial film and the compromise isn't how or what you do, the techniques you use, or even the content, but really the compromise is beginning to feel a lack of confidence in your innermost thoughts. And if you don't put those innermost thoughts on the screen then you are looking down on not only your audience but the people you work with. And that's what makes so many people working out there unhappy. They say: 'Well, I'll make a lot of money and then I'll come back and do this later on.' The truth of the matter is, of course, that they never do. These innermost thoughts become less and less a part of you, and once you lose them you don't have anything else. I don't think anyone does it purposely. It's just that a lot of people are not aware of losing those things. I found myself losing them too, and then suddenly I woke up by accident, by sheer accident of not getting along with something, with something inside."

mercial reality, Ben would rather talk trumpet than play it. He goes around feeling sorry for himself and pretending to be hip, but not really doing very much at all. He basically spends the entire film either getting into fights or attempting to pick up girls. The only thing that keeps him just this side of dislikable is Cassavetes' semicomic tone, which makes clear that his expressive thrashing about is more embarrassing to him than dangerous to anyone else.

The young sister, Lelia, becomes the de facto star of this film-without-stars. She steals most of the scenes in which she appears, not only because her part is so much more emotionally expressive than anyone else's, but because Lelia Goldoni, the actress who plays her (each of the figures plays under his or her real first name), is brilliantly able to use her face, voice, and body to express the smallest flicker of feeling. We follow Lelia through three romantic involvements – beginning with a relaxed, platonic relationship with an older writer named David, undergoing a crisis following a one-day stand with a seduction artist named Tony (who no sooner makes love to Lelia than he spurns her when he discovers she is black), and concluding with her being reluctantly enticed back into the dating game by a gentle, well-meaning admirer named Davey.

Because of its "sensitive" subject, the racial issues in the film have been emphasized by virtually everyone who has written about it,[5] yet it is revealing that the filmmaker was uncomfortable with that approach. He once told me that there was only one essay about the movie that he really liked – because it downplayed the racial angle to focus on what he called "the film's *human* problems." A suggestion of what he meant is provided by one of the character sketches he wrote out and gave to each of his actors to help them with their parts. The note for Bennie is the only one that survives:

> BENNIE: He is driven by the uncertainty of his color to beg acceptance in this white man's world. Unlike his brother Hugh or Janet [*Note*: The sister became Lelia after this was written], he has no outlet for his emotions. He has been spending his life trying to decide what color he is. Now that he has chosen the white race as his people, his problem remains acceptance. This is difficult, knowing that he is in a sense betraying his own. His life is an aimless struggle to prove something abstract, his everyday living has no outlet.

It is clear from this that the issue was not Ben's race in itself, but his uncertainty about his identity and his attempt to find an outlet for his undefined energies. When Cassavetes writes that Ben's "life is an aimless struggle to prove something abstract, his everyday living has no outlet," he

35

might be describing himself as a young actor before he began *Shadows*, or the expressive problems of many of the characters in his later works. The questions *Shadows* asks are the ones explored in all of Cassavetes' films: Who are we? Where do we find ourselves? How do we express ourselves? To what extent are our expressions of ourselves limited by other factors — whether they be racial stereotypes (as in this film), social conventions (as in *A Woman Under the Influence*), or bureaucratic pigeonholing (as in *Opening Night*)?

One of the things that makes Cassavetes' films notoriously difficult for viewers to get the hang of is the uninflected quality of the experience he offers. By that I mean that he studiously declines to take the viewer by the hand (or by the eyes and ears) by providing a stylistic map through the experience. The Hitchcock or Welles method is the opposite. With his virtuosic control of what the viewer knows and feels at any moment, the director has the viewer in the palm of his hand, spellbound in darkness, a passive consumer of a dazzling spectacle. The viewer sits back and is taken on a truly amazing ride. In contrast, Cassavetes' goal is rather to get us a little lost, to throw us back on our own resources, and to force us to blaze our own paths through the work, as different as one viewer's path may be from another's. He deliberately refuses to tell us what to feel or what we should pay attention to because he wants to make us full-fledged and coequal participants in the meaning-making process. Though it may sound paradoxical, his goal is nothing less than to free us from subservience even to his own narrative designs. He wants to empower us as active intellects, to stimulate us into a state of heightened awareness and independent responsiveness. In the service of doing that, he studiously avoids most of the standard rhetorical devices that other films use to italicize the importance of particular scenes, events, or interactions, or to help a viewer interpret them: the use of mood-music orchestrations, "editorial" framings, "expressive" lighting on characters' faces, key lighting or foreground positioning of "significant" props. For the same reason, the use of visual metaphors is also kept to a bare minimum. (There is nothing remotely corresponding to the constellations of image patterns in *The Trial*, *Vertigo*, or *Apocalypse Now*.)

There is one extended metaphor in *Shadows*, however. It involves a comparison of the "masks" we wear in public with the "faces" we hide beneath them. Yet it is typical of the film's rhetorical tact that it surfaces as an explicit visual image at only two points (and is so understated that, to my knowledge, it has never even been noticed in print before): first, when Ben admires a piece of sculpture in the Museum of Modern Art sculpture garden and refers to it as a "mask"; and second, when a tilt shot initiating the scene of Lelia and Tony's postcoital conversation begins by framing an African mask on the wall of his bedroom. In both shots, Cassavetes implicitly asks us to compare the mercuriality of living expressions with the fixity of sculptured ones.

However, the most resonant occurrences of masks in *Shadows* are not in terms of visual images, but in Cassavetes' presentation of his characters' behavior. Long before Ben calls attention to the MoMA mask, a viewer is made aware of how he wears an even subtler and more insidious mask – one that he is not aware of and that he can't remove. It is his "hipness." He hides behind beat-generation poses in an attempt to insulate himself from emotional vulnerability. That is why he spends all of his time cruising for pickups and spoiling for fights. As long as he keeps moving from girl to girl, he knows no deep emotional claims will be made, nor any enduring commitments required of him; as long as he keeps brawling, he won't have really to interact with anyone. He won't have to take off the mask and reveal the insecurities underneath it. Though Ben scoffs at the pretentiousness of a literary soirée to which he is invited, Cassavetes makes a viewer realize that in his everyday life he plays a role just as hollow as the poseurs who attend the party and babble on about "existential psychoanalysis."

Hugh, Rupert, Lelia, and Tony are also mask wearers, though in less obvious ways. As a professional jazz musician whose career has failed to get off the ground, Hugh has been reduced to playing clubs full of drunks, to introducing a chorus line to get on stage at all. As deeply wounded as he is by the compromises he has been forced to make, Hugh keeps his frustrations bottled up and puts on a brave face for his brother, sister, and Rupert, all of whom depend on him for both emotional and financial support. He plays the protecting older-brother role, suppressing his feelings to insulate himself from shame or vulnerability and to spare others grief.

Rupert does the same thing with Hugh that Hugh does with him. He declines to say what is most on his mind – his discouragement about Hugh's career and his inability to get Hugh better bookings. Given Hugh's insecurities, Rupert understandably turns himself into a cheerleader for his career. He is unflappably cheerful, upbeat, and positive.

Neither of them is stupid, however, which is to say that for both of them the optimism is just an act. They may fool others, but they don't fool themselves. As much as he accentuates the positive and talks a good line, Hugh knows that his career is dead in the water. Rupert, on his part, is too smart to believe his own press releases. Their smiling stoicism is a stance that many of the male characters in Cassavetes' subsequent work will adopt:

pretenses of male poise and confidence covering up self-doubt and feelings of inadequacy.

Lelia has found another way of protecting herself from pain and hiding her vulnerabilities. After first making the mistake of thinking that sex can be free from emotional complications (and subsequently being hurt by her impulsive fling with Tony), she goes to the other extreme, withdrawing into a camouflaging flirtatiousness, flamboyance, and self-dramatizing theatricality calculated to let no one get near her emotionally.

Although he is a less important character than the other four, Tony is also a mask wearer. He retreats from intimacy behind the role of wise male protector. He is too busy proving to the women in his life how experienced he is, how much he knows and feels, ever actually to allow himself to learn or feel anything.

Robert Frank's *Pull My Daisy* was made only two years after *Shadows* and is frequently compared to it. The two films have a number of superficial similarities, beyond being no-budget undertakings with rough production values: Both consist of anecdotal narratives that focus on the New York artistic and literary scene of the late 1950s, and both spotlight the performative flamboyance of beat-generation characters. The differences between the two works are more telling than the similarities, however. They sum up not only why Jonas Mekas's initial embrace of Cassavetes' work (he awarded *Film Culture*'s first "Independent Film Award" to *Shadows*) was a case of mistaken identity, but more importantly, why Cassavetes never fit into the New York avant-garde at all. His values were entirely different.

Frank clearly admires his characters' literary preening and their artsy role-playing, and wants a viewer to be charmed by it. Cassavetes views the identical behavior as figuring a profound emotional problem. Frank wants aesthetic pleasure to supersede ethical judgment. Cassavetes goes in the opposite direction: He wants aesthetic stances to be subjected to moral evaluations. He judges his characters and their Bohemian culture. He asks serious questions about the meaning of their lives and the values of their society. There is a moral seriousness to his work and a skepticism about cultural ideology that is completely absent from that of Frank and most other artists working within the New York cinematic and artistic avant-garde of the fifties.

As he often does, Cassavetes uses narrative events to point out the limitations of characters' imaginative stances. If we don't tell the truth about ourselves we must face the consequences. Lelia, Ben, Hugh, Rupert, and Tony each get into trouble because of the roles they choose to play.

Lelia is the most complex and interesting case. Cassavetes admires her

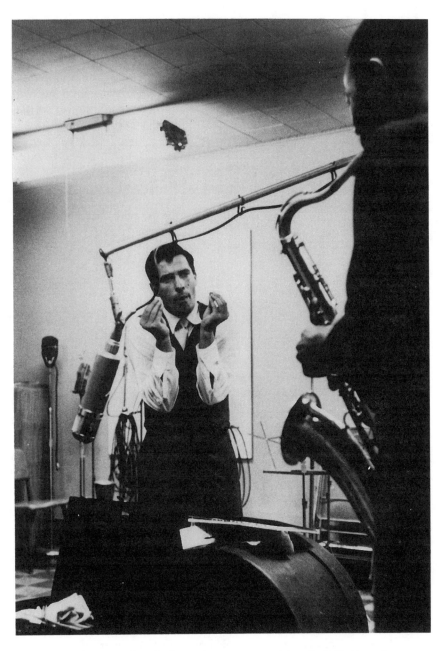

Creating the music for *Shadows*. Cassavetes coaching Shafi Hadi on the saxophone in the recording studio.

but carefully uses the plot events to indicate her limitations. On the positive side, she's spunky, sassy, and audacious. When she impulsively kisses Tony at a party, or runs through Central Park with him the next day, her expressive daring is more than a little dazzling. At least at the beginning of the film, she is absolutely fearless, and will apparently do anything, with anyone, anywhere. She is giddily free from expressive inhibitions or limitations, and her flamboyance not surprisingly makes her sexually alluring to each of the men around her – first David, then Tony, then Davey.

In terms of Cassavetes' own value system, all of the preceding is in Lelia's favor, but her expressive abandon is also a prescription for psychological disaster. Lelia treats all of life as if it were a stage for her outrageous performances, but she forgets that life is not theater, and that a relationship with a man is more than a matter of "making a scene." Sexual and romantic involvements have emotional consequences that a scene in a play doesn't. After she sleeps with Tony on a whim and he rejects her twice (first by refusing to say that he "loves" her, and second by showing his dismay when he discovers she is black), the irony is that her own emotions are the ones most out of control. She thought that having sex was no different from an actress trying out for a part, but she is the one who is unable to live with the emotional consequences of her levity. Cassavetes uses Lelia to ask whether expressive breeziness marks one as an emotional airhead, whether we can defy the gravity of our social responsibilities without becoming morally weightless. He wants us to wonder whether, instead of finding ourselves in vamping and voguing, we end up losing track of who we truly are and what we really need.[6]

Ben also gets into trouble in the course of the film by attempting to deny his feelings. He is the refrigerator ruler of his own ice kingdom of cool, but his problem is that since he freezes out anyone else, he reigns alone. Even as he endlessly searches for companionship, he shuts the door to intimacy. His "like a rolling stone" pose dooms him to go through life alone.

The glib optimism of Hugh and Rupert is yet another way of walling out reality. Up until their final scene together, they refuse to speak about the humiliation of Hugh's being yanked offstage in midsong, the cancellation of his bookings, or their shared discouragement that his career is going nowhere fast. It's all too painful to face; but the plot tells us that in order to get on with their personal and their professional lives they must open up to each other. They must admit their bitterness and frustration, and work through the painful emotions rather than keeping them bottled up. They must share their feelings with each other rather than hiding them.

40

The most obvious way we know that all five characters are covering up their emotional needs is that at odd moments their masks suddenly slip. Their pretended poise gives way to unexpected, violent explosions of feeling: tears, arguments, eruptions of anger, and fights (which seem even more shocking because of the gentle comedy of the scenes that precede and follow them). Just when the appearances have all been arranged precisely to prevent it, an abyss of forgotten or denied feelings opens to view. The repressed returns. What is bottled up in one scene is suddenly, violently spilled in another. Tony's macho-man cool gives way to racist panic when he discovers that Lelia is black. The morning after Tony wounds her, Lelia, who has pretended that she is not hurt, suddenly takes out her anger and grief on Ben in a screaming fit and flurry of tears. That evening, in the middle of a party, Ben suddenly gets into a fight with Hugh. Early the following morning, Hugh lashes out in discouragement against Rupert. The following night, Rupert, otherwise the mildest and most gentle of gentlemen, vents his own pent-up anger and frustration on Hugh.

Another of Cassavetes' favorite means of opening unspoken emotional depths to view is simply to hold a close-up on a character's face a beat or two longer than another film would, to allow a viewer to glimpse something behind the brave look he or she wears. Two of the most striking examples involve the conclusion of scenes featuring Hugh – the first in the dance studio, the second following his abortive performance in the nightclub. In both, Cassavetes ends the scenes with close-ups of Hugh standing silent and chagrined. When he thinks no one is watching, in his eyes we briefly glimpse the discouragement he otherwise successfully keeps hidden.

In that formulation, the emphasis belongs on the word "glimpse." While Hollywood melodramatically externalizes characters' emotional states, writing them in ten-foot-high letters in the form of actions, words, and mood-music orchestrations in order to maximize their visibility, the drama in Cassavetes' work is internalized to the point of being almost subliminal. (*A Woman Under the Influence* is the one exception, which is undoubtedly one of the reasons it appealed to a larger audience than Cassavetes' other work.) His scenes are characterized less by explosions of emotion than by acts of suppression or avoidance, to the point that some of the most crucial emotional events become almost invisible. It's not really surprising that most reviewers, accustomed to the Hollywood manner of presentation, couldn't see that there was anything at all going on in some of the films. I would emphasize that most of the emotional events I am describing in *Shadows* (concerning Hugh's bottled-up frustrations or Rupert's forced buoyancy, for example) are far from obvious on a first viewing, and pass completely unnoticed by most members of the audience; however, that is not a mistake on Cassavetes' part. The subtlety of the emotional suppressions is the point.

Shadows presents a continuous double text. The simple events, expressions, and gestures in a scene almost always paper over complex emotional depths. The scene in the dance studio near the beginning of the movie can stand as a summary of the film's pervasive subtextualizing. The events are simple and the scene itself is only a few minutes long: Hugh and Rupert are meeting with Jack Ackerman about the upcoming booking introducing the chorus line. Hugh is reluctant to accept the job because of the low status of the gig. Rupert looks on the deal more positively and urges Hugh to take it. At one point, Ben briefly interrupts the meeting to borrow twenty dollars from Hugh. That's all that there is on the surface; but the emotional undercurrents make the scene nothing short of fascinating. Cassavetes presents a dance of conflicting egos and shifting points of view – a drama that is played out completely underneath the spoken words and visible actions. None of the most important things are said; all are laid in between the lines:

Ackerman says he is frustrated with Hugh's reluctance to take the job, but the subtext suggests that he is taking out his frustrations on Hugh and Rupert because rehearsals of the song-and-dance routine Hugh is to introduce are going badly. Furthermore, though he tries to pretend that he has other singers interested in the spot (as a negotiating strategy to keep Hugh from realizing how desperate he is), his tones tells us that he very much needs Hugh to accept the job, and is panicky that he will not be able to get anyone on such short notice if Hugh turns him down.

Rupert, on his part, may seem to be there simply as Hugh's friend and advisor (and no doubt would explain his role in such terms), but so many other countercurrents of feeling are swirling under the surface that it is hard even to list them all: In the first place, Rupert is not simply functioning as Hugh's manager but is *playing* the role to the hilt, to impress Ackerman and to ingratiate himself with Hugh, whom he pointedly refers to as "his client." Additionally, though he never says so, Rupert is interested in closing the deal less because of the deal itself than because closing *any* deal is an affirmation of what managers are paid to do, and because in his mind any work for Hugh is better than none. At the same time, he also sympathizes with Hugh's reluctance to take this particular job. He attempts to bolster Hugh's self-esteem and to flatter him by calling him an "artist." He also attempts to assuage Hugh's hurt feelings by implying that a true artist can rise above the indignity of any situation in which he finds himself.

Hugh figures the most intricate emotional subtext of them all. He says his problem with the gig is simply his second billing to the girls and that he is a singer not an emcee, but there is much more to it than that: His pride is wounded by his being in this situation at all, reduced to negotiating with someone like Ackerman for such a paltry position. Furthermore, though he denies it, the low pay of the job matters very much to him, and adds to the insult of the offer. Ben's brief interruption of the moment by asking to borrow money turns the screw still tighter. Hugh is suddenly reminded that others are dependent on him and that it is selfish to think only of himself and his own pride. That recognition, and not Rupert's persuasion, is what finally tips the balance and induces him to accept a job that every fiber of his being rebels against.

In other scenes, such as the postcoital conversation between Tony and Lelia, Cassavetes' decision not to edit out the hesitations or false starts (as conventional editing practice would dictate) is another way of giving us a peek underneath the masks his characters wear. Since their line deliveries are important, I have indicated a few of the tones and pauses in brackets:

TONY: [*patronizing yet concerned*] Lelia – really, if I'd known this was the first time for you, I wouldn't have touched you.

LELIA: I didn't know it could be so awful.

TONY: [*trying to comfort her by pulling her toward him*] Don't be so upset, sweetheart.... Baby, it will be much easier next time.

LELIA: There isn't going to be a next time.

TONY: [*anything to change the subject and gain control over the beat*] Want a cigarette, huh? Come on, have a cigarette.

LELIA: No.

TONY: [*attempting to seize the initiative by playing hurt himself*] I'm sorry if I disappointed you. I guess I did.

LELIA: [*sympathetic and relenting*] I was so frightened. I kept saying to myself you mustn't cry. If you love a man you shouldn't be so frightened.

TONY: [*regaining his poise – on familiar ground*] It's only natural. [*a beat*] There isn't a girl in the world that wouldn't feel the same way. She's [*a beat, uncertain how to end the sentence*] ... got to.

LELIA: And what happens now?

TONY: [*at sea, taking a beat*] What happens? [*worried, another beat*] Um, well, [*yet another beat, then blurting out*] what do you mean what happens now?

LELIA: I mean do I stay with you?

TONY: [*frantic*] Lelia, uh. Stay with me? [*a worried beat, then suddenly deciding it's flattering*] You, you mean *live* with me?

LELIA: Yes.

TONY: [*tentatively*] You . . . want . . . to?

LELIA: No, I want to go home.

TONY: [*vastly relieved*] Okay, baby.

The beats, hesitations, and inflections are more important than the meaning of the words themselves. In allowing us to see their minds making themselves up as they go along, Cassavetes shows the viewer how uncertain and tentative their positions are. The pauses and tonal gymnastics expose cracks in the facade of knowingness. Particularly in Tony's case, the subtext not only enriches the surface text, but sets up meanings at odds with it. His silences reveal uncertainty underneath his pretended certainty, undercurrents of fear and doubt that contradict the braveness of his macho-man knowingness.

Another dimension of the scene (which is not apparent in my transcription of it) is the exaggeration of Tony's acting. His Method-influenced performance turns Brando's technique into a series of buttons to be pushed: First do the thing with your eyes, then clench your jaw, then take that pause in your line delivery. The "bad acting" here and elsewhere merits notice (and not mere dismissal) because it is one of the essential – if most misunderstood – expressive techniques in Cassavetes' work. Characters are *not* polished, smooth, articulate, and witty. Their performances are frequently heavy-handed, clumsy, or oafish.

In this scene and others, Cassavetes conflates the expressive limitations of the acting with the expressive limitations of the characters. When Lelia strikes the hackneyed melodramatic poses of the "wounded woman" after making love with Tony; when Tony comically overplays his scene of apology and remorse in front of Ben and Hugh ("Tell her I'm sorry. . . . Tell her there's no difference between us. . . . Tell her . . . ," etc.); when Ben costumes himself in an off-the-peg Method-acting slouch and shrug at Hugh's party, the acting is *meant* to be appreciated as clichéd. The formulaic quality of Tony and Ben's acting in particular – their exaggerated, Method-based beat taking, brow furrowing, and jaw tightening – is meant to communicate a formulaic quality in their lives. Their reliance on canned acting ingredients as a recipe for expression – a cup of James Dean stirred into a pint of Montgomery Clift – tells us how processed and precooked their expressions of themselves in life are. (That Tony is played by Tony Ray, the son of the director of *Rebel Without a Cause*, makes the indebtedness of Tony's performance to James Dean more than fanciful.)

This is one of the richest yet potentially most confusing aspects of the film. The problem is that any work that plays against conventional forms or incorporates deliberate expressive clichés, awkwardness, or badness into its characters' performances (certain scenes in *Husbands* and *A Woman Under the Influence* providing even more extreme examples of "bad acting") risks being dismissed as itself clichéd, awkward, or bad. In the case of both *Faces* and *Husbands* it sent viewers scurrying out the door and left Pauline Kael, John Simon, and other reviewers jeering in derision. "Acting so bad it's embarrassing," according to Kael, never known for her penchant for understatement. Cassavetes' use of deliberately "limited" performances backfired on him almost completely and continues to backfire, even in more recent academic evaluations.[7]

There are several ways we can be sure that Cassavetes detected the expressive limitations of his characters. The most important is that events in the narrative penalize them for their posturing. Ben, Lelia, Tony, and the others create problems for themselves because of the roles they choose to play. Beyond that, Cassavetes' photography of Lelia in hokey, expressive close-ups when she does her Joan Crawford imitation, and the use of the character David early in his film to poke fun at Ben's "beat-generation jazz," should convince even a skeptical viewer that the filmmaker was not taken in by his characters' posing.

Cassavetes' understanding of expression was an actor's. That is to say, for him, there was no essential difference between the expressive situations of acting and life: What happened in acting had its equivalent in life; what happened in life had its equivalent in acting. The artistic impoverishments of timid or derivative forms of acting were inextricably linked in his imagination with the disappointments of timid or derivative ways of living; conversely, the aesthetic excitements and challenges of original and brave acting were connected with the stimulations of original and brave living. Cassavetes understood that people hide behind dependable roles in their lives and relationships with others in the same way actors do in their performances, and that formulaic approaches to experience prevent us from learning anything onstage or off. Formulas are always the enemy of growth in his work. The characters and the actors playing them must dare to leave behind the protective cocoon of an established "technique." That means jettisoning the dependable mannerisms, predictable inflections, and prefabricated styles that we use to navigate a course through a difficult situation, and instead actually making ourselves vulnerable to its shifting, dangerous currents. Lelia's melodramatics, Ben's hipness, and Tony's knowingness, like the stilted "braininess" of the cocktail party habitués in an early scene, are fearful retreats from the challenges of real experience into the safety of formulated stances.

In Cassavetes' view of it, a related problem with most bad actors is that they want to "star" rather than to work as part of an ensemble. They want the pacing and emphases within a scene to respond to *their* rhythms, rather than making themselves responsive to its. The problem with Ben and Lelia is that they've got their acts together. They know who they are, and what they want. They've figured out their roles. Ben's beat-generation costume (black leather jacket and sunglasses, even indoors and at night), affectless tones (disillusioned, self-pitying, and already burnt-out at age 21 – "Maybe I'll join a little group in Vegas"), and tomcatting (on the prowl for a different girl every night) allow him to be the star of his own road show, but they deny him possibilities of emotional contact with anyone other than himself and his own problems. Lelia's extravagant self-dramatizations are more inventive and interesting than Ben's "cool, man, cool" posturing, but are ultimately no different from it. Her Garboism cuts her off from experience in the same way his Brandoism does: It gives her star billing in a one-woman repertory company in which she plays all of the parts and lets no one upstage her, steal her scenes, or get within a mile of her emotionally. Their acting is not interactional, not collaborative.

The issue goes beyond being open or closed to others. What's really wrong with formulas for acting is that they represent dead ends for self-development, while Cassavetes believed in ontological open-endedness, in acts of endless self-revision. The deepest problem with Ben's, Tony's, Lelia's, Rupert's, and Hugh's mask wearing and role-playing (both as actors and as characters) is that they attempt to close themselves off from change and movement. Their acting represents an effort to formulate a fixed, finished identity. To be finished in this way, however, is to be finished in every other sense as well.

This should make it clear that Ben's problem is neither his choice of acting models nor his ability successfully to mimic the model of his choice. Any model is a trap. Any act of imitation, however adroit, is an act of suicide. The difference between James Dean and Ben Carruthers is as absolute as the difference between Billie Holiday and a Billie Holiday impersonator, however brilliantly accurate the impersonator may be. The first time is tragedy; the second is farce. There is all the difference in the world between Charlie Parker inventively working his way through "Ornithology" on stage, and a later jazzman studying a recording and playing it note for note, beat by beat, identical to one of Parker's performances. The imitator is confusing the accidental tracks with the essential powers of the animal that made them. While Parker is testing his powers of recomposition against the continuous streaming decompositions of time, endlessly reconstituting his expressive identity on a racing razor edge, the Parker manqué is hiding out inside a blueprint Taj Mahal. Dean's slouches represented dangerous, system-breaking states of emotional exposure, but the identical slouches in Ben's imitation of Dean represent nothing more than a packaging of the self in a received style. (In terms of *Rebel Without a Cause*, that means that Ben is inadvertently closer to being the cross-dressing Jim Backus than Jim Stark.) As Emerson put it in *The American Scholar*:

> The sacredness which attaches to the act of creation – the act of thought – is transferred to the record. The poet chanting, was felt to be a divine man: henceforth the chant is divine also . . . as love of the hero corrupts into worship of his statue. . . . The one thing in the world, of value, is the active soul. . . . In its essence, it is progressive. The book, the college, the school of art, the institution of any kind, stop with some past utterance of genius. This is good, say they, – let us hold by this. They pin me down. They look backward and not forward.[8]

As a response to their pains, Ben, Lelia, Hugh, Rupert, and Tony each try to close up shop on who they are, so they won't have to keep working and responding. As actors and as characters, their goal is to work up a routine so good they won't ever have to depart from it. Having figured out a design for living, they try to move into it and lock the door behind them. Everything Cassavetes stood for was opposed to this sense of "canning" the self or its performances. He saw acting not as a matter of getting your part so down pat that you'd never have to think on your feet, but as the opposite: as a process of opening yourself up so completely that you could never say in advance where you were going to come out or what you were going to discover along the way.

The flip side of Cassavetes' conception of open-ended selfhood is that any social expression or role becomes an implicit constraint on our expressive possibilities. With respect to its words, actions, and appearances, the self is always elsewhere. Its energies are too inward and hidden to be brought to the surface except obliquely and fugitively, or too fluxional and intense to be figured in any practical social expression or role. At its best and most exciting, the self is not only unformulated, but unformulatable. It holds in suspension energies whose mobility and fugitiveness essentially resist representation.

47

In short, Cassavetes' appreciation of representation is radically skeptical. I have already alluded to one way in which representational skepticism is built into *Shadows* thematically: in the decision to make Ben's and Lelia's identities racially indeterminate. A viewer is forced to question basic social categories of understanding. If their skin is "white" but their genes are "black," are Ben and Lelia white or black? We are encouraged to ponder what such terms mean. Are they merely social conventions or representations of deeper, more essential qualities? How does one define one's identity? What does having an identity entail? Where does the self find itself? The questions Cassavetes asks are real ones, which is what makes *Shadows* far deeper and more mysterious than a movie like *The Crying Game*, where the gender switches are basically only a series of tricks played on the characters and the viewer, not fundamentally different from the mix-ups and reversals in movies like *The Stunt Man* and *F/X*.

Even more interestingly, Ben's and Lelia's identities are cinematically indeterminate. Insofar as *Shadows* violates conventional cinematic forms of representation (where a "black" would be represented by someone with clearly Negroid features and a "white" by a Caucasian), the viewer also enters into a less certain relationship with artistic conventions of representation. Cassavetes wants to get us a little confused. (In contrast, Douglas Sirk's *Imitation of Life*, which has a superficially similar plot and set of characters, works to keep us perfectly clear about representational categories and to reinforce conventional racial notions. In Sirk's picture, we are never in doubt about a character's race, or what it means. Sirk gives us confidence in our ability to understand things; Cassavetes makes us question it.)

By ensuring that the viewer undergoes the same delayed process of "discovering" Lelia and Ben's racial background in watching *Shadows* that Tony does as a character, Cassavetes brings Tony's problem home. The viewer doesn't merely entertain it as an intellectual possibility (which can be comfortably held at arm's length and be dismissed as happening somewhere else), but is forced to live through it, to see that Tony, the putative racist, is not someone else, but himself on screen. All of Cassavetes' films are "instrumental" in this sense. They are less interested in telling us *about* something than in putting us through the experience itself. To describe this in a way William James would have found congenial, Cassavetes presents experience not theoretically, but pragmatically. Experience means not something abstracted from it, but the process of having the experience. The meaning of this experience is for the viewer to jump to a false conclusion and subsequently be forced to realize his mistake.

The racial dimension of *Shadows* is really a fairly minor aspect of the

Rehearsing and directing the scene of the postparty conversation in *Shadows*. Note the microphone at the right end of the table. (Seated, from left to right, are Hugh Hurd, Victoria Vargas, Rupert Crosse, and Jacqueline Walcott; Cassavetes is standing.)

film, however. Even if it were stripped away, Ben, Lelia, Hugh, Rupert, and Tony would still induce a skepticism about the limits of social and artistic representation because Cassavetes makes them "role-players." Up to this point I have dealt with role-playing only in a limited sense as figuring an emotional problem insofar as it manifests itself as "mask wearing"; but it has a far more complex and less negative function in Cassavetes' work. Over and over again – from *Shadows* and *Faces*, through *A Woman Under the Influence*, *The Killing of a Chinese Bookie*, and *Opening Night*, to *Gloria* and *Love Streams* – Cassavetes' central characters are revealed to be wearing masks in a much more general sense: They strike poses, assume stances, and play with their identities and expressions, and their role-playing is one of the most interesting and complex aspects of their identities.

Ben and Lelia play expressive games in this more general way throughout *Shadows*. Virtually nothing Lelia says and does is merely "her." This is

49

obvious in her treatment of Davey in the second half of the film, but is the case even before Tony's brutality has prompted her self-protective coyness. Her behavior moves across a range of tones and moods, but to one degree or another it is all *acted*. Whether she is primping, preening, showing off, throwing a fit, or playing wounded, Lelia is always, in some sense, "on." She is posing, playing to an imaginary audience, watching them and herself, gauging the reaction and adjusting her performance accordingly.

Similarly, the most important fact one can state about Ben is that even beyond the ways I've already indicated – in his alternately annoying and touchingly clumsy Method mimicry – he is playing with his self-expressions. He experiments with stances and tones. He is never fully absorbed in anything he does because everything he does is in some respects a performance. That is why it is appropriate to call Ben's leather jacket and sunglasses a "costume," his sitting off to the side of Hugh's party a "pose," and Lelia's keeping Davey waiting for three hours on their night out an "act." One can only wear a costume, pose, or act in this way when one is not simply equivalent to one's clothing, stance, or behavior. The theatrical resonances of the words represent a recognition that the individual is not unproblematically identical with his expressions of himself. Ben and Lelia are separate from, and to some extent in control of, their expressions.

Needless to say, I am not suggesting that Ben and Lelia are insincere or hypocritical. Cassavetes locates us in a world in which such terms do not apply. The expressive games they play are serious, and they believe in them completely while they are playing them. Similarly, neither Hugh nor Rupert are any less sincere because they are acting so brave in the face of their mutual discouragements. Rather than say they lie, it would be more accurate to say that Cassavetes introduces a space between the performer's self-displays, and a self imagined to be somewhere just beyond, behind, or not entirely figured by the behavior. There is a gap between the self and its momentary expressions of itself. (The gap will open to the width of a chasm with Mabel Longhetti, the heroine of Cassavetes' *A Woman Under the Influence*.) Moral categories like "falsehood" and "deceit" are premised on the notion that there is no gap.

Reductive moral categories like truth and falsehood, honesty and deceit, can be used to describe the behavior of characters in most Hollywood movies because they have an essentializing notion of meaning. Characters clearly, easily, and repeatedly "speak" (in both the visual and verbal senses of the term) a few simple, essential qualities, and viewers just as easily decode their "speech" into simple moral and psychological terms. In those films, stylistic surfaces or characters' actions and words directly and unproblematically allow us to read reductive intellectual and emotional depths. Surfaces reveal essences, and the essences revealed are absolutely clear and unambiguous. The character knows his essential state of being. Other characters know it. The viewer knows it.

Things are never this simple in Cassavetes' work. Even love between two characters is not a pure, clear, definite emotion.[9] There is simply no stable, resolving depth behaviors can be traced back to, and therefore moral judgments can never be made in the reductive way other films encourage. Cassavetes' figures are "scene makers," but to create a character capable of "making a scene" is to register an intricate and oblique relation between the figure and a particular behavior or expression. There is discontinuity between depths and surfaces. Characters almost never directly speak their minds (or enact them). With a few minor exceptions, the films never merely translate the contents of consciousness into a charged glance, a mood-music orchestration, a key-lighting effect, or a visual metaphor. It can't be done, in Cassavetes' view, because translational problems arise at both ends for the artist, the actor, and the character. In the depths, consciousness is not static, simple, monotonic, or reducible to basic intentions and motives. On the surfaces, expressions are slippery, oblique, indirect, guarded, posed, and stylized. Needless to say, this does not mean that one abandons the act of translation (which artists, actors, characters, and viewers must continue in any case), but rather that one must conduct it in a more gingerly way than the other sort of film does. Hitchcock, Kubrick, Sternberg, and Welles believe in the existence of pure emotional states capable of being purely expressed; Cassavetes does not. For him, the emotion is confused and the expression is problematic. The result is that Cassavetes' actors, characters, and viewers have a more wary relationship with language (both cinematic and verbal). They wear it more lightly, hold it more loosely. Both cinematic and social forms of representation become less definitive and more provisional.

The representational skepticism that Cassavetes' work is premised on is simply absent from films superficially similar to his own. Characters in Paddy Chayefsky's *Marty* (which has plot similarities with *Shadows*) wear *clothes*, but don't wear *costumes*. They sit and talk and move, but they don't *pose* or *play* at sitting, talking, and moving the way Tony, Ben, and Lelia do. In short, for Chayefsky, one *has* an identity; one does not create it as Lelia and Ben do. For Chayefsky (and his characters) one's representation of oneself (in life or in art) is not fundamentally problematic.[10]

A more general way to put this is to say that in Cassavetes' movies there is a looser connection between "performed" surfaces and "intentional" depths. There is a degree of slack, play, or wiggle in the relationship between the self and its expressions. The social self becomes a loose-fitting Halloween costume with lots of room for independent movement, room for the positioning of a partly concealed inner self off to one side within the expression. The behavior that is presented to the world is *not* skintight, so as to reveal every wrinkle or bend in the deep self. Surface expressions are not snugly tailored to conform to depths, but rather represent a baggy heap of substitutions that are as likely to hide the depths as to reveal them. The space between the two realms, the shagginess of fit, makes room for imaginative games, jokes, role-playing, and pose striking.

The standard Hollywood production is organized in the opposite way: To facilitate legibility and prevent misreadings, it proposes the tightest possible fit between surfaces and depths, overdetermining psychological and emotional meanings with transparently revelatory surface expressions of "deep" feelings. The difference is what unsympathetic critics were responding to when they complained that Cassavetes' characters "clowned around," that his actors' dialogue seemed "rambling," "disorganized," or "winged," or that his scenes seemed "unfocused," "undisciplined," or got "nowhere." In a word, *Husbands*'s Harry could never be confused with Dirty Harry. The one figure's expressions of himself are as unfocused, elliptical, and oblique as the other's are overdetermined and charged with "deep" meaning.

While Hitchcock, Welles, and others practice an art of clarifying, resolving depths, Cassavetes offers one of intricate, shifting surfaces. The focus moves away from a belief in deep psychology, to call us to the appreciation of a world of fleeting, superficial (yet no less profound) expression. The way of profundity in Cassavetes' work is not in moving from surfaces to depths, but in breaking down the opposition between them. Rather than attempting to plumb depths, Cassavetes' viewers must learn to skate on shifting surfaces. In musical terms, the aesthetics of jazz performance replace those of classical symphonic structure.

Needless to say, in abandoning an essentializing presentation, Cassavetes took chances with the ability of his viewers to appreciate what he was up to. Many viewers felt lost when they were not able to trace the vagaries of surface expressions back to a stable psychological cause. Precisely to the degree that he freed his characters from monotonic motivations and empowered them to swerve away from reductive patterns of behavior, allowing them a wealth of complicating indirection in their surface expressions, they could seem vague, mystifying, or inconsistent to viewers accustomed to the focused intentionality and straight talk of characters in Hollywood movies. The ordinary viewer was bewildered, while sophisticated reviewers like

Simon, Kael, and Canby wrote off Cassavetes' work as an example of what happens when an actor-director lets his actors horse around on camera.

Nevertheless, even the most sensitive viewer could feel lost at times because of the tenuousness of the relationship between behaviors and feelings in Cassavetes' work. There is an essentially negative quality to Cassavetes' representational method that makes it incredibly difficult to understand his characters. As I have pointed out regarding the rehearsal studio scene, most of what matters is not said or done, but is suggested between the lines. The self is not the words it speaks. This is easy to see when Lelia puts on an air of exaggerated gaiety in order to conceal her sadness, or when Ben sullenly withdraws from a group precisely because he so dearly wants to be included in it. At other moments, however, the viewer is as much in the dark about the meaning of Hugh's or Lelia's words and actions as another character in the movie is. It may take many viewings of *Shadows* before some of the characters' expressions become intelligible, and in a film like *The Killing of a Chinese Bookie*, some expressions stay mysterious no matter how many times we see the movie. Late figures like Cosmo, Myrtle, and Robert stay mysterious even upon repeated viewings.[11]

When we notice that both Henry James and John Singer Sargent were similarly attracted to depictions of characters with "theatrical" qualities, and similarly fascinated with stimulating "loosenesses" of relation between surface expressions and deep identities, it suggests that Cassavetes' representational skepticism takes its place in a larger American expressive tradition. Lelia, Mabel, Gloria, and Sarah may be usefully compared with some of James's most memorable figures – *The Europeans*'s Eugenia, *An International Episode*'s Bessie Alden, *The Portrait of a Lady*'s Madame Merle, *The Spoils of Poynton*'s Fleda Vletch, *The Ambassadors*'s Madame de Vionnet, *The Golden Bowl*'s Charlotte Stant and Prince Amerigo – each of whose visible appearance and behavior leave an unusually large margin for the play of free interpretation about what is not visible.

Consider Eugenia, Baroness Munster, the main character in *The Europeans*, as an example of the intricate and oblique relation between impulses and expressions in James's work. While her straitlaced American hosts, the Wentworths, operate in a world in which feelings are directly and unproblematically translated into public expressions, Eugenia is much more like one of Cassavetes' masters and mistresses of obliquity. She is said to have "brought with her to the New World a copious provision of the element of costume"[12] (or as it is more comically and metaphorically put in another passage, to have surrounded herself with layer after layer of "curtains") with the result that "there were several ways of understanding her: there was what she said, and there was what she meant, and there was something, between the two, that was neither."[13]

Eugenia is consequently not only slightly mystifying to her American hosts, but frustrates many of their habitual ways of understanding, in particular the moral categories they seek to apply to behavior. Her theatricality is as much a mode of freedom as Lelia's is. It is a way of freeing herself from limiting judgments, defending herself from reductive readings. The effect is to create a far more complex relation between the self and its representations than simple moral categories can comprehend, to the point that judgments like "true" and "untrue" no longer obtain, as James takes pains to point out on several occasions: "Her declaration that she was looking for rest and retirement had been by no means untrue; nothing that the Baroness said was wholly untrue. It is but fair to add, perhaps, that nothing that she said was wholly true."[14]

Sargent explores a comparable ontological elusiveness in his greatest portraits: *Doctor Pozzi at Home*, *The Daughters of Edward De Boit*, *Madame X*, *Mrs. Fiske Warren and Her Daughter Rachel*, and *Charlotte Burkhardt (Lady with a Rose)*. The figures in each of these portraits are self-dramatizers who are revealed by their pictures to be "posing" for their pictures – which is to say we can't quite tell where "they" are in the pose, or whether "they" are there at all. The Charlotte Burkhardt painting is only the most obvious example of a figure breathtakingly missing in action. The sitter wills herself absent from her own portrait, striking a pose that declares she is precisely *not* where she apparently is.[15]

To avoid confusion, I would emphasize that although acts of imposture, impersonation, or disguise occur in classic Hollywood film, they almost always function in the opposite way from what I am describing in Cassavetes, James, and Sargent. Hitchcock's work, again, can stand as an illustrative counterexample. James, Sargent, and Cassavetes use role-playing to expand the boundaries of the self by proliferating it outward away from a unitary center into a kaleidoscopic display of alternative voices, expressions, and roles, none of which seems necessarily more true or more central than another. The self is made protean and plastic. Its boundaries are dissolved. Its identity is expanded. It is shown to contain multitudes. Hitchcock typically uses playacting in the reverse way: to affirm the inviolability of a single, central "true" identity. Disguises and mistaken identities abound in his work, but they always function to remind viewers and characters who the character really is separate from the disguise. Roger Thornhill and Eve Kendall in *North by Northwest*, Marion Crane and Norman Bates in *Psy-*

cho, Bruno Anthony in *Strangers on a Train*, and Scotty and Judy in *Vertigo* each assume various alias or disguises, or have alternative identities thrust upon them, but the viewer is never allowed to forget that the alternative identities are mistakes or acts of deceit. Hitchcock depends on the viewer's faith in the existence of an unposed, unacted, unembellished identity underneath and different from the disguise, a true identity that is always ultimately uncovered and affirmed. Once the plot twists have worked themselves out by the end of the film, there is never any question in the audience's mind (or a character's) what has been an act and what hasn't. We can know precisely at what points Bruno, Scotty, Eve, or Marion are acting because Hitchcock gives us a central unacted self from which to make all of the measurements. With Lelia, we can never quite say where the act ends and the person begins, because, as James's Madame Merle put it, the self "flows" and "overflows."[16]

In being allowed to play with their expressions of themselves, figures like Lelia and Ben are expressively more powerful and independent than characters in other films. The space between surfaces and depths leaves room for mystery, which is to say, freedom. The self is liquefied, its walls melted. Characters like Lelia and Ben are freed from the limitations of character itself (at least as it exists in other films – as a bundle of consistent behavior). Lelia's self-transformations are especially stimulating and awe inspiring. We can't predict what she is going to say or do next – whether she is going to go into a pet or laugh in our faces. She communicates the thrilling impression that she is making herself up and endlessly revising herself as she goes along, as if she could actually live the possibility that Emerson speculated about in "Circles," the life of being an endless "experimenter . . . with no past at [her] back."[17]

It is in the nature of Cassavetes' conception of character that it figures a state of unresolved energy that will not be reduced to a specific task, goal, or role – which in his view would represent an unacceptable limitation on imaginative possibility. In fact, as far as Cassavetes is concerned, if there *were* something in particular Ben and Lelia were supposed to do or say or become, or any final identity they were supposed to attain, they would not be worth saving. As a number of Cassavetes' supporting characters demonstrate – Ackerman here, and Benny Flowers, McCarthy, Zelmo, and Sil in other films (the last three played by Val Avery, Cassavetes' most dependable depictor of states of imaginative fascism) – there is no surer sign of damnation in Cassavetes' work than for a character to have a more or less predictable "character." His decision to focus on characters whose identities are racially indeterminate in this film anticipates his subsequent work, all of which is about characters whose identities are and must remain stimulatingly indeterminate in other ways.

For Cassavetes, the self is a loose bundle of unorganized energies and possibilities. Its lack of point is the point. It holds in suspension energies too volatile and mobile to be regimented into serving one specific goal or being limited to playing one particular role. That is why its most characteristic expressions partake of a certain degree of expressive excess or waywardness. Lelia's performative extravagance and theatricality, like Moskowitz's, Mabel's, and Sarah Lawson's in later films, is her way of declining to bring herself into reductive focus for others, and is Cassavetes' means of preventing her character from solidifying into a "character" in the conventional cinematic sense for viewers. To conform to normative standards of behavior and expression would be to betray the flowing truths of the imagination and emotions. That is why none of Cassavetes' most interesting figures will be stabilized. They stay in motion. Their expressions of themselves flicker and shift. Their selves must remain in flux and process to be true to themselves.

Cassavetes' understanding of selfhood did not originate in a study of advanced philosophy or psychology texts. It came out of his appreciation of the situation of the theatrical performer who creates and adjusts a role in front of an audience. In varying degrees, all of Cassavetes' most interesting figures are empowered to become artists of their identities in the same sense in which a dramatic performer is. One shapes oneself out of the materials that are available, and revises one's performance in accordance with the responses of the various audiences through which one moves, and one's own internal redirections.

Cassavetes' performative model of selfhood points a way beyond a false dichotomy of much modernist art, which imposes a forced choice on the individual: a choice between being trapped in and frustrated by a repressive social system, on the one hand; or breaking free and leaving it behind, on the other. Lelia's theatricality shows that the choice between enslavement and escape is an unnecessary one. One can function within an expressive system without giving up a margin of freedom. To use a concept that Richard Poirier has developed in great detail, Lelia shows that you can "perform" on and against the expressive structures in place around you without being imprisoned by them. In Cassavetes' performative model of freedom, the performer incorporates the resistances to his or her performance into the performance, replying to them, creatively bending them, moving freely within them. If, as an actor, he can't ever leave the scripted lines entirely behind, he can still inflect them in a creative direction. He can improvise on the margins of the text. Even if we can't escape a system, we can learn to use it creatively. Freedom can be immanent; it does not have to be transcendent. Cassavetes' figures (like James's and Sargent's) express their freedom in the forms of the world.

Nevertheless, we must pay for what we get. There is a negative side to this state of affairs. The dangers are exactly balanced against the opportunities. In the first place, as Ben and Tony demonstrate, insofar as one's identity is not natural and automatic, but artificial and achieved, a character faces expressive difficulties and runs ontological risks that characters in most other films do not. What is made can be a betrayal of one's true emotional needs. What is made can be badly made. What is made up can come undone.

Beyond that, the process of shaping a performance in the world, within the expressive structures of the world, asks an extraordinary level of energy and inventiveness from the individual performer. You cannot, as Hitchcock's characters do, withdraw into a state of insulated subjectivity when threatened. You cannot, as Woody Allen's characters do, imaginatively rise above social or expressive problems by moving into a state of vision or reverie. You must remain engaged with the forces that oppose you. That makes the life of the Cassavetean performer an especially strenuous one. The barely concealed tension of Sargent's figures, the high-wire stress of the performances staged by figures like Fleda Vletch and Maggie Verver in Henry James's novels, the nervous breakdowns and near-suicides of many of Cassavetes' figures, are testimony to the extraordinary demands this process of public performance asks of its participants.

Furthermore, insofar as one's identity is negotiated (and continuously renegotiated) in a process of interaction with others, it is fragile to a degree that it is not in most other films. The self is open to influences and vulnerable to wounding. It must remain actively in touch with and responsive to the very forces that continuously threaten to undo it. It must allow itself to be reached by, and therefore make itself susceptible to being hurt by, others. As Lelia demonstrates, in opening yourself up performatively, you open yourself to pain and grief. She and the later Mabel, Cosmo, Myrtle, and Sarah Lawson illustrate that in letting down the walls that hem in the self, you make yourself liable to be preyed upon or destroyed by others. In letting Tony and other men so deeply into her heart, Lelia pays the price of permeability.

The final challenge of Cassavetes' world is that there can be no rest stops on this journey. The ideal of freedom that his characters aspire to, and that he embraces, requires continuous, energetic renewal. For a creative responder, to stop noticing and responding even for a moment is to begin to die, since there is no role or pose that can be merely inherited or received from outside of oneself. Even more frightening, every past creative gesture becomes an implicit limitation on future creative movements. What starts out as creative and original forever runs the danger of becoming formulaic and mechanical. The performed self inhabits an eternal present. It must keep responding, changing, moving away from past stances and roles. The Cassavetean performer is open-ended and prospective, yet the stimulating, liberating liquidity of his experience is always on the brink of crystallizing into the rigidity of a confining pattern. This takes us to the heart of darkness in Cassavetes' imagination. He imagines a world in upheaval, a world of continuous imaginative compositions and decompositions, a world in which mechanical formulas everywhere threaten fluid imaginative ideals. That is the drama underneath the drama in all of Cassavetes' work.

Cassavetes' world is exciting precisely for the same reasons that it is dangerous. Indeed the pulse beat of his vision of life is that one aspect of the situation is inextricable from the other. We are continuously breaking free and just as continuously losing our freedom. For Cassavetes, as for the Emerson of "Circles," "Experience," or "Fate," life is this double, intertwined process of movement against everywhere-encroaching limitation, movement to a position which then itself immediately becomes a constraint, a limitation on future movement. Robert Frost once described a poem as being "like a piece of ice on a hot stove – floating on its own melting," and the metaphor might be aptly applied to Cassavetes' greatest characters and scenes. He imagines a heaving, surging universe in which meaning is continuously liquefying its own hardness (in the direction of freedom) yet just as continuously refreezing each of its own meltings (in the direction of what Emerson would call Fate). As Frost's metaphor brilliantly suggests, creativity and limitation are not opposed forces originating in different places or agents as they are sometimes imagined to be. They are not inner and outer, self and not-self, individual and society, us and them, but rather are the same energy in different states. Our freedom is continuously freezing and melting, our limitations continuously evaporating into steam or hardening into igloo walls. That ceaseless shifting of states is what life is.

Cassavetes' most interesting characters walk the knife-edge where this drama of composition and decomposition takes place: where free and eccentric impulses continuously congeal into processed, packaged expressions. To put it in terms of *Shadows*'s controlling metaphor, flexible role-playing is continuously on the verge of ossifying into the rigidity of mask wearing. Lelia shows us how mercurial playacting blurs into coy pose striking. Ben and Tony's Method-acting clichés demonstrate how the quest for free expression can end up trapping the self in formulas for expression. Ben and Lelia are empowered to form (and reform) themselves through various kinds of performance, but then run the risk of losing themselves in the roles they play. Ben risks becoming an epiphenomenon of his beat mannerisms and costume, his Method tones and styles. Lelia's flamboyant self-dramatizations can become a way not to express, but to deny her deeper needs and emotions even to herself. The mobility of our souls always runs the risk of hardening into the fixity of our roles. We continuously risk losing ourselves to the very styles that were intended to liberate us.

Cassavetes distrusts all systems of expression. Systems normalize and regulate expressions. Systems suppress or ignore fragmentary or fugitive impulses; they rob individuals of expressive uniqueness. The codes of Method acting are one such system. The codes of stoic male behavior are another. The codes of female sexual flirtatiousness are another. What makes Cassavetes' critique of systematization so powerful, however, is that it is ultimately directed against the systematizations of his own work. In this respect, he shows himself to be far more radical in his critique of abstract or intellectual forms of understanding than is Robert Altman. Although Altman's films also depict the tyranny of structures, they completely except their own structurings from the indictment. Altman's hell has only other people in it. For Cassavetes, his own cinematic systems of narrative organization are as much the enemy of truth as a system of acting or a system of personal expression is.

Narrative presentation depends on coherency, consistency, and continuity, but experience is lumpy, jumpy, and jagged. Life's truths come in unresolved impulses, disjointed pieces, and unfinished processes. The implicit concisions, clarities, and resolutions of narrative presentation are fundamentally at odds with the incoherence, obliquity, and muddlement of felt experience. In this sense, Cassavetes pits narrative against itself. His narratives disrupt their own legibility and delay their own comprehensibility. His entire stylistic project is an effort to fracture his narratives' own emerging regularities and coherencies in order to open them to the registration of expressive obliquities, eccentricities, and provisionalities.

That is why scenes in *Shadows* are so wildly unpredictable in their tones, moods, and directions. Fights and arguments break out in the middle of calm interludes. Romantic or comic impulses bubble up in the middle of tense interactions. The relationships of characters juke away from even the most alert viewer's ability to predict where they are headed.

As an extended illustration of tonal slipperiness, consider the sequence of scenes involving Lelia and Tony that begins with their lovemaking at Tony's place and continues on to the point at which they are necking on the sofa, when Hugh and Rupert interrupt them. The sequence moves from the comic pathos of Lelia's postcoital conversation with Tony ("I didn't know it could be so awful"); to the pseudosincerity of Tony's expressions of care ("It's only natural"); to Lelia's "wounded woman" melodramatics; to the zaniness of the cabbie's kibitzing over whether Tony will go upstairs with Lelia or take the cab back home, and his singing "I love you truly"; to Tony and Lelia's shared awkwardness when they first arrive in the apartment and find Ben and his friends there; to the tenderness of their dancing and kissing once they are alone; to the offensiveness of Tony's rejection of Lelia when he discovers she is black.

That sequence runs six or seven minutes, but even the briefest conversation in *Shadows* is liable to slip away from the intellectual structures within which we attempt to contain it. Consider two short interchanges: one from near the beginning of the film; the other from near its end. The first takes place between Tony and Lelia outside of Tony's apartment just before they go inside to make love:

LELIA: I feel like I'll never know things. Like ... like ...
TONY: What do you feel like, tell me what you feel like.
LELIA: I feel like I'm in a ... a ...
TONY: In a cocoon, and you can't get out.
LELIA: That's right. I didn't think boys were supposed to understand things like that. You see I *am* far behind.
TONY: Behind who?
LELIA: Now you sound like David.
TONY: I hope not.
LELIA: Why not? David is one of the most intelligent people I've ever met in my life.
TONY: But not very romantic.
LELIA: No, he's not very romantic.
TONY: You know, I'm not a very nice person. I mean I have romantic inclinations. I'm not one of those storybook characters who's supposed to be all noble and righteous. If I see someone I like and she likes me, we accept my romantic inclinations.

The conversation is quite loose and rambling. In fact, the first point to notice is the apparent casualness or aimlessness of the moment. Lelia and Tony are "just talking." Their talk doesn't have an overriding agenda or subject; but precisely because the moment is sprung free of an obvious narrative "point," the viewer is forced to encounter it with a specially heightened state of awareness. That we can't dive underneath the conversation to read a simple purpose or pattern out of it means that we must stay continuously "in" it and "with" its rhythms. Since it apparently doesn't exist to "go" somewhere, we can't merely wait to see how it ends. We must attend to the second-by-second progress of the interaction in the real time of its occurrence.

This is one of the most important aspects of Cassavetes' work. Just as he creates characters whose identities are in process, he creates scenes that don't exist to generate an endpoint. Rather, they locate us in what William James calls a process-oriented universe. They capture energies continuously on the move, and in their meticulous registration of movements, they honor impulses that won't be made to subserve a larger theoretical agenda or be made to trace a larger narrative trajectory. These tiny, unstable, mobile energies are the lost, forgotten, or buried impulses that Cassavetes devoted his career to bringing back to awareness. They are the truths of process that our lust for destinations makes us forget. They are the tiny emotional quiverings that most other films, in their commitment to getting to the next plot event, are forced to rush past or leave out altogether.

It is not too much to argue that Cassavetes is calling us to a new, invigorating form of seeing and feeling. The viewer is plunged along with the characters into a present-tense world in which one must live one step at a time, never seeing beyond the present step. In this respect, the conversations in Cassavetes' work have a lot in common with the thrusts and parries of a fencing match or the moves in a game of chess (compare the one I quoted previously between Lelia and Tony in bed). One never quite knows where a remark will lead or what a character's next "move" will be. Encounters are stimulatingly unpredictable and open to possibility.

There is another gamelike aspect to Cassavetes' dialogue passages: Characters' interactions do not organize themselves as a more or less direct logical or emotional progress along a straight line to a goal, but as a series of counterpoised tacking movements. The zigzag is the straightest line Cassavetes' characters know – not only because they can never see beyond the present moment, but because they must continuously take account of and respond to each other's continuously shifting positions and countermovements.

Even a single character's underlying meanings and intentions won't stop moving: Note that the conversational switchbacks not only are the result of the competition between Lelia's and Tony's different views, but occur even in one character's mind. Follow the shifting trajectory of the connotations Lelia attaches to David: In her first mention of his name, he represents stuffy intellectualism; in the second mention of his name, he is "one of the most intelligent people I've ever met"; in the third, he is "not very romantic."

Cassavetes' scenes communicate the impression of minds on the move and social relationships in flux. Nothing stands still. He captures states of continuous transition. Though in both scenes from which I have quoted Tony and Lelia are physically stock-still (in bed in the one scene, standing next to a lamppost on the street in the other), their intellectual positions are shifting at the speed of thought. Cassavetes creates an authentic dialogue in which not only are there two different points of view, but each individual point of view is put in motion. There are profound similarities between Cassavetes' sense of art and that of a jazz composition, and these scenes have a jazzlike quality to their form even more than they have jazz references in their content. As in a jazz improvisation, there is no foreseeing where each beat will lead. As in a jazz performance, impulse is not suppressed in order to maintain a straight line of development; in fact, the opposite happens – the pursuit of the impulse becomes the principle of organization. The purpose of the performance is not to maintain an overall continuity of development, but to display variations. That means that, like the listeners to a jazz performance, Cassavetes' viewers can only stay vigilant – open to continuously developing possibilities. This is the reason Cassavetes' scenes seem so alive and his characters appear so lively (and why his scenes feel improvised, even when they are not). While the characters in other films seem to be following a game plan, it always feels as if Cassavetes' characters are changing their plans from second to second, continuously swerving off track to pursue shifting impulses, continuously changing their stances to respond to other characters' changes. In the most profound sense, Cassavetes' characters don't exist, don't *have* identities, until they discover themselves and their possibilities in this process of exploring their differences. Talking at cross purposes, they function like jazz musicians "working it out" through dialogue interaction.

Notice how the control of the beats keeps shifting between Tony and Lelia. Who has the upper hand, who controls the pacing, who "directs" the scene keeps changing. Tony controls the first four or five lines; Lelia gets some leverage when she chides him that he sounds like David; Tony regains control with his put-down of David; Lelia reestablishes her solidarity with Tony by agreeing with him; Tony in turn then yields a degree of control to her with his final remark (which grants Lelia power by allowing her to decide the next move). They utterly resist being mapped onto a set of static positions (dominant–subordinate; initiator–responder; active–passive). We can't read a pattern out of their conversation that will stabilize their relationship. It is impossible even to say whether Lelia and Tony are generally in agreement or disagreement. All Cassavetes presents is process: They agree, then disagree, then agree. The social and intellectual movement of their interaction defies abstract description. The viewer and the characters are suspended in a present-tense, process-oriented universe that defies non-temporal descriptions.

That should suggest why Cassavetes' characters and scenes resist the designs of both deconstructionists and ideological critics of all stripes. Where energies are so coruscating and positions so fluid, there is nothing for them to get any critical leverage on. Where nothing is constructed, there is nothing to be deconstructed. Cassavetes' world of water won't give the sledgehammers of the feminists and Marxists anything to pound on, either. His work is similarly unavailable to students of popular culture, since the entire edifice of popular-culture studies is founded on a faith that works create meanings that are simplistic, static, detachable, and more or less allegorical.[18] The significances Cassavetes creates fail on all counts. Because his meanings are not portably packed up in such ways, the pop culture critic is left with nothing to unpack. Meanings that are so temporal, specific, and mercurial – true in one time, place, and set of circumstances, and false in another – resist being made to yield a sociological point. Whereas the conversations that take place between Dave and HAL, Charles Foster Kane and Susan Alexander, and Norman Bates and Marion Crane invite general and abstract interpretations, those that take place between Tony and Lelia defy them.

I would note, however, that although the interaction between Lelia and Tony is salutarily broken free from having its zigzag progress straightened out to conform to a more linear narrative trajectory, it isn't random or haphazard. Especially for a viewer listening to the tones and the emotional undertones, the conversations in *Shadows* have extremely complex shapes. It is nevertheless crucial to the impression of freedom Cassavetes orchestrates that a conversation's shape is usually visible only after it is over, or after one has watched it more than once. In this particular example, it becomes retrospectively clear by the end of the conversation that Tony, the consummate seduction artist, has been steering things in a very definite direction that he has decided on in advance. The apparently loose repetitions of the word "romantic" all lead up to his final proposition. On Lelia's part, in light of her decision to sleep with him, it becomes retrospectively clear that she has been entertaining his proposition all along, even as she attempts to

retain some degree of control over the situation with her coy argumenta-
tiveness. The shape, however, is apparent only later. Even if we can sometimes understand life backward, we are committed to living it forward.

For a final example of what a beat-by-beat, move-by-move universe feels
like, mark the beats in the brief flurry of disagreement and hurt feelings
that takes place between Davey Jones and Lelia on the dance floor near the
end of the film. It is the conclusion of a trying date, and both Lelia and
Davey have had difficult nights, though for different reasons. She is still
hurting from Tony's rejection, and holds Davey at arm's length to prevent
him from wounding her. Davey is smarting after hours of off-putting sar-
casm. I indicate some of the tones of the line deliveries, and begin in the
middle of the argument they are having:

DAVEY: [*firm*] Where I come from the men do the asking. The girls just go
yes or no.
LELIA: [*sassy*] Well, I guess I just don't fit into that pattern, now do I?
DAVEY: [*stern*] No, you don't. As matter of fact, you're just a little too
much for me.
LELIA: [*insulted and insulting*] Well then, why don't you take me home?
Or why did you ask me here in the first place?
DAVEY: Don't upset me, girl. [*self-pitying*] Do you always shout down your
boyfriends that way?
LELIA: [*shouting*] I never shout!
DAVEY: Well it does seem that way to me. Huh! Do you always go around
embarrassing people in front of strangers? [*wounded*] I mean laughing at
them in front of your family? [*sarcastic*] Keep 'em waiting for hours just to
show off how masculine you are?
LELIA: [*at her most feline*] Darling, I'm not masculine.
DAVEY: [*conceding the point by denying it*] Well, it would seem that way
to me.
LELIA: [*taunting*] Well, how do you want me to behave?
DAVEY: [*beating a strategic retreat after finding himself clearly out-
maneuvered*] Look. Just dance and be as lovely as you look.
LELIA: [*formal*] Look, David, I am what I am, and nobody tells me what
to do.
DAVEY: [*almost pleading for a little tenderness*] Look, I don't know who
you think you're fighting.... You know, I saw the way he [i.e., Tony, who
came to see Lelia as she and Davey were headed out] looked at you back
there, and I also saw the way he looked at me.
[*On the verge of tears, Lelia is unable to speak. A long silence ensues.*]

DAVEY: [*conciliatory, tender, trying to make a joke, realizing he has hurt her*] You know, despite your horrible exterior, it's you I like.

To pick up on Lelia's initial metaphor (and one of the governing concepts of the film), the meaning of this moment is that it "doesn't fit into a pattern." The liquidity of the experience is of the essence. Davey's temper flares. Lelia defends herself and strikes back. Davey defends himself. He is hurt. She is hurt. Lelia is suddenly reached, and becomes tender. Davey is himself deeply affected and becomes gentle. Experience is put on wheels. Emotional currents fluidly stream between characters. In this universe of oil, opportunities of relationship continuously slip into or slide out of existence. In the fluidity of Lelia's and Davey's tones, Cassavetes celebrates the imaginative movements that are possible even in the most physically confined or unpropitious settings. He shows us that momentous emotional transactions can take place even when nothing is apparently "happening" in terms of external events.

I would emphasize that the oscillations of feeling and relationship that Cassavetes dramatizes are not confined to conversational moments. What I've described in terms of the characters' conversations is true of Cassavetes' narrative procedures in general. Just as he breaks his characters' interactions free from narrative overdetermination in order to dramatize second-by-second movements of feeling, he breaks his film as a whole free from narrative tendentiousness in order (in his words) that the film's "small emotions . . . not be ground down in the plot." He refuses to straighten out narrative loops and twists so that individual scenes will smoothly advance the plot. The acting releases energies that the story can't control. The fidelity to impulse makes Cassavetes' films the Jackson Pollocks of cinema. He would rather be true to the scribble of his characters' inchoate expressions and to their undefined swirls of feeling than to the straight line of the story.

The goal is to make room, in the cracks of the plot as it were, for the expression of nonsystematic impulses of the sort that are squeezed out of other movies. Cassavetes brings unformulated impulses to light in many scenes simply by having a character make a face, throw off a casual gesture, or do something unexpected and undictated by the requirements of the plot. It is telling that most of these moments are purely *bodily* expressions; that is, they figure energies that are not brought to verbal consciousness (nor to consciousness at all). The characters themselves probably don't even realize they are doing these things. As always in Cassavetes' work, the body is the repository of truths to which the mind doesn't have access. The body tells the truth, even when the person wants to lie. A few examples should suffice to illustrate some of the specific ways unregimented energies surface in *Shadows*:

The weird bobbing motion of the girl who goes up to Ben to ask him to join the party and "get out of his mood."

Lelia's terrified gestures a few minutes later when she is caught standing too close to the fight that breaks out between Ben and Hugh.

The brief, zany theatrical "turn" Lelia and Ben do together and their shared laugh, while Davey is cooling his heels waiting for Lelia to finish getting ready for their date.

Ben's semicomic slouch after he is knocked out in the fight scene in the dumpster and the angularity of his arms as Tom carries him out.

Ben's strange pauses and jerky gestures throughout the film – two examples: the brief "beat" he takes as he walks into the dance studio where Hugh and Rupert are negotiating with Ackerman, and the irregularity of his timing and gestures in the film's final, nondialogue shot sequence.

These are the sort of oddball moments critics typically leave out of their accounts of a viewing experience because they do not function abstractly or systematically. Indeed, if they are mentioned at all they are assumed to be mere actorly exuberances, accidents, or errors. They do not lend themselves to metaphoric generalizations. They do not advance the plot. They do not "mean" superpersonal things, nor are they deeply revelatory about the intentions or goals of a character. They are personal, idiosyncratic, and fleeting expressions, eccentric to the overarching structures of the work.

But their eccentricity and evanescence are what most interest Cassavetes about them. That they function in an expressively opposite way than Charles Foster Kane's "Rosebud" utterance is the point. Insofar as they are unmotivated, unexpected, unpredictable, and stick out of the narrative, they express the triumph of impulse over system. They testify to his success in getting unassimilated, unsystematic impulses on film, and in so doing they let us see that life lies in that direction, away from struck poses and formulated styles of acting or of living.

In this sense, the style of *Shadows* criticizes the styles of the characters within it. Cassavetes' cinematic forms of scene making represent an implicit critique of Lelia's, Ben's, Tony's, Rupert's, and Hugh's personal forms of scene making. The conversational loops, jumps, and changes of direction, the unexpected eruptions of feeling, the tonal slippages, the glimpses under the masks, and the eccentric impulses that Cassavetes includes in *Shadows* give the lie to the forms of stylistic control and arrangement to which characters like Ben, Tony, Hugh, and Rupert devote themselves. While their

66

Spontaneous, exuberant eruptions of energy eccentric to the plot: the brief dramatic "turn" performed by Ben Carruthers and Lelia Goldoni while Davey Jones is waiting for Lelia to get ready for their date.

creator is in favor of the nonsystematic and unformulated, Tony, Ben, Hugh, and the others attempt to package themselves into coherent roles and conclusive stances. Specifically, Ben's endearingly idiosyncratic mannerisms and eccentric timing (in Cassavetes' photography of him) represent a surfacing of the vulnerable individuality that his "coolness" would deny. While Ben, Tony, Hugh, Rupert, and Lelia attempt to hide behind formulated roles, the interactions Cassavetes stages defy mechanical forms of presentation. The film's tonal and dramatic dislocations batter down the walls its characters erect to keep themselves safe from the dangers of unregimented experience.

It is important to the effect he is after that Cassavetes breaks his narrative away from the problem-solving structure that is customary in most movies. He does this in two different ways: with the plot and with the characters. In terms of plot, his scenes do not pose a concise series of narrative "questions" which are then resolved with a series of narrative "answers." In terms of characters, neither Tony, Hugh, Ben, nor Lelia has a specific "problem" to solve, nor a "solution" to be attained. They have no specific task to accomplish or sequence of actions to perform within the narrative. Their problems are deliberately kept as general and vague as any solutions to them would be. What they instead figure is a host of inchoate feelings that need to be worked through with no definite outcome in sight. Their task is nothing less than to learn how to be themselves and to get along with others. There is no particular action they can take or event that can happen to ease their job or mark their progress. How does one find oneself, anyway? Certainly not by doing something in particular.

The result is that viewers and characters must muddle through a series of scenes without really knowing what to pay attention to or where the plot or character is headed next. Since there are no schematic understandings to organize our processing of information, and no predetermined narrative destination or prescribed sequence of events along the way to mark our progress, at any one moment it is very hard to know where we are, where we are headed, or how far we have gone. Rather than being a negative condition, however, the consequence is that it creates an intense state of vigilance. Nothing is trivial; everything matters.

Think of the standard Hollywood feature film with its quest trajectory and its step-by-step presentation of a sequence of events that lead toward a particular goal as a jigsaw puzzle in which the clarity of the overall picture makes it unnecessary to scrutinize the shape of each piece very carefully. In that metaphor, Cassavetes' films are jigsaw puzzles without pictures (or with unfocused pictures). Following the bumps and curves of the individual pieces becomes the experience. No totalizing vision releases us from the fragmentary events. We piece things together in a piecemeal universe.

Cassavetes' films bring us to an acute state of present-mindedness. If we (or the characters) could simply wait to see how things turn out, or measure our distance from a defined endpoint, as we can in most other films, we would not be forced to pay such close and continuous attention to the present. To use a musical metaphor, in minimizing melody, Cassavetes makes his viewers attend to individual notes and shifts of key far more carefully. That makes his scenes as demanding, exciting, and unpredictable as a good jazz performance. In contrast, a more linearly plotted film, with its fixed trajectory of incremental buildups, confrontations, climaxes, and resolutions – more like Burt Bacharach than Charlie Parker – lets us coast most of the time, while we wait for the next high point to kick in.

Cassavetes had an essentially dramatic imagination, which means not

Directing by doing: blocking the action in *Shadows*'s final fight scene by playing it. Cassavetes, who is not himself in the scene, beats up Ben Carruthers prior to filming the scene with Cliff Carnell in the role Cassavetes is playing here.

only that experience is anchored in particular characters and specific situations (rather than being somewhat abstract, impersonal and generic as it is, say, in Kubrick or Hitchcock), but that it is extremely difficult to locate him as an unmediated presence in his work. There are very few moments in which one hears the filmmaker speaking more or less directly through a character. However, when David berates Ben and two of his friends in a conversation in a coffee shop with, "You never break your patterns," we come as close as we ever do to hearing the filmmaker's own words.[19] For Cassavetes, patterns are always hazardous to our emotional and intellectual health. They are forms of arrest. They stop the pulse-beat of life. They carry us away from experience by abstracting us from it.

Shadows's style forces characters to break their abstract patterns of behavior and viewers to break their abstract patterns of understanding. Part of opening up in this way means learning to navigate turbulent waves of expression without being able to stabilize our interpretations by anchoring them in "deep" insights. Cassavetes' superficiality is deliberate – and profound. As much as he defends his characters against having destinations for development, he prevents his viewers from tracing their situations back to origins. To move in either direction (ahead to the future or back to the past) would be to release oneself imaginatively from the stimulating excruciations of the present. That is why so many of Cassavetes' films begin without a beginning, and progress without giving us the background of events. Cassavetes doesn't tell us why Ben is the way he is, why Lelia thinks that her emotions can be disconnected from her actions, or why Hugh is a failure at his chosen career and is too weak to face it. He doesn't provide clarifying explanations or causes. He usually doesn't provide end points or resolutions to his characters' predicaments, either. The nostalgia for origins, the lust for destinations, is replaced by an appreciation of experience as process. In Cassavetes' view, all reasons, causes, origins, and destinations are conceptual avoidances of the temporally, emotionally, and socially flowing reality within which we live.

As is suggested by the way he initially veils Ben and Lelia's racial identities from the viewer, it is central to Cassavetes' narrative project that the viewer undergoes the same educational process in watching the film that the main characters do in living its events. *Shadows* teaches viewers and characters alike that however painful it may be, we have to give up our lived or theatrical "routines" – to abandon our designs for living (and our predetermined interpretative designs on a text) – and expose ourselves to the shocks and jars of an unpredictable series of events. We must make ourselves vulnerable to life – to unformulated, unassimilated experience.

Cassavetes creates a different kind of viewer than other films. We are asked to become faster, more intuitive, and more nimble in our responses. We must learn to live in a stimulatingly shifty world, leaping along a path of stepping-stones in the dark, unable to rise above the sensory and social particularity of specific moments. The conceptual shorthand that allows us to get a handle on events and characters in most other films only gets in the way here (or leads us to jump to false conclusions, as when we conclude Lelia and Ben are white because they look white). As with one's first experience of bebop, the first time out the experience can be bewildering (which is why Cassavetes earned the reputation as a confusing filmmaker), but once we get the hang of the new rhythms and pacings (which may take several viewings), it becomes invigorating and profoundly enlightening.

This is film not as storytelling, but as "an experience you are put through" (in Cassavetes' characterization of his own work) – a process of limbering up one's capacities of perceptiveness and sensitivity. Cassavetes' "creative writing" is an attempt to elicit the viewer's "creative reading." The viewer is educated to stay open and on the move. The filmmaker would have agreed with Emerson that emotional health is the result of "circulation." As *Faces* will even more emphatically demonstrate, Cassavetes' greatest scenes don't "get anywhere," or even try to. They only move through and compare a range of reactions, viewpoints, and emotions. When the three buddies, Ben, Dennis, and Tom, go to the Museum of Modern Art sculpture garden, Cassavetes' goal is only that we and they circulate through a number of different views of art and life. There is nowhere to "get." There is only a process of unceasing adjustment, and interaction.

Shadows's narrative enacts one of the master plots that occur many other times in Cassavetes' work: In response to their pains, Hugh, Ben, and Lelia close off their identities, close down their capacities for responsiveness, and shut down their emotions. Cassavetes' narrative thrust is always to force characters to reopen locked doors. They must make themselves vulnerable even if it hurts (and it usually does). For Cassavetes, the path to wisdom is always via the route of experience, which is to say, through involvement with and susceptibility to others, no matter how much we may want to protect our feelings. By this standard, *Shadows*'s final three scenes give us hope for the three main characters. Cassavetes depicts three acts of *anagnorisis* in the strict Aristotelian sense of the term – a fundamental recognition about one's nature and needs: Hugh and Rupert finally open up emotionally with each other and say what they have been feeling all along; Lelia opens herself to Davey (in the scene from which I quoted an excerpt); and even Ben comes to a realization that what he thought was self-creation is closer to being self-destruction.

Tony and Ben's semicomic wrestle with clichés of life and art demonstrates that even in his first film Cassavetes understood what a complex balancing act a free performance is. Freedom is hard. Our natural condition is unfree. Limiting intellectual, social, and emotional styles can rob us of our true selves. The characters' mortgaging of their identities to "beat" forms of behavior and Method intonations teaches us that in attempting to find ourselves, we can end up giving ourselves away to a preformulated style. What they teach us is crucial to an understanding of Cassavetes' subsequent work, all of which is founded on the conviction that characters are born into structures of expression that can't be avoided. Before we even arrive on the scene, cultural and artistic arrangements of knowledge are in place waiting to ensnare us. The world is not a blank slate on which we write our dreams: It is power saturated and convention imbued.

As *Gloria* will demonstrate by dramatically externalizing the concept, there is no escaping the system. You can't drop out of the expressive game or refuse to play it; you have to play by the rules, yet still find a way to win on your own terms. As Ben and Tony resoundingly demonstrate, if we fail to master the systems into which we are born, we will be enslaved by them. Anything that is not mastery is misery. That is another reason Cassavetes is not interested ultimately in characters' deep psychology or states of intentionality. In his view of it, creative expression takes much more than good will or noble intentions; it takes knowledge and work. Virtually all of the characters in his films "mean well" (just as Ben and Tony do) but meaning well is not good enough. Freedom takes much more than the desire to be free. We can be unfree and not know it. We can try to be free and fail. Creative expression must be wrestled from the forms in place around us, which always resist or betray our creative intentions. To paraphrase Lawrence, freedom takes a fine and complex knowingness. It takes heroic effort. Visions, dreams, and ideals are not sufficient.

As actors and as characters, Ben and Tony must find a way to use the influences that beset them – the conventions of acting and of life – in order to make original responses possible. They must learn to negotiate a free path through the expressive forms in place around them. Cassavetes would have agreed with Robert Frost that "the best way out is always *through*." Engaging and mastering the complex expressive inheritances of life (and their intricate entailments) is the only satisfactory course of action available to us. That process of hacking an idiosyncratic, individual path through a tangled undergrowth of "influences" (to allude to the title of one of Cassavetes' other works) is one of the other master plots of his films. His greatest characters must make their way through a jungle of intellectual, emotional, and social complications they can neither physically escape nor imaginatively rise above.

As the triple "recognitions" that end it suggest, *Shadows* is really quite upbeat and affirmative about this process. It is an optimistic film. It tells us that we can rediscover and express our true selves amid the everywhere-impinging conventions of expression. It further tells us that no permanent damage is done by our mistakes. Even at their most trapped, Tony's, Ben's, and Lelia's expressive clumsiness is more comic than tragic, more endearing than threatening, and causes more pain and embarrassment to themselves than to anyone around them. The wounds they inflict on others are minor and heal quickly. In short, it is the film of a young man with his hopes and dreams intact.

Cassavetes would never be this sanguine again. *Faces*, his next major work, is dark, somber, and almost despairing. It is a cry of horror and dismay at expressive possibilities lost and forgotten. Its characters have sold their souls to uphold a style they don't even realize is a style. They are hustlers and con men locked into an endless, draining battle for survival in a frightening, predatory world of expressive entrapment, frustration, and pain. They are imprisoned for life within dehumanizing forms of expression – mechanical styles that rigidify their behavior, rob them of their individuality, and inflict excruciating pain on them and everyone with whom they come in contact. Cassavetes moves from the lightness of *Shadows*'s semi-comedy to a tragedy of Shakespearean scale and resonance.

The shift might seem surprising and inexplicable, yet it is actually common to find such apparently contradictory visions in an artist's work. Precisely to the extent that Cassavetes entertains extreme ideals of creative self-expression for himself and his characters (as he does in *Shadows*), he is sensitized to the pervasiveness of cultural and intellectual conventions that regiment and frustrate expression (as he depicts in *Faces*). The extremity of the hope creates the extremity of the disillusionment. Even within *Shadows* itself, one might say that Lelia's expressive inventiveness brings Ben and Tony's expressive entrapment into existence. To be able to imagine Lelia's wonderful, stimulating, structure-breaking emotional extravagances is implicitly to recognize the potential of Ben and Tony's expressive imprisonment. In this sense, *Shadows* does not contradict *Faces*, but predicts it. The seeds of *Faces*'s tragedy are present in Ben and Tony's clumsy comedy.

With *Faces* and the films that follow it, Cassavetes' vision of expressive freedom becomes inextricably intertwined with a dread of expressive predation, coercion, and frustration. Murder, suicide, public humiliation, and shame haunt his later characters, many of whom seem on the verge of being pulled apart by the force field of stylistic pressures within which their films locate them.[20] Like Henry James in his late works, over the next two decades Cassavetes' exultant dream of expressive freedom alternates with (and at times becomes indistinguishable from) a paranoid nightmare of expressive entrapment.

2

Noncontemplative Art

Faces

My films are expressive of a culture that has had the possibility of attaining material fulfillment while at the same time finding itself unable to accomplish the simple business of conducting human lives. We have been sold a bill of goods as a substitute for life.... In this country people die at the age of 21. They die emotionally at 21, maybe younger. My responsibility as an artist is to help them get past 21.... *Faces* was a barrage of attack on contemporary middle-class America, an expression of horror at our society in general, focusing on a married couple – old fashioned in nature, safe in their suburban home, narrow in their thinking. The script gives them new situations to cope with, takes them out of their house, releases them from the conformity of their existence, forces them into a different context, when all barriers are down.

To tell the truth as you see it is not necessarily the truth. To tell the truth as someone else sees it is, to me, much more important and enlightening.... I absolutely refuse to judge the characters in my films and it is imperative that the [actors] neither analyze themselves nor others during the course of the filming.... I just want to record what people said, film what they did, intervening as little as possible, or, in any case, trying never to film inside them, so to speak.   – John Cassavetes[1]

In the early 1960s Cassavetes worked briefly in Hollywood on two studio pictures, *Too Late Blues* and *A Child Is Waiting*. Unfortunately, on the second project he got into a fight with the producer about the editing. Even more unfortunately, the producer was Stanley Kramer, one of the most powerful men on the West Coast. Kramer put out the word that Cassavetes was "difficult," and for the next decade he was more or less blackballed from working as a studio director.

But Cassavetes was never one to let lack of institutional support stop him, and by the fall of 1964, growing restless with a make-work job at

74

Screen Gems as a low-level producer, he decided he would make a feature film on his own. If he couldn't make a studio picture, he would make a home movie – working from his own script, bankrolling the film with his own money, employing friends as actors, and using his house as a set. Because he had already done more or less the same thing with *Shadows*, the idea probably didn't sound as outrageous to him as it would have to any other Hollywood director. As he often said afterward, "sometimes it helps not to know what can't be done."

In the years after his experience with Kramer, Cassavetes had written a number of unproduced stage plays (he had more or less given up on film as a hopelessly compromised commercial form). Late in 1964, he quickly rewrote one of them as a screenplay. It was a no-holds-barred indictment of the shallowness and hypocrisy of Los Angeles deal making. The film's ferocity is at least in part traceable to Cassavetes' personal struggles as a failed filmmaker in the six years that had elapsed since he finished *Shadows*. His emotional register had shifted. *Shadows* is sweet and sincere; *Faces* is unrelentingly hard and rough. The plot focuses on the disintegration of a marriage and the casual brutality of male–female relations. But that is a superficial description. *Faces* presents a view of a culture run psychologically amok. Contemporary upper-middle-class America becomes a harrowing world of jungle beasts on the prowl, preying on each other sexually and emotionally, thrashing about in their agony as they inflict pain or have it inflicted on them. The men in particular are completely out of control, brutalizing the women they let into the edges of their lives and insanely using business values to conduct their most intimate affairs.

The script went through various titles, from *The Dinosaurs* (which met-aphorically sums up the savageness of most of the characters), to *The American Marriage*, to *One Fah and Eight Las* (a reference to a song sung within the film), becoming *Faces* only after editing was complete. Cassavetes gathered together a mixed group of friends and relatives to appear in the movie, including his wife, Gena Rowlands, his closest personal friend, Seymour Cassel, former actresses like Dorothy Gulliver (whose previous acting career had ended around the time movies became talkies), and aspiring but untried actresses like Lynn Carlin, who was a secretary working across the hall from Cassavetes at Screen Gems.

The average undergraduate film student today has more sophisticated equipment and a more experienced crew than Cassavetes did when he began the film. Late in 1964, Al Ruban (who eventually wore hats as producer, director of photography, cameraman, and editor, and who would spend the better part of the next twenty years working with Cassavetes) was given a check for $8,000 from the filmmaker's savings and dispatched to New York to pick up as much used equipment as he could. In a week's shopping he managed to come up with a 16mm Arriflex, a few assorted heads and tripods, six lenses, a Perfectone recorder, two Lavaliers, a shotgun mike, and a pile of lights. Around Christmas time, he put everything into a U-Haul and drove to the West Coast, en route picking up George Sims, who would also work as cameraman, editor, and producer. Meanwhile, Cassavetes independently acquired a 16mm Eclair and some additional equipment on his own. (Though *Faces* was begun using both cameras, the Eclair completely replaced the Arriflex after a couple months of shooting because it was easier to hand-hold.) It was on-the-job training for everyone involved because no one except Ruban, who had experience free-lancing as cameraman on a series of low-budget New York films, even knew how to operate the equipment when it first arrived.

Everything about the production was strictly bargain basement. Though Cassavetes would eventually sink more than $200,000 of his own money into the production, *Faces*'s total initial shooting budget was the $8,000 given to Ruban for equipment and $2,000 more for film stock and lights, all from Cassavetes' savings. The actors agreed to work for nothing, which is to say for a share in the future profits, though no one expected there to be any. (The willingness to defer salary was something Cassavetes had to rely on in all of his independent productions.) The two principal shooting locations were the house of Cassavetes' mother-in-law (which became the apartment of the call girl, Jeannie Rapp) and the filmmaker's own home (which became the residence of the two main characters, Richard Forst and his wife Maria). To economize on the cost of stock, "short ends" – irregular-length pieces of film that the lab sold at a steep discount – were used as much as possible. The footage was edited and the sound was mixed at home as well, on a Movieola and a Magnasyne in Cassavetes' garage. (To give credit where it is due, Haskell Wexler pitched in at a crucial juncture to loan Cassavetes extra lights and equipment for scenes in the Loser's club, most of which were cut from the final print, and the Whiskey à Go Go.) Cassavetes earned the $200,000 that it took to get a screenable print by taking five acting jobs in the course of the three years it took for him, Ruban, Sims, Maurice McEndree, and a slew of volunteers to edit the film and synch the sound.

Since many of the participants held "real" jobs on other projects during the days, filming took place chiefly on evenings and weekends, and ran for six straight months, from New Year's Day through June of 1965. ("Deck the Halls with Boughs of Holly," which is sung by Jeannie, Freddie, and

76

Richard in the second scene, survives as a reminder of the time of year when filming began, as well as being connected with one of the working titles of the script.) As with all of Cassavetes' productions, shooting proceeded as much as possible "in continuity," which is to say, working in sequence from the first page of the script to the last, in order to help the actors develop the most emotionally resonant performances possible. One wonders how many of the cast and crew realized that they were assisting at the birth of one of the supreme works of genius in all of American film.

Faces offers a cinematic experience so different from what is provided by Hollywood that it is useful to begin a description of the film by emphasizing what Cassavetes does *not* do. In the first place, he rejects the fundamental premise of virtually all serious dramatic American film: the use of subjectivity as the basis of experience. From Griffith and Capra to Coppola, Scorsese, and De Palma, the main line of American feature filmmaking uses the consciousness of one or more central characters as the organizing center of the narrative, complemented by such conventions as expressive lighting effects, tendentious framings, mood-music orchestrations, and a character's own words to tell us what he or she sees, thinks, and feels. The narrative itself is propelled by changes in characters' states of feeling and knowledge. In *Psycho*, we see things largely from Norman Bates's, Marion Crane's, Lila Crane's, Arbogast's, and Sam's perspectives in succession. One after the other, we feel what they feel and know what they know. We enter into and participate in their points of view – optically, psychologically, and intellectually. Hitchcock's camera has such intimacy with his characters that it not only allows us to see into their hearts, minds, and souls, but often allows us to move inside and look out. At moments, we can virtually *be* Marion, Lila, or Norman. We see through their eyes and experience what they experience – squinting with Marion as she tries to make out the road through her rain-streaked windshield, jumping with Lila when she is startled by her own reflection in a mirror. The point-of-view shooting and editing convention sinks a visionary and imaginative mine shaft into a character's heart and brain. It allows consciousness to be shared in a way that life even at its most intimate never does. We can know the main characters the way we know ourselves. We can *be* them. We have access to their "visions" of life the way we have access to our own.

Cassavetes breathtakingly rejects that entire tradition. In his work we watch characters not the way we watch ourselves, but the way we watch other people. His pseudo-documentary camera and sound holds us on the outside. We look *at* his characters. We eavesdrop on their actions and words, but can't read their hearts and souls. As hard as we may try, we can never see very far in, let alone move inward and assume a vantage point inside looking out, as we do in a Hollywood movie. There is no access to simplifying, explanatory interiors – to motives, goals, intentions, or "true" feelings. We never see through characters' eyes, and they almost never tell us what they intend or mean. We can never know exactly why someone is saying or doing something. We are put in more or less the same situation we are outside of the movie theatre: uncertainly reading opaque, ambiguous surfaces.

Cassavetes' fundamental cinematic effort is to hold the viewer on the turbulent perceptual surfaces of life and prevent him from diving beneath them into calmer conceptual depths. His rejection of the point-of-view editing convention (and its subjectivizing tendency) was one way of accomplishing that, but it was necessary for him to prevent his scenes and characters from yielding themselves up to other forms of abstract comprehensibility as well. He defends his scenes and his characters' behavior against all forms of conceptual simplification (what he dismissively used to call "shorthand" understandings). The goal is to force the viewer to pay extremely close attention to the second-by-second progress of what he actually sees and hears, to bring him to his senses by keeping him in the realm of the senses. In the service of that goal, Cassavetes delays presenting clarifying background information and withholds categories of understanding that would simplify what we see by allowing us to fit into into a preestablished intellectual category. In Cassavetes' project of denying us conceptual shortcuts through the jungle of experience, even what might be considered perfectly innocuous categories of understanding (like a character's marital status, occupation, or how he or she is related to another character) must be guarded against. (In contrast, Hollywood movies take the opposing tack. They attempt to clear things up and keep them clear by relying on stereotypical characterizations and clichéd psychologies, by sketching in characters' backgrounds, situations, intentions, and narrative tasks as succinctly and as early as possible.) Cassavetes keeps us in the dark conceptually in the hope that we will open our eyes wider to what is in front of us perceptually.

Simply put, Cassavetes abrogates conventional "establishing" practice. Standard Academy "establishing" technique involves a series of codified cinematic and intellectual practices at the start of a movie, at all changes of scene within it, and at each point an important new character or setting is introduced: The goal is to keep the viewer informed of where the scene takes place, who the main characters are, and what is going on. Cassavetes deliberately goes in the other direction as far as possible, beginning films and scenes with characters who aren't introduced and doing things we don't understand for reasons not explained. Many of his films actually begin with an unexplained event already in progress: *Love Streams* in the middle of a heated argument between two unidentified characters; *Opening Night* with an unidentified actress rushing on stage halfway through the performance of a play; *Faces* with a character (whose name we later learn is Richard Forst) trotting down a stairwell, headed to an unexplained meeting at an unspecified location for an unknown purpose. That scene is itself followed by one in which Richard and another unnamed character drive with an unidentified girl to her house, more unexplained characters doing unexplained things. Five minutes into *Faces* the viewer is still pretty much in the dark about what is going on.

The veiling of information in Cassavetes' work is in the service of an ethical vision. He is a profoundly moral filmmaker and all of his effects are, ultimately, moral ones. His nonestablishing practice encourages us to suspend premature judgments. In the scene that follows the one just described, we watch the two men carrying on with the young woman. Cassavetes deliberately refuses to clarify their marital status or her social status as long as possible. He makes sure that we have been charmed and amused by Richard and Freddie's antics, and touched by Jeannie's tender solicitousness, before we discover that they are married men and she is a call girl. By the time we make the discovery it is too late for us to be able to shut them out of our hearts with a moral or intellectual category. The goal is to prevent the external, social understanding from narrowing our response to the spiritual possibility.[2]

The veiling goes on in different ways throughout the films. Not only is our knowledge of interiors blocked (what characters feel, intend, know, or essentially "are"); our view of exteriors also is frequently occluded (our ability simply to see or hear characters or to see or hear what they are responding to). All of these forms of veiling – intellectual, psychological, optical, and acoustic – run throughout Cassavetes' oeuvre: Much of the central character's performance in *The Killing of a Chinese Bookie* takes place in complete silence and near total darkness, and several key scenes in *Love Streams* involve conversations in which one of the participants in a dialogue is not visible on screen. Cassavetes protects his characters from the repressiveness of knowing by protecting them from the reductiveness of being too easily summarized in a cheap shot.

In *Faces*, characters frequently look, gesture, and move outside of the

79

frame without allowing us to see what they are looking at or doing. At key dramatic moments (precisely where another director would insert a close-up), Cassavetes occasionally turns a character away from cinematic view or moves him or her outside of the shot. At a climactic moment in *Faces*, after Richard asks his wife, Maria, for a divorce and calls Jeannie on the phone, Cassavetes withholds a close-up of Maria's face. Her protracted silence and turn away from the camera during and after Richard's call is much more imaginatively stimulating than her visibility would be. Similarly, in a subsequent scene involving the gathering of women in her house, Maria's silence and stillness speaks more complexly than speech and activity could.

A variation on this veiling technique occurs in other scenes in which background events are alluded to but not actually revealed or explained. Characters mention things that happened outside of the space or time of the narrative, whetting the viewer's appetite to understand them, yet denying him access to them. In *A Woman Under the Influence*, one of the most important conversations in the film (between Nick and his mother about his wife having slept with another man) is astonishingly revealed at a later point in the film as having taken place outside of the viewer's cognizance. To cite two smaller examples from *Faces*: After Richard and Jeannie spend the night together, they reminisce about what they did the night before and describe a series of events that Cassavetes has prevented the viewer from seeing. In another case, in the first scene in her apartment, when Jeannie crosses Freddie's remark, "Down with hospitals" with her retort, "Some hospitals are okay," a realm of possibilities to which she is alluding opens to view among which Cassavetes deliberately refuses to specify.

In its most extreme form, Cassavetes' nonestablishing becomes antiestablishing. The narrative doesn't simply withhold clarifying information, but provides misleading information, deliberately leading a viewer to jump to mistaken conclusions, jolting him from one false hypothesis to another. In the opening minutes of *The Killing of a Chinese Bookie*, when a friendly cabbie comes into a bar and offers to drive the main character home to his wife and kids, even an unsophisticated viewer recognizes it as important background information and seizes on the cabbie's words as a statement of fact. Cassavetes depends on our doing it; the hitch is that the information is false. It takes the next half-hour for us slowly to figure out that probably the single most important fact about that character is that he has no wife, no kids, indeed, no home to go to. Both *Love Streams* and *Minnie and Moskowitz* miscue and mislead the viewer so much that he quickly becomes wary of drawing general conclusions at all – which is of course the goal. Closure and resolution are the enemies. Absolute openness is the ideal.

Cassavetes stages a deliberate assault on our ability to sort events, expressions, and relationships into abstract categories and to pick up the experiences with conceptual handles. In Cassavetes' view, conceptions inevitably betray the experiences they attempt to grasp. Thought stops the motion of life. It smoothes the prickly particularity of concrete experience. It takes a step backward from the full reality of sensory perception. That is why, although intellectual understandings are ultimately unavoidable, Cassavetes' goal is to force a viewer to confront the full complexity of sensory reality for as long as possible before making the simplifying move from perceptions to conceptions. His cinematic agenda is very similar to William James's philosophical agenda. To draw on a few of James's metaphors, Cassavetes attempts to put the "thickness" back in human relations, to present the "full truth" of sensory experience (as an alternative to the "discarnate" truth of conceptual knowledge *about* experience), to give us art and life that won't be reduced to "outlines." As a flavor of James's own definition of the difference between the two kinds of truth, three paragraphs from his work follow:

> *Essential* truth, the truth of the intellectualists, the truth with no one thinking it, is like the coat that fits tho no one has ever tried it on, like the music that no ear has listened to. It is less real, not more real, than the verified article; and to attribute a superior degree of glory to it seems little more than a piece of perverse abstraction worship. As well might a pencil insist that the outline is the essential thing in all pictorial representation, and chide the paint-brush and the camera for omitting it, forgetting that their pictures not only contain the whole outline, but a hundred things in addition.

> Thought deals thus solely with surfaces. It can name the thickness of reality, but it cannot fathom it, and its insufficiency there is essential and permanent, not temporary. [If we are curious] about the inner nature of reality or about what makes it go, we must turn our backs upon our winged concepts altogether, and bury ourselves in the thickness of those passing moments over the surface of which they fly, and on particular points of which they occasionally rest and perch.

> Professor Bergson thus inverts the traditional Platonic distinction absolutely. Instead of intellectual knowledge being the profounder, he calls it the more superficial. Instead of being the only adequate knowledge, it is grossly inadequate, and its only superiority is the practical one of enabling us to make short-cuts through experience and thereby to save time. The one thing it cannot do is reveal the nature of things

.... Dive back into the flux itself, then, Bergson tells us, if you wish to *know* reality, that flux which Platonism, in its strange belief that only the immutable is excellent has always spurned: turn your face toward sensation, that flesh-bound thing which rationalism has always loaded with abuse.... We are so inveterately wedded to the conceptual decomposition of life that I know that this will seem to you like putting muddiest confusion in place of clearest thought, and relapsing into a molluscoid state of mind.[3]

James's humorous final phrase might stand as a summary of Pauline Kael's response to Cassavetes' films. As a connoisseur of the visual/visionary sublime, she was utterly blind and deaf to everything Cassavetes' nonvisionary cinema attempted. His breakthrough to a new way of knowing and being in the world was indeed for her only a fall into "muddiest confusion." While he attempted to turn our faces toward sensation, to get us to dive into the flux, she saw only a "relapsing into a molluscoid state of mind."

Cassavetes' attack on what James calls "intellectualism" involves much more than denying the viewer certain kinds of abstract knowledge about scenes and characters. Many other aspects of the experiences he presents are designed to make them resist intellectual containment. This happens in so many different ways that I can only touch on a few of the most important ones. The first to notice is how the sheer energy level of Cassavetes' characters and scenes prevents a viewer from getting intellectual leverage over them. *Faces* is a mountain range with all peaks and no valleys. Dispensing with the customary buildups, it moves from climax to climax, largely leaving out the in-between places within which most movies transpire entirely. Cassavetes plunges the viewer into a realm of such intensity and outrageousness that it is difficult to know what to think, or what to make of it. But that is the point. The *allegro furioso* disarms judgment. It's like watching an auto accident: the onlookers are thrown halfway into the same shock and bewilderment that the victims are.

What makes it still more difficult to get some emotional distance or intellectual perspective on the scenes is that the characters (and the actors who play them) are sprung free from the codes of decorum and normative expression that regulate behavior in most life and art. In *Faces*'s first extended scene, Richard and Freddie, two middle-aged businessmen, pick up a young call girl named Jeannie at a bar and go home with her. The men's state of inebriation and sexual excitement is an obvious pretext to justify the extremity of their carrying-on once they get there. Anyone familiar with Cassavetes' subsequent films, however, realizes that Richard and Freddie's nominal drunkenness merely allows Cassavetes and his characters to get to the place in which all his films are set – a place where characters give uninhibited expression to their wildest desires and most extreme impulses. When Freddie attempts to humiliate Jeannie in front of Richard in revenge for not having his way with her ("What do you think she is, some clean towel that's never been used?"), when McCarthy fights Richard, or when Richard's wife, Maria, attempts suicide near the end of the film, it is clear that *Faces* is set in a realm where characters say and do what most of us dare only fleetingly to think and feel.[4]

Excess is a mode of expressive liberation. The by-now tiresome complaint that Cassavetes' characters are "too extreme" or "crazy" misses the reason he made them that way. He attempted to put us and them in touch with a realm beyond the repressions of normative codes of thought, behavior, and expression. His goal was to gesture toward a state of feeling and being that exists before being intellectually tamed, expressively stabilized, or made socially acceptable. That is also why he was attracted to depicting states of surprise, shock, or disruption. He was the poet of breakdowns (in every sense of the word). The instances of shock or surprise in his work figure the breakdown of conventional understandings. He wanted to capture eruptions of emotion and imagination before they were repressively understood. He wanted to call his characters to truths of the body and emotions at odds with conceptual forms of understanding, and to break down cooler, more distanced ways of knowing in his viewers. This is what is fundamentally misleading about a psychiatric approach to any of Cassavetes' films insofar as it presumes a cure is necessary. Lelia, Chet, Moskowitz, Mabel, Sarah Lawson, and Cassavetes' other "crazy" characters do not need to be cured of their deviations from normalcy and normative forms of expression. In fact, their expressive excesses and extravagances are the most important and interesting aspect of their personalities. They, like Shakespeare's tragic protagonists, would be less without them.

Faces is extreme in more than its tones, however. It is extreme in its pacing. Experiences are too propulsively on the move away from any one position for us to be able to put them in a mental frame. Relationships between characters develop, flourish, and decay in *Faces* at a nearly insane pace. Scenes have an Emersonian "onwardness" that defeats our ability to use categories to stabilize our relationship with them. Experience boils over any cognitive container within which we attempt to hold it. Consider *Faces*'s first long scene again. Richard and Freddie keep changing (and their relationship with Jeannie keeps changing) so rapidly that we can't bring them intellectually into focus. They are gentle, sweet, and witty one moment,

83

then bastards the next. They are unguarded and intimate with her, then distant to the point of brutality a few minutes later.

The effect on the viewer is a little like that of Charlie Parker's playing. The speed of the changes is so accelerated that viewers/listeners tend to fall into one of three camps: The first consists of those who can't keep up at all, and are therefore bored to tears (since nothing seems to be happening). The second contains those who can keep up a little bit, but are unable to follow the logic of the changes in detail. They tend to be dismissive of the experience (since, to them, it seems merely chaotic and random). Finally, there is the small group who can both keep up and understand the incredible intricacy of what they are being presented with. Far from being bored, this last group is left almost breathless by the extraordinary speed of the experience; far from being dismissive, they are energized by and amazed at what they have witnessed. They temporarily participate in what can only be called an altered state of consciousness. Their perceptual capabilities are affected by what they have lived through. They are roused and heightened.

Finally, the embodied nature of meaning in Cassavetes' work makes it extremely difficult to deal with it conceptually or analytically. Most of the meanings in *Faces* are created not verbally or abstractly (and certainly not through systems of expression of the sort that Bordwellian formalists describe) but through assertively nonabstract, nonsystematic forms of expression: eccentric, unpredictable, jerky movements of the bodies in motion and collision; the pulsing expressions on their faces; the weird, sporadic gestures; and the fluctuating vocal tones. This sort of embodied, enacted knowledge defies intellectual analysis. It is too fugitive and darting to be glossed in terms of general categories of understanding. It won't hold still long enough for us to take a conceptual snapshot of it. And its tangibility resists abstract analysis. In the face of such robust, concrete physicality, thought is stymied; feeling is the only human capacity quick and capacious enough to deal with this material.

When Cassavetes brings Chet (Seymour Cassel), a young gigolo, into the suburban home of Maria (Lynn Carlin), a middle-aged married woman, and puts both of them in the middle of a group of Maria's upper-middle-class female friends, the emotional movements that take place in the room are even more difficult to keep up with than the physical ones. In a similar vein, the emotional adjustments of position among Richard, Jeannie, McCarthy, Stella, and Jackson in a later scene exceed most viewers' capacities to keep up with them on an initial viewing of the film. Every time we think we understand the relationship of the characters, Cassavetes changes it. During a five-minute scene that includes one of the great semicomic moments in the film, Cassavetes choreographs a complete reversal of the relationship between McCarthy and Jackson, on the one side, and Richard Forst and Jeannie, on the other. The two salesmen go from being snide and patronizing – before they know that Richard is the chairman of the board of a company they do business with – to being sycophantic after their discovery. They go from mocking Jeannie's request to be alone with Richard, to obsequiously bowing out in deference to her desire for privacy.

The tonal mercuriality of *Faces*'s scenes represents another form of resistance to abstract interpretation. The tonal cruise control that a studio film typically uses to guide a viewer's responses (serious moments are preceded by a gradual dramatic buildup; suspenseful moments by mysteriousness, etc.) gives way to continuous shifts of gears and changes of position in an Indianapolis 500 of the emotions. From second to second, it's impossible to tell where anything is going or what stance we should assume toward it. We must simply stay open and alert, picking our way cognitively and emotionally through an extraordinarily multivalent experience without signposts to indicate where we have been, where we are now, or where we will be in the next moment.

Consider the four- or five-minute sequence leading up to Maria and Chet going to bed together. How many different ways of feeling about the moment does Cassavetes present? Chet leaves the house to drive one of Maria's friends home, and the pressure-cooker tension of the gathering of Maria's friends that preceded is suddenly relaxed. The scene begins calmly and meditatively, with Maria jogging through the house turning off lights to the accompaniment of the only nonsource orchestration before the end of the film. That tone endures for only a matter of seconds, when Chet unexpectedly reappears, raucously tackling her in the hallway. For a second we don't know whether the tackle is ominous or playful; in fact, we don't even realize it is Chet at first. Then, as he and Maria laugh together and he playfully chases her upstairs, the film switches to a moment of pure, physical frolic. That too lasts only a few seconds; then the tone becomes romantic as Chet picks Maria up, carries her into the bedroom, and kisses her breast. The romantic mood is then interrupted by Maria's expressions of embarrassment; but Chet is undaunted and the scene turns shyly sexual as he carries her to bed and Maria arches backward in a moment of pure sexual abandonment. However, the opening to lyricism no sooner occurs than it is disrupted by Maria's now more insistent request to go into the bathroom to get herself ready. Cassavetes then intercuts shots of Maria in the bathroom nervously adjusting her makeup and dress with shots of Chet undressing on the bed, singing a naughty, comic ditty while he takes off his clothes.

When Maria finally returns to the bedroom, we have every reason to feel that at last there will now be a simple opening to a pure romantic mood. That tonal possibility is disrupted, however, by Maria's shyness and discomfort as she asks that the lights be turned off. The potential awkwardness of that moment is then dissipated as the sequence turns jokey, with Chet pulling the covers over their heads.

How many tones have we moved through in this brief sequence (which is all the more remarkable for being largely silent)? Rather than telling us how to feel about this odd couple, Cassavetes zigzags us through a range of emotional positions. *Faces* tonally twinkles like this in scene after scene. To adapt Lawrence's metaphor, Cassavetes never puts his thumb in the pan, and the scale never stops oscillating. As in a work of jazz, the refusal of the experience to pattern itself – the way it keeps swerving away from each incipiently emerging pattern – prevents the viewer from assuming a contemplative relationship to it.

As the preceding sequence also indicates, *Faces* denies us one other form of intellectual control over a scene: a controlling consciousness through which to filter events, weigh their importance, and organize our understanding of them. That is to say, it won't let us simply sublet a centrally located "starring" consciousness, move into it, and inhabit it. At any one moment, in any one scene, there are almost always two, three, four (or more) different points of view that must be shuttled between, no one of which is more authoritative or "correct" than any of the others. In a Hitchcock movie, we always know who we are supposed to "be," whose point of view we are supposed to sympathize with, whose perspective is the "right" one. In the bedroom scene with Maria and Chet, her embarrassment and shyness, his brashness and naughtiness, are honored equally.

Rather than following the studio notion of organizing the narrative around one or two figures with whom a viewer can "identify," *Faces*'s pseudodocumentary photography circulates the viewer through alternative optical, psychological, and imaginative views of a scene. While Hollywood is centripetal, *Faces* is centrifugal: It spirals away from any unitary center of interest. At every point at which we might narrow our view and focus in on one or two central characters, both the hand-held camera work and the kinetic editing broaden our perspective, forcing us to pay attention to other figures with rival perspectives.[5] Multiple, changing views replace the single, fixed views of other films. All of Cassavetes' work lives in muscularly counterpoised positions, endless corrections of view. Even though Maria is one of the most important figures in *Faces*, in the scene in which she brings Chet and her friends back to her house she almost drops out of our consciousness for about ten minutes. For the first five minutes or so, a character named Florence becomes the center of interest. Then Florence becomes less important and Chet's relationship with a character named Louise takes preeminence. Only at the very end of the scene does Maria again become an important figure.

Another way the focus is kept shifting is by parceling the narrative into a series of more or less separate episodes involving Richard and Maria apart from each other. *Shadows*'s jumping from Lelia to Hugh to Ben in pursuit of their different stories, *Love Streams*'s shuttling between narratives involving two apparently unrelated characters, as well as extended sections of the other films, do the same thing.

Even when Cassavetes does organize a narrative around a more or less dominant figure, as in *The Killing of a Chinese Bookie* or *Gloria*, one point of view does not reign supreme. There are always others to be reckoned with – completely independent views from characters who wouldn't even matter in another movie. Figures as lowly as a cabbie, employees at a bank, a limo driver, a waitress, a bartender, or a girl's brother briefly take over individual scenes, and weigh in with their own eccentric perspectives. In even the simplest human encounter (like a taxi ride or a hamburger order) Cassavetes makes it clear that there are other perspectives equal to (or arguably more valid than) the main character's. The taxi driver in *Shadows* who sings "I love you truly," the hysterical dental patient in *Husbands*, the waitress in *Minnie and Moskowitz* who "needs the table," the doorman in *Opening Night* who tells Myrtle Gordon she looks "frumpy," the three head-scratching cab drivers who deal with Sarah Lawson in *Love Streams* are each given their fifteen seconds of fame. In the scenes in which they appear, their points of view are absolutely as important as that of the principal character. No one is too unimportant, no part is too small to be reverenced. Cassavetes never puts down one figure to promote another. (What Cassavetes' critics failed to understand was that the reason Leona, the lady with the red hat in *Husbands*, made them squirm was that her point of view was respected, not denigrated. If it had not been honored, we wouldn't have empathized with it so acutely.) Even the most despicable characters are humanized and given their day in court to plead their case. They may hang themselves with the rope Cassavetes gives them, but they are never merely treated dismissively. Cassavetes celebrates the fact that there are at least as many different and equally interesting views of a scene as there are participants.

Cassavetes' films are sometimes described as being emotionally "edgy" in their moods, but these examples show that they are edgy in another respect as well: Individual perspectives don't merge, blend, and blur together as they do in conventional cinema, but rather edge each other out. The films and characters are pushy, not simply in the emotional sense of the word, but because one point of view pushes up against another, without absorbing it or melting into it. In *Psycho*, Arbogast, Sam, and Lila are interchangeable to a degree that Nick and Mabel never are.

In *Faces*, we never escape this linguistic, psychological, and dramatic perspectivism. Triangulation truth replaces tunnel-vision truth. The cinematic experience Cassavetes offers is close to the position William James articulates in "Humanism and Truth":

> The fundamental fact about our experience is that it is a process of change. For the "trower" at any moment, truth, like the visible area round a man walking in a fog, or like what George Eliot calls "the wall of dark seen by small fishes' eyes that pierce a span in the wide Ocean," is an objective field which the next moment enlarges and of which it is the critic, and which then either suffers alteration or is continued unchanged.... Owing to the fact that all experience is a process, no point of view can ever be *the* last one. Every one is insufficient and off its balance and responsible to later points of view than itself.[6]

The point is not that we take sides (as conventional Hollywood notions of identification dictate), nor that we attempt to clarify the discrepancies between different points of view, but that we circulate among truly irreconcilable perspectives that don't add up. The goal is not to conclude or resolve, but to move around and explore, to hold more than one thing in one thought. The outcome is a distinctive multiple mindedness that should make perfectly clear how *Faces*'s style teaches generosity and tolerance for different points of view without a single explicit reference to such things in the script.[7]

As James understood, what is at stake is more than a choice between many perspectives and few. The issue involves the *authority* of any or all views. The standard studio picture is premised upon the possibility of a view from nowhere: an ideal, absolute, complete view of reality. In a movie shot in this style (which includes all of the important work of Sternberg, Hitchcock, Welles, Kubrick, Coppola, De Palma, and many other filmmakers), everything a viewer needs to know in order to understand a scene is laid out in front of him, and its meaning absolutely indicated according to a hierarchy of importance. Films like *The Blue Angel*, *Citizen Kane*, *Psycho*, *2001*, *Blood Simple*, or *Blue Velvet* propose the possibility of a final or absolute state of knowing, a "best" or ultimate view of events and characters. The visions provided by the close-ups, lighting, camera angles, and mood-music orchestrations in those films have the authority of the director and his cinematic cohorts behind them. They tell us positively what the director wants us to know and believe. Even if the director doesn't intend it, the style of these works implicitly endorses the possibility of a God's-eye-view.

Since he relies so extensively on point-of-view shooting and editing conventions, it may seem that Hitchcock represents an exception to the preceding observations, and that the views in his work are fallible and personal, rather than absolute and God-like, but the fact that the view is often equated with the optical or imaginative viewpoint of a particular character does nothing to lessen its definitiveness and absoluteness. What Roger Thornhill sees in *North by Northwest* is absolutely everything the viewer ever needs to see and know. In the crop-dusting sequence, for example, however personal, his view is completely definitive. It's the only one we are even supposed to consider. (We are certainly never for a moment meant to sympathize with or participate in the point of view of the men in the airplane or that of the driver of the exploding gasoline truck.) Even when Hitchcock briefly lets us see through another character's eyes (as he does with the man waiting for the bus across the road from Roger), the other view invariably merely reinforces the view we already have (i.e., the man waiting for the bus feels Roger's standing alongside the road to be just as queer as Roger does). In sum, although we may be looking through the eyes of Thornhill, L. B. Jeffries, Scotty, Lila, or Norman Bates, we can rest assured that we are still seeing everything that matters, and seeing it in the simplest, most direct way possible. The proof of that is that when a character fails to notice something important (for example, when Norman doesn't notice the rolled-up newspaper as he cleans up Marion's room), Hitchcock doesn't hesitate to depart from the point-of-view editing convention to make sure that we notice it.

Cassavetes' work rejects the possibility of having such authority over experience, such intellectual distance from it, and such an abstract perspective on it. Because view succeeds view in a continuous process of revision, we are made aware that every view is partial and provisional. Each lacks authority. No knowledge is absolute or ideal. All knowledge comes in bits and pieces. We get it in time, with delays, interruptions, mistakes, and corrections. There can be no point of view above and beyond the incomplete views. There is no unitary "correct," "true," or "best" view; there are only views in the plural.[8] To adapt a few of James's other terms (this time from "A World of Pure Experience"), *Faces* locates us in a "pluralistic universe," with "a mosaic philosophy, a philosophy of plural facts."[9] Profiting from the photographic lessons of Italian neorealism in the 1940s (De Sica and Rossellini, in particular), and from what might be called "American neorealism" in the 1950s (the films of Morris Engel and Lionel Rogosin, and the live television dramas of John Frankenheimer and Delbert Mann), *Faces*'s style hints at a world in which more is always going on than can ever be understood or cinematically "grabbed." Cassavetes' style makes the same argument that James did in his philosophy: that lived, felt experience is richer, more mysterious and more "overflowing" than our intellectual containers can ever hold.

Two specific aspects of the film's pseudo–cinema verité photography and editing – one spatial, the other temporal – communicate a sense of each shot being only a partial view of a larger reality that defies more than provisional comprehension or stylistic containment. The spatial quality is that the photography is "open." In André Bazin's term, the frame becomes a "window" on the world, past which characters pass but within which they are not contained or defined. Objects and persons extend out of it. Others reach into it. The sound track picks up voices from characters who are not in the shot. Characters talk to others outside of the frame and react to persons and events we cannot see. The temporal dimension is that not only is there obviously more going on than can be taken in at any one view, but the roving camera work and jumpy editing keep changing the view. Even if we manage to bring things into focus at any one moment, the next unstable, unpredictable movement of the camera (or the next shot edited into the sequence) reveals something that the previous one did not show (and retrospectively changes our appreciation of its meaning). *All* framing efforts (intellectual, optical, emotional, personal, and cinematic) are limiting stances. The vision provided by the camera in *Faces* has no more authority than the vision of any of the characters in the scene. In fact, the camera's view has all of the fallibilities of a character's view: At times, it may be looking in the wrong place, or not be able to keep up with events. The view is unavoidably nontotalized and incomplete. The meaning of events must be pieced together from plural, inconsistent views. Understanding requires continuous revisionary reinterpretation.

The overall effect is humbling, yet also enticing and energizing. It is chastening because there is obviously more to see and understand than even the most sensitive viewer can take in at a viewing. Experience defies our power to control or understand it once and for all. Any knowledge we arrive at is local and subject to change. We are shown the limitations of any view, including our own; yet it is also stimulating because viewing is made active

Unbalanced relationships, mercurial movements, unformulated experiences slopping over the edges of the frame, bubbling over intellectual containers, breaking the forms that deliver them to us.

rather than passive. The viewer is empowered as a meaning maker – sorting, organizing, exploring experiences that have not been predigested and prearranged in hierarchies of meaning and importance. He (or she) becomes a "creative reader" in Emerson's and Whitman's senses of the term, actively engaged in making sense of these experiences, inventively creating meanings on the fly, and revising them as needed.

Up to this point I have been focusing chiefly on how *Faces* is shot and edited. It's time to turn to a few specific scenes in order to see how Cassavetes' aesthetic is implemented both in his scripting and in the performances he elicits from his actors. A good example is a scene that occurs about halfway through the film. It involves two traveling salesmen, Joe Jackson and Jim McCarthy, who are visiting the call girl Jeannie and a girlfriend named Stella. After they arrive, a third man, Richard Forst, calls

Jeannie to ask if he can spend the night with her. As Jeannie tries to get free from McCarthy, the next two or three minutes present a verbal dance of mutually adjusted psychological positions that is vintage Cassavetes; for while the plot is standing still in the realm of actions, events are taking place a mile a minute in the realm of emotional transactions. Typically for Cassavetes, the scene begins in midconversation:

STELLA: [*improvising a limerick, we realize sometime later*] She tucks it under her chin...

JACKSON: She plucks at her strings...

STELLA: [*continuing*]...Like angel wings.

JACKSON: [*ignoring her*] She plucks at her strings, among numerous things, and tucks it under her chin. [*leering*] Ha ha ha.

JEANNIE: Well, Mr. McCarthy.

MCCARTHY: Jim.

JEANNIE: [*Irish accent*] Jaimie McCarthy. Ah, that's a fine name, fine.

MCCARTHY: My mother used to call me Jaimie.

JEANNIE: [*continues Irish accent*] Did she, now? Say, how'd you like to call me mother?

MCCARTHY: Come on. I'm old enough to be your father.

JEANNIE: Listen. Listen. In that case, I'd like some fatherly advice.

MCCARTHY: Yes?

JEANNIE: You see, I have this terrible problem.

MCCARTHY: What's your problem, daughter?

JEANNIE: [*Irish accent*] Well, this fellow — a friend, an Irish friend. He just called me from a bar. He's in terrible trouble and wants me to come rescue him. Well, what do you think of that?

MCCARTHY: Well, what do you think of it?

JEANNIE: I'm asking for your advice. You're the wise one. Be a hero. Tell me.

MCCARTHY: Hey Jackson! Jackson! Remember the time we went to New Orleans on a bet?

JACKSON: Yes, sir. I do.

MCCARTHY: We stayed up all night, screaming at the top of our lungs. We had a...we had a...we had a...couple of bimbos. No, actually they were very nice girls. They remind me a lot of you two.

JEANNIE: Oh?

MCCARTHY: But they knew more dirty limericks than you could shake a stick at.

JEANNIE: [*chilly*] How nice!

The first thing to notice is how different each of the characters sound (differences that are even more obvious in performance). "Yes, sir" Jackson is deferential and knows his place. McCarthy is cocky and bossy. Jeannie and Stella sound different from each other and from each of the men. (Compare Stella's limerick line with Jackson's.) The diversity of the faces, voices, bodies, and perspectives in Cassavetes' work tells us that he celebrates the stimulating, energizing differences in our minds, our feelings, and our souls. His films are scripted and acted to accentuate the quirky, individual aspects of each character (in contrast to the characterizations in Hitchcock, for example, which are written and acted to create figures as generic as those in a dream or a psychodrama). Rather than leveling or homogenizing his characters, Cassavetes plays up their eccentricities and differences from one another. His scripting and the acting he elicits allow enormous scope for individual variation and expressive idiosyncrasy. For Cassavetes, as for Jean Renoir, not our similarities, but our differences from one another are what make us worth paying attention to. In Cassavetes' films, there is no eliminating the personal and idiosyncratic. All there is is quirky crotcheti-ness. Why become a fiction filmmaker in the first place if not to indulge in the delights of difference, the sounds of alternative voices, the weird indi-viduality of different personal perspectives?

We live in boxes of difference that we can never get out of, and, in his view, never should want to get out of. Our motives are different, as are our interests, our emotions, and our fears. Even if we use the same words we mean them differently. Even when we think we are communicating perfectly, it's impossible that we should be. And praise be the difference, he says. Cassavetes is showing us not only that there are different lives and interests behind our words, but also that there are different emotional and intellectual substructures within each of us that no amount of talking can erase or bridge.[10] Cassavetes' view of democracy is the opposite of a Tocquevillian leveling and homogenization. It is, rather, an Emersonian celebration of exceptionalism, not in theory but on an entirely practical ground, based on the different ways characters talk and the incompatible points of view they represent.

The conversation also illustrates a second aspect of Cassavetes' aesthetic: the even-handedness of treatment. Other films have characters who talk differently, but almost invariably one character and one way of talking, thinking, or feeling is preferred.[11] In all of *Faces's* scenes, there are no controlling figures. In this scene, McCarthy's point of view is just as im-portant as Jeannie's, notwithstanding that he appears only in this one scene, whereas she is in the entire film. Though it would be untrue to say that figures are treated with absolute equality – since one character or another may dominate a scene by sheer force of personality or by virtue of being given more lines and screen time than another (as Chet dominates the scene with the women in Maria's house), or may be relatively less important than another (as Stella and Jackson are in this particular scene) – Cassavetes scripts and edits the scenes as much as possible to present and respect the views of all of the participants. Just as we might in an actual social encounter with these figures, we are put in the position of following and entering into each of their perspectives. Cassavetes' style, like Renoir's, replaces an aesthetic of competition with one of cooperative relationship (even as the competitive individualism of a character like McCarthy pushes in the opposite direction to the style that delivers him to us). As much as Cassavetes' camera work and editing do, his scripting teaches the importance of sensitivity and supple responsiveness to multiple, changing points of view.

To the extent that they are adequate, the characters are asked to do the same thing the viewer does in watching the film. They must learn to become trick pony riders in a circus of shifting perspectives, nimbly jumping from one moving steed to another, denied a saddle of their own simply to plunk down on. That is what Jeannie and Chet both do in the group scenes of *Faces*, and what Mabel will do even more masterfully in the paired gatherings around the dinner table in *A Woman Under the Influence*: keep entering into different perspectives; keep in touch with, listening to, interacting with everyone; keep responding to one thing after another; never closing down their sensitivities; never shutting anyone out. As I pointed out in the Introduction, whereas conventional cinematic selfhood generally involves the maintenance of a stable point of view, Cassavetes defines selfhood as the capacity to allow oneself to be inhabited by other views. Cassavetes was not only opposed to the ruthless individualism of American society, but he was opposed to the forms of competitive individualism that stylistically underpin the scripting, acting, and photography of most other films. In those works, one acts (in both the social and dramatic sense of the verb) by capturing and holding a position; in Cassavetes' work, acting is interacting. For Cassavetes, as for Jean Renoir, to attempt to star as a character or as an actor – i.e., in the way of Jack Nicholson or Meryl Streep – is already to have failed. The soloist, however virtuosic, is doomed. To try to dominate a scene, to attempt to control the gaze of the viewer, to work to upstage others is to be fatally flawed. (In Cassavetes' view, that is what is horrific about McCarthy's and Freddie's performances in *Faces*: They don't relate; they dominate.)

As that suggests, Cassavetes' films define characters as members of groups.

Selfhood is social responsiveness. For him, as for John Dewey (whose values overlap his in many other respects as well), the nineteenth-century liberal/ Romantic belief in atomistic individualism was a temporary cultural aberration; our social interconnectedness is our true state. Experience is not something we have or feel alone, something that takes place almost entirely in our heads or hearts, as it is in the post-Shelly Romantic tradition (or in the Hitchcockian tradition, peopled as his films are with individuals engaged in solitary visionary pursuits, silently thinking and feeling, staring at something, or being stared at by someone). Life is essentially and unavoidably relational. It is something we work through with others (in *Faces* and most of the other films, chiefly in the form of bodily and conversational interaction).

A further point the McCarthy and Jeannie scene illustrates is one I described in *Shadows*: There is almost always a subtext to Cassavetes' dialogue, and the emotional and intellectual subtext is often at odds with the characters' spoken words. In short, what Cassavetes' characters say isn't what is actually being "said." Characters elide what is most on their minds, nervously jump from one subject to another, avoid issues that they don't want to deal with, and generally use words to accomplish purposes other than the manifest content of what they mean. In the passage I have just quoted, Jackson's smutty limerick is a sexual warm-up pitch. Jeannie's cutesy "Irish friend" routine is an attempt to elicit McCarthy's sympathy and cooperation with her plan to see Richard. His response by changing the subject ("Hey, Jackson! Jackson!") in effect tells her to drop dead with her request for help. The men's attitudes toward the two New Orleans "bimbos" is obviously the opposite of "they were very nice girls."

A related point that the conversations in *Shadows* also illustrate is that because the expression is only a superficial manifestation of a shifting, emotional subtext, interactions and personal expressions don't follow a logical progression, a straight and narrow conversational path. There's no such thing as straight talk in Cassavetes' imaginative universe, only obliquity. Straight talk would only be evidence of a character's flat-mindedness. While Hollywood gives us conversations as monotonic in their trajectory as the agenda for a meeting, Cassavetes presents conversational curlicues, doublebacks, ellipses, and dangling references driven by confusions of feeling. His goal was to make characters' talk responsive to movements of desire and swerves of impulse; doing that meant throwing out the surface clarities of logic and wit.[12]

Cassavetes shows us not only that each individual in a conversation has a different personal agenda, and not only that that agenda is confused by a subtextual swirl of inchoate, unconscious feelings, but that our agendas keep changing. McCarthy's position continuously shifts even in the few lines I quoted. His response to Jeannie's plea for help moves through a range of tones and moods, from potentially intimate self-disclosure ("My mother used to call me Jaimie"), to off-putting and patronizing ("Come on. I'm old enough to be your father"), to sympathetic ("Yes?"), to dramatically collaborative ("What's your problem, daughter?"), to emotionally guarded ("Well, what do you think of it?"), to a sudden repudiation of the dramatic collaboration ("Hey, Jackson! Jackson! Remember the time ... ").

In a world of such performative fluidity, it makes no sense to ask what McCarthy really, truly feels. Is he sympathetic or indifferent? Collaborative or dismissive? Kind or patronizing? Even he would not be able to say. He feels all of these things by turns, and none of them essentially. His self contains a host of tones, moods, and attitudes. As I have already emphasized, such questions presume a surface–depth model of expression in which surface fluctuations are clarified by reference to enduring deep purposes. For Cassavetes, as for William James, however, there are no deep truths. Surface truths are all that exist. There is no unitary, essential purity underpinning our various, expressive impurities. Truth in the world, truth in performance, sprawling, mediated, mutable, "thick" truth is the only truth we can know.

Since this is not only a crucial point, but one that seems somewhat difficult for some viewers to grasp, perhaps I can make it clearer with an example from the classroom. In classes, when I play the bedroom sequence in the course of which Chet undresses and sings a naughty song while Maria is in the bathroom fixing herself up, a difference of opinion about what is "really" going on sometimes arises among the students. One group (mainly the girls in the class) argues that Chet's risqué singing is evidence that deep down he is insensitive to Maria's delicate state of feeling at this moment. His singing is evidence of a typically "macho" way of controlling the tone of a romantic encounter and steering it toward his idea of sexuality. Another group (mostly the boys) argues just the opposite: That in belting out his off-color lyrics Chet is being thoughtful and considerate. This argument runs that he is attempting to assuage Maria's anxieties and to lighten the mood and ease the tension of their sexual encounter with his comical smuttiness. At that point, the discussion sometimes becomes quite heated, with each side accusing the other of missing the point, and failing to see what is really going on: the girls saying that the boys don't see how "macho" that attitude really is; the boys replying that the girls don't see how thoughtful Chet is really being.

What makes the argument illuminating is that, in its quest for the "real" Chet, the "essential" meaning of what he does, and its "deep" motivation or explanation, it is playing the very Hollywood game that *Faces* reveals to be fallacious. The very interest of the scene, its greatness as a scene, is that *both* (opposite) things are true. Chet is both sensitive to Maria's feelings (attempting to put her at ease), *and* is macho in the way he chooses to do it (by singing a dirty song). As much as we may want it, Cassavetes won't present expressions in a simpler form. He won't create a realm of "pure" intentions separable from the "impure" expression of those intentions. Chet's machismo and his kindness won't be expressively disentangled. That is what it means to say that expression is unavoidably impure, that our motives exist only in mediated forms.

There are very few films that attain this degree of expressive complexity. In works within the visionary/symbolic tradition, feeling or intention is cut away from the polluting mediations of practical, social expression almost entirely. Vision replaces speech in many scenes; and when characters do speak, their speech is direct, clear, and unproblematic. Contrast the tonal and semantic directness of Eve Kendall's romantic come-on to Roger Thornhill: "I'm twenty-six and unmarried," with the way Cassavetes' characters proposition each other. In *North by Northwest*, to the extent that they choose to, Roger and Eve can simply say what they mean. They can speak their feelings. They can talk directly. Cassavetes' characters inhabit a far more complex expressive world than that, one in which expression is oblique, throttled, indirect, problematic, muffled in layer after layer of mediation. Even the films of Woody Allen and Neil Simon, which put far more emphasis on characters' practical capacities of verbal expression than Hitchcock's do, ultimately allow good motives and desirable ideals to substitute for complex social expressions of those motives and ideals. Good intentions are good enough.

Allen's and Simon's characters figure a simpler and more direct relationship between intentions and expressions than do Cassavetes'. It's telling that characters in a Simon or Allen movie nearly always can explain themselves and their actions. If they are anxious or unhappy, they know it. If they have problems, they can talk about them. Even if all they understand is their failure to understand, they can comprehend themselves almost as well as a viewer does (which is why the way they talk about themselves is almost indistinguishable from the way a critic or psychoanalyst would talk about them). Cassavetes' work represents a fundamentally different understanding of our expressive relation to our own feelings, which is why his figures can't be as articulate and self-aware as theirs. The subtextual muddlements, surface inarticulateness, and shifting agendas of his characters suggest that the clarity of purpose and expression, the openness to emotional excavation that Simon or Allen present, is a lie about our emotional lives. We can't step outside of ourselves to understand ourselves that dispassionately. We can't remove ourselves from our feelings far enough to verbalize them. If we even knew we were confused, we wouldn't be as confused as we are. Figures like McCarthy, Richard, and Maria, Cosmo Vitelli, Gloria Swenson, or Robert Harmon don't even know when they are confused or mistaken or unhappy, and they certainly can't theorize about their desires or list their needs. As the filmmaker once said, "Most people live their lives not knowing what they want, what they are doing, or what they feel." The confusing swerves of the conversations in Cassavetes' films open to view a realm of emotional bewilderments and cross-purposes whose essence is that they won't be brought to consciousness and can't be understood by the victim of them (which is to say they are generated in a deeper place than reason, logic, and consciousness can plumb).[13]

McCarthy's "Hey, Jackson!" yell points to one of the most extraordinary aspects of Cassavetes' scenes, though it was misunderstood by virtually every reviewer in America. What it clearly shows is not only that a scene or a relationship can completely change direction at any second, but that any character can be the author of those changes. As William James might have put it, not only do "novelties" disrupt the most predictable moments, but it is within our power to make novelties happen. The relationship between Jeannie and McCarthy can be adjusted, corrected, destroyed, repudiated at any moment by either of the principals. In this particular scene, Cassavetes shows us that the dramatic collaboration McCarthy and Jeannie embark on together can be changed at any time. Jeannie proposes an improvisation around the theme of "Irishness" and "help for a friend." McCarthy is gradually teased into collaborating, and plays along with it for a few moments; but when it becomes boring or inconvenient, he is free simply to jog away from it, to go on to something else, to begin another collaboration on another theme with another character. The impression is exhilarating. We are free to move against, across, independently of the "scripts" of life. At the moment Jeannie attempts to force a particular response from him by asking a loaded question, McCarthy shows that questions don't have to be answered. Others may attempt to plot our responses, but we can improvise our own counterplots whenever we want.

Even more significant, the "Hey, Jackson!" yell demonstrates that Cassavetes' characters can make the countermovements not only against the scripts and plots within which others attempt to define them, but against the previous scripts and plots in terms of which they defined themselves. Richard, Freddie, McCarthy, Chet, Jeannie (and the actors and actresses who play them) continuously bounce off their own tones and stances. They push away from their own patterns of behavior (as McCarthy does in the later scene in which he suddenly realizes that Richard, whom he has been patronizing up to that point, not only is an important business contact, but outranks him in the corporate pecking order). They cut against their own grain. It would be hard to overemphasize the importance of this effect, or how rarely it occurs in other films. Cassavetes' characters are empowered to become their own self-movers. These conversational loops and swerves demonstrate that Cassavetes' most interesting characters are not only vulnerable and responsive to others' positions and movements, but to their own. It's a dramatic effect one encounters with any degree of consistency, to my knowledge, only in Shakespeare and Chekhov. Cassavetes' characters communicate the impression not only of listening to others, but, still more complexly, of listening to themselves as they shift their modes of expression, critique their own performances, comment on their own styles as they go along. They are, in a word, endowed with self-consciousness. They react to their own actions.

An example quite similar to McCarthy's outburst occurs in *Faces*'s first long scene, when Richard turns to Freddie in the middle of one of the dramatic routines they are doing for Jeannie and interjects, "This is a fine impression we're making on the lady." The effect far exceeds the moment's length or narrative point. It tells us that Richard is not captive to any particular form of behavior. His self-consciousness springs him free to comment on his own words and actions and to revise his expressions at any point. He meditatively turns around on himself, imaginatively pivoting in place. An even more complex and interesting illustration occurs in the scene that involves Chet's attempts to get Louise to dance. In the course of Chet's five-minute interaction with Louise (the most brittlely intellectual of the four women), Cassavetes choreographs a minuet of fascinated attraction and scandalized embarrassment on Louise's part. She is gradually teased, begged, and cajoled into dancing with Chet, only to have the whole episode end with her suddenly getting flustered, slapping him, and berating him for humiliating her.

What makes the sequence so fascinating is the impression it conveys that Louise is, at least momentarily, sprung free from definition – from ours or her own. Louise shows herself capable of leaving her own previous personality and behavior patterns behind. Though she begins her interaction with Chet as a profoundly limited character and ends it by withdrawing back into her limitations, for two or three minutes in the middle of their tentative "dance" it is as if she can be or do absolutely anything. She briefly shakes herself free from the constraints of her own identity. In an Emersonian sense, she opens up by temporarily "abandoning" herself, by forgetting who she is and what her past has been. She briefly becomes unformulated.

Identity shimmers. It fluctuates with possibility, without stabilizing itself around any fixed role or stance. The self is put in process. It represents less a formulatable identity than a capacity of energetic movement away from identities.[14] It is what breaks patterns, swerves away from received forms of expression, and resists summarization. In Cassavetes' open-ended and prospective view of identity, we are states of energy in motion that, to be true to ourselves, must remain in motion. There can be no destination for development because any goal would be a repudiation of the energies that made its attainment possible. Every achieved end point merely becomes a point of departure for movements away from it.

This is one of the most spiritually exultant aspects of Cassavetes' work. While many twentieth-century works tell us that man is weak or doomed, Cassavetes affirms the individual's essential power and creativity, and not only in theory: His use of actors and his trust in his viewers not to need hand holding tells us that he never doubted their creative power and inventiveness. As McCarthy's verbal ejaculation illustrates, one of our supreme powers, in Cassavetes' view, is our power to swerve away from the imposed scripts of life and to improvise personal counterscripts as we go along. Cassavetes dramatizes this process in dozens of ways throughout *Faces*. At various moments in the film, all of the major characters convince us that they are improvising their own personal scripts as alternatives to the scripts imposed on them. The effect is inspiring to the point of being frightening. As we watch Chet, Richard Forst, or Jim McCarthy performing in their various scenes, we have the impression that we are watching them improvising their lives and relationships in a process of continuous creation. The illusion they convey is that their individual expressions are being impulsively created, adjusted, and revised on the spot.

Cassavetes' minimalization of plot in his films heightens the effect. Since his narratives are not event driven (with each event dictating a fairly narrow range of responses by characters who then become more or less semiotic functions of the plot), characters can to some extent control the direction and pacing of the film's scenes. None of these effects would be possible if Cassavetes did not have a fundamentally different appreciation of acting from what one encounters in most other films. The contrast between his use of his actors and Hitchcock's or Welles's can illuminate both traditions.

So overwhelmingly determinative are extrapersonal stylistic effects (and so relatively unimportant are the independent, eccentric, personal expressions of the actor) that in many films, Hitchcock's actors can simply allow the stylistic effects to communicate the meaning for them. Since what is being presented in the most important scenes and moments is almost always merely a state of pure consciousness (figured by an act of looking, feeling, or thinking) and not an act of complex social expression (figured by a changing display of specific tones, stances, and facial expressions), the actor can play the role more or less as a pantomime, using facial, vocal, or bodily expressions at a minimum and allowing the style to do almost all of the talking. Take Tippi Hedren's performance in *The Birds* as an example. Beyond a few stock gestures and facial expressions, she does almost no acting during the course of the film. That might sound like a flaw, but Hitchcock's movie is not impaired by Hedren's inexpressiveness; indeed, it might be said to profit from it. The inexpressiveness of Hedren's face, body, and voice gives Hitchcock all the more free reign to deploy his stylistic effects. His style – his lighting, orchestration, and editing – makes her riveting precisely because it is not disrupted by her acting, which would only get in the way (incidentally vindicating Kuleshov's point that editing, sound effects, and contextualizing can make even the blankest face express an apparent range of emotions). Similarly, Jimmy Stewart more or less sleepwalks through most of *Vertigo* and *Rear Window*, to the ultimate benefit of the films. For a cinema of stylistically generated meanings, an actor's blankness or impassiveness is not a problem but an opportunity. It guarantees that nothing comes between the viewer and the director's stylistically created meanings. Actors are cattle in this expressive tradition (though concerning Hitchcock in particular, there were obviously additional personal reasons why he was attracted to actors with a degree of vacancy: Given his obsession with control, the passivity of the actor ensured that the director would be all the more completely in the driver's seat).

To suggest that Hedren or Stewart "don't act," however, is probably a misleading way to describe this expressive situation. The question is not whether there is or is not "acting" in some absolute sense of the term, but rather how an actor's acting relates to the larger stylistic structures of the work. The best way to formulate it is to say that Hitchcock's actors express themselves in ways that dovetail with the abstract semiotic structures that deliver them to us. They don't make independent movements against the abstract styles of their works. Unlike Stewart in *Rear Window* or Hedren in *The Birds*, Anthony Perkins turns in a fairly impressive performance in *Psycho*; but no matter how expressive he is, what is important is that he never "messes up" the abstract meanings the film deploys around him. If the lighting, the music, the framing, or the mise-en-scène tells us Norman Bates is dangerous and threatening, Perkins acts dangerous and threatening; if they tell us he is anxious and upset, he acts anxious and upset (or at least does not act against such meanings). In short, he either subdues himself to allow the extrapersonal stylistic effects to express him or expresses himself in harmony with them. The one thing he never – but never – does is move contrary to them or independently of them.

When Hitchcock's methods work, as they obviously do in *Psycho*, the actor becomes an epiphenomenon of the style. He "means" whatever the film's metaphors, photography, mise-en-scène, and editing tell us he means. The symbolic props and events (the rain on the windshield, the birds in Norman's office, his mop and bucket), the visual and acoustic effects (the low-angle photography of the house, the noises associated with the swamp, the lighting on characters' faces, the rhythms of the editing, the ominous music on the sound track) all "speak" for characters more emphatically than they (or the actors who play them) ever could to characterize their psychological states and to establish their relationships with others.

I am confining my examples to Hitchcock's work for convenience. The expressive tradition I am describing represents the dominant line in American film. Though Welles was often said to be an actor's director, *The Trial* and *Citizen Kane* obey the same rules as *Rear Window* or *Psycho*. The fairly unimportant difference between Welles and Hitchcock is that Welles replaces relatively "inexpressive" with relatively "expressive" acting; but the important similarity is that in Welles as in Hitchcock, the performances of the actors do not cut against the abstract semiotic structures, but mirror them. Whatever the mise-en-scène, lighting, framing, or sound effects tell us, the acting repeats in capital letters. Good acting or bad, expressive or inexpressive, it repeats and reinforces the abstract meanings within the work. It does not spring free of them or cut against them.

In Cassavetes' work, acting functions in the diametrically opposite way. It does not mesh with the extrapersonal stylistic effects, but rather pushes away from them. It introduces semantic instability into a scene. It interrupts and disrupts the abstract meanings. It complicates the interpretation. It slows down the reading process. The quirky concreteness of the actor's personal expressions (the eccentricity, particularity, and changeability of a character's face, bodily gestures, vocal tones, and movements) jostle against any of the abstract patterns that begin to crystallize within his own film.

There are two consequences of this state of affairs, both of which have already been illustrated by the scenes I have discussed. The first is that characters are not locked into schematic positions: They are freed to move, change, and adjust their performances. While visionary stylistics freezes characters into relatively fixed imaginative positions and relationships, the eccentricity of the personal expressions generated by the actors in Cassavetes' work melts them and gets them flowing. The overarching metaphoric patterns in *Psycho*, *Citizen Kane*, and *2001* necessarily create characters who are compelled to maintain more or less fixed imaginative stances that accord with them. Because he has to express himself in congruity with the abstract style of the film, Anthony Perkins/Norman Bates is anxious, creepy, and weird in every scene in *Psycho*. His relationship to other characters and his function within the narrative is as fixed and stable as if he were in an allegory. Richard Forst, Maria, Chet, and Jeannie are not semiotically frozen in place in this way. They are free to move and change, and they emphatically do.

The second consequence is that while the Hitchcock tradition implicitly communicates the passivity, weakness, and vulnerability of the individual, the effect of Cassavetes' work is to communicate an impression of extraordinary individual expressive power. Hitchcock's work represents an essentially Foucauldian vision in which the body is articulated, manipulated, and controlled by extrapersonal systems of significance. In this expressive tradition, which is essentially structuralist, the individual is "spoken by" the languages and styles in place around him, of which he makes himself the passive recipient and transmitter.

In Cassavetes, the individual character does not accrue meaning from participation in superpersonal institutional or technological arrangements of knowledge, but makes meanings on his or her own. The individual is the undeconstructable, uncoercible originator of meanings distinguishable from the technologies of cinematic presentation. (Indeed, insofar as Cassavetes' actors/characters give the impression of resisting being filmed – e.g., by breaking the line of the frame with their movements or moving in and out of focus – the meanings they generate might be said to be not only separate from but opposed to the technologies of cinematic arrangement and control.) Meaning is not inherited from or defined by preexisting cultural understandings, but is created anew, and revised minute by minute, by the individual actor/character in a series of independent moves across and against preexisting structures. As the William Jamesian resonances of this formulation should suggest, this is one of the most emphatically American aspects of Cassavetes' work. The individual is enfranchised as a free agent, an independent meaning maker. Cassavetes grants his characters the power to do the same thing in their lives that he grants his actors the power to do in their acting.

It is evidence of the creativity, inventiveness, and energy Cassavetes endows them with that all of the important characters in *Faces* function as artists of their identities and relationships, in dozens of ways. They do in life all of the things that actors do on the stage, playfully assuming false identities (McCarthy and Jackson become "the vice squad"), troping and playing around with their own words (talking with Maria, Richard unexpectedly twists "there's no place like home" into "have you ever been to Rome"), improvising dramatic routines on the spur of the moment (McCarthy puts on a little skit in order to impress Jackson with his having made love to Jeannie), and generally indulging in a wide range of verbal and performative extravagance, bravado, and posturing (from Richard and Freddie's theatrical performances in front of Jeannie, to McCarthy's taunts and threats to tear Richard limb from limb, to Richard's final over-the-top performance of outrage with Maria when he returns home at the end of the film). Even more obviously than *Shadows*, *Faces* is a tissue of acts of impersonation, role-playing, ventriloquy, and scene making. Theatricality is everywhere. Everyone is "on" almost all of the time. The characters are masters of dramatic effects.

Of course, in another sense, it is not Richard, Freddie, Jackson, and McCarthy who are staging these effects. Cassavetes and his actors are. There are, obviously, no characters; Cassavetes (as the script writer, director, photographer, and editor) and his actors (as the on-camera performers) are doing it all. They are the real tropers, transformers, and shape-changers. They are the ones who meditatively turn on their own previous expressions to comment on them and leave them behind. What Cassavetes shows Richard, McCarthy, and his other characters doing in their lives, he has already done and continues to do in his writing, staging, photography, and editing process. And that, then, suggests one of the deepest and most important truths about his work: that, for Cassavetes, there was an essential continuity between making art (i.e., the things you do when you write a script or act a part) and living life (i.e., the things you do in front of friends and lovers). As everything I have argued up to this point is meant to suggest, the energetic, self-delighting, self-conscious performances of Cassavetes' characters are absolutely of a piece with the energetic, self-delighting, self-conscious performances of Cassavetes himself in scripting and directing them (and of his actors in playing them). Art is not governed by special rules and constituted of distinctive materials. Cassavetes suggested as much, in a slightly different context, when he was once asked what made an actor good, and he replied by talking about the continuity between acting and life: "There's no such thing as a 'good actor.' It is an extension of life. How you're capable of performing in your life, that's how you're capable of performing on the screen."[5] Art is not a sacrosanct realm of harmony, clarity, and order separate from nonartistic life, but is absolutely continuous with life, quarried from life's materials, and shaped by the same processes by which we shape our lives. The character of Mabel Longhetti will represent Cassavetes' most extended attempt to demonstrate this truth, but it was already an article of faith when Lelia was created. All of Cassavetes' major characters are artists of their own lives and relationships in precisely the same way he is an artist.

A brief scene early in *Faces* can stand as another example of how Cassavetes (as the writer, director, and editor of the scene), his characters, and his actors all collaborate in the process of moving off of and against static structures. It involves Richard and his wife, Maria, lying in bed. He is telling her what the audience only gradually realizes are stupid jokes. Two different sorts of movement against fixed structures are taking place at once: The first form of swerving might be said to be originated by the characters; the other is originated and controlled only by the filmmaker.

At the character level, Richard is not really telling jokes to Maria, and she is not really listening to or answering them. They are playing a game that might more appropriately be called "antijoking." Richard asks a joke question (or delivers a joke punch line) and Maria deliberately either does or does not give the appropriate reply. A sample moment follows:

RICHARD: What's blue and whistles and hangs in a delicatessen? [*pause*] A herring! [*pause*] Aren't you going to say that a herring doesn't whistle? Aren't you going to say that a herring isn't blue? [*pause*] You're *not* going to say it?

The wit of the scene is not in the jokes (which, as the example illustrates, are infantile), but in the swerving away from the formula of the joke on Richard's part and the formula of the answer on Maria's part. At this first level, Richard and Maria do the same thing that Cassavetes does as the writer of the scene: All three use the established forms as something to be worked off of, something by which to gather momentum by moving against.

But there is a second level to the movement against structures that only the filmmaker originates or controls. It has to do with the tonal shifts within the scene. Just as he does in the bedroom scene between Maria and Chet, Cassavetes times his edit so that at every moment a viewer is about to catch up with the scene's meaning or tone, it slips out from under the current understanding. At each point we get "with" the feelings, Cassavetes changes the mood slightly and forces a readjustment in our reading process. While Richard antijokes, his creator antiedits.

Since the very essence of such a series of movements is to resist summarization, the only way to describe the effect of the scene is to walk briefly through the experience as we encounter it. As the scene begins, Cassavetes leaves us at sea as to how to respond to Richard's jokes. They are obviously not very funny, nor is the scene itself extremely amusing. Should we laugh with Richard? At Richard? With Maria? Should we laugh at all? It takes a minute or so for us to realize that the dumbness of the humor is intentional (on Cassavetes' part at least, if not on Richard's), and we finally start to laugh (less at the humor than at its stupidity, and at Richard's obvious delight in such idiocy). Our laughter is first tentative, then (as most dumb laughter is) increasingly raucous and contagious; but the edit is timed so that at the very moment we start to loosen up and hee-haw along with Richard, we also begin to realize that the scene is not funny after all, though for different reasons than we originally imagined. Although we might not be able to verbalize the recognition at this point, it slowly dawns on us that Richard and his wife interact with jokes because they have no other form of intimacy. By this point, however, we have been baited into laughing (and most of the audience in the theater is laughing loudly), and it is embarrassing to admit we're wrong and stop, so the laughter continues, even as Richard and Maria's hilarity becomes more and more hollow. At that point a deliberate state of cognitive dissonance is set up: The scene suddenly turns sad beyond words as Richard and Maria both drop silent, roll apart from each other, and stare off in different directions. Less than a minute later (when some members of the audience have just realized that the tone has turned darker), Richard asks Maria for a divorce. When Maria breaks into laughter at that point, laughter which is clearly not comical but hysterical, it's fair to say that for the first and only moment within the scene the tones stop changing. Cassavetes proves himself a master of moving against structures of emotional containment even more than Richard and Maria show themselves able to move against the structures of joke telling.

There is one final issue relating to the acting Cassavetes elicits that needs to be touched on: In light of the role-playing we saw in *Shadows*, one notices that the language, gestures, and stances of Richard, Freddie, McCarthy, and Jackson function a lot like those of Ben, Hugh, Rupert, Tony, and Lelia. That is to say, their words and postures are almost always not simply "them," but are "put on" and presented for effect. They are in a fundamentally oblique relationship to their own self-representations. They play with tones, stances, and words. They are almost never merely committed to their expressions. They use them; they toy with them. They are expressive experimenters, at a slight critical distance from each of their own expressions of themselves.

As an example of the obliquity of expression in the film, notice how in the first long scene, when Richard, Freddie, and Jeannie are dancing together, Freddie keeps adjusting his expressions to attempt to seduce Jeannie away from Richard. After his adjustments have given way to the brutality of insult, he then adjusts his subsequent apology, trying out several different tones in succession (none of which is truly apologetic, though all pretend to be so). As briefer illustrations, consider the following moments: Richard covers up his feelings of embarrassment when Jeannie washes his feet by singing a ditty. A few minutes later, he deflects attention away from his anxiety about spending the night with her by attempting to impress her with a series of set speeches. Jackson cheers up McCarthy after his wrestling match with Richard by ribbing him with a repeated joke about being "a son of a gun." McCarthy tries to cover his own later embarrassment about his previously patronizing treatment of Richard by making a series of awkward jokes about their mutual acquaintance "Stewie Ray."

As *Shadows* demonstrated, such expressive indirection is not evidence of the characters' deviousness or insincerity, but of the unavoidability of creative inflections in Cassavetes' work (inflections premised on the existence of a linguistic gap between the self and its always only partial, provisional expressions of itself). For Cassavetes, as for Emerson, "English is a language too." That state of affairs is not something to be regretted, but to be worked with. Our state of moderate alienation from our expressions is what makes creative performance possible. If these characters had a more direct, immediate, or naive relation to their own expressions of themselves, they would not be able to play with their self-representations so inventively and entertainingly. The gap between the person and the utterance is what makes room for role-playing, joke making, and game playing. Shape shifting becomes possible only when the self has a somewhat loosened and experimental relationship to its own expressions of itself. (Of course it takes actors of the acrobatic flexibility and quickness of Val Avery, Fred Draper, Seymour Cassel, and John Marley to communicate this effect, and a scriptwriter with the gymnastic imaginative musculature of John Cassavetes to create the material for them to perform with and against.)

There is a downside to all of this, however. The belief that the individual can be an autonomous agent for his own acts of self-creation is the most Jamesian aspect of Cassavetes' work, yet as James repeatedly acknowledged, our freedom is limited. For Emerson, James, and Cassavetes, the free movements we make are never entirely free. Patterns continuously encroach on us, threatening to mechanize our energies, to turn originality into derivativeness. The threat comes both from without and from within:

From without: Preexisting constructions of reality constrain our individual acts of creativity. As James put it in "Pragmatism and Humanism," reality is "resisting, yet malleable."[16] Or, in terms of the implicit dramatic metaphor that runs throughout Cassavetes' work, the ways others "script" our lives invariably limit the independence of our performances. (*The Killing of a Chinese Bookie*'s Cosmo Vitelli will be Cassavetes' most extended meditation on this limitation on our freedom.)

From within: Our own spontaneous, free inventions continuously congeal into received knowledge. As Emerson emphasized, our creative fluidity is always on the brink of coagulating into rigidity: "For it is the inert effort of each thought . . . to heap itself . . . and to solidify and hem in the life."[17] Every new performance, however creative in its original impulses, lays down a pattern that must be broken up by subsequent movements away from it. Tony and Ben showed us the dangers of being trapped by our own identities in *Shadows*; Freddie, Richard, and McCarthy demonstrate it in *Faces*.

In the face of both sorts of threats, in their different ways, Emerson, James, and Cassavetes imagine an unending drama in which "nature" (in Emerson's favorite term) and "man" (in James's) must endlessly decompose their own previous compositions, which are themselves continuously "hemming us in." Our deployments must continuously be energetically redeployed. "The new continents are built out of the ruins of an old planet; the new races fed out of the decomposition of the foregoing. New arts destroy the old."[18]

Richard, Freddie, and McCarthy are situated on the place all of Cassavetes' most interesting characters occupy: the razor-edge where flow meets fixity. At moments they inspire us with the audacity of their powers of self-creation and self-revision. They intermittently give the impression that they are making up their lines and their personalities as they go along, inventively improvising marginally new identities on the margins of the confining scripts of their lives. They fleetingly seem capable of realizing the dream of becoming artists of their own personalities. Every tonal swerve, every unexpected dramatic turn, every change of beat they display is a flexing of a muscle that tells us how truly strong and creative we are.

At other moments, however, they show us the opposite. They show us how our newly created faces harden into wooden masks; how flexible inventiveness can rigidify into a mechanical design for living; how laughter can become formulaic and hollow. They show us how a brave and creative performance can become a predictable, confining routine.

Cassavetes was under no illusions about how much energy the decomposing of past compositions asked of each of us. He understood the inertia of the human spirit, its tendency to stop with the past and to repeat itself in the future. In the end, it is the impression of crystallization and not of liquidity that dominates *Faces*. Like Louise in her interaction with Chet, virtually all of the characters in *Faces* withdraw in terror from the prospect of ontological openness. Like Richard, they no sooner have an opening night, a night of potential revelation and self-discovery, than they shut themselves down and flee from the adventure of insecurity that looms ahead. Like Maria, after daringly opening themselves up, they are so frightened by what they discover that they choose self-annihilation over life – imaginatively, by choosing self-erasure (and sometimes literally, by choosing suicide). They would rather die than learn something.

The way we know that most of the figures in *Faces* are profoundly flawed is that the effect of their personal styles is ultimately the reverse of the effect of Cassavetes' cinematic style. That is to say, while *Faces*'s style of scripting, photography, and editing moves us to appreciate free-floating flexibility, nimble responsiveness, and emotional openness, the performative styles of McCarthy, Freddie, Jackson, Forst, Billy Mae, and Louise reduce knowledge to formulas and their relationships with others to mechanical patterns. Whereas the film's style shows us how identity can participate in an open-ended adventure of continuous creation, they "can" themselves and package their performances in repetitious routines. While the style teaches a viewer the exhilarations of staying in motion, the joys of skating endlessly forward on the slippery surfaces of life, they attempt to stop the movement.

In this instance, as in so many other respects, Emerson mapped the possibilities. In "The Method of Nature" he wrote about futility of attempting to resist the flowing progressiveness of experience:

> The rushing stream will not stop to be observed. We can never surprise nature in a corner; never find the end of a thread; never tell where to set the first stone. The bird hastens to lay her egg; the egg hastens to be a bird. [The] smoothness [of the world] is the smoothness of the pitch of the cataract. Its permanence is a perpetual inchoation. Every natural fact is an emanation, and that from which it emanates is an emanation also, and from every emanation is a new emanation. If

anything could stand still, it would be crushed and dissipated by the torrent it resisted, and if it were a mind, would be crazed; as insane persons and those who hold fast to one thought, and do not flow with the course of nature.[19]

It would be hard to find a better illustration of both prongs of his argument than *Faces*'s cinematic style on the one hand, and the personal expressive styles of figures like Richard, Freddie, McCarthy, Billy Mae, and Louise on the other. Cassavetes' cinematic style is as propulsive as Emerson's rushing cataract; while they are crushed, crazed, and driven half insane by their attempt to stand still against experience's racing onwardness.

Every aspect of *Faces*'s cinematic style constitutes an implicit critique of the limitations of most of its characters' expressive styles. While the film tantalizes us with a vision of life's interactional possibilities, Richard, Freddie, McCarthy, Billie Mae, and Louise devote themselves to an ethic of domination and mastery. While its scripting and editing break down walls between characters, encouraging openness and intimacy, broadening views and perspectives, the characters withdraw into their own private worlds, fearfully and self-protectively closing down their range of responsiveness. While its cinematic style captures fluid shifts of tone and continuous adjustments of relationship, their expressive styles lock them into rigid positions. While the photography extols the virtues of circulation and movement, they freeze themselves into static intellectual and emotional stances. While the film attempts to make room for mysteries that allow characters to remain stimulatingly undefined and open to possibility, Richard, Billy Mae, Louise, Freddie, McCarthy, and Jackson package their personalities into mechanical routines and pigeonhole everyone with whom they come into contact. (People come from "musical backgrounds." Women are "bimbos." Teenagers are "college kids who wear sneakers." Businessmen are "golf men" or "tennis men.")

The very way *Faces* was made stands as a criticism of the performances of most of the characters in it. While the filming and acting style Cassavetes elicited from his crew and his performers was noncompetitive and egalitarian, Richard, Freddie, and McCarthy devote their lives to attempting to "star in" and "control" the scenes in which they appear. ("Hey boy, listen, I'm talking to you," McCarthy bullies Richard before discovering who he is.) While the way the film was made was premised on a belief in the importance of respecting multiple points of view, the characters attempt to force their own limited, personal points of view on everyone with whom they come into contact.

The only figures who deserve being excepted from the preceding generalizations are Chet, Jeannie, and, to a lesser extent, Florence. Alone among *Faces*'s characters, they have learned to live in Cassavetes' stylistic universe of process and provisionality, abandoning schemes for living, vulnerably experimenting with who they are, and staying open to emotional possibility. It is not surprising that Chet and Jeannie's personal styles are similar to Cassavetes' shooting and editing style. Cassavetes' camera is an all-observing eye and Jeannie is a rubber ear, paying attention to everyone, honoring everyone's feelings, and stereotyping no one. On his part, Chet represents a capacity of social movement, lubrication, and circulation that is the social equivalent to the way Cassavetes' shooting and editing moves from face to face around a room, respecting each individual perspective, dismissing none. Chet's wit and playfulness melt frozen positions and free up what is stuck, similar to how the wit and playfulness of Cassavetes' scripting forces the viewer to abandon categorical stances toward scenes and characters.

Chet and Jeannie's tolerance for differences is one of the things that links them most deeply with their creator. One of the most consistent and remarkable qualities of Cassavetes' work is its nonjudgmental quality. He is simply never scornful of or impatient with even his most benighted or apparently despicable characters. Unlike Robert Altman or Woody Allen, he never sneers or patronizes. Like Jeannie watching McCarthy and Richard compete for male dominance, or Chet watching the women establish their pecking order, as a director Cassavetes always seems to have a half-smile of amused delight on his face, no matter how weird the behavior of the characters. In fact, the more bizarre the behavior, the more it is relished. Rather than being outraged, he seems entertained by his characters' foibles and crotchets. (I would note that to the extent that the viewer is teased into the same state of half-amazed amusement, he is also freed from moralistic judgments.) Cassavetes' love of idiosyncrasy, his embrace of eccentricity, and his supreme respect for individual uniqueness are downright Renoirian.

Chet and Jeannie's acting styles repeat the lesson: They embody Cassavetes' own vision of "noncompetitive" acting, in which what matters is not controlling a scene, but responding to others within it. They are stars whose fondest goal is not to star but to interact. They treat their relationships with others as opportunities of true collaboration. Needless to say, their form of acting is much more difficult than that of Richard, Louise, or McCarthy. Ensemble acting is much harder to bring off than a star performance. It asks far more of an actor to stay open, to keep adjusting his performance to respond to another's, to avoid relaxing into formulaic positions, than it does for him merely to dazzle, to "take over a scene and make it his" (as Cassavetes once dismissively phrased the star attitude)[20] in the way of McCarthy (or, for that matter, of Jack Nicholson or Eddie Murphy).

Cassavetes' cinematic style does the same things in film that Chet and Jeannie do in life. It avoids categorical judgments. It enlarges perspectives. It cares about even those who don't want or deserve to be cared about – just as Jeannie cares about the feelings of even the boorish Freddie and McCarthy, and as Chet cares about Louise and Maria even after they berate him. It is a style of caring, a style of love.

One of the most paradoxical qualities of Cassavetes' work is that however difficult the films or the lives of characters within them, the films and the characters are never depressing. *Faces* is an anthology of acts of insensitivity and cruelty, yet it offers what can only be called a spiritually exultant experience. All of Cassavetes' work, no matter how painful, is inspiring and uplifting. It is extremely difficult to say why this should be, but I think that one reason is that (entirely unlike the work of Robert Altman, for example) Cassavetes' films are never about victims. Even his most doomed characters are the artists of their own fates. They have no one to blame for their problems but themselves (and they almost never do blame anyone else). Furthermore, Cassavetes tells us that however beset by pressures, we are essentially strong; we can swallow the worst that life dishes out. Even the most morally repugnant of his gallery of the damned still intermittently dazzle us with their wit, touch us with their glimmering awareness of their own deficiencies, and inspire us with their energy and indomitability. In this sense, no matter how tragic the films, they are profoundly hopeful and life affirming.

In *Minnie and Moskowitz*, in the midst of a self-pitying litany of his woes and disappointments, one of Cassavetes' most pathetic figures, Zelmo Swift, speaks a line that might be applied to all of Cassavetes major figures: "But I go on. I go on." No matter how awful their lives, they energetically carry on with them. No matter how much they lose, they never give up. The major ones (which leaves Zelmo himself off the list) never even pause to pity themselves, to weep and bemoan their outcast state. No matter how hard they struggle, they never slacken the energy of their efforts. Even the most doomed of them go through life holding nothing back, living completely in every moment, regretting nothing. In their occasionally pigheaded way, they never give up on their dreams, no matter how far from attaining them they may be. They never break up their lines to weep, which is why, in Yeats's sense, like Hamlet or Lear in their darkest hours, they are still gay.

In a postrelease interview, Cassavetes said something similar in response to a question about which character in *Faces* he liked the most. He said Florence was his personal favorite because, as he put it, she refused "to gripe and pine away in silence," no matter what obstacles she faced:

> I get a lump in my throat every time I see her. She tries everything and she doesn't care how ridiculous and pathetic it is. The point is that she tried. She fought for it, tied herself in knots. She wouldn't give up. And isn't it better to fight to realize your fantasies, to fight and to lose, than to gripe and pine away in silence.[21]

Cassavetes' works are the most personal and autobiographical of any feature filmmaker who ever lived – not literally, but spiritually. In the light of this quote, it should be obvious that the creator was more than a little like his greatest creations. Florence, McCarthy, Richard, Zelmo, and the crazy home-movie man who spent six months of his life filming in his own house, more than $200,000 of his own money, and three years editing the movie in his garage, all can say with gusto, "I go on. I go on."

3
Beating the System
Minnie and Moskowitz

For it is the inert effort of each thought, having formed itself into a wave of circumstances, – as, for instance, an empire, rules of an art, a local usage, a religious rite, – to heap itself on that ridge, and to solidify and hem in the life. But if the soul is quick and strong, it bursts over that boundary on all sides, and expands another orbit on the great deep, which also runs up into a high wave, with attempt again to stop and to bind. But the heart refuses to be imprisoned; in its first and narrowest pulses, it already tends outward with a vast force, and to immense and innumerable expansions. . . .

If you please to plant yourself on the side of Fate, and say Fate is all; then we say, a part of Fate is the freedom of man. Forever wells up the impulse of choosing and acting in the soul. Intellect annuls Fate. So far as a man thinks, he is free. . . . He who sees through the design, presides over it and must will that which must be. . . . Thought dissolves the material universe. . . . Every solid in the universe is ready to become fluid on the approach of the mind, and the power to flux it is the measure of the mind. If the wall remain adamant, it accuses the want of thought. To a subtler force, it will stream into new forms, expressive of the character of the mind. – R. W. Emerson[1]

Cassavetes' work is about intellectual pattern breaking and emotional opening. The dramatic form this process takes is usually romantic. As different as they are from one another, *Shadows, Too Late Blues, Faces, Husbands, Minnie and Moskowitz, Gloria*, and *Love Streams* each dramatize a character's shaking off limiting habits or relationships and opening himself or herself to new experiences as a result of a romantic encounter with another character.

The films are not just about opening up, however; they do what they dramatize. They attempt to induce the same changes in consciousness in the viewer that the characters within them undergo. Cassavetes' cinematic

114

agenda is assaultive; it is designed to break down the ways in which a viewer intellectually distances himself from experience. The problem is that we have become too good at reading movies. We hardly have to think to understand most of them. Twenty or thirty years of habitual responses stand in the way of learning anything. *Minnie and Moskowitz* is a frontal attack on our viewing habits. It is a wrecking ball directed at old ways of knowing in an attempt to make new experiences possible. As always in Cassavetes' work, destabilization is the path to growth, insecurity the door to discovery.

The "youth-picture" boom of the late 1960s and early 1970s gave Cassavetes an unexpected opportunity to work within a studio for the first time since his blowup with Stanley Kramer almost ten years before. At a time in which counterculture films like *Bonnie and Clyde*, *Easy Rider*, and *Five Easy Pieces* were making unexpectedly big money for the studios on small initial investments, Universal let it be known that they would welcome a script from him.

To mark his return to Hollywood, Cassavetes proposed a screwball comedy in the tradition of *It Happened One Night* and *Mr. Deeds Goes to Town*. He was probably attracted to the form not only because of all of the thirties genres it is the most zany and anarchic, but also because its drama is fundamentally psychological. It dramatizes developing consciousness. The important wars in Cassavetes' work are always inward (to paraphrase Marianne Moore), and screwball comedy is, with the exception of the woman's melodrama, the most "inward" of mainstream studio forms.

The master plot of the screwball form has three components: social and psychological unmooring as the initiating event; zany romantic conflict as a learning process; and psychological insight and emotional growth as the final outcome. To spell it out in a bit more detail: The central male and female characters are each asked to repudiate some aspect of their past lives and habits of behavior in order to enter into a bewildering relationship with each other. They are deliberately mismatched in every imaginable way, which creates arguments and misunderstandings between them and furthers their education. The end result of being bounced off of each other is that both members of the romantic pair are compelled to break their past patterns and forced to come to a new awareness of who they are.[2]

In the rough trajectory of its plot, *Minnie and Moskowitz* follows the formula. Minnie Moore is forced to break off her current romance and plunge head over heels into a free-for-all relationship with the crazy Seymour Moskowitz, with whom she has virtually nothing in common. She (and to a lesser extent he) come to a new appreciation of themselves and their needs for each other by the end of the movie. Cassavetes makes it clear at the start of the film that Minnie is the shell-shocked veteran of a series of failed relationships who has withdrawn in fear from ever making herself vulnerable again. (Like *Shadows*'s Ben, to whom she is distantly related, she wears sunglasses at night so that no one can see what she is thinking, and hides her feelings by wrapping herself in blankets of stillness and silence.) She is currently trapped in a dead-end romantic relationship with a boyfriend named Jim that is both physically and emotionally brutalizing; but as awful as it is, Cassavetes understands that even our anguishes become consoling if they are sufficiently long-standing. The known is almost always preferable to the unknown, and Minnie's horror-movie relationship with Jim has become as comfortable to her as a bad habit.

In line with the screwball agenda, Cassavetes forces Minnie to leave the predictable and plunge into the zanily unforeseeable. Within the comic premises of the film, it would be hard to find anything more shocking to Minnie's system than her hothouse romance with wild man Moskowitz. She gets emotionally tangled up with someone she would normally cross the street to avoid. The star-crossed lovers are as crazily mismatched as possible. Minnie is gentle, delicate, and from an obviously "good" background; Seymour is an aging, over-the-hill hippie with the manners of a sasquatch, whose idea of eating out is a sidewalk hot dog from Pink's. She is WASPish and beautiful; he is Jewish and dog faced. She is a museum administrator; he is a car parker. She is shy and reserved; he is brash and opinionated.

That is, as it were, only the surface story in *Minnie and Moskowitz*, however. As much as being about how personal styles limit our expressive possibilities, the film explores how cultural and artistic structures of understanding limit our experiences. Underneath the personal drama is a cultural and intellectual one. The drama within the drama is the one on which I want to focus. Let me give an example: Minnie's relationship with Jim is a romance from hell, but one of the things that binds her to him is that Jim (played by Cassavetes himself) fits the definition of a conventional cinematic lover. He is dark, handsome, mysteriously exciting, lady-killingly charming, and more than slightly dangerous. The dilemma with which Seymour Moskowitz presents Minnie is as much cultural as personal; the problem is not just that he acts goofy, but that his appearance, his behavior, and his forms of expression violate everything Hollywood has made us believe about romantic types.[3] He is neither conventionally handsome, articulate, nor suave. The reviewer for *Variety* (always a litmus test of how an experience stacks up against Hollywood's version of it) summed it up when he sarcastically wrote that Seymour "makes King Kong look like Cary Grant." What he failed to realize was that Cassavetes' point was to make us wonder why we prefer Cary Grant to King Kong as a leading man, or why for romance or adventure we prefer either to a nutty Jewish car parker. Cassavetes alerts us to the explicitly cultural predicament that Seymour figures by including many references on Minnie's part to how he violates her idea of romance. Many scenes in the film emphasize the extent to which Minnie's conception of love was shaped by at least three different sorts of cultural inheritance: Hollywood movies ("The movies set you up"), pop music ("Someday my prince will come"), and stories her mother told her ("That face is not the face I dreamed about").

Figures like *Shadows*'s Ben and Tony showed that, in his very first film, Cassavetes understood the danger of impersonal forms of identity edging out personal ones. In *Minnie and Moskowitz*, however, the characters have clearly moved into a more complex and dangerous expressive predicament than that faced by the characters in the earlier film. One sign of that difference is the change of venue: *Shadows* was an East Coast film with East Coast rhythms, emphases, and characters; *Minnie and Moskowitz* is L.A. all the way. (Even the precredits "New York" scenes have the staccato pacing of a music video.) In the Los Angeles of Cassavetes' imagination, characters are so "heaped" with cultural ideology (to use Melville's term) that they can never escape it. No data are raw, no experience is uncooked: Everything and everyone is relentlessly processed and packaged for mass consumption. *Minnie and Moskowitz* describes a world in which culture has replaced nature.[4] Or to put it more accurately, culture has convinced characters like Minnie that it *is* nature, which is why if Seymour doesn't look like a movie palace prince and act like a storybook hero, he can't possibly be one in Minnie's life. It seems hardly accidental that the three Cassavetes works which use Los Angeles as an important part of the story – this film, *The Killing of a Chinese Bookie*, and *Love Streams* – take the cultural processing of expression and identity as their subject. In this respect, it's fair to say that even though he lived in Los Angeles for more than thirty years, Cassavetes, a born-and-bred New Yorker, was no more imaginatively at home there than is his alter ego Seymour Moskowitz. (Accentuating the autobiographical dimension of the movie is that Cassavetes imagines Seymour to be an expatriated New Yorker who makes the same trip from one coast to the other at the beginning of the movie that his creator did a few years before in real life.) The East Coast boy never lost his distrust of West Coast forms of cultural packaging – most notably, of course, the forms of packaging called "the movies."

One of the principal metaphors for cultural processing in *Minnie and*

Moskowitz is the experience provided in films. They entomb us in a fantasy world. In an early scene Minnie indicates that she herself understands this, even if she is unable to escape it. She and an older girlfriend named Florence go to see *Casablanca*. They return to Florence's run-down apartment afterward and share a bottle of cheap wine. Near the evening's end, Minnie's inebriation prompts a rambling reverie. I quote from the final draft of the screenplay, which differs only slightly from the film:

> I mean, the world is full of idiots who crave your body and your soul and your mind and your heart. . . . They can't live without it 'til they get it. And when they get it, then they don't want it anymore. But you go to the movies – it's always different. I think the movies are a conspiracy. They set you up from the time you're a kid to believe in everything; in love, in ideals, in good people, in strength . . . in everything . . . you know? And then you go out, you keep looking . . . and you get a job, like us, we work in a museum, deal with pretty things, but they're not pretty. Spend a lot of time fixing up things, caring about nice things, pretty furniture and jazz, learn how to cook and be feminine . . . but there's no Charles Boyer in my life. I never met a Charles Boyer. I never met a Humphrey Bogart. I never met a Clark Gable. Or a William Powell. They set you up, you see? And I mean, no matter how bright you are . . . and we're bright, we're geniuses compared to the rest of the people. I mean look at you . . . and look at how tasteful you are – you're smart and nice and I look at the sum total of your life . . . and it's a room and you're alone with diminishing sexual returns. You don't even have someone that's just a pal. You know? Isn't that crazy? Go to the movies and you see a man die for a woman just because he wants to see her again. That's good. Kill the son of a bitch. If it could only be that way. You know?[5]

The ironies are multiple and obvious. These painful recognitions are precisely what are left out of *Casablanca* or *Algiers*. Nevertheless, Cassavetes knows that to recognize a problem and to be able to escape it are entirely different things. Minnie can rail against the influence of the movies, but even her complaints are evidence that she is still under their imaginative thrall, a fact that an earlier version of the screenplay makes even clearer. Here is the exact same moment in an earlier draft of the script:

FLORENCE: I thought it was good, but I didn't think it was great.
MINNIE: Well, I thought it was great. I told you how I felt. I don't know why you keep contradicting me, Florence. I know movies. I know movies

better than I know art. Because I've lived with movies...and Charles Boyer is the best...because he loves women and he always looks like his heart is breaking and his hands are tender.

FLORENCE: Tender?

MINNIE: That's right, tender. His hands are tender...you can tell when a man's hands are tender and when they touch you how they're gonna feel. That's when you know if a movie's good – when you want to be kissing the man. Don't you know that? God, anyone knows that. I thought you knew that. Because probably the only thing that's really good, and I'm talking about good, you know, outside of breathing, is being desired. And the way he came down there and he knew he was going to die, even if he didn't know it...I knew it.

FLORENCE: But she didn't know it.

MINNIE: No, she didn't know it...but he knew it and I didn't know it... and that's what made it a good movie because he wanted her so much to be happy. It's so great to cry. I think that's why I don't cry anymore. I'd just be terrified that I would go to a movie and find myself dry. Aw, that's not true, Florence. I cry. We all cry. But the damn movies are so much better 'cause you feel for everybody, not against them. You know what I mean.[6]

This version shows Minnie so completely blending movies with life that it is hard to know which she is talking about at any particular moment. (Notice also the pronoun confusions, suggesting that Cassavetes deliberately scripted in the grammatical errors and inconsistencies that were usually attributed to his alleged improvisatory methods.) A comparison of the two drafts also reveals something stranger still: Minnie apparently learns something between them. It is as if, like her creator, in the later version (the one printed here first) she has read her own earlier screenplay (the one printed second) and come to understand something about herself that then allows her to move to a more sophisticated critical position.

However, Cassavetes was always less interested in theoretical statements about an experience than in having his characters and viewers undergo the experience itself. That is why he not only makes reference to movies in *Minnie and Moskowitz*, but edits a number of clips directly into the film:

Seymour goes into a movie theater and watches a clip of Bogart and Mary Astor in *The Maltese Falcon* (which we see).

Minnie and Florence watch *Casablanca* (we watch the final minute or so of the film along with them).

Later on, Seymour and Minnie watch *Casablanca* (we hear the ending of
the film a second time on the sound track).

There is also a series of other implicit or explicit references to movies:

Seymour goes into a restaurant and talks with a character named Morgan
Morgan who declares his love for Wallace Beery. Seymour says he prefers
Bogart.
Several allusions are made to Rouben Mamoulian's *Dr. Jekyl and Mr. Hyde*.
Seymour does a Bugs Bunny imitation to get a child to eat a carrot.
Two allusions are made to the Indian head that appears in the nighttown
sequence of Frank Capra's *It's a Wonderful Life*.
Seymour tells Minnie that she looks like Lauren Bacall.
A swimming pool scene is meant to remind us of a related moment in
Nicholas Ray's *Rebel Without a Cause*.
In the most extended and important sequence of all (which I will discuss
in detail below), Cassavetes models three or four minutes of *Minnie and
Moskowitz* on one of the spaceship sequences in Stanley Kubrick's *2001*.

Vincent Canby's response to these sequences was typical of most reviewers. He treated them as acts of homage to previous Hollywood films, and
as implicit expressions of Cassavetes' gratitude to be participating in the
studio tradition. There is a germ of truth to both points. Cassavetes was
quite fond of some of the movies to which he alludes, and insofar as this
film marked his gingerly reestablishment of diplomatic relations with a
mainstream studio, it is understandable that he might have had Hollywood
on his mind when he made the picture. Speaking still more practically,
having the backing of a studio permissions department is the only reason
he was able to include these clips at all. He would have been neither able
to get the rights to use them nor to afford them had he been working in
his usual capacity as a complete independent. In short, Canby was partly
right; but his response typically did not go deep enough. In his characteristic
focus on style, he ignores the meaning of the clips, which tells us that if the
allusions are in part a token act of genuflection and gratitude, they are even
more a display of power and mastery over his studio precursors.

Cassavetes is acknowledging his indebtedness, but also declaring his independence. Like Minnie in her drunken ramble, he acknowledges the sway
of Hollywood forms of experience over his imagination. Unlike her, he has
a witty, playful, critical perspective on them. Consider an early example:
Seymour declares his fondness for Humphrey Bogart, and we watch him
watching a scene from *The Maltese Falcon*. Cassavetes is acknowledging

the power Bogart has over our imaginations and urging that we regard Seymour as a version of Bogart. But he is also declaring his ability to rewrite Bogart wittily and perversely, to imagine a wildly different vision of maleness. The differences between Bogart and Moskowitz are far greater than the similarities. The clip gives us a Bogart who stands tall and stoic against an emotional Mary Astor. Seymour, on the other hand, is more like the woman than the man in the scene: passionate, involved, uncool. The clip gives us a Bogart who is poised, aloof, expressively guarded and emotionally controlled; by contrast, Seymour is sweaty, expressively excessive, and at least half out of control. Cassavetes is less tugging his forelock than sticking out his tongue.

In a similar vein, as their emergence from *Casablanca* together is meant to tell us, Minnie and Florence *are* Rick and Renault. As the sex-change operation Cassavetes does on Curtiz's buddy-boys suggests, however, Cassavetes' characters don't inhale, but rather inflect, their cinematic inheritances. Far from bowing nostalgically in the direction of *Casablanca*, Cassavetes flaunts his ability eccentrically to redeploy its images. He parades his ability to bend Hollywood's figurations in ways Hollywood could never have imagined. This Rick and Renault do not stride arm in arm in the mist together, but take a bus home. And home is not an exotic nightclub, but a dingy walkup apartment with an empty refrigerator. When they get there, they do not drink champagne (or Vichy water), but rather wine out of a screw-top bottle. When Curtiz's grandiloquent concluding crane shot is echoed in a later scene, Cassavetes significantly reverses its direction of movement. Its swoop does not carry us from the earth up into imaginative clouds (the rhetorical inflection Curtiz gives to all of *Casablanca*'s scenes), but downward.

Cassavetes' redeployment of Hollywood's forms of experience is never more puckish or perverse than in the extended parody of Kubrick's *2001* at the center of the film. It involves a three- or four-minute director's sequence first showing Minnie and Seymour cruising down Hollywood Boulevard in Seymour's pickup, then sitting parked near the cliff at the top of Mulholland Drive. In the first half of the sequence, as the truck goes down the street, Cassavetes positions the camera to pick up moving reflections on the pickup's back window of colored neon lights from the street, so as to mimic Kubrick's shots of lights reflecting off the spacesuit visors of his astronauts. In the second half the truck stands still, and Cassavetes slowly moves the camera above and around the cab, then downward toward it (in the reverse crane shot already mentioned), to mimic Kubrick's shots of slowly moving or docked space vehicles. Minnie and Seymour inside the dimly lighted truck cab resemble the spacemen inside the ships in *2001*'s process shots. Both sequences are accompanied with the signature orchestration of Kubrick's movie, the swelling strains of Strauss's *Blue Danube*.

Contra Canby, what is clearly taking place is not awestruck imitation but sassy parody. Cassavetes offers a deliberately distorted reflection on Kubrick's images. Spaceships on Hollywood Boulevard? Interplanetary exploration in a dilapidated pickup? Cassavetes takes the emotions that *2001* associates with extraterrestrial experience and brings them down to the sidewalks, the streets, the parking lots of life. He relocates Kubrick's out-of-this-world exaltations in the realm of the visible and tangible. Far from paying homage to *2001*, Cassavetes is inverting its value system. Kubrick used these images to blast off intellectually into rarefied realms of thought; Cassavetes pilots a path downward, plotting a course of reentry into the density and resistance of earthly close encounters. Cassavetes transforms Kubrick's visionary releases into social involvements. He domesticates Kubrick's sublime.

The final seconds of the *2001* allusion wittily sum up the light-years separating Kubrick from Cassavetes. The crane shot moves from high up in the air down to the ground of a dirty lot. Seymour abruptly switches off the Strauss (which we suddenly realize was coming from the truck radio all along), reminding us how not only Kubrick's objects but his sounds too were sprung free from such expressive contingencies. Minnie accidentally drops a lighted cigarette onto the seat, and a not-entirely comic scurry to locate it ensues. An argument follows about whether they are right for each other. One is reminded that Kubrick's astronauts were cut free not only from the effects of terrestrial gravity, but also from the emotional gravity of this sort of moment. Their interactions were as emotionally weightless and merely visionary as Cassavetes' are sweaty and passionate. Kubrick's high-tech world is spacey, frictionless, and bloodless to a fault; Cassavetes' is crowded, frictional, and hot-blooded. Cassavetes is telling us something not only about Kubrick, but about ourselves as well: about how our lust for imaginative escapes from worldly expressive complications (our love for movies like *2001*) is part of what makes our lives back on earth so complicated.

Cassavetes' use of Kubrick's images is a display of both power and knowledge: power idiosyncratically to borrow and inflect, and knowledge to make new, arguably even more interesting meanings than were present in the original. It is important to distinguish the realms not only because they are different, but because they may actually be opposed, as Emerson suggests in "The Poet":

An imaginative [work] renders us much more service at first by stimulating us through its tropes, than afterward, when we arrive at the precise sense of the author. . . . The poets are liberating gods. . . . They are free and they make free.[7]

The distinction between "stimulation" and "sense" leads to one of the most important yet difficult aspects of Cassavetes' work to which to do critical justice. A critic's job is one of understanding, but one of the things that must be accounted for is how Cassavetes delays and at times deliberately prevents clarifying understanding. In Emerson's terms, while Cassavetes stimulates viewers with his tropes, he often leaves them uncertain about their sense. The critic consequently runs the danger of giving a false impression of how the films feel by clearing up (and cleaning up) the experience. It is in the nature of the experience Cassavetes provides that it does not become clear for many screenings, and sometimes not ever. It is as if knowledge itself were one more form of repression to be guarded against. Insofar as knowledge systematizes the energies that power releases, Cassavetes' working premise seems to be that it is better to leave viewers wondering than knowing.

Most of the cinematic allusions Cassavetes offers in *Minnie and Moskowitz* are presented so deftly, unobtrusively, and rapidly that viewers don't identify them the first time they see the film. Even the rare viewer who does "get" one usually doesn't attach a clear meaning to it for a long time after leaving the film. A viewer's response to these references is less a state of knowing than of half-bewildered provocation: What is *Casablanca* doing here anyway? Why is it in the film twice? Why does Seymour briefly pause in front of an Indian head on a doorway and turn in profile? What is the weird but unnameable familiarity we feel with some of the images that accompany the Strauss? How odd that the sounds of a nineteenth-century Viennese waltz should suddenly appear in a movie otherwise scored with all-American jazz.

If the viewer happens to see *Minnie and Moskowitz* more than once, the second or third time through he may have a little more opportunity to ponder some of these meanings, but many of the allusions probably still won't make a lot of sense. Our responses at this point might run approximately as follows: How strange to think of Seymour and Bogart in one thought. How bizarre to bring Kubrick's spacemen down to earth in this way. *Are* those other scenes actually referring to Capra and Nicholas Ray or is it only my imagination? To be true to the actual experience that Cassavetes offers, even at this stage, what the viewer most feels is still not the precise sense of the tropings, but the stimulation of their weirdness and the provocation of their unresolved tone. They keep us guessing, wondering, and uncertain – which, as far as Cassavetes is concerned, is never a bad state to be in.

In short, the "stimulation" of the moments is always more important than the "meaning" they provide. Even once we have finally "figured out," more or less, the complete range of significances in the *2001* sequence, what we still most feel is not the fixity of meaning, but the shocks and jars of movement: the jolting launch of the Kubrick comparison with the cut to the truck cruising down the street and the unexpected strains on the sound track; the sudden changing of its terms with the cut to the crane shot; the upending of the comparison when the cigarette is dropped and the radio suddenly switched off. That is to say, even after we finally understand these events as knowledge, we still feel them principally as displays of power. Cassavetes' performance has the audacity of a circus act. The stability of the meanings proffered is counteracted by the imbalance and idiosyncrasy of the movements that deliver them to us. The genuine sincerity of the comparison of the truck to a spaceship is counterbalanced by the bizarreness and eccentricity of the redeployment of Kubrick. Whereas meaning formulates and resolves, Cassavetes' idiosyncratic movements deliberately provoke and arouse; whereas meaning figures arrival, what Cassavetes most puts on display is his powers of departure. He and Seymour both show us the "vehicular and transitive" nature of truth (to adapt Emerson's metaphor): They flaunt the creative individual's ability to use expressive U-turns and swerves to avoid having his performances limited by the rules of the road.[8]

This is even more obvious in the second form of troping in *Minnie and Moskowitz*: the bendings not of specific cinematic icons, images, and scenes, but of general cinematic structures. In scene after scene, Cassavetes employs a series of visual jokes that tweak received forms of cinematic knowledge. These range from the way movies withhold the director's name until the end of the credits sequence ("Directed by..." appears further into *Minnie and Moskowitz* than it does in most James Bond movies), to the way space and time are elided in scenes involving travel (Seymour's flight from New York to Los Angeles consists of two library shots of planes taking off and landing, edited almost back to back), to the way directors choose one take over another to edit into a film (two takes of the same moment – Jim's "I've gotta go" – are spliced one after the other). The target Cassavetes takes aim at most frequently is the way cinematic syntax functions to control the viewer's interpretive process and create the sort of "shorthand" meanings he himself shunned.

Consider a ten-minute sequence early in the film. It begins just after the late-night drunken reverie already quoted and ends bright and early the next morning. Cassavetes choreographs a series of miscues, disruptions of expectation, and reversals of tone that teasingly invert or parody most of the rules we have internalized about how to read a movie. Normal forms of cinematic understanding are turned upside down and inside out. Crucial facts about characters' backgrounds and relationships are suppressed. Clues are supplied about what is going on that deliberately lead the viewer to jump to mistaken conclusions. Tones and moods are established one moment, only to be completely reversed the next.

As the sequence begins, it's fairly early in the film and we know nothing about Minnie except that she is an attractive blonde in her late twenties or early thirties. We see her at *Casablanca* with Florence, then going back to Florence's run-down apartment where the two women talk about men and the bleakness of the singles scene. Minnie then takes a cab back to her own place sometime around midnight. We have every reason in the world to conclude that she is a single, unattached woman with no man in her life when the first of several surprises occurs: There is a man standing in her kitchen when she walks into her apartment.

We haven't seen him before, and Cassavetes presents our initial vision of him as the merest glimpse so that we have time for no more than a quick surmise. Probably we jump to the conclusion that he is an intruder. But when he slowly walks up to Minnie in her living room, we rapidly change our working hypothesis and decide that he is a husband or a lover who has let himself in with his key. It comes as a considerable shock. It means that we are forced to revise everything we have assumed up to that point about Minnie being "single" (including revising our understanding of the passage about men that I quoted), but we hurriedly make the cognitive adjustment. It is not the last one we will have to make.

But instead of embracing her as we expect, the still unnamed and unidentified man beats Minnie brutally to the floor. We are again forced to revise our conclusion. He is obviously not a boyfriend. However, just when we feel we may have finally caught up with the scene and the mood (which is as violent and dark as can be imagined), it veers into comic-pathos, as the still unnamed stranger suddenly stops hitting Minnie, fixes her a drink, helps her up, makes jokes about the beating he has just given her, and protests how much he misses and "loves" her. (Even more bizarre, he's obviously deeply sincere – though intentions count for nothing in Cassavetes' work.)

The next instant, in one of the many astonishing jump cuts in this masterpiece of cinematic jumps and worldly cuts, Cassavetes cuts to the stranger getting dressed upstairs and preparing to leave after he and Minnie have obviously made love. "Jim" says he's "gotta go," and Minnie begs him, "Please don't go." That is followed by another disorienting cut, and another "I gotta go." (This is the moment in which Cassavetes edits two takes of the same scene back to back.) This time Minnie is singing and hugging him and walking him to the door (following what the viewer concludes is apparently still more hugging, kissing, and lovemaking in the gap between the two shots, so automatic is our habit of reading a shot sequence narratively rather than purely formally). Now, Jim is Minnie's wonderful lover.

By this point, numbed and assaulted by the visual outrages and emotional shocks, we naturally enough assume that there can be no more surprises. The sequence is obviously over. But just as we are starting to settle back in our seats, Cassavetes follows the two previous jump cuts with a third, even more outrageous one in which we watch the man pulling into the driveway of a house in which there is another woman waiting up for him. When he goes inside and kisses her, it suddenly dawns on us that she is his wife. The topper comes a few seconds later when their kids troop in and start up a chipper, comical breakfast table conversation over the Frosted Flakes about his missing a Little League game the night before. Cassavetes has played free and loose with everything we are used to about how a film presents information. Where did the wife and kids come from? What kind of movie is this anyway? (There is one more unexpected switch that ends the scene, which I will avoid giving away, except to say that this "ending," which involves the wife, rather than resolving the sequence, is itself switched into meaning something else in a later scene between Minnie and Jim, as the series of disruptions continues merrily along.)

I have emphasized the cognitive switches and swerves, but Cassavetes yanks our feelings around as much as he does our understandings. The sequence zigzags tonally as much as it does intellectually, going from the genuinely touching meditativeness of Minnie's conversation with Florence about her disillusionment with men, romance, and the singles scene; to the slapstick of her falling down Florence's steps; to two bits of comic business that take place between Minnie and the cab driver who takes her home; to the horror-movie resonances of Jim's attack on Minnie; to the bizarre lyricism of the moments following their lovemaking; and finally to the inverted Norman Rockwell gothicism of the breakfast scene at the end.

The screwball genre is noted for its tonal slides, but Cassavetes pushes his movie beyond anything even Preston Sturges ever attempted. One of the reasons the beating Jim gives Minnie comes as such a shock is that this sort of movie is just not supposed to have that sort of scene. No one is supposed to really get hurt in screwball; the sparring is supposed to be merely verbal; the falls merely slapstick. In this movie, however, all of the ground rules are off. Anything can happen, and most things do.

It is a breathtaking sequence, and I employ the adjective not only in its vague, honorific connotation, but more to the point, in its literal sense. This series of scenes leaves many viewers actually gasping with bewilderment and dismay. In fact, in describing the sequence verbally I have perhaps made it seem slightly less shocking and confusing than it does to a viewer. Describing it slows it down and makes its progress seem somewhat more coherent than the actual viewing experience is, where we don't quite know what to pay attention to, where we are emotionally at any moment, or where we are headed next. The sequence is a tumble of incongruous impressions, a cascade of astonishing events, coming at us with a rapidity at or beyond the limits of our ability to process it.

Seldom has there been a more stirring cinematic illustration of Emerson's observation in "Circles" that "the universe is fluid and volatile. . . . This surface on which we stand is not fixed but sliding."[9] Emerson's allusion in "Experience" to the Galilean recognition that nothing on earth can stand still almost perfectly captures the feelings of the viewer of this onrushing sequence: "Gladly would we anchor, but the anchorage is quicksand. This onward trick of nature is too strong for us. *Pero si muove.*"[10] We can't sit back and relax into a predictable mood for a second. Cassavetes puts us on the edge of our seats, unsure what to think or feel about anything.

Rather than look at these cinematic events from the perspective of the viewer's half-bewildered, half-exhilarated responses to them, however, we can understand them as displays of the artist's power to make them. Cassavetes treats the structures of previous film not as something with which we must bring ourselves into conformity, but as a platform on which the artist can perform. As Emerson proclaimed in "Fate": "[Our] sound relation to these facts is to use and command, not to cringe to them."[11] Preexisting forms are something we joyously, energetically move on, through, and against. Movement is the operant concept. As the *2001* and the Jim sequences illustrate, Cassavetes' movement among and against the forms is almost an end in itself – an end that can never really be an end, since there is nowhere to get that would not be a negation of the movements that got you there. That suggests a crucial point. Cassavetes' tropings are *not* an attempt to replace old forms (Hollywood's Bogart, Kubrick's visionary sub-limities) with new forms (Seymour as a "new Bogart," a pickup truck romance as a "new sublime"). That would only be to substitute a new fixity, a new pattern for an old. These tropings do not represent new forms, new pat understandings, but capacities of movement that break all forms. All rigidities – new or old – need to be moved across and against.[12]

Just as we saw in the 2001 sequence, one of the forms of coagulation that Cassavetes works against in the scenes with Jim is meaning. Meaning stops movement. It is opposed to the energies performance releases, which is why at every point at which we think we catch up with the meaning of the scene between Jim and Minnie, Cassavetes has it slip away from our categories of understanding. The point is to delay clarification, to defer conclusion, to disrupt knowledge. Each meaning we attach to an event is successively revealed only to have been a snapshot of an experience inexorably on the move. We must learn to live provisionally and tentatively, in space and in time, going from one thing to another. Experience is preferred to explanation. On the evidence of the films, it is fair to conclude that Cassavetes simply did not believe in enduring, essential, or "deep" meaning. To him, reality offered only a slippery set of sliding experiences.

That suggests why it is wrong to read the experience of *Minnie and Moskowitz* (or any of Cassavetes' films) backward: to interpret the uncertainties of earlier scenes in light of the discoveries that occur in later ones. The instabilities of tone, style, and understanding *are* the experience we are meant to have. To understand an earlier moment by reference to what happens later is to substitute concepts for percepts, and to betray the truth of phenomenal reality. In the case of Jim, this means that we can't read his married status as discrediting his earlier profession of "love" for Minnie. Later in the film, we can't read the beginning of Zelmo's lunch date with Minnie in terms of his final explosion of rage. That would be like interpreting a jazz performance as "meaning" wherever its final chord came to rest when the very point of the performance is to force us through the contortions of getting there without being able to see beyond the present moment.

We *can* be sure that wherever we and the characters are at any one moment, we and they are sure to be somewhere else the next. Cassavetes continuously disrupts each successively emerging understanding. He creates knowledge in *Minnie and Moskowitz* and in all of his other films, but it is knowledge not as a state of closed-off understanding, but as an invitation to remain open. Cassavetes implicitly argues that only when experience is recollected in tranquillity can it be presented in terms of fixed forms. The actual feel of experience is a streaming becoming, and a fidelity to that (and not to any fixed idea about it that it can be mangled to fit within) means that he is committed to presenting a series of semantic and emotional compositions and decompositions. To use terms William James would have found congenial, he replaces "substantive" experience with "participial" experience. Verbs replace nouns.

A final illustration of Cassavetes' fluxing of fixities is provided in the sequence that begins with Minnie meeting Zelmo for lunch in the lobby of the museum and ends with her and Seymour eating hot dogs in Pink's. As even that truncated summary indicates, there is no telling where a scene is headed. A date that starts off with one person can end with another. A lunch that begins in an upscale Italian restaurant can conclude in a fast-food hot dog stand. It would take several pages just to list all of the changes of beats in this ten-minute sequence, but let me touch very briefly on two moments to bring out the shiftiness of Cassavetes' scripting and editing.

At the start: How many changes of position take place even in the first thirty seconds? As Minnie strides across the lobby where Zelmo is waiting, she is initially furious with Florence for having arranged the blind date without asking her permission. Florence volunteers to go up to Zelmo to call it off. Minnie insists that she herself will put an end to it. Instead of calling it off, however, she and Zelmo talk. She agrees to have lunch with him. By the end of the scene, only seconds after her previous irritation, her voice is shy, almost tender.

Jump ahead to the lunch date itself: Minnie and Zelmo are in a restaurant together. How many positions are cycled through in the first three or four minutes of their conversation? How many different emotions surface? How many different tones are used? How many times does the control of the beats change? Minnie is successively gentle, shy, reserved, politely critical, bewildered, embarrassed, thoughtful, upset, wounded, afraid, and outraged. Zelmo is by turns patronizing, smug, arrogant, rude, self-pitying, badgering, nasty, abusive, and hurt.

What makes the shifts of position and relationship in Cassavetes' work all the more difficult to keep up with is that he suppresses transitions and explanations. Characters jump from one tone or mood to another almost instantaneously, with no point between. Furthermore, no psychological motivation for the jumps is offered. Why does Minnie suddenly change her mind and go out with Zelmo after she berates Florence for arranging the date? Pity? Loneliness? Friendliness? Indifference? Why does Zelmo suddenly go ballistic at the end of the lunch date? Just as Henry James does with his late style (which uncannily mirrors the "process-oriented" universe of his brother's philosophy), Cassavetes denies us "deep" explanations in order to compel us to negotiate the surfaces of life all the more attentively.

He not only provides no answers to the questions I posed, but keeps us so busy responding to the beat-by-beat changes that we don't even have time to ask the questions. In this whirl of events and relationships we have to run just to stand still. The question his work asks – without asking – is whether this is a world too hard for us to function in. Does it require too much of us to keep up with it? Many viewers apparently answer in the affirmative by walking out of the theater, but Cassavetes didn't think so. As far as he was concerned, his scenes' liquidity and his characters' capacities of movement were empowering. Insofar as Jim and Minnie and their relationship can't be understood, or any one moment's understanding of them is corrected by that of the next, they are open to possibility.[13]

Cassavetes was attracted to the wild, eccentric, unclassifiable, and unpredictable in human nature and relationships for the same reason that William James was attracted to the unformulatable and unsystematic in philosophy. In James's words, these resistances "to verbalization, formulation, and discursification" embody "the genius of reality that escapes from the pressure of the logical finger, that says 'hands off,' and claims its privacy, and means to be left to its own life."[14] The same suspicion of the ways systems of understanding betray the true experience of life is played out in *Minnie and Moskowitz* in terms of Cassavetes' distrust of received systems of artistic and social expression. For both James and Cassavetes, it is impossible simply to escape those inherited systems, but our capacity to trope and flux them defines a margin of freedom. In a continuation of the passage I just quoted, James exhorted philosophy to "pass from words, that reproduce but ancient elements, to life itself, that gives the integrally new," and Cassavetes similarly exhorts film to pass from established formulas of presentation and received categories of understanding to grasp energies that essentially defy formulas and categories. Even as we may resist the effort, his dislocations of cinematic syntax force us to free ourselves from the tendency of his own presentations of experience to rigidify into new understandings. He wants to liberate us even from his own structurings.

Not only are scenes, events, and relationships put propulsively on the move; personal identity is also. When "the only sin is limitation" (to quote Emerson again), the "self" (at least as it is defined in most films, plays, and lives, as an essential core of coherent, predictable expression) becomes one more limitation that must be left behind. Each of the characters stays "in character" (as the phrase goes), but Cassavetes shows us how spacious character can be at its best, and how oppressive and confining it can be at its worst. Cassavetes suggests the possibility of breaking free from the closed-off, unitary self in several of his films through the pairing of expressively "limited" characters with expressively "unlimited" ones. Minnie takes her place in a long line of expressively conservative and socially withdrawn figures (including *Shadows*'s Ben, *Faces*'s Louise and Maria Forst, *A Woman Under the Influence*'s Nick Longhetti, *Opening Night*'s Sarah Goode, and *Love Streams*'s Robert Harmon) who are contrasted with socially promiscuous and expressively extravagant figures in the same works (Lelia, Florence, Chet and Jeannie, Seymour, Mabel, Myrtle, and Sarah Lawson).

Cassavetes imagined the contrast between the two kinds of figures in terms of several metaphors. In the spatial image that is developed in a few of the films, expressive conservatism is linked with static blockings or with states of physical or visual withdrawal behind doors or walls, while expressive daring is linked with plunging-forward movements through space and across boundaries. In terms of that metaphor, characters who are socially, psychologically, and physically "moored" (to pun on Minnie's last name) are usually paired with characters who unmoor them. Seymour scares Minnie precisely because he asks her to cut her ties to her previous values and assumptions. He wants to "un-Moore" her identity.

The other metaphor that applies to many of the same figures is a theatrical one. In its terms, the limited characters package their acts and identities, withdrawing into a series of canned routines so that they will never have to take expressive risks or be forced to rethink their parts. By contrast, the unlimited characters turn themselves into inventive, wacky improvisers of unpredictable and wildly creative performances. One never knows where an improvisation will lead. One of the ways a viewer knows that characters like Morgan and Zelmo are limited in Cassavetes' mind is that they are predictable. They have their acts and their characters worked out in advance. Like the earlier McCarthy, Forst, and Jackson, they have turned their lives into long-running shows in which they always star and control the readings of the lines.

At a superficial glance, there might seem to be little difference between Morgan, Zelmo, and Seymour; all three are confident, outgoing, loud, and brash. The difference is that while Morgan and Zelmo are ontologically and theatrically closed off, Seymour is wide open. While they know who they are and have decided in advance what they feel, he is an improviser who holds himself open to possibility. Indeed, he may be too open for his own good, as the disturbances he causes and fights he gets into at the beginning of the film suggest. When the "closed" characters interact with Seymour or other "open" characters, it is significant that the former show themselves to be masters of dramatic monologue, while the latter specialize in dialogue. Seymour does not control a scene and unilaterally impose his pacing upon it, but rather makes himself available to the energies coursing within it. He allows the currents of the universe to flow through him, but without losing himself to them. He responds and interacts.

Although she is not nearly as wide open as Seymour, it is significant that Minnie similarly shows herself fundamentally to be a responder, even as she simultaneously attempts to withdraw from others in pain or dismay. One of the things that makes her lunch date with Zelmo so upsetting to her (and so painful to watch) is that Minnie does not merely screen out Zelmo's obnoxiousness. She makes herself vulnerable to his rudeness and cruelty. She actually listens to him, and lets him reach her emotionally. (All of which should suggest how much more pain the responders of life let themselves in for than the controllers do.) In fact, one of the things that makes Cassavetes' version of the lunch-date scene so different from the routine "lover's quarrel in a restaurant scene" as it occurs in Hollywood cinema is that the two characters actually do open to each other (though Zelmo much less than Minnie). In the standard-issue version of this scene, the lovers argue, but never really touch each other emotionally – no more than Emily and Kane get to each other in their breakfast table montage. The characters in these other movies are emotionally armor-plated. They talk at each other, but they don't listen. They get mad, but do not really get hurt.

As we saw in *Shadows*, Cassavetes conflates the actors' acting strategies with the characters' interactional strategies. As actors, Tim Carey (Morgan) and Val Avery (Zelmo) take refuge in identities that have been worked up and packaged into predictable, mechanical routines before their scenes even begin, much as the characters they play do in their lives. Cassel gives us acting as improvisatory collaboration. As an actor, Cassel discovers his purposes as he goes along in the same way Moskowitz does as a character. Carey's and Avery's forte, as actors, is their ability to hold forth and dominate a scene with the power of their personalities; Cassel's is his ability to listen, to respond to, to interact with another person. It's not accidental that Seymour's (and Cassavetes') ultimate putdown in the film is to say that someone "has no sense of timing." Timing is something that involves more than one person. To care about timing is to care about relationship.

Though much of Cassavetes' work is indebted to Method influences and examples, he goes against Lee Strasberg's interpretation of Stanislavski's *An Actor Prepares* in this respect. Strasberg encouraged actors to create their characters alone, in their imaginations, apart from the sensory specificity

132

and timing of the actual performance. Actors from Brando and Dean to DeNiro, Nicholson, and Streep have followed Strasberg's lead and learned to go deep into themselves and hold on to an essentially private imaginative identity. Cassavetes embraces a different ideal. Whereas the Strasberg form of acting means that the actor is essentially alone, even in the middle of a crowd, Cassavetes' greatest actors, even at their most private moments, reach out to each other (to their benefit or dismay). Their acting is as relational as their characters' identities. As the production processes of both *Shadows* and *Husbands* demonstrate, for Cassavetes, an actor's character can never be something worked out in advance, in private. It emerges gradually, hesitantly, in the actual activity of onstage and offstage collaboration with others. It is brought into existence in the process of interaction with other actors and continuously adjusted according to the second-by-second progress of the actual performance.

To be a responder like Seymour is to realize that identity is not a fixity but (in Emerson's term) a "capacity," that is, an ability to keep including new impulses and possibilities, to move through styles and experiences without becoming trapped by them. The self is freed from boundaries and definitions. It is transcendental in the authentic Emersonian sense. (Cassavetes' next major character, *A Woman Under the Influence*'s Mabel Longhetti, will go even further in the direction of opening herself. Even more than Seymour, she will figure an extreme ideal of vulnerable openness and unresolved responsiveness.)

The most demanding aspect of the process of breaking free from patterns is that it can never end. Since patterns are continuously crystallizing within the flow of experience, pattern breaking has to go on continuously. If, as Emerson emphasized, "we have no sooner spoken than we are committed men,"[5] Cassavetes' goal is to spring us free from the prison house of ever-encroaching structure. Even the consistency of one's own previous performances must be broken up and left behind. We must be brave enough to "live ever in a new day," and not look backwards. "Consistency," in Emerson's view, is only another name for "terror."[6]

The practical consequence is one of the aspects of Seymour's personality that is most confusing to critics. Cassavetes commits him to swerving away even from his own previous tones and stances. We no sooner conclude that he is crude and insensitive than he surprises us with tenderness; we no sooner decide that he is considerate and thoughtful than he shows himself to be daffy, impulsive, or slightly dangerous. He fulfills Emerson's conception of power as movement: "Power ceases in the instant of repose; it resides in the moment of transition from a past into a new state, in the shooting of the gulf, in the darting to an aim. This one fact the world hates, that the soul *becomes*; for that ever degrades the past."[7]

However, it is one thing to meet with such conceptions on a page of Emerson, and something quite different to watch the consequences played out in life or film. Emerson's level of abstraction is a Trojan horse that conceals much of the threat of the ideas he presents. His Lyceum lecture tone moves them off to a distance from life that makes them seem relatively innocuous. Cassavetes brings Emerson down to earth, which is a potentially scary place to have him. The films "realize" his ideas and put them in action in a way that the essays don't. That is why the films seem shocking and assaultive. The consequences of Emersonianism dramatically *enacted* results in characters and experiences that are, it has been said by critic after critic, just too much, too extreme, too undisciplined. So comfortable has Emerson made us with merely theoretical stances that, to my knowledge, the Emersonianism of Cassavetes' films has passed unnoticed.

For similar reasons, most avant-garde films don't arouse the degree of resistance from a viewer or a critic that Cassavetes' work does because they also implicitly marginalize their own insights. They stylistically contain the dangers they dramatize; they do not release them into life. Their assaults are formal, their fragmentations are stylistic, their disorientations are intellectual. Cassavetes moves avant-garde imaginative disruptions off of the screen and into the world. He persuades us that the dangerous, stimulating, structure-breaking energies that he presents occur in our everyday lives. They are not merely stylistic effects created by a film's writer, director, or editor. When his characters go to pieces, he convinces us that it is something that can happen in our relationships with others, not just in our imaginations or our works of art.

Furthermore, as I pointed out in my discussion of *Shadows*, while avant-garde art is generally disengaged from ethical considerations, Cassavetes does not back down from pursuing the disturbing moral consequences of his vision of selfhood. Seymour not only breaks free from conventional codes of expressive propriety but from conventional codes of ethical behavior as well – with potentially troubling moral consequences. As a case in point (though only one of these scenes survives in the release print), in the course of the shooting script of the film, Seymour sleeps with three different women. Minnie's boyfriend Jim is relatively monogamous in comparison.

Minnie and Moskowitz is energized by an uncertainty that crops up in most of Cassavetes' work. Like *Shadows*'s Lelia, *Faces*'s Chet and Jeannie, *A Woman Under the Influence*'s Mabel, or *Love Streams*'s Sarah, Seymour figures Cassavetes' uncertainty about whether there can be a "home" for the liberated imagination. What makes these characters free makes them potential social outcasts. They are also exposed and vulnerable. They take chances with their lives and relationships that border on being reckless and dangerous to themselves and to others. Call it the "Cleopatra syndrome" (after the Shakespeare character). Precisely to the extent that we gloriously liberate ourselves from normative restrictions on expression, we may also doom ourselves. Precisely to the extent that we are creative, we may also end up destroying much of what is valuable in our relationships. There is a dark side to breaking free from structure, a nightmare flip side to the American dream of transcendental freedom. Seymour is stimulatingly open and spontaneous. He gives free reign to his impulses, but that also makes him more than a little frightening at times, especially in the small explosions of violence he indulges in during the first half hour of the movie. The radicalism of his freedom also defines him, for most of the film, as a loner. As Henry James wrote about Dickens, a community of eccentrics is no community at all.

To change the Shakespearean reference point to Iago, one can see the same syndrome through the other end of the telescope, this time in terms of the nominally negative depictions in Cassavetes' work. The defining quality of Shakespeare's Iago is not that he is morally reprehensible, but that he is one of the most expressively brilliant and dazzlingly creative figures in his creator's oeuvre. In short, he is one of the figures closest to his own author in his powers of improvisatory self-reformation. Yet, needless to say, Iago is absolutely, utterly damned. That paradox informs the work of Cassavetes as well. *Faces*'s Freddie, McCarthy, Jackson, and Forst, *Minnie and Moskowitz*'s Morgan, Zelmo, and Jim figure the same double state of affairs: They are brilliant *and* damned. They represent the "Iago" aspect of Cassavetes' imagination insofar as they show us that the free movements of the unfettered imagination inevitably do threaten truly valuable and desirable moral and social structures. They suggest that there is no ethically acceptable social role for performative virtuosity. The fluidity of the liberated imagination is at odds with the responsibilities of home, family, and history. There is something in us at war with the very stabilities that we need to survive. Our most exciting energies make us immoral (or to put it the other way, morality is repressive of our freest capacities of performance). Perhaps freedom and morality can never be reconciled.

That is why, just as in Shakespeare, it is impossible to draw a hard and fast line between the con men and the free spirits. As the Iago and Cleopatra analogies suggest, one person's liberation is another's hustle. The same imaginative extravagance that sponsors Seymour's entertaining zaniness grants the others the capacities for their heartless, fascistic performances. If social and moral unmooring makes possible the expressive creativity of Moskowitz, and of *Faces*'s Chet, it also makes possible the emotional blackmail of Morgan, Zelmo, and Jim, and the social savagery of McCarthy, Forst, and Freddie.

Cassavetes has Zelmo, Seymour, Jim, and Morgan trade lines and scenes because he wants us to realize that they are disturbingly much more alike than they are different. At various moments, Seymour's behavior is more or less indistinguishable from that of each of the sleazy characters in the film. When he yells at Morgan in the restaurant, it is echoed a few minutes later by Zelmo's yelling at Minnie on their lunch date. When he goes off and spends the night with someone else the day before he proposes marriage to Minnie, he repeats Jim's infidelity. When he yells at Minnie after taking her to lunch or peels away from her in the dance hall parking lot, both scenes are meant to remind us of her lunch date with Zelmo.

Seymour, Zelmo, Morgan, and Jim embody a radical dream of expressive freedom. They make their identities and expressions of themselves freely responsive to their shifting desires, saying and doing what most of us only think or feel. Cassavetes nevertheless understands that to open up the self and its expressions is to open oneself up to dangers from which one was previously protected. If nothing holds back your shape changing, by the same virtue nothing holds you together. Free to make themselves up as they go along, these characters are equally free to go to pieces before our eyes, free to destroy each other at will. Cassavetes breaks down the walls of understanding that repressively define the self as well as the walls of decorum that separate individuals and moderate their behavior, but he also recognizes what Robert Frost did when he wrote that "good fences make good neighbors." The expressive "roughness" that Cassavetes favors liberates his characters to a larger, looser expression, to a freer play in their relationships; but, as the scenes with Morgan, Jim, Zelmo, and Seymour demonstrate, it also makes one's life and relationships with others incredibly rough and rocky. An ungrounded life – the life led by *Love Streams*'s Sarah, by *Faces*'s Jeannie and Chet and by *Minnie and Moskowitz*'s Seymour, Zelmo, and Morgan – is one of imaginative and social insecurity.

To the bewilderment and delight of his acquaintances, the filmmaker was more than a little like the works and characters he created. In occasionally exasperating ways, like his own masters and mistresses of mercuriality, Cassavetes played with his identity and expressions rather than merely promoting them. He didn't always buy what he sold. He slipped away from being pinned down.[18] It was as if in his life as well as his art, the fun of playing around with his identity, of moving from one stance to another, was more fascinating to him than any destination the movements eventuated in.

A corollary is that by all accounts the films themselves apparently mattered much more to him as a path of creation than as a goal to be achieved. Cassavetes almost always talked about his movies – even long after their release – not as results, but as activities. When pressed in conversation, he would say, with just the least bit of a twinkle in his eye, that the films didn't matter. What mattered was the process of making them: the surprising turns of events, the discoveries, the fun, the scrambling, the unexpected things that happened along the way. Seymour Cassel (Cassavetes' closest personal friend) and Al Ruban (his long-standing cinematographer and producer) only half-facetiously used to joke that Cassavetes liked the process of making his movies so much that at times they were convinced he never wanted to release them.

In terms of writing the scripts, that meant not only that he actually liked rewriting, but also that, rather than being a gradual process of refining an original, each of the revisions more commonly functioned as a series of tangents away from the previous versions. Each draft was less a refinement than a reimagining of the story. (This is what I meant by suggesting that Minnie learns something between the two drafts of the scene with Florence.) The same thing was true in terms of editing. Cassavetes would wear out most of the people he worked with by his refusal to let well enough alone. Even after a perfectly acceptable version was achieved, he would keep editing new versions of sequences just to play with the differences. Prior to their release, he recut his films over and over again, experimenting with their rhythms, changing their tones, fiddling with the relationships of the characters. *Shadows*, *Faces*, and *Husbands* were assembled in numerous entirely different versions. Even following their release, Cassavetes continued to recut some of the movies. Two different prints of *Minnie and Moskowitz*, *Husbands*, and *The Killing of a Chinese Bookie* exist. In the case of *Bookie*, the most extreme example of Cassavetes' revisionary insatiability, the versions represent two completely different edits with different shot selections and different scenes.

The point is that Cassavetes' performance as a writer-director-editor in a film like *Minnie and Moskowitz* was not only staged on and against the forms of previous Hollywood movies, but against the crystallizations of his own previous narrative and cinematic arrangements. He couldn't remain in a passive relation even to his own text. He had to keep moving against the structures that emerged within it. Relentlessly decomposing his own text's compositions, and recomposing its decompositions, Cassavetes fluxed the incipient solidifications of his own imagination in the same way his most mercurial characters do.

What sealed Cassavetes' commercial doom is that the supreme challenge of his work is directed at the viewer. Cassavetes asks his audiences to make the same double act of renunciation in watching the films that he did in creating them: not only to leave outlines for knowing behind at the beginning of the process in order to be able to enter into the openness of having a fresh experience in the first place; but then, even more challengingly, to keep tearing up each of the understandings that emerge in the course of the film in order to remain fresh. Like the characters, we must open ourselves to a state of not-knowing. We must allow relationships to be uncertain, tones to remain unresolved. We must unmoor ourselves cognitively and put to sea on an arduous, countertacking voyage of discovery.

This is the transformative aspect of Cassavetes' work that separates it from the merely diacritical or analytical work of other filmmakers. He intends to change our lives, not merely to criticize them. His goal is nothing less than a transformation of his viewers' consciousnesses. He demands a radically active and energetic viewer. Rather than sitting back and being passive consumers of his texts, he asks that we become energetic meaning makers – sorting, organizing, piecing things together. Even to the end of his life, and after all the criticism he came in for, he still fervently believed in the existence of audiences of such athletic and engaged viewers. His work is profoundly optimistic in this respect.

Cassavetes' films offer the opposite of what a viewer who is used to merely kicking back and being taken for a ride wants or expects. They force us into new and uncomfortable positions, just as the events in the films do to the characters in them. Cassavetes works to create a state of freshness, openness, and responsiveness that is possible only when we leave habitual categories of response behind. It's not hard to calculate the commercial consequences of such an artistic agenda in a culture in which television programs, ad campaigns, and Hollywood movies command space on the ground floors of our museums and universities.

It's not surprising that Cassavetes was avowedly antipathetic to theoretical stances in both the creation and the interpretation of his work. Gena Rowlands has said that one of the few taboos on a set was for one actor to talk to another about his character or performance. In an interview, Peter Falk said that he personally believed that, at times, Cassavetes deliberately gave a confusing answer when Falk would ask him for advice about how to play a role, in order to deny him refuge in intellectual categories that might short-circuit deeper understanding. ("He never wanted you to understand up here. ...He was dreadfully afraid if you understood it, you would translate it into a cliché.") As far as Cassavetes was concerned, analysis and theory could only stop the motion he was interested in getting going.

The one sort of theoretical pronouncement that the filmmaker was not hesitant to make was about his indifference to the kind of theory called history or ideology. As he once put it:

> Life is men and women. Life isn't, say, politics. Politicians are only bad actors grubbing around for power.... I'm a revolutionary – but not in the political sense.... In my opinion, these people and these small feelings are the greatest political force there is.[19]

That sort of antitheoretical pronouncement is actually belied by Cassavetes' practices. His films are not just about "people" and "small feelings." They *are* ideologically informed, but in a subtler way than most movies with explicit historical or sociological subjects. All of his work is historically anchored, but in structures of consciousness, not in historical persons, places, or events (which is why it may not seem to be historical). There is a superficial realism that involves presenting facts, details, and events, and there is a deep realism that involves capturing the emotional rhythms, intellectual textures, and ideological tendencies that formed the facts, details, and events. While explicitly historical filmmakers give us history as the bric-a-brac of life, Cassavetes gives us the cognitive structures, emotional forms, and cultural understandings of which the bric-a-brac are, as it were, merely an accidental and relatively unimportant emanation.

In *Shadows*, Ben and Tony's James Dean imitations, and Ben's "beat" poses and costumes, demonstrate how the self can lose itself in historically specific cultural formations. Many of Cassavetes' films reflect on the ways the twentieth-century business culture of America has corrupted personal relationships. *Shadows, Too Late Blues, The Killing of a Chinese Bookie,* and *Opening Night* include portraits of small-time entrepreneurs (Ackerman, Frielobe, Cosmo, and Manny Victor, respectively) who attempt to organize their intimate relationships the way they run their businesses. Most of the male characters in *Faces* – Richard, Freddie, McCarthy, and Jackson – are flawed in just this way. They insanely try to make "deals" with friends and lovers the way they might close a real-estate transaction. *Husbands, The Killing of a Chinese Bookie,* and *Love Streams* present views of other psychological aberrations of being male in contemporary America. These films are all historically grounded and ideologically informed, in this respect.

Cassavetes' allusions to other films and his bendings of cinematic syntax in *Minnie and Moskowitz* demonstrate that history can be in a text's style in far deeper ways than when merely the subject of a text. The forms of history that Cassavetes captures in a single scene of *Faces* tell us more about America, late-twentieth-century capitalism, the business ethic, and the mid-sixties than does the content of the complete works of Oliver Stone and Paul Schrader. The cinematic forms troped by *Minnie and Moskowitz* represent far more profound personal responses to the history of our culture than the meticulous reconstruction of a historical period in a David Putnam, John Hughes, Barry Levinson, Paul Schrader, or Paul Mazursky movie.

Their history is the furniture of life – the clothing people wear, the songs they listen to, the cars they drive. In contrast, the history in *Shadows*, *Faces*, *Husbands*, and *Minnie and Moskowitz* is the history of forms of consciousness that create the furniture and everything else, whether this consciousness takes the form of personal images (the tough-guy stoicism encapsulated by Bogart; the hysterical women played by Mary Astor), or as more general ways of understanding our place in the world (the unworldly visionary sublimities of *2001*; Minnie's "someday my prince will come" notions of romance). The deepest history is the history of subjectivity.

The difference between Cassavetes and Stone, Levinson, or Schrader reflects contrasted conceptions of the individual's relation to history. Because history represents a system of objects, facts, and events external to the individual for these other filmmakers, it is almost entirely beyond the individual's control. Because history exists as structures of consciousness for Cassavetes, it is something upon which we can perform countermovements of consciousness. Stone's, Levinson's, or Schrader's history is deterministic: Social systems limit meaning and control what can be expressed at any moment. Cassavetes' history allows extreme possibilities of free performance within and upon the system. That is after all what *Minnie and Moskowitz* is: a declaration of independence from the studio system, spoken from within the studio system and presented within its terms of understanding.

Robert Altman is one of the only major American filmmakers who captures some of the inner forms of history in the same way Cassavetes does, but Cassavetes' work is not recognized as engaging ideological positions as generally as is Altman's due to the far more complex and oblique relation the individual has with ideology in Cassavetes' work. Whereas the relationship between persons and structures is fairly direct in Altman (with the structure more or less dictating the personal expression), Cassavetes includes two kinds of countervailing, structure-resisting energies within his films.

The first is the performative energy by means of which individual characters (in *Minnie and Moskowitz*, most notably, Seymour) are empowered to break away from forms that would otherwise normalize and rigidify their identities, behavior, and expressions. Altman's characters are never comparably empowered. From *Nashville* to *The Player*, they more or less operate as semiotic functions of the structures in place around them. They are trapped in them, and, as with the character of Griffin Bell's assistant in *The Player*, the very best they can do is to walk away from those systems. They can never perform creatively within or upon them. To allude to the first epigraph to this chapter (from Emerson's "Circles") Altman ultimately despairs of the quickness and strength of the soul to burst boundaries. He is cynical about the heart's desire or ability to escape its imprisonment. Cassavetes is neither despairing nor cynical. The difference in the two filmmakers' beliefs about the power of the individual is the reason that Altman's work feels chilly, depressing, and negative, while Cassavetes' – notwithstanding the pain or difficulty of his characters' situations – is paradoxically hopeful, encouraging, and inspiring.

The second way Cassavetes countermoves against the structures in his own work is through his own artistic performance within them, as this chapter has been devoted to showing. As Altman never does, Cassavetes builds into his films swervings away from their own tendency to stabilize meanings, define identities, and bring events into focus.

That double movement ultimately represents Cassavetes' inspiring affirmation of the freedom and power of the human spirit (his own and that of his most interesting characters), while a structuralist like Altman communicates his characters' ultimate weakness and victimization. Cassavetes may be quintessentially modernist in the antisystematic and antifoundational qualities of his work; but he is exultantly antimodern in his faith in the individual's ultimate power and authority over the systems around him.

Minnie and Moskowitz teaches us an invigorating new way of being in the world, in which we place ourselves at a critical distance from the structures of knowledge in order to perform with them. In Cassavetes' view, we cease to be passive victims of cultural ideology, and are transformed into active responders to it. History, language, critical interpretations, and the inherently stabilizing tendencies of narrative itself all represent forms that must be moved against: They normalize the eccentric, rigidify the fluid, and formulate the unformulated. Yet, if we are strong and inventive enough, we may turn their resistance into a platform for performance by troping them, moving among them, and fragmenting them. There may be no escaping the forces around us, but there is performing with them, as Mabel Longhetti will even more ebulliently demonstrate in the film Cassavetes makes in 1972, immediately following this one. The shape-shifting, structure-defying energy that creates comedy in *Minnie and Moskowitz* makes for tragedy in *A Woman Under the Influence*, without being any less spiritually exultant and uplifting.

4

An Artist of
the Ordinary

A Woman Under the Influence

Oh, yes, my body, me alive, *knows*, and it knows intensely. And as of the
sum of all knowledge, it can't be anything more than an accumulation of all
the things I know in the body.... Those damned philosophers, they talk as
if they suddenly went off in steam, and were then much more important than
they are when they're in their shirts. It is nonsense. Every man, philosopher
included, ends in his own finger-tips. As for the words and thoughts and sighs
and aspirations that fly away from him, they are so many tremulations in the
ether, and not alive at all.   – D. H. Lawrence[1]

As the greatest lessons of Nature through the universe are perhaps the lessons
of variety and freedom, the same present the greatest lessons also in New
World politics and progress. If a man were ask'd, for instance, the distinctive
points contrasting modern European and American political and other life
with the old Asiatic cultus...he might find the amount of them in...two
main constituents, or sub-strata for a truly grand nationality – 1st, a large
variety of character – and 2nd, full play for human nature to expand itself
in numberless and even conflicting directions.... I say that democracy can
never prove itself beyond cavil, until it founds and luxuriantly grows its own
forms of art.... It may be argued that our republic is, in performance, really
enacting to-day the grandest arts.... Are these not better than any utterances
even of the greatest rhapsode, artist, or literatus?   – Walt Whitman[2]

A Woman Under the Influence is the final work in what has been called
Cassavetes' marriage trilogy – a series that, with *Faces*, began at the end of
everything, with *Minnie and Moskowitz*, looped back to detail the beginning
of a romance, and, with *Woman*, ends with a view of a married couple in
the middle of a muddle, denied the clarification of being granted either a
beginning or an ending to their love.

Like *Minnie and Moskowitz* and *Gloria*, *A Woman Under the Influence*

143

is the story of a mismatched odd couple whose task is to learn how to "act" together (in both the dramatic and the ordinary senses of the word), not by erasing their differences but by making something of them. It's also a hallmark Cassavetes "family film" in that it features a very small group of characters and is set almost entirely in one location, an ordinary house where Nick and Mabel Longhetti (Peter Falk and Gena Rowlands) and their three children, Angelo, Tony, and Maria, live. As their last name suggests, and the names of the children emphasize, the family is a working-class Italian one, but to notice that is immediately to confront a potential question about Cassavetes' relative indifference to "realistic" representation.

Cassavetes provides a few token indications of the Longhetti's ethnic background, but the point to notice is how few. Nick and Mabel live in a small house in a working-class neighborhood. Nick is a construction worker. He and Mabel eat spaghetti in one scene; a crucifix is visible in the kitchen, and a statue of Mary on a mantle in the living room in a couple of others. However, beyond a few other sketchy reminders of the Longhetti's economic and social status, there is only the limpest attempt at sociological verisimilitude. Compare five minutes of A Woman Under the Influence with five minutes of The Godfather or Moonstruck, and everything that Cassavetes does not bother to include is obvious. There are no distinctive ethnic rituals, accents, gestures, language, or clothing. Nick and Mabel don't even look Italian (and, needless to say, neither Falk nor Rowlands is). And there are no references to Italian culture, traditions, or history.[3]

Though virtually everything ever written about Cassavetes characterizes him as being concerned with "nitty-gritty realism" (as Stanley Kauffmann recently put it), what is left out of A Woman Under the Influence defines a crucial difference between him and the authentically "realistic" filmmakers with whom he is usually compared – Martin Ritt, Paul Schrader, Paul Mazursky, Barry Levinson, Sidney Lumet, Sydney Pollack, and others. These filmmakers spare no expense to recreate the props, costumes, and sets appropriate to their characters' periods and types because their works define life as a matter of what suits you wear, what car you drive, and what house you live in. Such things were as unimportant to Cassavetes as they were to Henry James (which is why James seldom bothers to describe his characters' physical appearances, how they dress, or what they do for a living).

It is significant that in the rare scenes in which props or costumes do figure prominently as conveyors of meaning in A Woman Under the Influence – as Mabel's wacky, mismatched clothing does in the school-bus scene – it is not sociologically to stereotype her, but to indicate how she eludes

A nongeneric, unclassifiable identity: Mabel, the mismatched mistress of the unconventional, waiting for the school bus.

categorization. Far from defining her as a representative of a group, the weirdness of her appearance suggests energies that defy economic, ethnic, religious, or ideological categories of understanding. To quote Isabel Archer from chapter 19 of *The Portrait of a Lady*, what Mabel's clothes tell us is that they "*don't* express me, and heaven forbid they should!"[4] For Cassavetes as for Isabel, sociological categories of understanding represent "perfectly arbitrary" limitations on one's imaginative identity. The "reality" in which he is interested is a character's feelings, ideals, and visions (which in his view usually has almost nothing to do with the so-called reality represented by his or her physical and social trappings). Mabel creates her own identity; it is not created for her by her clothing or ethnic background. If we want to understand her, we must look at her performance, not the furniture of her life.

The differences between Cassavetes and authentically realist work define contrasting conceptions of the relationship of the individual to the expressive structures around him. The basic premise of realism (in film, literature, or painting) is the acceptance of the fundamental authority of extrapersonal structures of expression. A character in *The Best Years of Our Lives, Anatomy of a Murder, Norma Rae, Tootsie, Bob Roberts*, or *A Few Good Men* (to name as wide a range of realist works as possible) may have a difficult time learning how to manipulate established expressive forms to his or her advantage, but the character and the director never question whether they are *fundamentally* limiting or repressive. The process of learning to express oneself adequately within existing expressive systems is, in fact, the basic plot of most realistic dramatic works. In the films of Martin Ritt, for example, the narrative consists largely of the central character's gradually learning how to use the expressive codes with which he is confronted – frequently the special rules governing discourse in the institution of which he is a part – on behalf of various desirable social changes. The basic assumption underpinning such a process is that the individual *is* ultimately able to express himself completely, clearly, and satisfactorily within the reigning codes – able to express himself adequately to himself, to others in his film, and to viewers of it. Any expressive gap that exists between ideals and actions, between desires and words, is ultimately closed in the course of the narrative.

In the tradition in which Cassavetes is working, however, the expressive wound is never – and can never be – healed. Social systems of expression are *essentially* compromising and untrustworthy. The structures of language and society are fundamentally at war with our fluxions of feeling. They inevitably betray or subvert the expression of our finest impulses. Cassavetes honors imaginative energies inevitably disruptive of the very forms of understanding and expression that realist filmmakers accept. That is what it means to say that, for him, the self is not social, but transcendental.

This is, however, too much an external description. The chilly reception Mabel is accorded when she asks the time of passersby in the school-bus scene suggests the extent to which her expressions of herself are doomed to be misunderstood by others. The more profound expressive problem Mabel figures is that she is in a fundamentally unstable and oblique relationship to *her own* representations of herself. Even if the opinions of the world changed, her expressive problem would not disappear. As we have seen in *Shadows* and in *Faces*, Cassavetes' characters are unable simply to be who they are, or to say what they mean. There is a gap between the expressive ideals of a character and the always more or less limiting expressive realities available to him or her.

Much of the greatest American art takes this "expressive gap" as its subject. Hawthorne, Poe, James, and Faulkner (in American literature), Sargent, Eakins, Homer, and Hopper (in American painting), and Capra,

Loden, May, and Rappaport (in American film) have each explored the vexed transactions between the imagination and the forms of expression available to it.[5] For each of them, turning feelings into expressions involves a problematic act of translation, in which at times it seems as if not less than everything is lost. The evidence of the difficulty of that act of translation is the various forms of stylistic disturbance in their works, which is another reason it is more appropriate to compare Cassavetes' work with certain forms of stylistically anxious and imaginatively exorbitant writing, and in relation to various sorts of melodramatic or operatic filmmaking, than to view it under the rubric of "realism."

One of the stylistically agitated forms that Cassavetes not only acknowledged his indebtedness to in interviews, but directly alluded to in his films, is the body of work that includes the classic Method-acting performances of the fifties – specifically the two most important films in which Montgomery Clift appeared, *A Place in the Sun* and *Wild River*, and the two most important James Dean movies, *East of Eden* and *Rebel Without a Cause*. Both Clift and Dean are more than ghostly presences throughout Cassavetes' oeuvre: Cassavetes wrote the lead in *Too Late Blues* specifically for Clift (although Bobby Darin, who was a student in the acting class where *Shadows* originated, ended up playing it). *The Killing of a Chinese Bookie*'s Cosmo Vitelli and *Love Streams*'s Robert Harmon are distant cousins to Clift's Clyde Griffiths and Chuck Glover, and Mabel Longhetti is a fraternal twin to Dean's Jim Stark (and was modeled on him). *Woman* also briefly "quotes" *Rebel* in several scenes.

Clouding the issue is the fact that the work of Method actors and directors has been misunderstood in the same way Cassavetes' own work has been, in terms of the superficial "realism" or "naturalism" of its effects. Although films like *A Place in the Sun*, *East of Eden*, *On the Waterfront*, and *Rebel Without a Cause* may seem to be taking "realistic" social problems as their subjects and are frequently set in "nitty-gritty" surroundings, the effect of the performances of their central characters is to turn our attention away from the social realm. These films are not examinations of social or political issues except in the most superficial sense; they are about extreme states of consciousness and feeling deprived of satisfactory forms of expression. In short, they are artistically closer to the writing of Henry James and William Faulkner than to that of John Steinbeck or Sinclair Lewis.

The Method's self-proclaimed emphasis on depths in place of surfaces, its focus on the importance of being in touch with private states of feeling, its nurturance of fantasy, its psychotherapeutic bent, and its deemphasis of socially regulated codes of representation (the codified tones, gestures, and stances used in traditional British acting) all mark it as a form of American Romanticism. One does not have to subscribe to the inevitability of these oppositions or agree with these artistic preferences in order to recognize that they represent a distinctively Romantic conception of the relation of the individual impulse to social expression.[6]

Underneath their veneers of social realism, *A Place in the Sun, East of Eden, On the Waterfront*, and *Rebel Without a Cause* are essentially romances, dream films, or melodramas of inexpressible consciousness (in Peter Brooks's sense of melodrama). They play as melodramas because they share similar assumptions with standard melodrama about the repressiveness or irrelevance of social expression. The states of expressive disenfranchisement, social displacement, and imaginative alienation that became identified with the greatest performances of Dean, Brando, and Clift are related to those in a Bette Davis or Joan Crawford picture. The Method teenage-boy-in-love movie is the male version of the woman-in-love weepie. Indeed, one of the reasons the Method took such firm root in American soil was that its expressive agenda coincided with the established expressive tradition in American art. Film was mining this imaginative territory in the forms of melodrama long before the Actors Studio influenced Hollywood. The great Method and post-Method acting tradition defined by figures like Marlon Brando, Montgomery Clift, and James Dean, and continued by Jon Voight, John Malkovich, Richard Dreyfus, Ben Gazzara, Peter Falk, Seymour Cassel, Charles Grodin, and Gena Rowlands (as well as by the acting of Cassavetes in his own and others' work) is a deepening and continuation of the pre-Method traditions of American acting practiced by figures like Barbara Stanwyck, Jimmy Stewart, Gary Cooper, and Humphrey Bogart.

The cultivated inwardness of Method acting represented a commitment to the expression of imaginative and emotional states whose very privacy, intensity, or fugitiveness defied translation into the tones and gestures that traditional forms of acting relied upon to communicate meanings. The nuanced intonations and verbal sophistication of a Lawrence Olivier performance were replaced by states of fumbling inarticulateness, agitated silence, and stuttering emotion. The key Method scenes involve subterranean states of feeling too tiny, mercurial, and unformulated to be translated into the decorous continuities, stabilities, and coherencies of technical acting. These feelings can surface, as it were, only in the space between the lines and actions – in an actor's muttering, murmuring, grimaces, grunts, cries, and shouts. It's not accidental that Mabel Longhetti's most memorable moments are ones in which she is either entirely silent or is laying in bodily or tonal meanings distinguishable from her scripted lines. Both Cassavetes' and the

Cassavetes handholding the final scene of *A Woman Under the Influence.*
Note the shabbiness of the chair seats and how such "nitty-gritty realism" is
never allowed into the film at all. The marginality depicted is imaginative
rather than sociological.

major Method works move us to the edges of what can be said in a work
of art. What William James believed about philosophical language, Cassavetes felt to be true of cinematic and dramatic language: It inevitably
betrays the expression it exists to facilitate. Expression in his films is always,
at least in part, pitted against the medium that makes it possible. Dramatic
language inevitably tames, systematizes, and abstracts the surging fluidity
of our feelings. Central to all of Cassavetes' work is the issue of how
identities as unformulated and fluid, and experiences as unresolved as he
wants them to be, can be presented at all in the forms of art. Most of
Cassavetes' central characters, including Mabel Longhetti in this film, flirt
with representational illegibility to one degree or another. Their deeper
selves, desires, and motivations are veiled not only from the view of other
characters, but from the view of the audience as well. Cosmo Vitelli, the

main character in *The Killing of a Chinese Bookie*, is the most obvious illustration of a character who withdraws not only from the representational forms of his own life, but almost from those of his film.

I have mentioned that Mabel Longhetti resembles *Rebel Without a Cause*'s Jim Stark in many respects. Both he and she are socially alienated, expressively estranged, and in pain; yet the differences are as important as the similarities. Stark's expressive alienation is so complete that it leaves him silent, socially withdrawn, and unable to function within any group but the fantasy family of his own creation. Mabel doesn't have the luxury of his grand alienation. She, after all, has a biological family and children. She couldn't be a loner even if she wanted to be. As is true of all of Cassavetes' characters, her identity is relational. She finds herself in a group. She is more socially embedded, more trapped and encircled but also more supported than Ray's protagonist, which means that for better or worse, she can only be "moderately alienated" (to use a term of George Kateb's). That is in fact the more creative place to be. Stark is on the outside looking in, but Mabel is half-within, half-outside a system, which is to gain perspective on it and a small degree of leverage over it, even while remaining in contact with it. Her marginality becomes a position of potential power. In the specific metaphor of her film, Mabel is the head of a resident repertory theater company made up of her family and friends.

Many of Cassavetes' main characters function as alter egos for their actor-director creator, but none more obviously than she. Rowlands/Mabel is the most dazzling theatrical presence in all of Cassavetes' work. She is an off-balance ballerina of intricate choreography, an eccentric entertainer, parodic pantomimist, and comical mistress of ceremonies. (Though Gena Rowlands is best known for her intensely serious roles in her husband's films, her exuberant, mugging performance here and in *Gloria* reminds us that she began her acting career as a comedienne in *The High Cost of Loving*.) Mabel's deepest similarity with her creator is that she is an improvisatory writer-director of family scenes – not only herself performing, but sponsoring performances in others. She gets hard hats to sing opera and encourages her own and neighbor children to become actors and actresses of their own lives, imaginatively transforming themselves into cowboys, dying swans, and pirates, by turns.[7]

What interests Cassavetes about Mabel is not just that she is a kind of director, but what kind of director she is. He makes a number of points about her directorial style. In the first place, she is never merely mechanical or technical in her direction, which is to say, she is less interested in the details and the surface polish of a performance than in the depth of emotional exploration it represents. She shows us that there is no "best" way to direct others or no one "right" response she is after. She will do just about anything to move the figures around her into a deeper place than merely scripting, blocking out, or dictating their actions ever could. Sometimes she proceeds by mimicry (as when she comically parodies her mother's gestures and tones of voice when the kids return home for their books). At other moments she badgers and nags (as she does with Mr. Jensen, when all else fails). She can direct with expressions of tenderness (as when she caresses Billy Tidroe's face or her son's hand). At still other times, she directs by not directing (as when, in the final gathering, to cut the tension, she changes the subject away from her hospital stay and tells jokes to get Mama Longhetti to lighten up).

Mabel knows that the route of discovery lies in moving off the beaten path of conventional expression. Even more radically, she tells us that it is only the movement that matters, not anywhere you get as a result of it. Any attained end becomes a dead end that must itself be left behind by subsequent movements. It may be extraordinary to get Italian opera from a black sewer worker, but watch Mabel's response carefully: Hugh Hurd's *Aida* aria becomes a springboard from which to launch an even more daring performance with Billy Tidroe. There can be no end to this process, which is why every time a tone is about to stall into a fixed position, Mabel shakes it up. She is a principle of social and imaginative lubrication that "unsticks" people and scenes. In her view, for things to stop moving even for a pulsebeat is for them to begin to die.

Another point about directing that Mabel illustrates is that in order to keep opening up others in this way, you must yourself remain open. That is to say that much of her directing (especially at the spaghetti breakfast) simply consists of responding freely and passionately to others' performances. Directing is not dictation but dialogue, a relationship between two people. Mabel is a great listener and an amazingly alert viewer. Even as she pushes herself and those around her away from expressive clichés and conventions, she continuously adjusts her own directorial performance to take account of their discomfort or anxiety. Even with a cause as lost, an actor as blockheaded and uncooperative as Mr. Jensen, she keeps changing her performance to respond to his. It's not accidental that Mabel's idea of directing Mr. Jensen (or, earlier, Billy Tidroe) is to dance with him. She doesn't impose her vision on others but asks for a kind of mutually responsive partnering.

That leads to the final and most important point about Mabel's directing, which is that it is for others, not for herself, that she is ultimately working.

Rather than making the actors an extension of her personality, her direction attempts to elicit answering responses that express *their* needs and desires. She encourages her "actors" and "actresses" to dare to give the performance of their lives, not so that they will realize her vision, but that they may explore unrealized parts of themselves and enlarge their own possibilities. She doesn't want to change them or make them over in her own image, but to use their possibilities, their differences from her.

Needless to say, Mabel sometimes succeeds (gloriously, as when Hugh Hurd sings Verdi or Billy Tidroe comically lists his kids), and sometimes fails (abysmally, as she does with Mr. Jensen and with Mama Longhetti at the final gathering). Her material frequently resists her imaginative enrichments, her vision of it, but that is part of the game, and it is telling that she never stops trying or gives up on even the most limited actors and actresses around her.

As should be clear by now, Mabel *is* John Cassavetes, not in a superficial biographical sense, but as an embodiment of his vision of life's collaborative expressive possibilities. Mabel gives us our deepest view of how Cassavetes actually performed on the set. She aspires to dance with her actors, and in a metaphoric sense of the term, Cassavetes "danced" with all of his, partnering them in different ways to elicit original and fresh responses. (It is not coincidental that many of the most evocative scenes in Cassavetes' work actually involve dancing, including a wonderful ballroom sequence cut from the final print of *Husbands*.) It was in the nature of Cassavetes' conception of dance – and direction – that each actor was partnered differently.

Like Mabel, Cassavetes used every trick in the book, yet always adapted his methods to the individual actor's needs: begging, pleading, and explaining sometimes, rallying, provoking, or chiding at others. There are dozens of stories about the occasional tricks Cassavetes played on his actors, not all of them fond or charitable. He would do anything from provoking a deliberate argument to get an actor's emotions where he wanted them (as he did on occasion with Val Avery or Fred Draper), to using mild threats to raise the performer's energy level (as he did with Jakob Shaw in *Love Streams*), to talking philosophically about the role (if an actor needed that sort of explanation to help his performance). There were no hard and fast rules on how to direct. Cassavetes did whatever it took to get an actor to go deeper into himself or to jog his emotional memory.

Critics are fond of quibbling about the ethics of these sorts of practices, but the proof is in the tasting: in the final result on film, and in the actors' final feelings about working in this way. Though at one moment or another probably every actor Cassavetes ever worked with vowed that he would

Peter Falk waiting for a shot in the upstairs children's bedroom as Elaine Goren goes over the script with the filmmaker in the background.

never work for him again, once they saw the result on screen, all of them expressed their desire to be in another of his movies.

On rare occasions Cassavetes was even known to fool actors in certain ways to help elicit less self-conscious or more sincere performances. Leola Harlow (the woman who wears the red tam-o'-shanter in *Husbands*) tells the story of how Cassavetes confused her about when a scene was being rehearsed and when it was being filmed, so that when Gus (the character the filmmaker plays) yells at her in the course of her scene, she didn't quite know whether it was the character or the director criticizing her singing and giving her new "directions." The result is an astonishingly authentic performance. Others involved in the production process have told me that Cassavetes occasionally (though rarely) would film when an actor thought a scene was merely being "walked through," in order to capture an especially unselfconscious moment.[8] Another technique he employed to keep a performance fresh was the old silent-era practice of calling out redirections in midscene (and then removing his voice from the sound track during post-production). Some of the uncanny freshness of his actors' performances is undoubtedly attributable to the fact that at such moments they were actually thinking on their feet and responding to an unexpected suggestion during filming.

All of these techniques go to illustrate what the filmmaker was getting at when, queried for the hundredth time by an interviewer about his alleged improvisational methods, he offered a typically unhelpful explanation: "The emotion was improvisation. The lines were written."[9] As that suggests, the critics were following the wrong scent. They assumed that the authenticity and apparent spontaneity of the performances could only be the result of the actors leaving the script behind to make up their own lines, when in fact, the freshness of their performances was the result of Cassavetes' ability to get them not out of, but more deeply into, their lines – more intimately, more emotionally, and more personally than other directors were able. By moving his actors' emotions around (and supporting them emotionally), he and they could make even routine lines or actions *feel* personal, passionately believed, and amazingly convincing.

In the service of getting the actor to originate fresh emotions (and not merely "indicate" them mechanically), one thing he almost never did was to tell the actor what he wanted from a scene or character, or how to play a role. Rather, he attempted to find out what the actor saw in it, how he or she wanted to approach it. He did almost anything to get the actors' responses rather than impose his on them. He pushed the actors to go deep into themselves, and knew that the way to do that was to leave them alone to solve their own equations, rather than dictate an answer. (Gena Rowlands has told many stories about how Cassavetes would turn the character that the actress was playing over to her, and would insist that she really knew more about her character than he did. He would decline to give suggestions, saying he was just there to observe, be ready, and be filming when the most interesting and revealing moments happened – which wasn't quite true, but was empowering to an actor.)

On the other hand, that didn't mean he wasn't critical or was easily satisfied. If he wasn't happy with a take, he wasn't reluctant to express his dissatisfaction, and he had occasional bursts of anger. His way of correcting was nevertheless not to dictate a solution, but rather to throw it back on the actor to come up with one during a subsequent take. Cassavetes was relentless about reshooting. He would have the actor do a scene again and again until he was satisfied, but the point is that the changes almost always came from the actor going deeper into himself and the character as the shooting proceeded, not from the director imposing superficial suggestions about tones or gestures. Cassavetes didn't offer more specific direction because he really wanted to learn from the actors. He didn't want them to be clones of him. He didn't want to homogenize their differences. Direction was a process of holding himself open to discovery. One of the most important aspects of Cassavetes' directorial style was simply his ability to elicit these eccentric, idiosyncratic performances and to keep the camera running to preserve the best of them. Of course, knowing what to preserve, what moments to wait patiently for, is no small accomplishment. Cassavetes watched his actors with amazing sensitivity, listened to them astonishingly closely, and allowed himself actually to learn from them and from the material. By all accounts, he saw things no one else could see. He frequently exasperated crew members or actors who couldn't understand why he wanted take after take of a scene that they thought had already gone perfectly well the first time. Of course the vindication of the sensitivity of his eyes and ears is in the films themselves, in the moments he was single-minded enough to elicit, patient enough to wait for, and alert enough to succeed in getting on film.

Like Mabel, Cassavetes was his actors' own best audience to their performances – laughing, smiling, jumping out of his seat, whooping with delight when interesting and unexpected things happened (just as she does with the construction workers). Moskowitz has a genius for unprogrammatic responsiveness, but in her performance as a hostess Mabel goes far beyond him, and Cassavetes surpassed both as a director on the set. For him, direction was not about control, but responsiveness. It was an invitation to shared exploration. Direction was dialogue, just as Mabel's ideal of life is dialogic.

Acting and directing were never competitive for Cassavetes. His actors always said that they gave their best performances for him because they knew they would never be exposed on film. To be an actor for Cassavetes was to be a member of a cooperative, mutually supportive group, and Mabel shows us the fundamentally cooperative aspect of Cassavetes' own interactions with his actors as well as their interactions with each other. She illustrates what it really means to say that Cassavetes' view of direction was not a relation of superior and inferior, of boss and worker, but of equals working together in a surprisingly intimate public way.

Cassavetes' vision of directing was the opposite of a display of power in the vein of Sternberg or von Stroheim (in which the jodhpur-clad director, riding crop in hand, functioned as a cross between a French aristocrat and German general). It was not done from on high or with a bullhorn. It was a whispered tête-à-tête in the midst of a crowd of people and equipment. It was a private moment shared between two people, an island of intimacy carved out in the middle of the pressure and bustle of a shoot.[10] Direction was the model for all intimate personal relationships in which one person opens himself to and responds to another's needs and feelings. It is suggestive that one of Mabel's most memorable qualities as a "director" was also Cassavetes': her childlike violations of adult standards of spatial decorum by bringing her face "too close" to the faces of others – Hugh Hurd, Billy Tidroe, or Mr. Jensen. Many photographs of Cassavetes on the set show him doing the same thing (usually with his arm over an actor's shoulder – another of Mabel's gestures).

There is, however, one absolutely crucial difference between Mabel and her creator that needs to be pointed out: Cassavetes exercised a single-minded determination in the pursuit of his vision that Mabel entirely lacks. He was willing to do anything to realize his particular agenda of expressive exploration, and he let nothing swerve him from his basic purpose if he had resolved upon it (neither the resistance of the actors, nor complaints from the crew, nor the opinions of his closest personal friends). He was willing to stand completely alone against the world. Mabel cares too much for others' opinions of her. The result is that the tone of their respective performances is entirely different. On the set, Cassavetes was a man possessed, a force of nature, absolutely driven, focused, and uncompromising in his quest for the emotionally revealing moment. She is much weaker and more susceptible to breakdown. He let nothing stop him or distract him from his goals. She lets everything get to her. He worked and fought – tooth and nail, if necessary – for his vision and never flagged in the pursuit of it, in a way that Mabel is not tough enough or determined enough to do. (Of course, Mabel is a woman and a mother, not a man and a director, and that makes a difference. It makes her directing and her attempts to take charge of her universally male crew much more difficult. She has it much harder than her creator did, and he clearly wants it that way.) In comparison with the directions Cassavetes gave to his actors, Mabel's seem scattered, undisciplined, and tentative. Proof of his amazing focus and determination abounds: That the films were made at all is the most striking evidence of his astonishing strength of character. The way they were made is further evidence: Cassavetes shot as much as a million feet of film per picture, and would think nothing of asking for ten, twenty, thirty, or more takes before he was happy with what he saw. (The end of the scene with Richard, Freddie, and Jeannie in *Faces* ran to more than fifty takes, and much of the rest of the film required ten or twelve takes per scene.) Though he listened to his actors and responded to them, Cassavetes was also extremely demanding and thought nothing of removing them if they were not performing up to

Making moments of privacy and intimacy in the midst of a crowd: (*top*) The director (far right) has a tête-à-tête with Peter Falk and Gena Rowlands about the scene in which the kids unexpectedly come home for their schoolbooks; (*bottom*) Cassavetes quietly talks with Rowlands about her attempted suicide scene while the crew prepares to film it.

his standards. (Cassavetes flew into a rage, wrapped the production, and threatened Seymour Cassel with dismissal ten minutes into his third day of acting on *Faces*.) Members of the crew were more than occasionally fired (most frequently the director of photography). At least in public, Cassavetes displayed none of Mabel's vulnerability and self-doubt. He was unswerving in the pursuit of his vision, and would fight to the death rather than sacrifice it or change it (which is a difference from his later alter ego, Cosmo Vitelli, also).

If one needs a counterposition to bring Mabel's and her creator's genius into focus, Mabel's husband, Nick, can stand as a point of contrast. He is the opposite of his wife and Cassavetes himself in almost every respect. (In the realm of biography, if Mabel figures Cassavetes as a director, Nick might be Roman Polanski, whose clashes with Cassavetes during the filming of *Rosemary's Baby* were the stuff of Hollywood legend.) While she gets close, whispers in others' ears, puts her arms around them, or otherwise physically touches them, Nick stands back and issues bulletins from the front, shouted orders from headquarters. While she frees her actors to explore themselves, he is a tyrannical director who cuts others to fit his view of their role. While Mabel accentuates differences, Nick partners everyone the same way, and treats everyone – his children, his coworkers, his wife – the same. It's not that Nick is an unkind or mean-spirited man, but his anxieties and insecurities about himself and others lead him to be obsessed with clarity, control, and order. While Mabel elicits creativity from situations of mess or confusion and, like Cassavetes, seems positively stimulated by states of energetic disorganization, Nick destroys any possibility of original response by imposing limiting scripts and spirit-dampening structures on everyone and everything. While she relishes individual eccentricities, he forces people and events into homogenized patterns of expression.

A series of parallel scenes repeatedly contrast Nick's performance as a director with Mabel's. His performance in a bar in the opening scene is contrasted with hers in a bar that evening. His performance at one end of the table in the spaghetti breakfast is contrasted with hers at the other. Her performance at a backyard party is contrasted with his at the beach. The most revealing moments in terms of his explicit function as a director, however, are the film's two final gatherings (the first in the living room, the second around the dining room table) following Mabel's return from the hospital. Cassavetes registers the true awfulness of the acting that Nick elicits from his "repertory company." It has been said that it took a choreographer of George Balanchine's genius to choreograph recognizable awkwardness and to be able to use it for artistic effect. Similarly, it might be argued that it took a director of Cassavetes' sensitivity to great acting to make *bad* acting a meaningful expressive event. (Beyond that, most other films don't have acting uniformly good enough to make the badness of specific moments count.)

Proof of Nick's directorial ineptness is that he works from the outside in, attempting to use external mannerisms and lines to mask the absence of motivated feelings. Like Sarah Goode in *Opening Night*, he thinks that "all you have to do is say the lines" and truth will emerge. He thinks if he can get Mama, Zepp, and Mabel to *say* the right things, the feelings will take care of themselves. Cassavetes believed the opposite. As he explained over and over again to his actors: "Don't worry about the words – the words don't matter." The words were only a kind of afterthought. They could easily be changed (or dropped altogether). It was getting the feelings into the right place that was important. For Cassavetes, as for Emily Dickinson (who was a Method theorist before the fact): "The outer from the inner derives its magnitude / 'Tis duke or dwarf according to the mood."[11] In this "deep" view of it, acting was not a matter of feigning what wasn't there, but of revealing what most truly was. Acting was a technique of sincerity, a barometer of truth. It never lied. The hammy and insincere performances of Zepp, Mama Longhetti, and Nick in the two group scenes are evidence that they are devoted to the opposite notion: They attempt to use acting not to exhume, but to bury the truth.[12]

Cassavetes' commitment to acting as a process of emotional excavation and discovery is obviously indebted to Method concepts of expression, but that does not mean that external technique, discipline, or control are ignored, as critics of the Method and of his work have charged. His films underwent weeks of rehearsals; his sets were extremely disciplined; and, as previously noted, his scenes were shot in many more takes than those in the typical Hollywood film. Cassavetes was under no illusions that adequate expression could be "uncontrolled." Mama Longhetti is present in *Woman* as a cautionary example of what "direct" expression looks and sounds like. Her gaucheries, shrieks, mistimings, and hysterical gestures contrast with Mabel's extraordinarily disciplined, delicately modulated, sensitively paced, and complexly self-aware expressions during the two gatherings around the table. Nick's fight with Mr. Jensen, his shouting match with Dr. Zepp, and the injury he inflicts on Eddie make a similar point: Adequate expression is never the result of losing control of oneself. For Cassavetes, we express ourselves adequately only when we work to understand ourselves complexly.

Filmmaking as a form of social interaction and intimate relationship (even as Nick demonstrates his own inability to have a moment of intimacy with his children). Cassavetes and Mike Ferris shoot the scene in which Nick brings the kids home from the beach in the back of the truck. Notice how Cassavetes leans on the children, assumes their physical positions, and enters into their optical and imaginative perspectives.

Truth takes profound self-awareness and strenuous self-knowledge. (*Husbands* mounts the same dramatic argument, though most reviewers missed the point and took the opposite moral from it.)

The idea that the woman on the street can function as an actor-director of her own life is one of the most radical concepts in Cassavetes' work. Cassavetes goes decisively against the grain of high modernist tradition (including that of most European art films), which conceives of the role of the artist and the function of art as being socially marginalized. In the tradition of Baudelaire, Borges, and Calvino, the artist is priestlike and oracular, deliberately establishing himself off to one side of society. He and his creations place themselves at a calculated distance from the experiences of ordinary life and cultivate a state of meditative or visionary disengagement from the forms and forces of everyday existence.

Cassavetes participates in an entirely different expressive tradition. Rather than going up the mountain, the artist goes down the Open Road. Rather than rising above the temporal and physical contingencies of ordinary life, he expresses himself in and through them. Rather than calling us away from social duties and familial obligations, he calls us to them, and himself participates in them. In Cassavetes' view, the way we become artists is the same way Mabel does — not by disengaging ourselves from expressive messes and social muddles, but by diving into them and making something humanly valuable out of them. The artist is not figured by the social disengagements and disembodied states of heightened consciousness of the fictional alter egos of Flaubert, Proust, and Virginia Woolf, but can be an inarticulate construction worker talking to his buddies (Nick), a housewife putting on a party for her kids (Mabel), the impresario of a strip joint (Cosmo), a call girl (Jeannie), a gigolo (Chet), or a woman searching for love (Sarah Lawson). While the art of the European modernists is almost always implicitly (and frequently explicitly) world fleeing and world denying, Cassavetes' films are world embracing and world loving.

For Cassavetes, artistic expression not only takes place in the world, but draws its materials and forms of organization directly from the activities of everyday life. This aspect of Cassavetes' work is implicitly a reply to the aesthetic assumptions underpinning the entire fine arts tradition, in which, in the words of John Dewey, "art is remitted to a separate realm, where it is cut off from that association with the materials and aims of every other form of human effort, undergoing, and achievement."[13] Mabel Longhetti and the film she is in are, in effect, Cassavetes' response to Dewey's challenge "to restore continuity between the refined and intensified forms of experience that are works of art and the everyday events, doings, and sufferings that are universally recognized to constitute experience."[14]

Dewey saw the "segregation [of works of art] from the common life"[15] as part of a larger cultural malady that is worth considering, since it is useful to an understanding of some of the cultural implications not only of this film but of the films Cassavetes makes following it. In *The Killing of a Chinese Bookie*, the main character, Cosmo Vitelli, is, in effect, a representative of the fine-arts tradition that Dewey and Cassavetes repudiate, and figures its general imaginative fallacies:

> The factors that have glorified fine art by setting it upon a far-off pedestal did not arise within the realm of art nor is their influence confined to the arts. For many persons an aura of mingled awe and unreality encompasses the "spiritual" and the "ideal" while "matter" has become by contrast a term of depreciation, something to be explained away or apologized for. The forces at work are those that have removed religion as well as fine art from the scope of the common or community life. The forces have produced so many of the dislocations and divisions of modern life and thought that art could not escape their influence.[16]

In *Experience and Nature*, Dewey traces the roots of the fine-arts tradition back to the classic Greek opposition between theory and practice, and to "the classic disparagement of the practical in contrast with the theoretical," which in post-Platonic thought became the favoring of contemplative life over active:

> The depreciatory view of experience was identical with a conception that placed practical activity below theoretical activity, finding the former dependent, impelled from outside, marked by deficiency of real being, while the latter was independent and free because complete and self-sufficing; that is, perfect....
>
> Objects of rational thought, of contemplative insight, were the only things that met the specification of freedom from need, labor, and matter. They alone were self-sufficient, self-existent, and self-explanatory....
>
> If Greek philosophy was correct in thinking of knowledge as contemplation rather than as a productive art, and if modern philosophy accepts this conclusion, then the only logical course is relative dis-

paragement of all forms of production, since they are modes of practice which is by conception inferior to contemplation.[17]

Cassavetes follows Dewey in rebelling against this entire tradition. He de-idealizes art. In opposition to the visionary/symbolic line of disembodied expression, he demands that vision be practically enacted in the forms of the world. He insists that the work, its characters, and their expressions of themselves represent acts of engagement with the world. Art is not somewhere else; it is in life, and absolutely continuous with it. To quote Dewey again, for Cassavetes the individual's experience "of struggles and achievements in the world of things [is] art in germ." For Cassavetes, as for Dewey, the artist and his characters are emphatically *not* "shut up within [their] own private feelings and sensations," but are engaged in an "active and alert commerce with the world, [which, at its height, involves] the complete interpenetration of self and the world of objects and events."[18] Artistic expression is taken out of the realm of refined consciousness and restored to contact with the rough-and-tumble of lived experience in all of its expressive contingency and disarray. Cassavetes calls us to the ideal that Emerson articulated in the final sentence of "Experience": "The true romance which the world exists to realize will be the transformation of genius into practical power."[19] Or perhaps the apt comparison would be to Whitman. Cassavetes' pragmatic form of American modernism is Whitmanesque in its spirit. Like Whitman, it celebrates the gusto of the senses; it loves the world of men and events; it relishes the social and emotional involvements of mothers, fathers, and children. Unfortunately, far from helping win recognition for his work, Cassavetes' similarity to Whitman probably counted against him critically. In a universe of critical discourse that takes its conception of modernism from the cerebralism and worldly renunciations of Eliot and Pound, to be world embracing in a Whitmanesque way is to doom oneself to be misunderstood.

For Cassavetes and Dewey, the location of meaning shifts from the mind to the body – from being figured as ideas, beliefs, and visions, to acts of speaking, moving, and acting. Truth becomes a form of doing, rather than a way of knowing. It becomes active and pragmatic, rather than passive and visionary. Art moves out of "texts" and into the world. It is not confined to "works," but slops over into the work of everyday life. Cassavetes views Mabel and each of the figures around her as being, at least potentially, as much an artist as he himself is. That is Mabel's view of the people around her as well. Flaubert wants us to appreciate how different he is from Emma Bovary; Cassavetes wants us to see how similar Mabel Longhetti's life is to

164

his own as a writer-actor-director. She figures the glorious possibility of being an artist of ordinary life. That is why her means of engagement with other characters is usually an artistic one, but an art that won't be marginalized on the page or stage. Like Cassavetes and his actors, Mabel blurs the lines between life and art; where one ends and the other begins becomes impossible to say. Children dance ballet with cowboy gestures in the backyard, and costume themselves as a way of playing. Mr. Jensen and Billy Tidroe are asked to dance as a way of getting acquainted. And Hugh Hurd's performance as a singer stirs together Mabel, Aida, and Mighty Mouse.

The hope that Mabel figures is that our imaginations do not estrange us, but can knit us into the social fabric of the world. She and her creator attempt to translate their most idiosyncratic impulses into actual social expressions. Mabel attempts it in the spaghetti breakfast and the backyard children's party; Cassavetes attempts it by creating Mabel.

As I've suggested in previous chapters, if one thing most distinguishes Cassavetes' work from other American film, it is that expression is *embodied*. Meaning is generated by and anchored in the actors' bodies – their physical movements, tones of voice, facial expressions, and gestures. That may sound like a truism: After all, every movie has actors and characters who have bodies and faces, and who speak and gesture. In most other films, however, expression is subtly detached from the physical body of the performer. Meaning is lifted above the physical world and relocated in the abstract perceptions of the eye, ear, or mind. It is taken out of the realm of gestures and motions and turned into words and looks. One sign of that process of derealization is that in those films knowledge can be communicated for long stretches independently of the actor (in terms of stylistic effects of light, sound, and metaphor); but even when the actor is part of the process of meaning making, his physical presence almost always matters less than his words, ideas, or visions (both optical and imaginative).

It's only because the habit of abstraction is so inveterate in our art that most critics aren't even aware of it (not to mention its bizarre skewing of what counts as "knowledge" and "meaning"). This aspect of Cassavetes' work was one of the things that most blocked critical appreciation of it. Precisely because the meanings in his films were *in* bodies, there seemed to be no meanings at all. When critics looked for visions, ideas, symbols, metaphors, or abstractions – the sorts of generalized allegorical figurations that leap out of works like *Citizen Kane*, *Psycho*, and *2001* – and were unable to find them, they simply assumed that there was nothing there.

They couldn't imagine that these bodies, facial expressions, and voice tones represented an entirely different kind of meaning. Cassavetes' films offered meanings not abstract, excerpted, and contemplative, but active, embedded, and physical. *Casablanca* lofts us above our bodies to the realm of souls; *A Woman Under the Influence* reminds us not only that our souls have bodies, but that our spirits can be expressed only in the flesh.

There are several references to bodily knowledge in the dialogue of *A Woman Under the Influence*. In an early scene, Mabel asks her children to give her a back rub, and, while they do it, wonders out loud, "Why do hands feel so good?" Of course her children don't have an answer, and she is not really looking for one, but the answer is implicit in all of Cassavetes' works: Bodily knowledge brings us to our senses (in more than one meaning of the phrase) and represents a deeper way of interacting and a truer way of knowing than minds alone provide.

Yet it is crucial to the effect of this scene that, even as it touches on a central concern in *A Woman Under the Influence*, it does not (to use current critical jargon) "thematize," "foreground," or "metaphorize" the concern with bodies. The abstractness of an intellectual or symbolic presentation would contradict the concreteness of the knowing. Cassavetes' meanings are not delivered to the viewer as abstractions and metaphors. They exist in performance, and only in performance. They will not be cut free from the faces and bodies and voices that bring them to us. The casual obliquity of the unfurling of meaning in Cassavetes' work, and the shifting sensory particularity of *how* his scenes and characters mean is inextricable from *what* they mean. He declines to make metaphoric moves or to massage events stylistically (laying in a musical strain on the soundtrack, moving in for an emotional close-up on a character's face, or expressively lighting a shot or framing it) in order to make a moment function more abstractly and generally, because his very point is to make it mean concretely and particularly.

That is why, while a description of the abstract styles of scenes in *Citizen Kane* or *2001* would adequately summarize most of the film's effect on a viewer, the same sort of stylistic or thematic summary would leave out almost everything that matters in *A Woman Under the Influence*. What we really see and hear in the scene on the porch is not an abstract presentation

(facing) Temporarily going out of your head to speak the language of the body and the senses: Harry (Gazzara), Archie (Falk), and Gus (Cassavetes) clowning around on the street in *Husbands*; the film equipment in the background of this shot is not visible from the camera angle used in the film. Gus frisking with Mary (Jenny Runacre) in the same film; note the boom and mike above them.

167

of themes, but something like the following: Mabel is out of breath and says she has a headache. Her kids give her a back rub. She asks a question and looks at one son's hand. She asks the other son to make a muscle so she can feel it. He objects but complies. In the end, they all go inside. Nothing is rhetorically heightened or stylistically emphasized. The back rub, the talk about hands, the making a muscle are emphatically not Norman Bates's stuffed birds, Kane's "Rosebud," or Kubrick's match cut of a bone and a space station. The bodily events pass before the eyes of the viewer in such a rhetorically undeclarative and sensorily embedded way that, in comparison with other films' abstractions, they may not seem like knowledge at all. (What viewers are more likely to feel is that events in Cassavetes are harder to figure out, less clear in their meanings than they are in other movies.)[20]

Two other kinds of moments run throughout the film relating to bodily knowledge, but again, because Cassavetes doesn't rhetorically freight them, not a single review I am aware of treated them as expressive events at all: a series of "falling-down" and "standing-up" movements that run throughout the film, and particular arm movements and bodily postures associated with Mabel. To make a sample list of "falling" movements from various scenes: Mabel and Garson fall in the front hall of the house; food falls on the floor; the kids fall down, imitating the dying swan; Nick pulls Mabel's mother and she falls onto the bed; Mabel is pulled down onto the children's bed by Dr. Zepp; Eddie is injured in a fall at the construction site; Maria falls down on the beach; the kids fall down in the front yard after Nick gets them drunk; Mabel misses a chair and falls on the floor; Mabel is knocked onto the rug by Nick. One might make a parallel list of characters' acts, attempts, or pleas to "stand up."

Though there is no space to go into detail, the various downward and upward bodily movements are subtly linked to remind us of one another. To give only two examples: Maria's baby steps down the stairway at home (to come to Mabel's aid when she is lying on the living room floor) mirror Nick's awkward stutter-steps down the hillside to come to Eddie's aid after he falls. Mabel's dying swan impression on the sofa near the end of the movie similarly echoes the childrens' dying swan imitations in the backyard. There is too much to say about these moments to summarize their meaning here; suffice it to say that one of the things Cassavetes' "dying falls" do is to bring both viewers and characters to a ground floor of sensory reality. Events involving falling down or getting up, and those involving the body in general, are important in many of Cassavetes' films because they take characters out of their heads and force them to put both feet imaginatively back on the ground. They are compelled to recognize a place beneath in-

The soul has a body: Nick threatening to hit Mabel if she doesn't get down off the couch, with Cassavetes standing to the left of them filming it; Mabel being knocked to the floor a moment later.

tellectual flights of fancy. The process of bringing characters to their senses takes place in many different ways throughout his work. When Bennie gets beaten up in *Shadows*; when Jeannie Rapp massages Richard Forst's feet in *Faces*; when Harry gets into a fight with his wife in *Husbands*; when Flo beats up Cosmo in *The Killing of a Chinese Bookie*; when Myrtle is brought down to her knees in a drunken stupor in *Opening Night*; or when Robert Harmon is knocked down on the ground and kicked and punched in *Love Streams*, each of the different forms of "physical therapy" is meant to teach both the character and the viewer truths that the mind might otherwise overlook. In Cassavetes' view, the reality of the body savingly corrects the assumptions of the intellect as much as the dreams of the imagination do.[21]

That is made even more clear in the other set of physical expressions that run through *A Woman Under the Influence*: Mabel's use of her arms and hands in scenes involving sleeping, lovemaking, dreaming, and in her nervous breakdown. There are not many of these moments, but they are some of the most important in the film. Five instances come to mind (though there are probably others I am not recalling): when Mabel clenches and unclenches her outstretched hands in half-sleep the morning after spending the night with Garson; the stretching movements she makes as she comes out of the bedroom to greet the construction workers; the movements of her arms when she and Nick are in bed together later that day; the tortured, angular positions of her arms during the scene of her breakdown; her gestures standing on the sofa doing the dying swan impression.

It is not accidental that the half-gawky, half-elegant positions of Mabel's arms and torso at such moments remind a viewer of some of the specially intense states of physical and emotional abandonment that occur during sexual rapture, or that several of the moments are themselves linked with scenes of lovemaking. Mabel's unposed, unselfconscious, angular gestures come from a place inaccessible to awareness, anterior to intention, deeper than the neocortex, a place we move into only at certain uniquely vulnerable and exposed moments in our lives — moments of unguardedness that occur for most of us, if they occur at all, only during sleep, sex, or dreaming.

These gestures surface only if we are able utterly to leave the world and all that's in it behind, to forego all of culture's public stances and poses. But it takes a second step beyond leaving the looks and judgments of others behind. Even more important and challenging, we have to leave our pasts and past consciousness behind, to renounce the excess baggage of memory and experience that usually weighs us down. We open this completely only when we are able to forget ourselves, to give ourselves up to the expression of our deepest and most secret impulses. Cassavetes makes Mabel a kind of ballerina, and at these moments she truly is like a dancer, allowing herself to speak from a deeper place than the brain.

Emerson celebrated such possibilities in "Circles" when he wrote that "the way of life is wonderful; it is by abandonment," and Mabel shows us that even a nervous breakdown can represent such a moment of liberated self-forgetfulness.[22] But Cassavetes also emphasizes how rare such moments are, how hard it is to forget ourselves in this way, and how fiercely society defends itself against such acts of self-abandonment. Not only society, but even our language and our art implicitly war against such expressive possibilities. It is significant that at the moments Mabel is most liberated from the fetters of self-awareness and self-consciousness, she drops almost completely silent and stands still. The script has nothing for her to say and almost nothing for her to do. An early reviewer of the film characterized it as "a movie of facial tics," and in a sense Gena Rowlands's entire wonderful performance exists to show us that our facial muscles, flickering expressions, and body language reveal truths far more profound, alluring, and elusive than words can ever plumb. Her body and face speak from a place far beyond where words and actions can reach, and speak energies too evanescent and mobile to be captured in language. All of Cassavetes' work is interested in the ways we break free of normative codes of behavior and understanding, and the body, in all of its expressive mercuriality, idiosyncrasy, and concreteness, is a realm of freedom.

When we hear something as basic as the sound of breathing in scenes in *Faces* (in the fight between McCarthy and Forst), in *Minnie and Moskowitz* (when Zelmo and Seymour fight), in *The Killing of a Chinese Bookie* (when Mickey hunts Cosmo down in the warehouse scene), and in this film (in the scene I described with Mabel and the children), it may suddenly dawn on us how thorough the process of derealization is in other movies. While Cassavetes' art is performative, Hollywood art is essentially conceptual and contemplative. As different as they are in other respects, Allen and Simon, Hitchcock and Welles believe in the validity of ideas, the importance of meditative stances, and the possibility of abstract solutions. They provide conceptual shortcuts through experiences. Along with their characters they aspire to rise above the clutter of perceptions by moving into a realm of conceptions. They want to escape from the physical and temporal confusions of felt experience by moving into a realm of understanding. Cassavetes utterly declines to make the meditative move. He asks that his viewers and characters dive into the world of sensory experience to know it for the first time, not rise above it. His films ask his viewers and characters to learn how to function within the contingencies of space and the provisionalities of time.

Every metaphoric transformation in *Vertigo, Citizen Kane,* or *2001* proclaims that the life of the body and emotions is less important than the life of the mind. Every imaginative effect in the work of Hitchcock, Welles, or Kubrick tells us that the physical world of actual people, places, and events wasn't sufficiently interesting to hold their attention. Cassavetes had an entirely less abstract interest in life. For him the visible world was far more mysterious, wonderful, and important than the invisible. The three buddies in *Husbands* – dancing down the sidewalk, bodies bouncing off each other, juking and jogging their way through the film – teach us physical truths that Hitchcock, for all of his obsession with bodies, never even touches. All of Cassavetes' characters, and none more than Mabel, live in their bodies as much as their minds. They are alive to their fingertips. Their very pores speak their meanings. Like Cassavetes as a director working on the set, their body language is at least as vivid and expressive as their verbal language, and frequently more so. Cassavetes worked with his actors by touching and moving them to explain what he meant, and Mabel works with her "actors" in the same way. Cassavetes' crew occasionally complained about his "inarticulateness" on the set, but what they failed to appreciate was the extent to which the nonabstract, nonconceptual meanings he was attempting to capture essentially defied verbal forms of articulation. A choreographer might also have difficulty explaining his ideas in words; that is neither artist's shortcoming, but rather the reason his art exists.

A Woman Under the Influence puts the heft, stickiness, sloppiness back into experience: Spaghetti glops onto your shoes when you spill it (in the spaghetti breakfast). Doors stick in their frames (when Nick tries to close the sliding doors in the scene when he brings his construction-worker buddies home). Telephone cords get tangled around your legs (in the call from Nick's mother that concludes the spaghetti breakfast). Beer fizzes over when you open a can (in the scene with the children in the truck). Maria's glass tips and splashes her (in the film's final gathering).

Fights are not weightless allegorical duels but result in drippy cuts and blood-splotched towels (in the scene just before Dr. Zepp arrives at the house). Characters not only have bodies, but their bodies are nonabstract and nongeneric (most comically and touchingly in the scene in which skinny Angelo and tubby Maria model their swimsuits for their dad). Physiques (e.g., the more-than-portly Vito Grimaldi wearing Mabel's bathrobe at the beach), faces (e.g., Billy Tidroe's), and voices (e.g., Adrian Jensen's) are emphatically not from Central Casting. Even characters' ways of walking

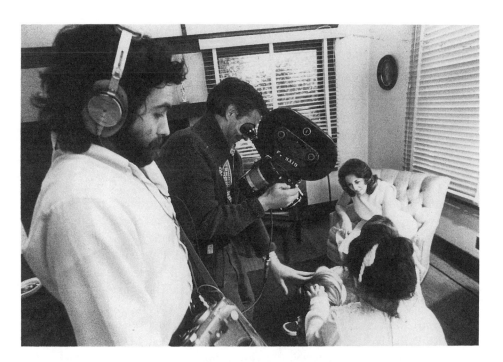

Cassavetes shooting a scene (cut from the final print) with the children, with Bo Harwood recording the sound on a Nagra. Notice how Cassavetes reaches down and touches Matthew Cassel's head. Notice his smile.

are not normalized: What can one say about the touching way little Maria goes down the steps one at a time, except to point out that this and dozens of other moments couldn't occur in a film featuring child actors with homogenized good looks, voice-coached intonations, and scripts that script any of the child that remains out of them?

However, I risk giving a misleading impression. Most of the oddball moments don't even stand out because the eccentric detail or event is swamped by the overall eccentricity of the scene in which it occurs. That is why a term like "comic relief" is inappropriate to describe the effect of these events. For the comedy to be a relief from something, there would have to be an overarching tone or mood to be played against, but there is nothing to be departed from when a scene is all departure.

Cassavetes' scenes are eccentric in more than details. They are eccentric in their shape, in a root sense of the word: They spiral away from tonal or intellectual centers. When Emerson wrote that "there must not be too much design," he knew that to keep his writing alive (and true to life), he had to counteract the tendency of logic to level his argument and overdetermine its progress. Similarly, Cassavetes continuously countermoves against the tendency of narrative logic to overorganize experience. Even more subtly than in *Minnie and Moskowitz*, he interrupts and disrupts the progress of his own scenes to prevent them from patterning themselves. The experiences in scene after scene overflow cognitive or emotional forms of containment. Just as the beer fizzes out of its can and the water spills, every moment we attempt to scoop up a scene or relationship and hold it in a mental container, Cassavetes has it suddenly slosh away from us.

One of the principal ways this effect is created is that the tones won't stand still long enough for a viewer to stabilize a relationship to the material. Consider the five minutes or so that conclude the spaghetti breakfast. A straight and narrow tonal path through the experience no sooner starts to emerge than Cassavetes yanks the scene in a new and unexpected direction. With his "it's in the air" meditation on babies, Falk is endearingly sheepish and comically clumsy in his best Columbo manner. The construction workers' interjections about strontium 90 and golfing on the moon push the tone toward the outright cartoonish. With the opera singing, the scene veers toward the lyrical and romantically evocative. When Mabel attempts to include the shy Billy Tidroe in the conversation, she is first considerate and thoughtful, and then tender (when she gets up and caresses his face). But Tidroe's flustered embarrassment and Nick's abuse (escalating from "that's enough" to "get your ass down") turns the mood unexpectedly black. That shift is startling enough to make an audience gasp and squirm in its seats, and would seem to have pushed the scene into painfulness irrevocably, when Cassavetes proceeds to undo what he did. While embarrassment and shame still hang in the air, Falk answers the phone and proceeds to do an Elaine May routine about "You ate *fish* at *Hamburger* Heaven?" The comedy is then itself interrupted by Nick's moving and earnest, if syntactically awkward, aside, "–how, you know when your mother is ill, comes to mind you're not going to live forever." As Nick gets up from the phone, Cassavetes moves the scene toward slapstick (with Nick's leg getting tangled up in the phone cord), followed by argumentation (between Nick and Mabel), zany parody (Mabel's "pip, pip, pip" mimicry of a grande dame), poignant pleading ("Tell me what you want me to be"), and ending with a moment of sublime calm and tenderness (the blackout to the sex scene). In one scene, we've traveled more places tonally than many entire films go.[23]

It is of the essence of Cassavetes' vision of life that narrative non sequiturs and loose ends are not scripted or edited out of a scene, but are deliberately included. Cassavetes let the dirt and confusion of life *in*, in a way D. H.

Lawrence would have appreciated, as evidenced by his animadversions in *Reflections on the Death of a Porcupine* against artistic purity, and in favor of impurity:

> Somehow, you sweep the ground a bit too clear in the poem or the drama, and you let the human Word fly a bit too freely. Now in the novel there's always a tom-cat, a black tom-cat that pounces on the white dove of the Word, if the dove doesn't watch it; and there's a banana-skin to trip on; and you know there is a water-closet on the premises. All these things help to keep the balance.[24]

That is why events do not "come clear" in Cassavetes' work. They come cloudy and dirty. Insofar as knowledge is tangled up in space, time, and the body, it is unavoidably flawed, provisional, and multivalent. Ideal understanding is possible only in the realm of ideas. In the realm of experiences, one can't get rid of phenomenal clutter, temporal mutability, and perceptual mystery.

What was true of Cassavetes' scripting and editing process was true of his production process as well. The filmmaker virtually never called "cut" in midscene, and his actors and crew were instructed never to stop no matter what happened in the course of it. As Gena Rowlands explained in an interview (coincidentally using the same metaphor Lawrence does): "John never stopped a take, no matter what. If a glass fell over and broke you dealt with it, like life. You went out and got a broom and cleaned it up [on camera]." Sometimes the messy moments were sheer on-camera accidents like the fizzing beer or the spilled glass, and the actors' response was fresh because the event was genuinely unplanned. There are, however, only a few actual unscripted accidents preserved in the films. More often, the confusion a viewer sees was carefully choreographed. Cassavetes scripted disruptions into his scenes to break up straight dramatic lines and to spiral a viewer and a character off on multiple tangents. He worked to mess up overly tidy expressions. Weird excurses and divagations are the weave of his work because, as he once phrased it, "Something happens all the time, even at the height of tragedy, even in a prison or insane asylum, there's some kind of life continuum."[25]

This is true not only of the overall development of his scenes, but even of the line-by-line progress of his characters' dialogue. For two purely verbal examples, ponder the dramatic effect of Cliff Carnell's "Hey, Nick, can I use a glass?" (just prior to the spaghetti breakfast) and an unnamed woman's "Hi, Mabel. You don't know me. I'm a friend of Vito Grimaldi's" (as Mabel pulls up in the car bringing her home from the hospital). The pointlessness of both moments is the point. Experience does not occur in a straight line but as a series of jagged crisscrosses. Even at a moment of high drama (as when Mabel is returning from the hospital) our experiences are interrupted and detoured by a zillion, silly-ass distractions.

That's the wrong way to put it, however. There really are *no* tangents or distractions. Cassavetes is telling us that the interruptions and detours are the experience itself. There is no purer experience behind the spatial and temporal mess; there is nothing but the mess. What would be a distraction in a more conceptually organized work is the experience itself here. Whereas concepts, ideas, dreams, and metaphors lift us above space and time, for Cassavetes experience *is* spatial and temporal, and therefore cluttered and unsettled. Thought can be "thin" and "straight" (and can therefore be messed up or bent by the interruptions of nonconceptual experience), but the experience here is always already "thick" and "crooked."

Not only is there no telling where a scene will go from second to second, but at any one instant it is hard to know tonally or intellectually where we are. One of Cassavetes' favorite ways of creating the density he is after is through a visual layering in which too many things are going on at once to be subsumed under an analytic heading.[26] In the brief scene in which the children return for their school books, while Nick is pulling Mabel's mother onto the bed, she is seriously resisting, the kids are clowning around, Nick is smiling, and Mabel is mugging. In Cassavetes' "pluralistic universe", there is no dominant, unifying tone or meaning; there are only tones and meanings.

At other times, Cassavetes simply pitches a character's performance at an in-between place where it defies reductive point making or understanding. How are we supposed to understand Nick's "it's in the air" meditation? In one respect it's merely nutty and shows us what an intellectual midget he is. His overinsistence about it also shows us his inflexibility, his tendency to stop a conversation in its tracks. In another respect, however, it's surprisingly thoughtful, forcing us to recognize that, sewer worker that he is, Nick is also a kind of poet. How are we supposed to understand Mabel's decision to go out alone when Nick stands her up? Or to bring Garson home and spend the night with him? These moments stay mysterious no matter how many times we see the movie.

Mabel Longhetti is Cassavetes' most extended attempt to explore the practical consequences of open-ended selfhood. Whereas most of the important figures around her, and certainly Nick, organize their lives around maintaining and projecting a more or less stable identity, Mabel's achievement is to hold herself open and responsive to all of the "influences" around her. Leaving fixities behind, she reforms herself in each new context, endlessly moving away from past positions. She shows us that a self is less a definition of oneself than the ability to elude definition: to wriggle free from anyone and anything that might limit or straitjacket you. To know who you are, to have decided who you want to be, is to stop living. To be finished in this way is to be finished in every other.

Mabel embodies Keats's ideal of negative capability not merely as an imaginative stance, but as a lived course of action. In this regard, Cassavetes goes further than Keats. The English Romantics knew enough to write poetry. It was only Americans like Whitman, James, Emerson, and Cassavetes who were foolish enough to attempt to translate poetic ideals into the prose of life.[27]

Mabel contains multitudes. At the simplest, Cassavetes shows us that she is many different people – mother, wife, housekeeper, playmate, lover, and hostess (with markedly different functions in each role). Still more interestingly, he shows us that she refuses to keep her various selves in airtight compartments. She creatively mixes up her roles, playing with Nick's co-workers and with Mr. Jensen the way she might play with her children, or talking as philosophically with her children as she might with an adult. She violates the unspoken rules that dictate what self, what tone, what style is presented at what moment to what person: attempting to open intimacies where others would maintain distances (as when she asks Mr. Jensen to dance, or caresses Billy Tidroe's face), making personal remarks where meaningless chitchat is called for (as with her comment about Mr. Jensen's first name), verging on profanity when tea-party politeness is expected ("screw the tea"), or vulnerably reversing roles of parent and child (asking her children whether they think she is crazy).

But Mabel doesn't merely violate expressive norms and conventions; her more radical function is to reveal that they are *only* norms and conventions. She repeatedly steps back from a situation to comment on it, to disclose what Derrida might call "the structurality of its structure." These are some of the most remarkable moments in the film because they indicate that her consciousness allows her actually to stand aside from her own performance, watch herself and her audience's reaction, and comment on both – as when she analyzes her own behavior after the spaghetti breakfast ("Tell me what you want me to be"); when she talks with Nick after his fight with Jensen and summarizes what happened ("OK. You got upset and made a fool of yourself"); or when she comically comments on her own craziness near the end of the movie ("You know, sometimes I think I really am nuts"). Like *Faces*'s Richard or McCarthy, but much more disciplined, intelligent, and analytical than they were, Mabel shows that she is not captive to her own behavior and expressions. An imaginative ballerina even more than a worldly one, she imaginatively pirouettes on her own premises.

She shows others (and herself) that the expressive games they play are only games, and that the rules by which they play are only rules. In this sense, Mabel doesn't simply cycle among different selves; she reveals that selves (and the behaviors through which the self expresses itself) are social constructs. She mugs, parodies, and plays so much that she might be said to leave all roles or identities behind. She keeps the doors on her identity open to the point that her identity becomes a revolving door – which is why her idea of a party is to play games with who you are (as she does by having the children role-play), and for her, routine dinner-table interaction is experimenting with breaking free from customary forms of identity (as when she gets Nick's buddies singing or tries to get Billy Tidroe to dance). Her self, like her greatest performances, is dialogic. It is brought into existence not unilaterally but in conversation with others. There is no personal limitation on what it can do or be because it is brought into being collaboratively.

Mabel wants everyone to be able to realize a self as rubbery as her own. She wants to shake people up, to loosen their identities, to lubricate their interactions, to make them as fluidly relational as she is. Needless to say, Cassavetes was under no illusions about how society reacts to such an effort: It resists it to its dying breath. As the visual images of the school-bus scene suggest, while Mabel offers loose and baggy costume-party identities, people prefer snugly tailored suits. When she tries to free them, she finds chained minds, chained identities, and even chained shoes.

The school-bus scene illustrates another aspect of Mabel's personality. When faced with resistance, like the stand-up comedian to the world that she is, her response is not to screen it out, but to "work with it" – to build it into her performance. She does the same thing Cassavetes did as a film-maker in *Minnie and Moskowitz*: Like a practitioner of judo, she turns the resistances into fulcrums to generate leverage for her own displays of power. Confronted with the rudeness of the woman with chains on her shoes, she parodies her walk and mannerisms. Insulted and abused by Nick at the spaghetti breakfast, her ultimate response is not to close her spirit to him, but to engage his concerns by parodying his attitude with her "pip, pip, pip" performance.

The flip side of this situation is that precisely because she opens herself to opposition rather than shutting it out, Mabel is in danger of being lethally wounded. Because she plunges into resistances and works through them, she makes herself vulnerable to suffering. So open is her spirit to the influences around her that she allows even her own children to hurt her feelings (when Maria won't come over to hug her when she returns from the hospital, or when she asks Tony to tell her what he thinks of her). In holding herself so profoundly open, like Myrtle and Sarah Lawson later, she opens herself to profound pain and confusion. In not retreating into the shell of a formulated self, she risks being torn apart by the predations of others. She puts herself on the razor-edge where her openness and sensitivity to the influences around her border on making her susceptible to being destroyed by her own states of awareness. Emotional and spiritual suicide is an imaginative possibility for Mabel long before it becomes a physical event.

One of the recurring subjects of Cassavetes' work is the tightrope that his characters walk between honoring their own feelings and responding to others' claims upon them. Where do an individual's responsibilities to others end, and her responsibilities to herself begin? In "Poetry and the Imagination," Emerson imagines the poet as straddling the boundary where centeredness meets sympathy: "The poet is rare because he must be exquisitely vital and sympathetic, and, at the same time, immovably centered."[28] For brief moments, Mabel, Myrtle, Sarah, Moskowitz, Chet, and Jeannie are "poets" in Emerson's sense – they fleetingly reconcile fluid responsiveness with rock-solid independence of spirit. The balance is an unstable one, however, and more often than not even the greatest of Cassavetes' "poets" of responsiveness – Mabel, Myrtle, and Sarah – mix up their needs with their obligations; they sell their feelings to pay their responsibilities.

Cassavetes asks to what extent a performer empowers his audience to define him against his own best interests – how far he sells himself out to suit its needs and expectations. It's a question that would obviously occur to any independent writer-director-producer. *The Killing of a Chinese Bookie*'s Cosmo Vitelli, a cheery, bromidic Rotarian to the cosmos, *Opening Night*'s Myrtle Gordon, a crowd-pleasing professional actress, *Love Streams*'s Sarah Lawson, a "professional" mother who takes it on herself to keep everybody happy (even the relatives in Dallas!), and Mabel each confront the problem of distinguishing their needs from their need to please. All of them flirt with giving up a self apart from the one needed by those around them – or more than flirt.[29] In giving herself to others so completely, Mabel risks giving herself away.

Cassavetes imagines a very difficult universe. In this film, only the children offer Mabel a society that is genuinely unpredatory and uncoercive. Every

Keeping the crew as small and intimate as possible: (*above*) Cassavetes squat-
ting on the floor, shooting into the bathroom with an improvised camera
stand, while the script girl keeps track of the shots and the dialogue. (*facing*)
Cassavetes in the right foreground handholding the final party scene, with Bo
Harwood holding the mike and carrying the Nagra at left. Peter Falk and
Joanne Moore Jordan (who also played Louise in *Faces*) embrace.

other group she encounters is potentially hazardous to her health, no matter
how much its members declare they "love" her. It is a sad recognition, but
the children are the only ones who ultimately knit Mabel back into the
fabric of the family at the end of the film – not her husband, not her father,
and not her mother. Mabel's own childlike qualities link her with them, yet
Cassavetes shows us that even they are sometimes embarrassed by her (as
when Angelo and Tony both express concern for her in the course of the
film) or feel estranged from her (as when Maria initially keeps her distance
when Mabel returns from the hospital).

It is further revealing that Mabel exists most joyously and passionately
in groups (like that at the spaghetti breakfast), and is at a loss for what to
do or be when alone. Like the consummate performer she is, it is as if she
has no self when she has no audience. (Though, for reasons I have given,
it is as if she has no self when she has an audience, either.) Mabel has only

a performed identity, not a private one. Cassavetes organizes *A Woman Under the Influence* around scenes that alternate between Mabel in a crowd and Mabel alone, and it is significant that, notwithstanding the unremitting pain that others cause her, she feels most threatened when alone.

It is not accidental that her initial crisis is precipitated by her inability to remain alone in the house when Nick stands her up on their planned night out. Later in the film, her children are no sooner trundled off to school than she goes to the door and declares "I can't wait for the kids to get home." When she is outside of the home or among strangers, she desperately attempts to create an instant society around herself: in the bar with Garson Cross, waiting for the school bus, or when the Jensen kids come to her house. It is as if she feels she would disappear if she went more than a few minutes without interaction with others. The self that creates itself in collaboration with others is in danger of lapsing out of existence when others are not around to support it. Nick tells her to "be yourself," but what he doesn't understand is that, like the later Sarah Lawson, Mabel has no self to be except the one she finds in others. She exists only for herself in her relationships with others. Like many women, in a promiscuity of love, she gives herself away.

Rather than telling us that Mabel has an infinite number of selves, Cassavetes suggests that she potentially has no self (of her own) at all. To notice that she can be and do almost anything is to point out that she is never really there in any of her roles and parts. Her problem is not only that she proliferates herself into so many stances, roles, and tones that she seems to lose control over (or contact with) any central self apart from them; it is also that she forever seems to be just beyond *any* of the roles she plays, not quite expressed by any of them. Like Sargent's sitters or James's heroines, in living forever in the "optative mood," Mabel has only what Emerson called "a referred existence" – her physical presence marked only by signs of her imaginative absence. Any place she is, any role she plays, her imagination has already moved beyond.

That is why it is impossible to satisfy Mabel's wants or needs, and why we can't name her problem or find a solution to it. There is nothing she can be or do in the actual world that is not an unacceptable limitation on the intensity and mobility of the energies she figures; nor is there anything anyone else can do for her, even her husband.[30] Her situation is created by the nature of her identity, not by Nick or by "gender oppression" (as the cant of certain feminists would have it). It is not created by society either (as Marxist critics would accuse). Nothing in particular can actually express or fulfill Mabel because she is beyond every role she plays, any role she can play. Proliferating herself outward in moving waves of fluid sensitivity, she is imaginativeness on the move that has to stay on the move; but that means she is doomed to be forever homeless. Cassavetes shows us that her identity becomes transcendental, but he also wants us to ask if that is different from being existentially missing in action.[31]

One of the things that makes *A Woman Under the Influence* so provocative, and Mabel's situation so complex, is that her triumph is her tragedy: Her willingness to make herself available to others brings her to the brink of losing control over an identity separate from their definitions of her. Her sublime sensitivity to the "influences" around her is what makes her so susceptible to breakdown. It would be easy to sentimentalize the film and turn it into feminist polemic, but Mabel is not a victim. However much others unintentionally work to destroy her, her destiny is chosen, not thrust upon her. In that sense, like Shakespeare's Cleopatra, she is heroic and in control of her fate, not controlled by others. Her strength, not her weakness, is what undoes her. The profundity of Cassavetes' vision lies in his perception that Mabel's tragedy is not contrasted with, but inextricably linked to, her heroic capacities of sympathy and responsiveness. She can't have one without the other. Cassavetes balances each side of Mabel's predicament against the other: Her acts of self-creation depend on her willingness to risk self-destruction. Her emotional sensitivity to the claims of others on her imagination yields exhilarations that are inextricable from her agonies. Cassavetes is certainly not suggesting that Mabel would be better off by freezing out the world, by shutting down her vulnerabilities. That way defeat lies. Her open-endedness is her genius as well as her pain. She goes much further than Moskowitz in the direction of beautiful responsiveness, and consequently much further than he does in the direction of self-annihilation as well.

Critics sometimes talk about "tragic flaws" in characters like Mabel, but Cassavetes reminds us that the greatest tragedies interest us because they occur to characters who are not flawed in the Aristotelian way, but superior to us in every way that counts. Lear and Cleopatra are better than we usually dare to be: more passionate, more imaginative, more daring, more courageous. Mabel is braver, more creative, more inclusive in her love than most of us have the courage or capacity to be. Her superiority, not her inadequacy, precipitates her crisis of selfhood. In the program note for the 1974 New York Film Festival, Cassavetes called this profound tragedy his "most optimistic film to date." Who could not be hopeful about a world that has such possibilities in it, no matter if they doom us?

5

The Path of
Greatest Resistance

The Killing of a Chinese Bookie

All my life I've fought against clarity – all those stupid definitive answers.
Phooey on a formula life, on slick solutions. It's never easy. I think it's only
in the movies that it's easy...I won't call [my work] entertainment. It's
exploring. It's asking questions of people....A good movie will ask you
questions you haven't been asked before.   – John Cassavetes

One wearies of the aesthetic quality – a quality which takes the edge off
everything, and makes it seem "boiled down."...Art is still to us something
which has been well-cooked – like a plate of spaghetti....The peculiar lurid,
glamorous style which is natural to the great Americans...comes, I think,
from the violence native to the American continent, where...the life-force is
so strong that it tends to come forth lurid and clumsy....It causes a savage
desire to go to extremes, whether of idealism or of violent action.

– D. H. Lawrence[1]

From the beginning of Cassavetes' career, it was clear that the last thing
that mattered to him was currying favor with critics or viewers. Jonas Mekas
had no sooner awarded *Shadows* a prize, than, to Mekas's astonishment
and chagrin, Cassavetes repudiated the movie, and reshot and reedited it.
The moment is emblematic of the way Cassavetes inadvertently alienated
even his would-be fans over the course of the next thirty years. It seemed
that they no sooner praised something he did, than he would either disown
it or go off in a different direction with his next work.

Cassavetes aimed to please no one but himself, and one way to keep
himself interested was to avoid repeating himself. Picasso once said that the
ultimate form of escapism was imitation, and the ultimate form of imitation
was to imitate one's own past work. Cassavetes refused to escape from the

challenges and stimulations of the present by imitating anyone, even himself. The celebrator of pattern breaking kept breaking his own patterns. He confounded the critics not only by making a different kind of movie, but by refusing to make it different the same way twice. You just couldn't predict what he would be doing next, and you certainly couldn't prepare yourself in advance for the experience. That made it hard even for his admirers to keep up with him. The few critics and reviewers who did manage to tune their brain waves to *Faces*'s jittery movements, pressurized pacings, and crowded frame spaces were left gaping when it was followed by *Husbands*'s static blockings, editorial *longeurs*, and visual airiness. Viewers who succeeded in slowing down their biorhythms enough to be able to sympathize with the T-group earnestness of Harry, Archie, and Gus were in turn thrown for a loop by *Minnie and Moskowitz*'s genre-film zaniness, jerky jump cutting, and jazzy syncopations.

In short, a year after *A Woman Under the Influence*, audiences were ready for anything but *The Killing of a Chinese Bookie*. With every reviewer in America primed for another domestic melodrama, Cassavetes switched to film noir. The Longhetti house was replaced by a strip joint, and gangsters and con artists took the place of *Woman*'s children and relatives. Even the visual style was turned inside-out: The "Cosby Show," fill-lighted beiges and pastels were replaced by garish kick-lighting schemes, blinding spotlights and velvety blackness, and shots slashed through by the internal reflections of a camera shooting into the light.

Bookie is the story of Cosmo Vitelli, the owner of a cheezy L.A. strip joint who gets over his head in debt at a mob gambling casino one night and is forced to murder a bookie to clear the debt. At least that's what Cosmo thinks is going on. In fact, it's a setup: The "bookie" is really a West Coast godfather protected by bodyguards and watchdogs around the clock. The mobsters intend that Cosmo be killed in the impossible hit so that they can take over his club, which they've had their eyes on for a while. The only problem is that Cosmo accidentally double-crosses the double-cross: By sheer luck he succeeds at the murder and gets away, which leaves the mob in the uncomfortable position of having to do the dirty work of rubbing him out themselves.

True to form for Cassavetes, however, the plot summary is only loosely connected with the actual viewing experience. Viewers who expected a "shoot-em-up" were left as much out in the cold as those who expected a sequel to *Woman*. (Cosmo fires his gun a total of three times in the entire movie.) Cassavetes uses the gangster-movie premise as a mere frame in which to hang his most shadowy psychological portrait. *The Killing of a Chinese Bookie* is one of Cassavetes' most profound works, but its truths were hidden so deep that most viewers couldn't see there was anything there.

Cassavetes' early films depicted intricate group interactions. They were presentations of the complex calculus of interpersonal relations. That changes after *A Woman Under the Influence*. All of his important late work focuses on loners whose principal societies are visionary, and whose most important forms of expression are imaginative. (With its profoundly alienated yet relentlessly encircled ballerina-heroine, *Woman* is clearly transitional in this respect.) Consequently, like the other late films, *The Killing of a Chinese Bookie* is largely a one-man show, yet what makes it such a challenging viewing experience is that the "star" of the show almost succeeds in turning himself into an invisible man. Cosmo's strategy for survival is the opposite of Mabel's. Beleaguered by the "influences" in her life, she stages a series of self-affirming, self-sacrificing public performances. She becomes a performing artist to the universe, proliferating her identity outward into a succession of audience-pleasing roles. Cosmo has none of Mabel's theatrical panache. Confronted with pressure, he self-protectively withdraws inward. He hides himself from view. He wraps himself in darkness and hugs silence.

Cosmo almost drops through the cracks not only of the society *in* his film but of the expressive forms *of* his film. He won't quite come into focus. He remains slightly beyond our grasp to the very end of the movie, inscrutable even upon repeated viewings. His elusiveness drove reviewers from the theater muttering and complaining, but rather than using it as a stick to beat Cassavetes, we need to allow ourselves to learn from it. Cassavetes deliberately holds Cosmo just slightly beyond definition.

Cassavetes' cinema is antiessentialist. Behavior is not reducible to origins, causes, intentions, motives, goals, or desires. What is true of Cosmo is true of all of Cassavetes' most important figures: Their characters won't be summarized in terms of a simple problem (or solution). What do Mabel Longhetti, Myrtle Gordon, or Sarah Lawson *really* want or need? Why does Mabel undergo her nervous breakdown or slash her wrists at the specific moments she does? What exactly precipitates Myrtle's final emotional collapse and alcoholic binge? These questions remain questions to the very ends of the films. All that is presented are mysteries of uninterpreted behavior. Yet it's not only that the depths (a character's intentions, desires, and needs) are less accessible in Cassavetes' work than in other films; it's also that the surfaces (a figure's words, eyes, face, voice tones, or body language) are less defined, more slippery and shifting, more open to multiple interpretations. The viewer must negotiate a series of fluxional surfaces without knowing precisely what they mean even as transient, local, expressions.

This leads to a crucial point which, insofar as it is at odds with the assumptions that inform almost all American filmmaking and criticism, requires a brief explanatory excursus. To put it succinctly, it is that the mysteries, uncertainties, and vaguenesses in Cassavetes' work are real. They are not feigned, arranged, or calculated. The questions he asks are ones for which he does not have answers. It was not merely a rhetorical pose when Cassavetes insisted that he only made movies about things he "didn't understand," or when he argued that "you have to guard against knowing – because knowing is a form of closure." To know something is to foreordain its trajectory, to limit its possibilities, to short-circuit the learning process. While every tendentious angle in Hitchcock tells us how he merely uncovered the sermons he had already hidden under his stones, for Cassavetes filmmaking was a matter of diving into confusions and uncertainties and actually learning something. The experiences Cassavetes filmed were as mysterious to him as they are to a viewer.[2]

Two entirely different ways of making art are figured in the difference between Hitchcock and Cassavetes: on the one side, a "blueprint" model of creation as the execution of a preformulated plan; on the other, a sense of creation as a process of exploration and discovery. Process is the key word. Cassavetes was not describing feelings, attitudes, or beliefs that he had worked out in advance and that were then summarized in his writing, shooting, and editing: He was exploring and discovering them in the process of writing, shooting, and editing; in the activity of re-reading his scripts, watching and listening to his performers, studying take after take as scenes were being filmed and edited. Cassavetes' work shows us what it is to think *in* film – not to use film to package and present a series of predetermined ideas that exist outside of the movie and anterior to it, but to use filmmaking as a means of thought. For him, film does not represent the contents of thought, but figures the actual process of noticing, wondering, and understanding.

We take for granted that practitioners of the other arts naturally work this way, discovering things as they go along. It is the way writers use writing, composers and jazz performers use playing, painters use painting, choreographers use dancing, and chess masters use their playing. In a misguided attempt to get cinema taken seriously, however, film critics have become knee-jerk neoclassicists, glorifying a notion of artistic control and planning that not even Flaubert actually practiced. They praise Hitchcock because he "storyboarded" camera angles and character movements long before the actors showed up on the set, as if a blueprint sense of art were proof of a "real artist" rather than the opposite. Cassavetes, by comparison, made films the way Picasso painted, Balanchine choreographed, or Robert Frost wrote – pursuing an impulse, adjusting and revising his path as he went along.[3]

The difference in the two ways of making movies reflects a fundamental difference in the conception of the nature of expression. While Hollywood's truth exists outside of or anterior to its particular expressions, Cassavetes' can never be cut free from specific facial, bodily, and vocal expressions because it doesn't exist except as a specific personal utterance. This is, incidentally, why it was impossible for Cassavetes to do what Hitchcock, Welles, Kubrick, or Spielberg do: to sketch out or to know the meaning of a performance or scene in advance of the casting, rehearsing, and filming process. Meanings and relationships in the films of these and other directors can be storyboarded, blocked, lighted, and metaphorically worked out before the actors come onto the set because these directors believe that meaning can exist independent of and be understood apart from actual acts of expression; Cassavetes didn't. Hitchcock was a Platonist who believed that meaning could be detached from fallible, local, bodily expression; Cassavetes was a pragmatist for whom meaning is brought into existence only within the contingencies and partialities of particular social and physical expressions. For Cassavetes, apart from the specifics of the actual performed expression, there is and can be nothing. It would be as inconceivable to him that meaning could be worked out independently of the actor's voices, bodies, and faces, and in advance of their actual performances on the set, as it would be for Sargent or Eakins to decide on the meanings and forms of their portraits before they met the sitters.

In specific respects, *The Killing of a Chinese Bookie* is clearly indebted to Welles's *Citizen Kane*, but the difference between the kind of mysteries Cassavetes presents and the mysteries in Welles's film tells us important things about the difference in the two directors' conceptions of expression. *Kane*'s mysteries obviously were all figured out in advance. Welles (and Herman Mankiewicz, his cowriter) took an originally clear experience and fragmented it to make it less clear – suppressing particular bits of information, misdirecting the viewer's attention, presenting events out of chronological order, and introducing slight biases through pseudo–point-of-view narration. Functioning like the prestidigitator he was, Welles creates the illusion of suspense, mystery, darkness where there actually is none. It's a stirring, wonderful act; but an act nonetheless – sleight-of-hand. It is marvelous hokum, but still hokum. The mystery is only mystification.[4] Hitchcock's use of MacGuffins and his deliberate suppressions and miscuings figure the same process.

The style, as always, tells the deep story. No matter how much the nominal subject of their work is uncertainty or confusion, the style of Welles's or Hitchcock's films is never, even for a moment, uncertain or confused. On the contrary, it is crystal clear. It is utterly knowing. It is coolly manipulative. It is "smart." It is clever and witty to a fault. Their stylistic coolness testifies to how merely rhetorical all their questions are. Admittedly, Welles and Hitchcock were virtuosos; they were masters of sorting, organization, and control. By the same virtue, however, their visual and acoustic mastery tells us how they were never really threatened by their own stage-managed mysteries. They were masters of special effects who kept their work in the realm of special effects. Far from being subdued to the thing it worked in – troubled by it, moved by it, or wounded by it – the dyer's hand clearly never even came into messy contact with it.

In contrast, Cassavetes' work displays a truly unresolved, uncertain style. The filmmaker can never remove himself to a sufficient emotional and intellectual distance from an experience to get the kind of control over it that Welles, Hitchcock, De Palma, the Coens, Spielberg, and the vast majority of mainstream American filmmakers routinely display. Cassavetes' style shows us what it looks and feels like to be *in* an experience, puzzling over it, emotionally involved in it, intellectually responding to it (and adjusting one's responses to it) as it happens. His camera work and editing are not magisterial and poised, but tentative and alert – noticing, comparing, and wondering. He doesn't glide over the world as Hitchcock does, but jumps into it, probing and exploring it.

This is true of all of his work. In *Faces*, his editing unstably jumps around in space, comparing characters' responses and views, studying what is happening from different angles and perspectives. In *A Woman Under the Influence*, he uses focus racking to make experimental slices through different planes of experience, almost as if he were a researcher studying a tissue culture under his microscope and comparing different levels of cell structure. (I would emphasize, however, that Cassavetes' examination of this culture has none of the clinical detachment of doing a biopsy; it is sweatily *in* the experience, responding to its fluxions. Detachment is always a vice in his work, as Robert Harmon's authentically clinical attitude toward his own experience will demonstrate in *Love Streams*. Harmon treats experience the way Hitchcock does – as something one voyeuristically looks

at, but never dirties one's hands by getting mixed-up with emotionally.)
Many of the most memorable moments in *Bookie* also involve the use of
a hand-held camera making uncertain, exploratory movements through inky
darknesses. This is filmmaking not as mastery, but as a profession of humility, a form of learning.

On the other side of the equation, movies like *Citizen Kane, Psycho,
Dressed to Kill,* and *Blood Simple* can provide obvious cognitive satisfac-
tions that Cassavetes' work does not. Welles, Hitchcock, De Palma, and
the Coen brothers not only make sure that they ask questions to which they
already know the answers; they make sure they ask questions that have
answers – short, pat, definitive ones at that. Their works provide the viewer
with the gratification of a controlled problem-solving experience; Cassavetes
does not. Watching their movies is a little like doing a crossword puzzle;
bit by bit it all works out. Watching Cassavetes' films is more like hacking
your way through a jungle; not only do you not know where you're going,
but you don't know whether you're going anywhere at all. They ask concise,
clear, identifiable questions with concise, clear, identifiable answers. Cassavetes does not. They present knotty situations and show us how the knots
may be untied, while for Cassavetes, experience is more like a ball of yarn
without an end. He doesn't tell us what the knots are, what caused them,
or what can undo them. His characters' problems are not traceable to
discrete origins, causes, or intentions; nor are they correctable by means of
a specifiable series of events, actions, or statements. Boiled down, what is
Richard Forst's basic problem, or Cosmo's, or Robert's, or Myrtle's, or
Mabel's? Boiled down, what exactly should they do to straighten out their
lives? The answer is that their problems and their solutions cannot be "boiled
down."

Cassavetes' characters are as complex, mixed-up, and multivalent as people we meet outside the movies. As I argued about Chet in my discussion
of *Faces*, their vices and virtues are so blurred together that they can't be
sorted out. The good, the bad, and the ugly of them are too tangled together
to allow them to be slipped into a convenient psychological or intellectual
pigeonhole. Cassavetes shows us that genuine love can express itself in
hateful, tormenting ways (Mama Longhetti), that professional integrity and
personal idealism can be so fierce that they become indistinguishable from
arrogance and self-destructiveness (Myrtle Gordon), and (in the case of
Cosmo) that a character can be both heroic and pathetic, strong and weak
at the same time. Cosmo has the vices of his virtues: His desire to do good,
to keep everyone happy, and to stay out of trouble results in his doing
precisely the wrong thing for everyone, especially himself. With figures as

complex as these, even repeated viewings won't let us sit back and relax into a clear judgmental stance. We can't put them in our pocket intellectually and say we know them. Like people in life, they keep surprising, disappointing, delighting, and disconcerting us out of simple evaluations of them. The snap moral judgments other films allow us to luxuriate in just can't be made. Our lazy categories of understanding break down under the strain. That, of course, is Cassavetes' goal.

It's not hard to see why the one kind of film would be more popular than the other. The characters in the puzzle-solving film are never allowed to become as confused or confusing as are Cassavetes' – to themselves, to others in their films, or to their audiences. They ultimately flatter a viewer's capacities of analysis. We can understand them without too much work (the character himself frequently tells us what his problem is), and we can feel good about participating intellectually in their salvation (figuring them out and intellectually "solving" their problem even if they can't do it themselves). Cassavetes' characters resist abstract understanding as much as real people do, however. A viewer looking for the satisfaction of "figuring something out" is bewildered, frustrated, and disappointed.

There is another respect in which Cassavetes' work was a genuine technique of exploration that deserves mention. He not only wrote his scripts with particular actors in mind, but used them to explore off-screen aspects of his own and their lives. The films became ways of understanding particular actors' personalities and his feelings about them. Peter Falk, Ben Gazzara, and Seymour Cassel (in starring roles), and Val Avery, Tim Carey, Meade Roberts, and Al Ruban (in supporting ones) were all used in this way. In the films in which they appear, Cassavetes poses questions about them, not simply as characters, but as actors playing those characters. He tries to understand what makes them tick as real people, and invites them to explore themselves. Falk's cautiousness and need for clarity are explored in the character of Nick Longhetti. Gazzara's emotional inwardness and quiet intensity are explored through the characters of Cosmo and Harry. Ruban's emotional guardedness and no-nonsense drill-sergeant toughness, Cassel's boyish roguishness and cocky flamboyance, and Avery's argumentative edginess and volatile insecurity become the subjects of their roles. The result is a far more authentic and intense engagement with the role. The actors were not only able to express themselves more personally, but were encouraged to draw on the deepest parts of this their personalities in their performances – even if not fully aware of what Cassavetes was doing.

It would be hard to overstate Cassavetes' daring in this respect. He used acting and filmmaking as genuine techniques of exploration and discovery.

Needless to say, a devotion to film as actual exploring (rather than as a paint-by-numbers process, as in the blueprint model of creation) takes courage, perhaps even a little foolhardiness. You never know where you are going to come out, what you are going to discover, or how painful or unpleasant it may be. What Cassavetes said of himself and his costars (Peter Falk and Ben Gazzara) in *Husbands* is true of all of his films:

> We started working on *Husbands* as a natural extension of people wanting to continue their lives in work: use what you think you've learned and deepen it.... From the very beginning we made a pact that we would try to find whatever truth was in ourselves and talk about that. Sometimes the scenes would reflect things that we didn't like to find out: how idiotic we were, how little we had to do with ourselves, or how uptight we were. We felt that it was important to ...have the courage to put that out on the line for whatever it was, even if the picture itself would not be exciting.... You have to have the courage to be bad and really express what you want to say.[5]

This is film as a way of exploring and understanding people and experiences outside of the movies, but American film criticism – from Manny Farber and Andrew Sarris to David Bordwell and beyond – has never been intensely interested in film as a form of truth telling. It is always easier to describe movies in terms of semantically empty aesthetics (the "beauty" or "virtuosity" of the photography, the "signature of the auteur" or the "stylistics" of the work); to talk about a movie's relation to other movies (its conformity to or violation of "genre conventions," its "intertextual" connections with other films); to describe it in terms of contentless cognitive arrangements (value-neutral "structures" of meaning and emotionally empty "diegetic strategies"); or to reduce it to a series of de-authored, impersonal "ideological" predispositions (as much feminist and politically engaged criticism does). Such criticism unconsciously internalizes the values of Hollywood filmmaking (the values it is supposed to place in critical perspective). It parades its knowledge of lighting, photography, and editing, but has virtually nothing to tell us about life or the relation of art to life. Like the typical high-concept pitch session, it is keen on connections of one movie with another, but falls silent if we dare to ask why any of this matters.[6]

Since the explorations in Cassavetes' films never remain merely formal, since his style is always in service of moral values and human meanings, his work raises issues with which such criticism simply cannot deal. His films explore new human emotions, new conceptions of personality, new possibilities of social relationship. He explores new ways of being in the world, not merely new formal "moves." His films are not walled off in an artistic never-never land of stylistic inbreeding and cross-referencing. Cassavetes gives us films that tell us about life and aspire to help us to live it. He shows us that art can be a form of knowledge, the finest, most complex form of knowledge, and of its communication, yet invented. We learn things when we watch his movies, about our culture, ourselves, and our relations with others, that we never knew and that can't be communicated in any other way. This passed relatively unnoticed and uncommented upon during his lifetime because the knowledge we acquire is not didactic, but stylistic. We don't learn new facts or observations or beliefs, but new ways of seeing, hearing, thinking, feeling, and being in the world.

The experiences in Cassavetes' films were mysterious to him and his actors when he began them, while he made them, and after he was finished with them, and they stay mysterious for a viewer no matter how many times he sees the films. The mysteriousness is the experience itself; it is not something added to it in the writing, shooting, or editing process, nor is it something eventually to be gotten beyond by figuring it out. As in a Charlie Parker performance, the experience Cassavetes presents exists only in all its speed and density; it never existed in outline form and can therefore never be subsequently translated into outline form, so it stays complex no matter how many times we have it. It may take from three to five viewings of a particular work to get the hang of it, but even when that happens, the complexity is not something we leave behind. Mastery doesn't involve rising above the soupiness, the opacity, and the uncertainty, but learning to live *in* them, responding nimbly enough to stay with them, not to drop out of them for even a second. As in listening to the best of Dizzy Gillespie or watching a Balanchine piece like *Symphony in Three Movements*, it's when we haven't mastered the experience that we keep dropping out of it in a quest for simplifying essences, origins, destinations, or resolutions. Understanding Cassavetes does not consist of moving from confusion to clarity, from thickness to thinness, but rather of eventually learning how to live with particularly intricate and interesting forms of uncertainty, weight, and clutter.

Cassavetes' procedures were the furthest thing imaginable from following a blueprint. His cameramen, producers, and actors all tell stories about how many different ways he wrote, rehearsed, shot, and cut his films, continuously rethinking the material. He was always ready to change in order to pursue a discovery. If he shot a scene and noticed something unexpected that interested him along the way, he might change everything to pursue it. Since he filmed in continuity, as he worked, he was truly watching and wondering, studying and learning about his scenes and his characters. As an example, Cosmo's meeting with the gangsters in the casino after his night gambling was shot over and over again with Gazzara "thanking" the gangsters for their kindness to him using almost imperceptibly different tones of voice, gestures, and facial expressions. Cassavetes later said that he regarded this as one of the key moments in the film, and wanted to understand how someone like Cosmo could carry off the experience of losing absolutely everything while still holding onto his self-respect. He wanted to understand what kind of person can "thank" someone for ruining his life. As he was editing, he repeated the process: comparing alternative takes, studying the unplanned gestures or spontaneous expressions that might have unexpectedly surfaced in a particular take for what they might mean or reveal, playing with the footage to shift the tone or to change the emotional effect slightly.

In these respects (but *not* by minimizing the importance of scripting, rehearsal, and planning during the shooting process), Cassavetes functioned like a documentary director, allowing his characters and events to teach him things as he went along, learning about his movie from the previous day's work, changing his mind as he worked on it. For some reason, that an artist would work this way seems illegitimate to certain critics, but it is the way Beethoven composed, Michelangelo painted, and every writer writes: beginning by pursuing a planned course of action, then continuously adjusting it according to the possibilities discovered in the process.

That openness to exploring possibilities at any stage of an experience (and not out of the artistic self-indulgence and laxness with which he was absurdly charged) was what made Cassavetes so willing to rewrite on the set, or to change the ending of a film after he had already begun shooting it. Of course, this is something that is possible only when the director and the writer are the same person, and when the filmmaker is willing to change his plans and schedule in midstream, something most union-dominated, budget- and schedule-obsessed studio shoots will not and cannot allow.

The reason all of this matters, beyond simply getting the facts straight, is that Cassavetes' performance as a director embodies his philosophy of life. His characters and actors are asked to do the same thing in functioning within the films (and his viewers are asked to do the same thing in understanding them) that he did in making them. They are asked to remain open to unformulated impulses and undefined imaginative possibilities. The films show us the importance of being willing to revise ourselves and our purposes at every moment. They are demonstrations that the attempt to formulate experience – by planning, concluding, or resolving – is the enemy of life and creation. They are celebrations of the abilities of their characters, their

"Tell me what you want me to be. I can be anything. I can be *that*." Cassavetes as Mabel in *A Woman Under the Influence*, miming her gestures and facial expressions as she leaves the bathroom, as Gena Rowlands looks on.

creators, and their viewers to learn things by accepting states of not-knowing.

None of Cassavetes' works goes further in the direction of keeping a viewer in the dark and frustrating reductive interpretive designs than does *The Killing of a Chinese Bookie*. The drama of understanding what a viewer goes through in trying to make sense of the film is incorporated into the plot as the drama of understanding what Cosmo Vitelli goes through in trying to make sense of his life. Cassavetes' goal is to teach us to live in a stimulating condition of confusion and uncertainty – even as he knows how upsetting a state of cognitive irresolution can be. Cosmo represents an example of how *not* to survive in this world. He gets into trouble because of his need for clarity and resolution in his life, just as a viewer will get into trouble if he wants the viewing experience of this film to be clear. The intention is that we learn from Cosmo (as a negative example) – that we learn the virtues of living in the dark and the vices of trying to escape from uncertainty. We need to learn that vision can blind us, and blindness grant us insight.

Cosmo's entire life is devoted to a quest for clarity, harmony, and coherence. He is the proprietor of a strip joint, the Crazy Horse West, and though his club is not the only expression of his blessed rage for order, it is the most obvious one. He attempts to live the Romantic dream of creating an artificial environment within which the self can wall out confusion and pressure. Cosmo's club may seem tacky and trashy, but Cassavetes intends that we appreciate that, in its working-class way, it is a Stevensian Key West of the imagination. The imaginative function of the Crazy Horse is emphasized by the fact that it is a private repertory theater company with Cosmo as its artistic director.[7] The waitresses and bartenders wear western gear, and the strippers do "artistic" numbers. Cassavetes goes to considerable lengths to make us aware that it is not just a bar or sex joint: At the beginning of the film he has Cosmo wander into a hole-in-the-wall bar in order to remind us how dingy and sad such a place can be; later on he has Cosmo briefly pause on the sidewalk in front of a porno-movie house to remind us of how much more romantic Cosmo's view of sex is than the gynecological one of an XXX-rated movie.[8]

Cosmo flees from the confusions of a world he can't control, to one in which he can script and direct his life and the lives of everyone around him. In the Crazy Horse, Cosmo does it all, onstage and off. He writes, casts, choreographs, directs, and emcees the shows that take place on his stage. Behind the scenes, he plays all the parts as well. He is everyone to everybody: *padrone*, father-confessor, therapist, cheerleader, sugar daddy, and Romeo to his "girls." Playing all the instruments in a one-man parade is a lot of work, but it is the only way to control every beat. Cosmo lives a masculine dream of power, mastery, and control. (It is one of the recurring fallacies under which Cassavetes' male characters labor – from Hugh, Tony, and Ben in his first film to Robert Harmon in his last.)

Mix a little Walt Disney with a lot of Wallace Stevens and spice the whole thing up with a dash of MTV soft-core porn, and you've got the Crazy Horse West, where the realities of actual sexual and social life are checked at the door, and a gauzy, alternate reality is brought into existence through sound effects, costumes, and lighting. The acts on Cosmo's stage define a universe separate from but parallel to and mirroring (in a fun-house way) his life outside of his club: The day after he makes a final protection-money payment to the Mob, his strippers introduce a new routine with a gigantic hundred-dollar note as a backdrop, in which they sing "I can't give you anything but love" and throw dollar bills to the audience. While he is being corralled into the Mob hit, his strippers stage "The Gunfight at the O.K. Corral." While he is traveling on a surreal imaginative journey through nighttime Los Angeles, they mount "An Evening in Paris." The routines are bizarre externalizations of Cosmo's offstage life, but, more significantly, they are clarifications and fantasies of fulfillment. They round the edges of reality. The art is orderly in a way that life, especially Cosmo's, never is. Onstage, things are brightly lighted, the dramatic conflicts are well-defined, and the resolutions are clear. Onstage, Cosmo (present through his doppelgänger, Mr. Sophistication) is not a goat, but "a star."

Like the Sternbergian artist he is, Cosmo lives through his eyes and his "vision," and invites the audience in his club to live through theirs, while declining the difficulties of converting that vision into social expression. (A series of references to *The Blue Angel* explicitly link Cosmo's artistic agenda with Sternberg's Disney-like "cinemagic" kingdoms.) Disney is a relevant reference point insofar as his entire magic kingdom (from cartoons to amusement parks to movies) was founded on our culture's separation of imagination from social involvement and action. This is the split Dewey described. As Charles Hartman puts it: "Once that division has been instituted [the separation of poetry from thought, reality, truth, or any profound responsibility for or to the human situation], the province of imagination shrinks to recreational fantasy."[9] In short, Disneyland, the films of Steven Spielberg, the voguing of Madonna, genre criticism, and Bordwellian formalism are alternative manifestations of the same phenomenon. So is the life's work of Hugh Hefner, to sharpen the metaphoric focus on the realm Cosmo presides over. Like Hefner's, Cosmo's life and art are terrified retreats from the mess of complex sexual and social involvements into the lazy sublimities of *Playboy*'s adolescent world of wet dreams and airbrushed fantasies. It's not at all accidental that Cosmo's greatest stage piece is a paean to the transforming power of the imagination.

Cosmo's airbrushing of experience, however, is neither confined to the shows his girls put on nor circumscribed by the walls of his club. Like Charles Foster Kane, whom he resembles in many respects, Cosmo's troubles begin in earnest when he attempts to treat the whole world as a private repertory company. He tries to arrange his life as if it were governed by the same rules as one of his stage routines. Cosmo's life, like that of Kane (or Welles), is an all-American attempt to let form do the work of content. As in contemporary Hollywood "deal making," contact with messy realities is pretended away: What matters is not truth but "style" or "class" (which, needless to say, are not the same things as style or class). Life is turned into a series of performances by actors who are never offstage. As long as no one blows your cover, "reality" (which Vladimir Nabokov, a Sternbergian artist in another medium, typically enough said should always be enclosed in quotation marks) never rears its ugly head.

The embarrassing discrepancy between Cosmo's grandiose vision of himself as an artist and a lover, and his clumsy expressions of himself in his life and on his club's stage, take us to the heart of the work. Unlike Mabel, Cosmo is a "romantic" in the slack sense of the term, someone who attempts to uncouple imagination from reality, not to translate from one to the other. He attempts to escape from the confusions of the physical world into a realm of "pure" imagination, while Cassavetes is the poet of the stimulating impurities of transactions between the realms. One of Cosmo's most important deficiencies is that, rather than translating from one realm to the other, he tries to use imagination to screen out the disturbances of the physical world. (Note that his escapist impulses as an artist are of a piece with his denial of the reality of his own body when he is wounded in the shoot-out. He treats even his death as if it could be stylistically arranged for maximum artistic effect; but *The Killing of a Chinese Bookie* is not *The Saga of Anatahan*, as much as Cosmo may think it is.) Like their creator, Cassavetes' greatest creations – Mabel, Myrtle, and Sarah Lawson – translate between vision and reality. Cosmo's belief that imagination can provide an escape hatch out of the bewilderment of reality is the flip side of his faith that charm can replace substance and style do the work of emotional involvement in his offstage life. He is an escapist in both his life and his art.

One of the ways Cassavetes communicates the fallacy of Cosmo's attempt to build a Coriolanean "world elsewhere" of the imagination is by having plot events disrupt his dreams. When Cosmo attempts to use the Crazy Horse to wall out worldly pressures, Cassavetes brings gangsters into his club. When he tries to play out his fantasy of being a high roller, the plot has him lose $23,000. While Cosmo thinks committing a murder is merely a matter of sleepwalking through a scripted role (you just "say the lines and go through the motions," to paraphrase *Opening Night*'s Sarah Goode in the film following this one), Cassavetes makes sure he takes a bullet in his body that no amount of boutineered stylishness can pretend away. In Cosmo's vision of life, it's not supposed to be that way. "You can't shoot me; I'm the star" is one of the lines he writes for his alter ego, Mr. Sophistication, to say in "The Gunfight at the O.K. Corral." That may be true in most art, especially in popular film; but the Mob is convinced that Cosmo, star or no star, can be killed anytime they want. In short, even as Cosmo devotes his life to the opposite conviction, his film's bullet-in-the-body plot is designed to suggest the limits of disembodied stylistic arrangements.

"There are some things that cannot be talked...away," as Emerson put it. "Style" (in Cosmo's sense of the word) is *not* everything.

Cosmo's sense of style is, however, only half of the film. The other half is Cassavetes'. What makes *The Killing of a Chinese Bookie* such a complex viewing experience is the double vision Cassavetes induces: His style is the opposite of Cosmo's. The difference takes us to the heart of the film. While Cosmo airbrushes, Cassavetes focuses on the blotches in reality. While Cosmo sands rough edges, Cassavetes deliberately makes things rough on Cosmo and the viewer. While Cosmo tries to treat life as a glorified costume party, Cassavetes devotes all of his efforts to ripping off the costumes and sneaking a peek under the masks (just as he did in *Shadows*). While Cosmo devotes himself to the art of comfort and composure, Cassavetes offers us an art of disturbance and decomposition.

One of the filmmaker's favorite ways of rubbing against the nap of Cosmo's stylistic velvet is simply to reveal the fictionality of Cosmo's fictions. What Cosmo wants us to regard as truth, Cassavetes reveals to be artifice. If the success of the tuxedo Cosmo wears at the beginning of a big night out with his girls depends on the people around him not perceiving it as a costume, then as the evening proceeds, Cassavetes gradually reveals its "costumeness." First Cosmo's shirt is shown to be just a tad long in the sleeves; then his tuxedo jacket is removed. Finally, his bow tie is taken off and revealed to have been a clip-on. The props Cosmo depends on for his special effects – a limo, a driver, even a bottle of Dom Perignon with which he tries to impress one of his girls – are similarly shown to be "props." At one particularly revealing moment, when Cosmo takes the champagne bottle from the ice bucket, we see that it is half-empty (and presumably half-flat). We suddenly realize that this is a lower budget production than we thought: The bottle is a leftover from a high roller who visited the club the night before.

Another way that Cassavetes ruffles Cosmo's artistic feathers is in a comparison of the difference between "looking" and "touching" that runs throughout the movie. Like Hugh Hefner and Josef von Sternberg, Cosmo construes experience as a matter of purely visionary understandings and relationships (in both the optical and the imaginative senses of the adjective), while Cassavetes throws tactile and physical reality in his face (and in the viewer's). As Cosmo systematically "derealizes" reality, Cassavetes "rerealizes" it. The difference is wittily summarized in the corsage scenes at the beginning of the big date. Cosmo is interested in having his girls *look* great ("How's that look?" he asks Lamar, the limo driver, about a corsage), but as Cassavetes comically presents the situation, Cosmo is too shy to touch the girls' skin and attach the flowers to their evening gowns himself (delegating the duty to Lamar).

The absence of instances of touching is expressively significant. There are only two brief moments in which Cosmo actually touches Rachel, the girl with whom he is in love: Early in the film, he gingerly rests his hand on her bare back as he escorts her out of her house on the way to the gambling casino; near the end of the film, he reaches up to the stage and takes her hand – but again only for a few seconds. The only moment in the film in which Rachel initiates a touch (in the casino scene, when she momentarily puts her hand on Cosmo's leg), he barks at her to stop it because it distracts him. It is understandable that a strip joint is a world of "look but don't touch" for its patrons, but what Cassavetes wants us to realize is that Cosmo has bizarrely internalized its voyeuristic ethos. Sexy gestures, tones, and appearances take the place of real sexual intimacy and involvement. Long before MTV made the connection clear, Cassavetes equates postmodernist style-surfing with the superficiality and intangibility of adolescent masturbatory fantasy.

There are similarities between Cosmo and an earlier character in Cassavetes' oeuvre in this respect. *Too Late Blues*'s aptly named "Ghost" Wakefield similarly declined to make the move from vision to action. He would rather think love than make it; he would rather have romance than sexual involvement because sex required that he leave the pure world of his imagination and grapple with more complex realities. However, the character Cosmo most obviously asks to be compared with is the one who preceded him: Mabel Longhetti. Cosmo inverts her value system. Mabel embodied love; Cosmo disembodies it. In her own person, with every flicker of emotion in her eyes and face, Mabel showed herself to be a mistress of bodily and facial expression; Cosmo figures stoic impassiveness and emotional suppression. Whereas she realized love in actions, movements, and bodily positions, he derealizes it. She translated it into practical, personal expressions with her children, her husband, and her acquaintances; he withdraws into a set of purely imaginative constructions and visionary relations. While she hugged or touched people and things, he presides over a realm of vision where touching is forbidden. (Note how even his fussiness and fastidiousness – early in the film with a wet glass in a bar, and at the end with the blood on his blazer – is part of his desire to wish away physical realities.) Subsuming all of the other distinctions, Mabel and Cosmo go in opposite directions as artists: She brings the energetic messes and confusions of life into her lived art. She makes art tactile, mobile, and energetic. He tries to

Cosmo signing his "acting contract" with the men who want to "produce" his life and work (and to profit from it). Note the costumeness of his costume: Cosmo has a carnation in his lapel, a clip-on bow tie, and a rented shirt too big in the collar and too long in the sleeves. His job will be to attempt to improvise a free performance in the margins of the script he has just committed himself to playing.

take the mess, the movement, the bodily knowledge out of both his art and his life.

In summary, while Cosmo moves out of the realm of the body and into the imagination, Cassavetes moves his film in the opposite direction. While Cosmo pretends that clothes make the man, Cassavetes reveals the difference between the person and the costume, the performer and the performance. While Cosmo devotes his life to upholding the smoothness of style, Cassavetes' goal is to reveal the cracks that appear when we try to varnish over angularities of truth. While Cosmo uses costumes, lighting effects, and makeup to hide the wrinkles in reality, Cassavetes focuses in on the seams and shabbiness. What's wrong with Cosmo's merely visionary relationship with reality is that it *is* beautifully weightless and frictionless. For Cassavetes, truth is always and essentially frictional – as Angelo's back rub in *A Woman Under the Influence* previously told us. While Disney, Hollywood, MTV, and postmodernism all put experience on ball bearings, Cassavetes was in favor of restoring the scrape, squeak, and stickiness to life.

A few of these metaphors surface at several points in *Bookie*. Near the end of Cosmo's night out with his girls, Lamar goes to close the limo door and it momentarily sticks; in the next scene, when he attempts to open it for Cosmo, it scrapes the sidewalk. *Bookie* is riddled with such moments. A third and fourth example: In a scene about five minutes after the two limo events, there is a fight between two girls at Cosmo's club and one of them bolts for the door half-dressed, hurriedly putting on her clothes as she runs. In her haste she drops the shirt she is pulling over her head and has to go back and pick it up off the floor. A second or two later she has to yank twice at the door to get it open because it sticks the first time. Both "mistakes" appear in the same shot, which is less than ten seconds long, and they are obvious. A fifth example: A few minutes later, when a car full of gangsters pulls up in front of Cosmo's club, we hear their tires screeching against the curb. There are dozens of similar instances in this film and in Cassavetes' other works, most of which were either criticized by reviewers as "mistakes" or charitably overlooked as an unavoidable consequence of apparently not having a big enough budget to do things "right" – meaning the studio way. Far from being errors, the so-called sloppy or unpolished moments are a crucial component of Cassavetes' expressive project.[10]

A studio director would have instantly called "cut" during every one of these moments – while the limo door hinges were greased in the one scene or the tires run up on ramps to provide adequate curb clearance for the door closing in the other, while the club door was planed so that it wouldn't stick, or while the gangsters were told to pull in again so their car's tires wouldn't rub the curb. Even if the glitches were not noticed during the shooting, and the takes were accidentally printed and edited into the film, the sound could easily be manipulated during postproduction to eliminate at least the rubbing and scraping noises. Cassavetes was an absolute fanatic about getting things right, and could easily have reshot any of these moments or cut them in editing.

It's interesting that such events virtually never occur in a mainstream film. I would argue that most American films can't handle such moments and don't include them because, as I asserted in the Introduction, they are essentially allegories (though it is precisely because of this that we don't recognize them as being so). Their expressive project involves moving away from "impure" sensory realities into a realm of "purer" ideas and emotions.

Really expressing something by making mistakes. Cassavetes behind the camera shooting the scene in which the waitress, Trisha Pelham, first drops her shirt and then momentarily can't get the door open.

To put it the other way around, they remove the sensory content from experience and substitute an abstraction in its place. They replace the roughness of sense experience with the smoothness of an idea about reality. The visionary impulse implicit in the Academy style (especially as it was practiced by masters of subjectivity like Hitchcock, Welles, and Kubrick) subtly but relentlessly abstracts and metaphorizes objects, events, and characters. The objects and architectural spaces in *Citizen Kane*; Ilsa's face in *Casablanca*; the mop and bucket in *Psycho*; and the costumes, props, and sets in *North by Northwest, Vertigo, Rear Window, Dr. Strangelove, 2001,* and *The Shining* do not have the tangibility of actual physical objects; they figure the contents of consciousness (either a viewer's, a character's, a director's, or all three). They are almost purely metonymic and symbolic.

If the difference between the sensory and the intellectual forms of filmmaking is not perfectly clear, compare the cafe scene in De Sica's *The Bicycle Thief* in which Bruno eats and makes some financial calculations on a napkin, with the scene in Hitchcock's *Psycho* in which Marion Crane eats a sandwich in Norman Bates's office and then goes to her room to calculate how much money she needs to repay. (Cassavetes made no bones about being profoundly influenced by neorealist film at the start of his career, and by De Sica's films in particular, so it is entirely appropriate that one finds similar qualities in their respective works.) Bruno's bread has crumbs, his mozarella stretches, his pencil and fingers are stubby, his napkin has wrinkles and is difficult to write on. Marion's sandwich is symbolized by a single slice of bread that she never actually swallows; her process of eating involves nothing more physical than three or four abstracted chewing motions; and her calculations consist of a few doodling motions of her hand paired with an insert shot of numbers being written.

Hitchcock inhabits Plato's simplified heaven of forms – abstraction heaped upon abstraction, unsullied by contact with messy or resistant reality: His characters are generic, allegorical abstractions. Their experiences consist of states of abstraction (looking, seeing, thinking, and feeling plenty, but never actually doing or expressing very much). They inhabit a world of abstractions (as this example illustrates, their reality is weightless, hygienic, and highly symbolic). And they are played by actors who themselves merely abstractly "indicate" the occurrence of emotions and events. In contrast, De Sica thrusts us into the complexity of felt sensory reality. He shows that life is lived not only with the imagination, but in a world of the senses that is potentially at odds with our imaginative appropriations. His scene captures the resistance of reality to our mental and emotional possession of it – even in details as minor as the way stretchy cheese makes a piece of toast difficult to eat or how the flimsiness of a napkin makes it hard to write on.

The world of Hitchcock's characters (at least in all of his major postwar work) is defined almost entirely in terms of disembodied visions, thoughts, and feelings. De Sica's (and Cassavetes') world includes the body and the senses. Whereas Hitchcock asks us to dive into sensorily invisible depths – into realms of deep psychology, buried reasons, socially unexpressed feelings, and hidden causes, De Sica and Cassavetes tell us that the really complex events of life are actually all on the surface, if only we understand the surfaces complexly enough. Cassavetes shows us what a nonallegorical, nonabstract, nonmetonymic cinema looks like. He restores the tangibility, the clout, and the thickness to experience. While Hollywood film is engaged in derealization and disembodiment, Cassavetes brings sensory tangibility, specificity, and oddity back to representation. He brings characters and viewers to their senses. He turns away from imaginatively transcendent stances. Immanence is our lot. Even the most exalted moments in our sexual relationships are frictional; in fact, without the friction there would be no exaltation. (The sex scene between Mary and Gus in *Husbands* demonstrates that in another way.)

In terms of the examples from *Psycho* and *Bicycle Thief*, Cosmo's problem might be said to be that he attempts to be a Hitchcock character in a De Sica movie. He tries to ignore the resistance of reality to his imaginative appropriations – something he could get away with in a Hitchcock film, but never in one by De Sica or Cassavetes. The touching, semicomic recognition Cassavetes urges on us is that even as Cosmo aspires to turn his entire life into a "stylish" work of art, he doesn't reign as a supreme fictionalist even on his own stage. He can't screen out life's confusions even within the enchanted circle of his own dramatic productions. He attempts to use his stage productions to figure Romantic dreams of beauty, to loft himself and his audience imaginatively above bodily realities and emotional complications, but life keeps getting in the way. Mr. Sophistication and the strippers muff their lines, quibble about their parts, throw dressing-room fits of temperament, and generally goof up the productions in every way. Their bad acting and their personal rivalries and jealousies keep messing up the ideas and ideals the fiction is abstractly supposed to represent.

The issue is dramatized in many different ways. The easiest to see is by noticing how the bodies, faces, and expressive identities of Cosmo's actors and actresses won't be neatly absorbed into the work of art. At every point at which Cosmo (functioning as a Hitchcockian artist in this respect) wants his performers to represent abstract figurations of his vision, to disappear in their roles, instead, the personal particularities of their bodies, faces, and expressive capacities stick out like proverbial sore thumbs.

The point is the difference between Cosmo's conception of a work of art and his creator's. Cosmo casts his strippers in depersonalized genre pieces like "An Evening in Paris" and "The Gunfight at the O.K. Corral," but his creator makes us notice all the rough edges where the character won't slip cleanly into the mold of "character." A stripper's plainness, the unshapeliness of her body (in comparison with conventional standards of cinematic beauty), or the way she muffs her lines ("Mr. Sophistication" becomes "Mr. Fascination" at one point) puts a crease in the oilcloth of fantasy. Even onstage "Mr. Sophistication" won't simply *be* the role he plays. He repeatedly destroys the illusion of illusion by speaking directly to the audience in his own person (something Myrtle Gordon will also do in the film following this one), deviating from the script, reminding us that he is a person, not just a dramatic functionary. Near the end of the film he even throws a little fit of artistic pique and refuses to go onstage until Cosmo calms him down.

Although Cosmo wants the person to disappear in the persona, Cassavetes wants the opposite. He not only tolerates expressive idiosyncrasy, he celebrates it. As he once said about his own work, it is only by "*not* having the actor be better than he is, that he can really express something. The mistakes you make in your life are assets on film.... I try to have the actors *not* clean themselves up."[11] For Cassavetes, the individual performer's distinctive expressive identity – the ways in which the individual body and voice inflect the role and change it – was what made the role mean anything at all. Whereas Cosmo cringes at the missed cues and muffed lines, Cassavetes obviously relishes them. While for Cosmo the personal fallibility of his actors and actresses dooms his productions, for Cassavetes it is the only thing that makes them worth saving. The idiosyncratic tones and unplanned expressions that sneak out between the scripted lines are much more interesting than anything in the script.

If we don't see this from Cassavetes' lovingly patient and amused tone toward the foibles of the strip-show performances, we can see it from the way Cassavetes stages every scene in *Bookie*. Behavior, faces, and voices are emphatically nonnormalized, nonstandardized, and nongeneric. While Hollywood movies represent homogenized, corporate, group-think forms of expression (organized around allegorical characterizations, abstract conflicts, and standardized forms of speech), Cassavetes was the poet of the idiosyncratic and personal. For Cassavetes, as for De Sica and Renoir, our individual expressive differences and peculiarities, not our abstract imaginative or intellectual similarities, were what made us worth knowing.

Cassavetes is the same kind of artist that Mabel Longhetti is. He raises bodies out of the narrative plots in which they normally are buried. He incarnates; he translates backward from spiritual experiences and generalized intellectual understandings into the world of faces and voices, gestures and tones. The word is made flesh. He reverses the unfortunate direction of most Western philosophy and academic criticism. The Chinese godfather Cosmo murders is an anonymous game piece in a depersonalized Mob plot (and would be a faceless semiotic function in any other gangster movie's plot – the one kind of plot not being very different from the other), but Cassavetes restores his physical particularity and idiosyncratic expressive identity. As we and Cosmo are uncomfortably forced to observe, he is an embarrassed old grandfather with fogged-up glasses, sagging dugs, and a wrinkled abdomen. The gangsters are fascinating precisely for the reasons that they would never make it through the casting call for a *Godfather* sequel: They have hooked noses, weird voices, bad haircuts, and carbuncled faces. Even the figures in the club's audience are not turned into impersonal

Non-Hollywood, nonidealized standards of beauty and performance. Cassavetes makes sure that the actress does *not* look better than she really is, that she does *not* clean up her act and get her lines down pat, as Cosmo futilely devotes his life to the opposite artistic agenda.

members of a Central Casting crowd: In one scene a man has a facial tic, in another a girl dabs sleep out of her eye.

Cosmo is in love with glamour, style, rhetoric; Cassavetes fights against them. One of the most extraordinary qualities of Cassavetes' work is its courage to leave rhetoric behind in the pursuit of truth. Even at Hollywood cinema's very best (*Citizen Kane, Mr. Smith Goes to Washington, Some Like It Hot, Humoresque, Now, Voyager, Casablanca*), it never dares to take the sheen off its characters and their situations. We may agree that Charles Foster Kane and Rick Blaine are flawed and fallible, or that the characters played by Bette Davis and Joan Crawford have emotional problems, but their very shortcomings are made romantic. Even their suffering is alluring. There isn't a viewer in the theater who wouldn't trade places with them for a week or a day. They flatter us. If this is us, we look great even when we are miserable. The studios knew they had to do that to keep audiences coming back. They softened the edges of truth to sell enchantment. Cassavetes does not. None of his characters are romantic, attractive, or glamorous. He was fully aware of this aspect of his work. There is even a scene in *Love Streams* where he mocks the "glamourousness" of suffering as it occurs in works of popular art. One character gushes to a writer: "I *love* your novels. They make loneliness seem *so . . . so exciting*." It is telling that the film itself shows that loneliness is not in the least exciting, but sad and painful.

Furthermore, while Hollywood encourages (and depends upon) a viewer's identification with the protagonist, Cassavetes frustrates it. The goal is to prevent us from "falling into" the film or the character in the Hollywood way, as if we were merely living our lives through the main characters, because the merging of identities on which that identification depends is premised on a lapse of critical judgment, a suspension of our independent analytical faculties. Cassavetes wants to put us at a slight distance from what we see – a critical distance that empowers us as independent thinkers and forces us to assume a critical perspective on what we are watching. Rather than have us blend into the characters, he wants to compel us to maintain an adversarial, diacritical stance with respect to them. Rather than asking us to "become" them, he wants to hold us outside of them so that we will have to wrestle with and come to grips with them.

Cassavetes' central figures are not in the least generic Everymen into whom the viewer can plug his pet theories or fantasies. In the first place, they aren't representative or archetypal. As Cosmo and Myrtle Gordon in *Opening Night* most obviously illustrate, the occupations, backgrounds, and interests of many of Cassavetes' main characters are completely alien to the experiences of the average viewer. They are highly individualized, distinctive, and eccentric. The consequence is that we can't kick back and passively "be" them the way we can "be" Rick and Ilsa, Indiana Jones, or Roger Thornhill in *North by Northwest*. Beyond that, they aren't ciphers or Rorschach ink blots; nor are they generic outlines that we can simply color in with our personal fantasies. They are not passive and receptive to fantasy, but strong, active, energetic creators of their own meanings and identities who actively resist the imposition of others' meanings – including those a viewer may want to impose on them. Rather than opening themselves and making themselves available to us, they make us work to understand them, and keep changing and breaking their own patterns independently of what we may want or expect. They will not yield themselves up to formulaic or categorical understandings. We have to bend and twist and fold our minds to get them around them, and keep changing our understanding to keep up with them.

Cassavetes' view of life is frictional. Characters resist the viewer's imaginative appropriations. They hold the viewer at arm's length and alienate him. Whereas characters in Woody Allen or Neil Simon solicit our sympathy and care, those in Cassavetes' work repel it. Allen's and Simon's films embody their creators' empathetic, confessional points of view, their love of and faith in analysis (especially self-analysis), whereas Cassavetes' movies and his characters despise and distrust it. His figures won't let us cozy up to them. They scorn our sympathy. They won't put themselves on the couch and open up to us; they won't tell us what's wrong with them. They cover up (or deny) their problems and pains. Since they won't take their own pulses and tell us their secrets on camera, we have to make an enormous effort to understand them – which is exactly the position in which Cassavetes wants to put us. In order to read these difficult, resisting, opaque texts, we have to become active, engaged, critical thinkers. Cassavetes makes things hard on viewers because he wants them to come to grips with a hard world, one that resists imaginative appropriations and expansions.

Cassavetes' characters usually aren't even superficially likable. They are as prickly, cantankerous, and difficult as people we meet in real life. Who would want to be Cosmo Vitelli, Nick Longhetti, Archie Black, Richard Forst, or Robert Harmon? The men in *Husbands* make complete asses of themselves. Nick Longhetti is a jerk in many respects. The businessmen in *Faces* are obnoxious. Cosmo is extremely hard to like. Cassavetes wanted his characters to be imperfect.[12] Yet, on the other hand, to be flawed and fallible is not a sign of damnation in his work. It is merely evidence of one's humanity. Unlike the villains in a Hollywood production, none of these characters is meant to be dismissed. Each of them is taken utterly seriously. Each is us. Cassavetes gives us ourselves in our crusty idiosyncrasy and imperfection, then asks us to find a way to love, respect, and understand ourselves and each other, warts, wrinkles, and all.

For Cassavetes, resistance is a law of life. All of *Bookie* might be said to highlight the pinch-points at which our glorious fantasies rub up against the resistances of nonimaginative life. The scraping of the limousine's door on the sidewalk, the rubbing of the Mob car's tires on the curb, or the sticking of the club's door is nothing, however, compared to yet another kind of friction that runs throughout the film – the frictional relation of characters and the resistance they put up against each other. If characters don't open themselves to a viewer's imagination, they equally resist each others' maneuverings. Cassavetes imagines a brick-wall universe. In place of the visionary blending or romantic merging of other films, every character we meet and interact with presents a brick wall we must either batter down or find a way around. Not even the simplest human interaction is weightless or frictionless; no relationship is automatic or easy. Think of the gauntlet Richard Forst has to run before he can have his evening alone with Jeannie. In *Gloria*, even something as simple as going to the bank to withdraw your money involves a host of complications, a series of fragile egos to be taken account of. Work, struggle, friction can never be avoided. The briefest phone call or most perfunctory conversation takes effort and a degree of finesse to bring it off.

In *Bookie*, consider the sequence that begins with Cosmo calling a cab from a pay phone on the street after his car breaks down on the freeway. He gets into a brief argument with the dispatcher about where he should be picked up. He calls his club and gets into a flurry of disagreement with his own bartender about which act is onstage. When the cab arrives, he gets into a spat with the driver about where he wants to take the cab. He arrives at a restaurant to pick up some hamburgers to take out, but not before there is a disagreement with the waitress about how they should be wrapped, followed by an awkward conversation with the bartender about the waitress's personality, followed by another uncomfortable conversation in which the waitress apologizes for her previous behavior.[13]

The roughness of the relations between the characters is one of the reasons many critics concluded Cassavetes was a cynical or depressing filmmaker, and it is not hard to see why it is easy to misunderstand the meaning of these arguments and disagreements. Cassavetes' view of expression goes diametrically against the official party line of post-1960s liberal culture. It contradicts every variety of "I'm OK, you're OK," feel-good thinking from

"Sesame Street" to *Everything I Need to Know I Learned in Kindergarten*. That culture espouses the compromising of positions and the homogenizing of roles. It is in favor of the avoidance of conflict and the erasure of differences. Cassavetes celebrates differences. Like William James in "The Moral Equivalent of War," and Emerson throughout *The Conduct of Life*, he tells us that struggle and opposition are not only unavoidable, they are energizing.

Cassavetes' characters understand this as well as he does. None of the differences of opinion Cosmo is forced to negotiate in the sequence I described is malicious or ill-intentioned. The context establishes that the taxi dispatcher, the bartender in the club, the cabbie, the waitress, and the bartender are not being unpleasant or disagreeable; rather, each is actually trying to help Cosmo. Cassavetes would have agreed with the author of "On a Certain Blindness in Human Beings" that differences in point of view will loom in the most direct and forthright encounters. Even the most minor characters with whom Cosmo interacts, no matter how briefly, have their distinctive prickliness and eccentricity. Gaps open that must be bridged even between intimates like Cosmo and his lover, Rachel.

Far from being something to avoid or minimize, resistances are important in Cassavetes' view because they stimulate us to answering responses. As both *Minnie and Moskowitz* and *A Woman Under the Influence* demonstrate, our greatest performances are shaped out of the process of negotiating our differences, and indeed require a certain amount of resistance in order to be staged at all. In being met head-on with independent expressions, we are stimulated into clarifying our expressions. That process of not eliding, but of working through the resistances around us, is the most interesting part of life for Cassavetes. Differences are energizing. In fact, agreement is positively undesirable. When everyone agrees, conversation dies. (Both *Faces* and *A Woman Under the Influence* actually include scenes in which this happens.) Harmonies are boring; discordances are stimulating. In *Woman*, while Nick seeks the former, Mabel specializes in the latter. As Cassavetes himself explained: "You want a little friction, because that shows there's something alive there. Something worth saying."

Minnie and Moskowitz shows that the artist does the same thing the characters in the films do, creating new expressions through struggle against the resistance of preexisting forms of expression. As I've already suggested, in this respect, and notwithstanding his complete indifference to recreating specific historical events in his work, Cassavetes' understanding of experience was essentially historical. He didn't need to evoke the past in order to grapple with history, because, for him, history saturated the present moment. We are reminded of history by every movement we make across and against received forms of expression seeking to have their way with us. Like the personal struggle the characters stage with others, this struggle with resistant forms is the fundamental fact of all creative activity. If there were no resistance, there could be no creation.

Speech itself is different in Cassavetes' work. The Hollywood tradition, including the work of Hitchcock and Welles, is as implicitly Platonic in its understanding of spoken language as it is in its understanding of nonlinguistic expression. When characters talk, they all speak the same language (or, more accurately, the same language speaks them). An ideal realm of pure ideas, feelings, and beliefs exists into which the characters simply plug themselves, and which they frictionlessly transmit to each other in the form of words. Meaning is not enacted, it is declaimed. The characters might as well be communicating by semaphore or with flash cards. Such films subscribe to the possibility of an ideal meeting of the minds (even if it is only an agreement to disagree) – the minds of characters with each other and of viewers with characters.

It is inconceivable to Cassavetes that his characters could communicate so perfectly and completely with each other (or with the viewer) because he does not believe in the possibility of depersonalized ideas, feelings, or beliefs. Expression can never be cut free from the expressive contingencies that everywhere impinge on it and inflect it. All meanings are mediated. None is abstract, absolute, or universal. There is no realm of meaning above and beyond the personal. The consequence is that while Hollywood conversations can figure frictionless meetings of minds, Cassavetes reminds us that we are too different from each other ever to interact frictionlessly, nor should we want to. Since their identities are so purely mental and abstract, Hollywood characters can mesh perfectly, as if they were gears cut to an identical pattern (and they generally are, since most of them talk and think the way a Hollywood writer or director thinks). Cassavetes' conversations are displays of the sparks that fly when gears don't mesh. The nongeneric, unhomogenized bodies, faces, and voices of his characters are only, as it were, the outward and visible sign of their nongeneric, unhomogenized minds and feelings. Characters who are truly individualized and absolutely distinct can never come together without jagged gaps and rubbing overlaps.

As a result, interaction becomes a matter of expressive work – with an emphasis on both the adjective and the noun: "expressive" because the grounds of interaction are moved out of the mind and into the voice, face, and body; "work" because nothing can happen effortlessly or instantaneously. Since every interaction is staged against expressive obstacles and resistances, it takes enormous effort. This commitment to expressive work is one of the crucial, defining differences between Cassavetes and filmmaking contemporaries like Woody Allen, James Ivory, Henry Jaglom, and David Lynch. Their films are fundamentally about possibilities of imaginative and visionary relation (or nonrelation) between characters and between characters and the viewer, which is to say they finesse the labor of practical expression. Since characters relate to each other in terms of feelings and ideas, goals and intentions, they are spared the complexities of practical expressive acts.

Cassavetes has an entirely different sense of the meaning of truth and of our relation to it. For him, a character's success (or failure) is never a matter of mere ideals, dreams, or intentions. Cosmo is the most clear-cut demonstration of this in all of Cassavetes' oeuvre. His intentions are terrific. He means well. In a Woody Allen movie, with its focus on states of feeling and contemplation, its willingness to let sentiment substitute for action, that would be more than enough; it would be everything. For Cassavetes, however, intentions count for nothing because they represent a purely imaginative relationship with reality. For him, victory (or defeat) is never imaginative, but active. Salvation involves engagement with and mastery of the resistances of life. It involves expressive work and struggle. In that sense, Cosmo is a failure. He is a failure precisely because he attempts to retreat from the difficulty of expressive action into the easiness of private vision. He thinks that good intentions can take the place of good, hard struggling resistance against the mob. The filmmaker would have agreed with Emerson, who wrote in the "Worship" chapter of *The Conduct of Life* that "the only path of escape in all the worlds of God is performance."[4]

When truth is not available as a visionary or imaginative relation, it becomes a matter not of seeing, but of doing. A performative model of truth replaces a contemplative one. Truth is not set in the realm of the intellect and imagination, but in that of action. Negotiation, not transcendence, is our highest destiny. In "Natural History of Intellect," Emerson is explicit about the frictional nature of the expressive events that result from a non-contemplative relation with reality: "Genius is not a lazy angel contemplating itself and things.... Man was made for conflict, not for rest."[5] In "The Pragmatist Account of Truth and Its Misunderstanders," William James extends Emerson's point in a direction Cassavetes would have found congenial by contrasting "discarnate" truth (of which he and Cassavetes indicate the limitations) with "full truth," which in James's (and Cassavetes') view necessarily "does battle":

All discarnate truth is static, impotent, and relatively spectral, full truth being the truth that energizes and does battle. Can any one suppose that the sleeping quality of truth would ever have been abstracted or have received a name, if truths had remained forever in that storage vault of essential timeless "agreements" and had never been embodied in any panting struggle of men's live ideas for verification?[16]

Our expressive engagement with obstacles inevitably involves real struggles against real resistances. We have to dirty our hands expressively. Adequate expression can never be smooth, automatic, or unearned. This suggests yet another difference between Cosmo and his creator. As his big night out tells us, Cosmo aspires to the ultimate in performative smoothness and polish, while Cassavetes believed that all creative activity involved expressive dirtiness, roughness, and bumpiness. Whereas Cosmo embodies a "go along and get along" philosophy of life, Cassavetes (as he once described himself to me) "relish[ed] the fights." Whereas Cosmo wants to paper over differences in order to deny the roughness of reality, Cassavetes tells us that all of our important meanings must be made within the resistances of ordinary life, not to escape life's roughnesses but to help us to live in them and with them. (I'm reminded of his reply to the pleasantry a journalist inflicted on him about how he hoped things were "going smoothly" on a shoot: "Who *wants* it to go smooth? You want things to go *rough*.")

Although Cosmo devotes his life to smoothing away difficulties and avoiding ruffling feathers, Cassavetes was always in favor of taking the path of greatest resistance. He wanted his actors, characters, and audiences to have to take the long way round, the hardest way through, which meant denying actors various actorly shortcuts in their playing (the satchel of clichéd indications that every experienced actor has at his disposal), denying characters emotional and intellectual shortcuts out of difficult situations (e.g., by being able to take some clarifying, resolving action in the plotty American movie way, as if an action ever solved an emotional problem), and denying audiences shortcuts through their viewing experiences. In place of quick fixes and easy solutions, Cassavetes proposes a course of work, labors of expression and interpretation. To appropriate Henry James's appreciation of Conrad in "The New Novel," Cassavetes might be said to be "a votary of the way to do a thing that shall make it undergo most doing."[17]

But Cassavetes would undoubtedly have hated such a theoretical description of his purposes. The level of abstraction implicitly betrays the things it talks about. As I already mentioned, for him, meaning was never made verbally or theoretically, but in action and performance. It is enacted or it is nothing. His own work never tells, but shows. To see what performance against and within resistance looks and feels like, we only have to watch Cassavetes working through and against the spatial and temporal structures of this film. Not unlike what he did with the screwball form in *Minnie and Moskowitz*, he chooses a standard Hollywood genre, not in order to plug into its narrative conventions, but to have something hard and firm to bend his muscles against. The film noir form becomes a scaffold upon which Cosmo and his creator, in their different ways, stage unbelievably eccentric, idiosyncratic temporal and spatial performances.

In the first place, faced with the most plot-heavy, action-centered form, Cassavetes shifts the drama from action to reaction, from event to the space between events. He skips over showing what Cosmo *does* (staging the actual killing of "the bookie" perfunctorily, almost as an afterthought) in order to lavish attention on the states of thinking and feeling leading up to and following the killing. He focuses in on the emotional and psychological black holes most narratives simply zoom past in their rush to the next event, the moments of stillness and silence that punctuate our dark nights of the soul.

Second, faced with the most causally overdetermined form, Cassavetes plays against its tendentiousness by programming in a series of narrative interruptions, divagations, and delays. At every point we think we're going to get somewhere, he derails the story. Every time we think something is about to happen, he postpones or elides it. If things begin to resolve even a little, he confuses them. The ellipticalness of *Bookie*'s scenes, the dilatoriness of its pacings, and the murkiness of its events make Cassavetes' other work look downright conventional by comparison.

Cassavetes' goal is similar to William James's when in "The Stream of Thought" James said that he was interested in "the reinstatement of the vague to its proper place in our mental life."[18] The vague represents what does not fit into a system of thought or expression. Cassavetes knew that all narrative presentation represents an act of simplification. It selects one thing over another to see, to listen to, to care about. It directs our understanding. It tells us that these events and figures belong together and are separable from those. It establishes clear causal links between things. It provides purposes and goals. His goal was to move us into the places that conventional narrative, by its very nature, excludes because they won't be harnessed to advance the plot or to contribute to the concise characterization of a figure: places of uncertain, ambiguous, undefined, contradictory feelings and states of awareness. These are the nonverbalized, nonlogical, discordant aspects of experience that most of our waking thoughts are devoted to keeping from rising into consciousness; but as Cassavetes knows, they are the very heart and soul of our emotional lives. He forces us to confront the uncertainties and mysteries that most of life is organized to avoid. He moves in on the places our understanding breaks down.

Consider Cosmo's dreamlike voyage through Los Angeles on his way to and from the murder of the Chinese godfather as an example of how Cassavetes punches psychological holes in the seamlessness of narrative. The action would have been simple to dramatize if Cassavetes had wanted to do it directly: All it involves is Cosmo going from his club to "the bookie's" house, bumping him off, and getting back to his club. It could all be done in a couple of minutes if Cassavetes had chosen to do so; but of course he didn't. What he presents instead is a labyrinth of confusing instructions, double-crosses, changes of plan, pauses, diversions, and interruptions. The "killing" exists only in order to give the filmmaker and his hero something to avoid doing, to diverge from, to delay. Here is how the scene actually begins:

Cosmo is yanked out of his club in the middle of a show by one of the gangsters; but instead of simply being given his marching orders (nothing happens simply here), he is taken into a side alley and beaten up (to indicate that his friends are not in a joking mood). He is then wedged into the front seat of a car full of mobsters. What the viewer and Cosmo are next put through is deliberately made too dizzyingly complex to be followed. Cosmo is given a mind-boggling series of convoluted, overly specific directions and instructions (by four gangsters talking at once) on everything from the difference of the safeties on a .38 and a .45, to how to break into a house, to the intricacies of navigating the L.A. freeway system: Cosmo has two guns forced into his hands and is asked to choose one. He is instructed on how to release the safeties, and how to use them. He is told to drive a hot-wired car that has been stolen just for him. He is given a series of bewildering directions on how to get to the Chinese godfather's house. He is offered advice on how to get past his bodyguards and Dobermans. He is warned about searchlights and trip wires. He is handed a key stolen from a lock-smith. He is given directions on how to get to the particular room in the house in which the man sleeps. He is handed the mortgage papers to his club and told to inspect them. To add to the confusion, the scene is staged in almost complete darkness. Along with Cosmo, we glimpse odd angles of gnarly faces we can hardly see, listen to voices and accents we can barely make out, and try to keep up with what in the world the overlapping dinosaur grumblings mean. If it were not tragic, it would be hilarious – a

A man trapped in a bureaucracy, an actor trapped in a nightmare part, constrained by a script that keeps going against him and unable to redeem his role. Cosmo in the gambling casino, in the recurring situation in which he finds himself throughout the film: surrounded by others who make all the rules and dictate all of his moves.

combination of tones in which Cassavetes specializes because it puts the viewer into such an unresolved, unstable relation to what he is watching.

Cosmo eventually gets into the car and drives off; but now that he is actually cruising down the freeway, Cassavetes does his best to prevent him from getting anywhere. Cosmo no sooner gets going than the stolen car blows a tire, swerves out of control, and stops dead on the highway. Needless to say, Cosmo doesn't have the key to the trunk. He is stranded in the middle of nowhere. The moment is characteristic: Just when the movie was getting somewhere, Cassavetes screeches it to a halt. Nothing in *Bookie* happens without a dozen interruptions and delays. Even more than Cosmo's automobile, Cassavetes' narrative is sprung free from the expressway of straight-line progression (though his critics thought that, like the car, it was just dead on the road or pointlessly idling). Rather than presenting a simple sequence of events, Cassavetes puts Cosmo (and the viewer) through an obstacle course designed to sidetrack every action. A drive down the freeway is liable to take us anywhere except where we thought we were going, namely, to a climactic action. In this strung-out universe of experiential interruptions and narrative digressions, detours are the straightest path between any two points.

With his car still sitting on the highway, Cosmo has to find a pay phone in a deserted gas station and call a cab; but we know better by now than to think that the next shot will have him arriving at the godfather's house. While he's waiting for the cab to arrive, he calls his club to check on the progress of one of his shows. When his bartender can't identify the act on stage, he does a Bob Newhart routine into the phone, eventually singing a chorus of "I can't give you anything but love . . ." to explain which act he means. The cab finally arrives; but before Cosmo can get anywhere, there is a flurry of argument with the cabbie about where he wants to go.

Even now, Cosmo still has a ways to go before he gets anywhere. He is next in a restaurant, where he has a series of awkward conversations with a waitress and a bartender. There is a cameo of a Greek short-order cook. (Only sometime in the middle of this scene do we realize that Cosmo has gone to the restaurant to pick up a bag of hamburgers to distract the Dobermans.) He finally arrives at the house of the Chinese godfather, walking up the driveway puffing away at a cigar. Cassavetes stays with Cosmo, literally and metaphorically step by step, as he feeds the Dobermans, goes up some stairs, makes his way across the patio, goes up more stairways, through a doorway, through dark corridors, into the inner sanctum of the man he is supposed to murder. It has taken something like twenty minutes to get to this point.

The trip back from the hit is as move by move and zigzaggy as his trip there, but I'll summarize it more briefly. It consists of a run down a flight of stairs, then across a patio, then down another flight of stairs. There is then a jog down a street and around a corner. Then there is a bus ride, a cab ride, a brief stop in front of a movie theater, a second cab ride, a side trip to Betty's house (Rachel's mother), and yet another cab ride back to the club.

The shortcoming of the preceding descriptions, however, is not only that it is impossible to capture the impression of duration that Cassavetes orchestrates, but that naming an event clears it up in a way the experience of the film doesn't. That is to say, Cassavetes keeps us even more in the dark than the preceding description indicates. Like Cosmo, we have to feel our way through space and time, from one point to another, from moment to moment. Cosmo and the viewer are yoked together in a second-by-second existence, moving from one event to another, from one place to another, step by step, without being able to predict what the next one will be or where it may lead. We pick our way through the narrative dark, event by event, literally and imaginatively proceeding one step at a time, "leaping from one floating cake of ice to another on an infinite sea" (in William James's phrase from "Pragmatism and Religion").[19]

Bookie is the opposite of what Cassavetes once pejoratively described as a "shorthand" film. All of its experiences are longhand. Nothing is elided, summarized, or skipped. Not even the simplest event is presented simply, obviously, or in summary form. Take the blowout on the freeway as an example. It's a simple, stock event that has appeared in scores of movies; but not in Cassavetes' hands. He does not present the typical clear, concise shorthand formulation of "a blowout" (say, by providing an intercut close-up of the tire wobbling on the road), but rather makes the viewer experience the same state of uncertainty, surprise, and confusion that Cosmo does as it happens. A viewer sees Cosmo going down the highway, suddenly hears a noise, hears other noises, watches his car jerk in an unexplained way, and sees other cars threateningly bearing down on it with horns blaring. We watch Cosmo jump out of his car, run around and try the trunk, run off the highway, and then reverse himself and run back onto the highway to raise the hood. What is going on is not really clear until the sequence is over and the film is on to other things.

It would be hard to overstate the originality and importance of what Cassavetes does narratively. Whereas the narratives of other movies, especially gangster pictures, are fundamentally totalizing or essentializing – presenting a series of events hierarchically arranged to serve a larger purpose and build to a climax – Cassavetes presents a fragmented story that stays fragmentary even upon repeated viewings. Whereas gangster pictures are usually about tying narrative knots as tight as possible, *Bookie* presents a series of loose ends, unraveled relationships, and dangling and unresolved encounters. As long as there is an impulse that can be pursued, the plot is put on hold, because plot is precisely what suppresses the registration of eccentric impulses and reactions. Narrative events, cinematic views, and characters' actions are broken free from the support of (or subservience to) larger structures of organization. The overarching narrative point exists only to be fractured, interrupted, and swerved away from.

We are in a world of temporal process. Beyond that, the progression is sequential and evenhanded: there are no climaxes, resolutions, or clarifications. This is a world of *and* and *and*, of one thing next to another, not of heights, depths, ultimates, or essences. *Casual* relations replace *causal* development. The result is a uniquely demanding (and rewarding) viewing experience. Since there are no climaxes or buildups, time and events are leveled. Sprung free from the accents of plot, every small moment becomes potentially of equal importance. We can't relax anywhere.

Cassavetes is realizing narratively what William James philosophically described under the rubric of "pluralism" or "radical empiricism," and which he distinguished from "post-Kantian" or "transcendentalist" systems of knowledge. Experience is not traceable back to essences. It is not generative of climaxes and conclusions. It is received in bits and pieces, unfinished actions, and uncertain conclusions. Totalizing visions or essential understandings are not available. In this view of experience, nothing ever is (or can be) revealed. Two representative passages from James follow (the emphases are James's):

> Humanistic experience is pluralistic, and its parts lean on each other *from next to next*, whereas in all these post-Kantian systems, however conceived, it is *through the whole* that they get connected with each other, that being the logical *prius*. In "Humanism" as I understand it, no whole need be *realized* at all, and the largest ensemble that is realized may be a *sum* or *result*.... *Continuity* rather than *in* or *of* an absolute "whole," [is] the secret of the one and the many.[20]

> For pluralistic pragmatism, truth grows up inside of all the finite experiences. They lean on each other, but the whole of them, if such a whole there be, leans on nothing. All "homes" are in finite experience; finite experience as such is homeless. Nothing outside the flux secures the issue of it.... The world we live in exists diffused and distributed, in the form of an indefinitely numerous lot of *eaches*...[21]

It goes without saying that this strung-together state of affairs drove many of Cassavetes' viewers and reviewers out of the theater, and even for those who remained and to some extent got the hang of what he was offering, it was easy to mistake his position for a form of nihilism, so powerful is our craving for visionary clarifications, so automatic our habit of understanding experience in terms of essential meanings.[22] James's philosophical stance was accused of the same negativism or defeatism for the same reasons. As much as James did, however, Cassavetes intends the "next to next" experience he offers to be profoundly stimulating, energizing, and affirmative.

James's philosophy has both spatial and temporal ramifications. Where the view stays partial, knowledge is something that occurs in time and through time, not out of it or above it. He argues in "A World of Pure Experience":

Life is in the transitions as much as the terms connected; often, indeed, it seems to be there more emphatically, as if our spurts and sallies forward were the real line of battle, were like the thin line of flame advancing across the dry autumnal field which the farmer proceeds to burn. . . . According to radical empiricism, experience as a whole wears the form of a process in time, whereby innumerable particular terms lapse and are superseded by others that follow upon them by transitions which, whether disjunctive or conjunctive in content, are themselves experiences, and must in general be accounted at least as real as the terms which they relate. . . . The only function that one experience can perform is to lead into another experience. . . . So the notion of a knowledge still *in transitu* and on the way joins hands here with the notion of a "pure experience". . . . Why insist on [knowing] being a static relation out of time when it practically seems so much a function of our active life? For a thing to be valid, says Lotze, is the same as to make itself valid. When the whole universe seems only to be making itself valid and to be still incomplete (else why its ceaseless changing?) why, of all things, should knowing be exempt?[23]

Where experiences are joined not through their centers, but only one to the other at their edges, what James called "the process-aspect" of experience becomes one of its defining attributes. One thing leads to another only in the gradualness of its happening. Only in thought (or the unnaturally accelerated editorial pacings of other films) can we jump directly from one thing to another without traversing the distance between them. In the experience Cassavetes offers, there are no spaces or gaps, and there is therefore no jumping. Logic and thought have discrete, separable terms, but lived experience is thick, clogged, and full. To cite James one more time, as he argues in "Bergson and His Critique of Intellectualism," a spatially and cognitively "mosaic reality" is necessarily one of "intolerable intervals" that must be temporarily negotiated: "To get from one point to another we have to plough or wade through the whole intolerable interval. No detail is spared us, it is as bad as the barbed-wire complications at Port Arthur, and we grow old and die in the process."[24]

All of *The Killing of a Chinese Bookie* could be cited to illustrate what it feels like to have "to plough or wade through barbed-wire complications." Cassavetes works to complicate our reading process throughout *Bookie*. The progress of scenes is never telegraphed. In fact, their meaning is that meaning is not available in a telegraphic way – in a verbal statement, an establishing shot, a summarizing metaphor, or an abstract vision. Meaning is transmitted one bit at a time, with switches, swerves, and changes of direction. Like Cosmo's running off the freeway, then back on, then off again during the blowout scene, meaning is expressed with delays, mistakes, reconsiderations, and reversals of conclusion. Far from weeding them out, Cassavetes includes error and revision into his film. He celebrates them.[25]

In place of a logic of buildup, confrontation, climax, and resolution, Cassavetes offers a logic of postponement, elision, and anticlimax. After Cosmo unexpectedly succeeds in murdering "the heaviest man on the West Coast," he himself is set up for a Mob hit in a deserted warehouse. A hired gunman named Mickey stalks Cosmo with pistols blazing. He works methodically from room to room, closing off spaces behind him as he goes. In a four- or five-minute action sequence, Mickey gradually makes his way to the upper floor and the final room of the building. The tension mounts. We are apparently headed to an inevitable emotional and narrative climax as pointed and cathartic as the shoot-out in *Gunfight at the O.K. Corral*. A confrontation between Cosmo and Mickey is unavoidable. Or is it? In a shot that is so brief and so murky that it is almost impossible to make out what is going on, as Mickey shouts for Cosmo to come out and fight like a man, Cassavetes has Cosmo simply walk down the back stairs and out of the building. Mickey is left yelling into the darkness, blasting away into an empty room, not knowing that Cosmo isn't even there anymore. (Many viewers do not realize it either.)[26]

The entire movie consists of a similar series of nonevents and anticlimaxes. We want life to have crises and confrontations. We crave shoot-outs with winners and losers. We lust for apocalypse. But *Bookie* relentlessly frustrates our quest for eschatological ultimates and resolutions. Every time a clarifying or resolving moment seems about to occur, the film elides, confuses, or defers it.

As another example: Prior to his interrupted journey, Cosmo is ordered by the Mob to use his girls to seduce another target for a Mob hit. This bookie lives in Chinatown. Cassavetes cuts to Cosmo and the strippers in Chinatown the next day. We see them having a Coke at a restaurant, attending a movie together, and subsequently returning to the club. We naturally assume we are seeing them passing time before or after the assigned task, only to discover later on that neither Cosmo nor his girls ever visited the person they were sent to see. Cosmo's "action" (and his film's action) consists of *not* acting. He is ultimately forced to murder the Chinese godfather in the sequence I described only because he has managed to avoid doing anything else up to that point. Where other movies are driven by events, *Bookie* is organized around nonevents.

It's crucial to realize, however, that these nonevents in the eyes of the gangsters (and in the eyes of the reviewers who scoffed at the "slowness" of the film) are not in the least nonevents in Cassavetes' view. The most important moments in *Bookie* are, in fact, those when nothing is happening according to gangster and reviewer standards of eventfulness. In the middle of an action, Cassavetes (or Cosmo) will simply insert a pause: Cassavetes will put the narrative briefly on hold, or Gazzara will take a beat in his acting. These delays are among the most important expressive events in the film.[27]

Like Cosmo's stalling tactics in Chinatown, and Cassavetes' sidetracking of his movie's plot, they are only delays of the inevitable, but all the more important because it is inevitable. However doomed, they are registrations of resistance. However small and fleeting, they are declarations of independence. The Mob may control Cosmo's body. The film noir plot may dictate his actions and the events Cassavetes is ultimately committed to presenting sooner or later. But Cosmo's and his creator's consciousnesses are their own. The timing of it all is still open. The inevitable may be unavoidable, but *when* it comes is up to them. Timing may not be much, but it is everything; it is all they have left. Cosmo and Cassavetes show that even when one's actions are blocked and scripted in the most horrific and pre-destined way, an actor-director can still improvise an eccentric performance in the margins of the text. Needless to say, this is a different notion of performance than the Mob is prepared to appreciate. For them you either bump someone off or you don't. They function like most reviewers. They have an on–off, black–white sense of life. Your "contract" (narrative or gangland) entails a particular series of actions and events. Performative inflections, temporal retardations, and stylistic bendings don't exist. Cosmo and Cassavetes live in a more complex world than that, which is why neither the gangsters nor the reviewers had a clue what either was up to.

Life bizarrely imitated art in the making of *Bookie*. According to Al Ruban, who was one of the film's producers and who plays Marty Reitz, one of the goons who pressures Cosmo, on the evening designated for "shooting" the Chinaman (in both the cinematic and the murderous senses of the word), Cassavetes, like Cosmo delaying his appointment with destiny in Chinatown, took his crew out to a restaurant and kept putting off the time of the shoot. In Ruban's words: "John just didn't want to go through with it." It was only hours later, after Ruban badgered and pressured the filmmaker (just as Ruban's character does in the movie – life imitating art in this way as well), that Cassavetes reluctantly and halfheartedly went through the motions of an event his heart was not in, but which could not really be avoided if he was going to continue making his film. The point is that *Bookie*'s plot committed the filmmaker to a series of actions he would rather not have performed, in exactly the same way that the gangsters' plot committed Cosmo. And both responded identically: What could not be avoided could at least be postponed.[28]

To delay clarifications, postpone resolutions, and defer endpoints is a way of keeping possibilities open. That should help explain why Cassavetes wants moments in *Bookie* just slightly to resist comprehensibility. He wants to keep a viewer *not* knowing, because knowing is a limitation on possibility. For Cassavetes, as for Cosmo, in darkness and irresolution there is opportunity. When Cosmo shoots Mort (the gangster played by Seymour Cassel) in the warehouse, Cosmo slams the door of Mort's car at the same instant he pulls the trigger of his gun; at least that's what we figure out later. We are kept absolutely in the dark about what is going on. Neither Mickey nor a viewer even knows that Mort has been killed until after the fact. (Compare the way our knowledge of Cosmo's own gunshot wound is delayed.) The moment exists not only to allow Cosmo to demonstrate that he truly is a master of low-budget special effects (just as his hiding from Mickey in the scene following this one allows him to prove himself a master of low-budget lighting effects); even more important, it is a display of how Cosmo and Cassavetes control time. Even in the face of an event as definitive as death, Cosmo and his creator flaunt the fact that they can stylistically manipulate and slow down our interpretive process.

These moments of interpretive uncertainty remind us where we are. This is a world shrouded in darkness where nothing is obvious or certain. The visual world of *Bookie* is one of uncertain movements through inky darkness, murky passageways, and mysterious spaces. Cassavetes uses a moving, hand-held camera and cluttered sets to communicate the density and mystery of the spaces through which we and Cosmo pick our way. The lighting is either complete fill (in the dressing room scenes and Betty's house) or the lowest of low key (in the gangsters' car and the passageways leading to the lair of the Chinese godfather); but whether uniformly bright or dark, the effect is the same. In either case, by eliminating lighting accents Cassavetes denies us visual shortcuts. As is most emphatically demonstrated by the scene of Cosmo making his way through the undefined, twisting corridors of the house of the Chinese godfather, this is a world in which we must gingerly feel our way toward outcomes we can't possibly foresee.

Moreover, in this world, lights blind as much they illuminate; they threaten as much as they protect. One of the visual leitmotifs that runs

The shot Cassavetes did everything he could to delay shooting. The director is behind the camera shooting Cosmo; Cosmo is in front of it shooting the "bookie." The viewer is implicitly asked to compare the filmmaker's ability to resist the plot imposed on him by the film noir genre with Cosmo's ability to resist the plot imposed on him by the gangsters. While Cassavetes barely succeeds, his protagonist barely fails.

through *Bookie* is the positioning of the camera so that it is shooting into the light (rather than across it or with it, as most other films, including Cassavetes' own, usually do). The unconventional placement of the camera with respect to the light source captures a complex mix of feelings about cinematic and theatrical illusion. As a filmmaker and as an actor, Cassavetes knew that lights are silent partners to every actor's performance, sometimes working for and helping him, at other times working against and dooming him. Some of the lights facing the camera threaten Cosmo's life (like the gun firing into the camera at the godfather's house or the headlights of the cars coming at Cosmo during the blowout scene). Others save it (as when Cosmo uses his stage-trained knowledge of light and shadow in the warehouse scene to hide in the brightness). Cosmo's dapper appearances on his own stage (even at the end of the film, when he has a bullet in his side), like his cocky stroll up the stage-lighted driveway of the godfather's house, show that he is a master of working the lights.

There is nevertheless another side to this issue. That Cassavetes calls our attention to the lights in these scenes and others reminds us how much everything we are seeing consists of artistic illusions – sometimes Cosmo's, sometimes his creator's. In terms of Cosmo's life, Cassavetes makes us aware that the events he appears in are almost all entirely staged. Cosmo is always onstage, never more than when he is offstage. But beyond that, the presence of lights in many of the shots reminds us that we are watching a *movie*, a movie created with lights and cameras that is itself a series of staged effects.[29]

The effect is a complex, double one: Sometimes it seems to discredit the reality of what we are seeing, as, for example, during Cosmo's pep talk about "comfort" when Cassavetes (or is it Cosmo?) positions the light so that we can see it the whole time Cosmo bathetically holds forth. The lights tell us that the theatrical set speech *is* a theatrical set speech. We are made skeptical about the "special effects" we witness in the same way we were made skeptical about Lelia's or Ben's theatrical effects in *Shadows*. At other times the visibility of the lighting seems a celebration of how imaginative bendings of reality through special effects are available everywhere. For example, Cosmo's performance under the lights in the warehouse almost convinces us that the whole world *is* a kind of stage for theatrical illusions. Cassavetes' goal is not (as in Godard or Altman) to disillusion us or to rob illusion of its power, but rather (as in late Renoir or Rivette) to remind us both of art's illusionistic magic and of the boundaries of that illusion. We need theatricality, beauty, and imagination, but we can't use our fictions to deny or displace actual bodies and lived realities either.

In this illusionistic meditation on the wonders and limits of illusion, it is fitting that many of the "spaces" Cosmo moves through and past in the film were themselves "special effects"; they don't exist outside of the cinematic experience. Though Cassavetes set virtually all of his preceding works within one or two specific, actual locations (in *A Woman Under the Influence*, the Longhetti house was a real, rented house; in *Faces*, the house of Richard and Maria Forst was Cassavetes' own, and the apartment of Jeannie Rapp was his mother-in-law's; in *Opening Night*, the theater and hotel were a real theater and hotel), in *Bookie*, with the exception of the nightclub (which was an actual, but now defunct club called Gazzari's), virtually all of the other spaces are synthetic. For example, the stage-lighted driveway Cosmo walks up to reach "the bookie's" house is actually miles away from the location of the house. The guard house is not even in the same city as the house it is supposed to be guarding. Cassavetes imaginatively bends and warps space, creating mysterious, eccentrically distorted imaginative spaces where there are no actual worldly places.

The most mysterious space of all, of course, is the black hole called Cosmo. A viewer is left attempting to read a blank slate in many of the scenes. Why does Cosmo perform the Mob hit? What alternatives does he consider and reject? Does he really think he is going to live to tell about it? Does he believe the absurdities he preaches about "comfortableness" near the end of the film? Cosmo's blending of theater and reality makes it impossible to say where "he" is in all of the costuming and posing. As is said about Hollywood, once you've learned to fake sincerity, you've got it made; and Cosmo seems to have genuinely lost the capacity to tell the difference between stage effects and life. His four curtain-closing speeches (to Flo in the warehouse on what it means to be "a pro"; to Betty at her house about "rivers"; to his strippers in their dressing room on "comfortableness"; and to his club audience on "beauty") are sheer Bovarism. Cosmo is not only talking to others in order to cheer them up; he is also talking to cheer himself up. He can no longer tell the difference between rhetoric and reality. Like a bad politician or Hollywood "actor" (or a politician-actor), he apparently believes his own press releases and campaign speeches. That is why, in this deep view of Los Angeles, there is no "there" there. There is no one inside Cosmo's costume, behind his voice. The mask has become the face. He has become a series of disembodied stage effects. He erases himself in acts of conspicuous theatricality. Cosmo's acts of self-protective camouflage are acts of self-destruction.[30]

The difference between Cosmo and Cassavetes as artists is summarized in that whereas Cosmo devotes his life to keeping up his guard, to polishing his patina of unflappable cool, Cassavetes devoted his to breaking down protective veneers and exposing realms of weakness, uncertainty, and confusion. It was ironically fitting that the few reviewers who had anything at all good to say about *The Killing of a Chinese Bookie* chose to praise the "restraint" of the performance of Gazzara/Cosmo (as contrasted with what they had considered to be the over-the-top excessiveness of Gena Rowlands/ Mabel Longhetti, for example). The only problem was that this missed the entire point of *Bookie* (and of Cassavetes' other work as well). No filmmaker was more opposed to performative coolness (in actors and characters). For Cassavetes, emotional poise and the desire to stay in control were the enemies of discovery. *Shadows*'s Tony and Ben are cool; *Faces*'s McCarthy, Forst, Louise, and Billy Mae stay emotionally in control; *Minnie and Moskowitz*'s Jim is cool – in fact, he breaks off his relationship with Minnie when it threatens to get too hot; *Love Streams*'s Robert Harmon is unflappable and poised to a fault.[31] Cassavetes regards the coolness of these characters under fire not as a positive achievement, but as figuring a state of emotional derangement.

The virtues of the five decades of he-man cinema from Humphrey Bogart to Clint Eastwood are vices in Cassavetes' work. Cassavetes is enthusiastically in favor of Seymour's emotional extravagances in *Minnie and Moskowitz*, of Mabel's pitch of desperation in *Woman*, of Myrtle Gordon's refusal to compromise or accept her situation in *Opening Night*, and of Sarah Lawson's bet-everything-on-love daring in *Love Streams*. In Cassavetes' own words, the countess's virtue in *Husbands* was that "she is *not* cool." The basic premise of *Husbands* itself is that three men's attempts to stay "cool" are salutarily disrupted.[32] Florence's virtue in *Faces* is that "she tries everything and doesn't care how ridiculous and pathetic it looks."[33] Cassavetes was always in favor of characters who took expressive risks and opposed to those who didn't. In taking real chances and risking undesirable outcomes there is possibility.

For Cassavetes, our attempts to stay safe and comfortable are what prevent us from being truly safe and comfortable. Real development and growth come only from plunging into our places of danger and discomfort, which he often said was the secret of great acting as well. Like Nick Longhetti, Cosmo cares too much about looking ridiculous or pathetic to avoid being ridiculous and pathetic. Like *Love Streams*'s Robert Harmon, he is ultimately doomed by his attempt to play it safe. Caution is the only real danger, risk the only way onward for all of Cassavetes' greatest characters. We have to take enormous chances, risk terrible losses, and gamble everything (like the highest of high rollers, never risking more than when we are down in our luck and on the verge of losing everything), in order to gain anything.

"Gambling" is a resonant metaphor in Cassavetes' work in both the emotional and the financial senses.[34] Scenes of gambling or betting occur in *Too Late Blues*, *Husbands*, *The Killing of a Chinese Bookie*, and *Love Streams*. Even more important, each of Cassavetes' major characters are asked to take emotional gambles at crucial points in their films: Lelia, Maria Forst, and Minnie Moore each take a chance on love in opening themselves to new lovers after suffering with old ones; Gus, Harry, and Archie are asked to take chances by breaking their patterns of life; and, most gloriously of all, Mabel, Myrtle, and Sarah actually do risk everything in their attempt to stay true to their feelings, rather than making deals and accepting safer bets in which less would be at stake. These characters live on the edge and pay the price in anxiety and uncertainty, but they also reap the benefits of risking it all. What we stand to gain is what William James called "novelty." If we dare to gamble, we make real, fresh opportunities possible that wouldn't have existed otherwise. Sarah meets Ken (in *Love Streams*) and Minnie meets Seymour (in *Minnie and Moskowitz*) only because both dare to take real chances with their lives.

What Cassavetes' view of life takes, above all, is effort and work. William James summarized the "strenuousness" of a life lived in this precarious state of possibility in "The Absolute and the Strenuous Life":

> [The world of pluralism] is always vulnerable, for some part of it may go astray; and having no "eternal" edition of it to draw comfort from, its partisans must always feel to some degree insecure.... The pragmatism or pluralism which I defend has to fall back on a certain ultimate hardihood, a certain willingness to live without assurances or guarantees.[35]

Art and life are never separate in Cassavetes' mind. Cosmo's personal timidity and conservatism are linked with his escapist impulses as a Sternbergian (or Disneyesque) artist. His fear of emotional involvements, his dislike of arguments, in short, his cowardice in life is inextricable from his escapism in art.

It should be obvious that there are profound similarities between *The Killing of a Chinese Bookie* and *Citizen Kane*. Cassavetes' film is a conscious remake of Welles's. Cosmo is a working-class reincarnation of Kane, a man attempting to stage-manage his life and live out an American dream of self-reliant self-sufficiency. Xanadu and the Crazy Horse are both monuments to their creators' Coleridgean ideals of imaginative autonomy; and, like Coleridge's Xanadu, both end up being mausoleums commemorating the death of their dreams. Both Welles and Cassavetes suggest that their respective protagonists' Romantic ideals are deluded and dooming. To that extent the two films might be said to share common values.

As a ten-second comparison of the actual viewing experience of the two movies suffices to demonstrate, however, the differences between *The Killing of a Chinese Bookie* and *Citizen Kane* ultimately loom much larger than the similarities. To put it simply, Welles is a lot more like Cosmo (and his own Kane) than like Cosmo's creator. Welles is in love with beauty and artifice; Cassavetes distrusts them. Welles is enchanted with imaginative transformations of reality and seduced by special effects; Cassavetes is deeply skeptical of both.

That is to say, there is an artistic contradiction at the center of Welles's movie. Even as he pretends to be criticizing Kane, Welles does the same thing in his movie that Kane does in his life: He relentlessly "processes" and "packages" experience so that it will reflect grandiose imaginative meanings. In the deepest view of *Citizen Kane*, it is impossible to distinguish the character from the director: Both are equally convinced that as long as an experience is wrapped in a thousand layers of glitzy acoustic and visual packaging, rough-edged, gawky, clumsy truth will never have to be dealt with. To put it in concrete terms, what Kane does to Susan Alexander in the opera production is no different from what Welles does to her and to every other character and experience in his entire movie.

Welles *is* Kane in senses he could not have intended, and his movie is as much a Xanadu as Kane's retreat is. Welles is as addicted to crafting a self-contained, self-justifying, self-referential imaginative world in his film as Kane is in his life. Welles is as devoted to substituting P. T. Barnum hype, cartoon characterizations, stylistic razzle-dazzle, and empty rhetoric for truth in his cinematic style as Kane is in his personal life, his run for political office, and his newspaper career. Welles is as much the Faustian information manager and manipulator of meaning in his direction as Kane is as a human being. Welles is as convinced as Kane that Spielbergian special effects and carnival showmanship can displace awkward realities.

In short, although *Kane* pretends to criticize the excesses of capitalistic arrangements and manipulations in its content, it collaborates with them in its form. The style of *Citizen Kane* is an extension of the value system of MTV and *Advertising Age*, not an alternative to it. As a filmmaker, Welles sells his soul to a public relations attempt to let rhetoric do the work of truth as completely as Kane did as a newspaper man. The values Welles pretends to indict, he in fact enthusiastically participates in. After all, life, art, journalism, show business – it's all the same thing, isn't it?[36]

It goes without saying that all of this defines a decisive difference from Cassavetes' film. *Bookie* criticizes PR forms of human relationship without collapsing into PR forms of presentation. It points out the limitations of capitalistic forms of processing and packaging without repeating them in its form. It shows the utter fatuousness of Cosmo's quest for contentless stylishness, charm, and elegance without itself playing the same game in its visual and acoustic effects. In brief, Cassavetes is far more radical and more thoroughgoing in his critique of American Romanticism than Welles is. He gives us an art devoid of gorgeousness. (The only beauties we find in *Bookie* are "terrible," in Yeats's sense of the word.) He embraces an art that repudiates special effects and stylistic dazzle. He presents an art that turns away from rhetoric to embrace truth. He declines to allow us to retreat from the untidiness of reality into a world of grandly coherent imaginative resonances. He offers us an art that does not even aspire toward clear, harmonious, grandiloquent meanings.

As his political rally indicates, Kane would love the style of his own film (even if he might have problems with its satiric point). Cosmo would hate his movie's style. Cassavetes has an entirely different conception of art than that of his character. Cosmo's creator refuses to do what Cosmo's art is devoted to – lofting his audience into a world of abstract significances and visionary relations. Cassavetes forces us to live in provisionality, concreteness, and muddle. The form and style of presentation, the effects that compose *Bookie*, teach us how to make the most of a mess, not how to rise above it.

It is essential to Cosmo's conception of art that it takes place in an imaginative realm cordoned off from the ordinary lives of his audience. It is set up on a stage off to one side of life and slightly above it. Like sculpture before Duchamp or painting before Pollock, Cosmo's art is lifted off the ground and surrounded by air. Its meanings are clear and definitive in a way life's never are. The stories it presents are disconnected from ordinary experience and governed by special rules that obtain only within the magic circle. In short, Cosmo's conception of art (like that of Kane or Welles) is what passes nowadays for an "advanced" one. Like the art of formalist film critics, it is premised on the belief in a gap separating artistic from ordinary language, and on the absolute distinctiveness of the forms and styles that structure the artistic experience. It continues the world-forsaking, body-renouncing, physicality-denying tradition of Pater, Tennyson, and Woolf.

Cassavetes' own view of art is the opposite, so it is not surprising that he attacks forms of artistic marginalization in all of his work. In *Bookie*, whereas Cosmo wants to keep his audience's attention on what happens onstage, Cassavetes takes viewers backstage and upstairs into the strippers' dressing room (and into their homes to meet their families) to reveal the evasions of the onstage fictions, the frayed seams in the apparent seamlessness of narrative. Everything that the gorgeous arrangements of conventional narrative suppress, all of the emotional complications that our public and our private fictions leave out, are what Cassavetes devotes himself to bringing to light. *Opening Night*, his next film, will be almost entirely set in the backstage space we only glance into here. The entire movie will be devoted to anthologizing what does *not* get on stage. The context is restored to the text. Cassavetes raises the curtain to reveal what is hidden or repressed in the name of art – giving us a peek behind the scenes, letting us glimpse the personal sacrifices and agonies of which beautiful effects are made.

Cosmo of all people should know better than to think that art can be some kind of purely imaginative game played apart from life. All the while his artistry is devoted to creating an enchanted theatrical realm freed from the pressures and confusions of life, his own life is demonstrating the impossibility of walling out pressure and confusion. If nothing else did, the fact that he dates and sleeps with his actresses should show him that art and life are inevitably in bed with each other. The realms are stimulatingly confused in his own life, even as he attempts to deny it.

That is why every time that Cosmo, his art, and his characters attempt to hide behind the theatrical "fourth wall," Cassavetes batters it down. He deliberately destroys the illusion of illusion. He has Mr. Sophistication get into arguments with the audience, the audience kibitz with the actors on-stage, and Cosmo get heckled onstage by his club patrons. In the most general sense of the concept, all of Cassavetes' work might be said to be about breaking down the transparent wall that is usually thought to separate art from life. For Cassavetes, art does not define a world unto itself. Its rules are not different from the rules of life. Characters and works are not set in (or made in) Hollywood's fantasy island, but in real streets, real homes, and real nightclubs. But even if we don't respond to that, the emotional intensity of Cassavetes' work makes it impossible for a viewer to hold it at arm's length emotionally or imaginatively. We can't watch it as escapist entertainment. Every shot and scene is an attempt to reach into viewers' lives and to encourage viewers to reach into the work for ways of understanding.[37]

As an artist, Cassavetes went in the opposite direction than did Cosmo: not trying to screen out worldly accidents, contingencies, and particularities, but rather finding ways to use them expressively. He put his actors' expressive idiosyncrasies under the lights rather than trying to erase them. For him and his actors, art was not an escape from life but an extension of it. It was a means of thinking about and working through life's problems. The subjects of art are quarried from life's concerns, and the forms and structures of artistic experience are embodiments of the forms and structures of non-artistic life. We must find our salvation and our art must find its truths, not in a realm of clarity and beauty above and beyond the world, but in the uncertainty and resistance of negotiating the same sorts of problems that we encounter in everyday life.

Cassavetes' reply to Sternbergian and Wellesian conceptions of art as a realm governed by different rules from life. The gaffes of Mr. Sophistication and the strippers and their kibitzing with the audience break down the walls that separate life from art, and blur the line between the scripted and the unscripted.

Needless to say, this is not an easy form of art for audiences or critics to appreciate. Cassavetes' artistic pragmatism makes demands that more intellectual art does not. *Bookie* is much harder to enjoy (or understand) than *Citizen Kane*. Its meanings are much more elusive and slippery. It is murkier and less clear than *Kane*. Like Cosmo or Kane, we all crave clarity and resolution. We prefer abstractions to perceptions, static truths to moving ones. We resist the educational process; but if we truly open ourselves to the experience Cassavetes provides, we may, almost against our wills, just learn to live in a world of in-betweenness, uncertainty, and irresolution.

Cassavetes tells us that we must learn to live through the whole damn mess (the "barbed-wire complications"), rather than aspiring to skip from point to point intellectually. We must learn to function in states of not-knowing. We must give up our lust for resolutions and answers and learn to accept movement and change. We must admit the limitations of the life of the mind and the imagination, and acknowledge the complicating richness of the body and the senses. We must make what sense we can of experience taking one baby step at a time, feeling our way through the dark, never able to see beyond the present moment. The very things that Cosmo's life and art are devoted to denying, Cassavetes' style brings into robust existence.

6

Compositions and Decompositions

Love Streams

Nothing interests us which is stark or bounded, but only what streams with life, which is in act or endeavor to reach somewhat beyond.... Beauty is the moment of transition, as if the form were just ready to flow into other forms. Any fixedness ... is the reverse of the flowing, and therefore deformed.... To this streaming or flowing belongs the beauty that all circular movement has; as, the circulation of waters, the circulation of the blood, the periodical motion of planets, the annual wave of vegetation, the action and reaction of Nature; and, if we follow it out, this demand in our thought for an ever-onward action, is the argument for the immortality.   – R. W. Emerson[1]

The universe is like Father Ocean, a stream of all things slowly moving. We move, and the rock of ages moves. And since we move and move for ever, in no discernible direction, there is no centre to the movement, to us. To us, the centre shifts at every moment. Even the pole-star ceases to sit on the pole. *Allons!* There is no road before us! ... Each thing streams in its own odd, intertwining flux, and nothing ... is fixed or abiding. All moves. And nothing is true, or good, or right, except in its own living relatedness to its own circumambient universe; to the things that are in the stream with it.... We should ask for no absolutes, or absolute. Once and for all and for ever, let us have done with the ugly imperialism of any absolute. There is no absolute good, there is nothing absolutely right. All things flow and change, and even change is not absolute. The whole is a strange assembly of apparently incongruous parts slipping past one another.   – D. H. Lawrence[2]

Cassavetes' final film, *Love Streams*, was shot in the summer of 1983 and given a limited American release in the autumn of 1984.[3] The two main characters are a writer named Robert Harmon (played by the filmmaker) and a recently divorced woman named Sarah Lawson (played by Gena Rowlands). For the first half of the film their situations and personalities seem unrelated, and the narrative jumps between their independent stories. However, not only do Robert and Sarah's destinies become narratively intertwined in the second half of the film, but the success of *Love Streams* can be measured by the extent to which at some point in the second hour it gradually dawns on the viewer that, in effect, Robert and Sarah figure the same imaginative problem viewed through opposite ends of the telescope. They are brother and sister in a far deeper than biological sense.[4]

By worldly standards, Robert and Sarah are opposites. He is a rich, famous writer, ensconced in a hilltop mansion, surrounded with fawning, beautiful women, and apparently able to buy (or take) anything he wants.[5] Sarah, in contrast, has everything that matters to her taken away from her shortly after the film begins. Her marriage reaches a shattering end in a contested divorce and her one remaining intimate relationship (with her teenage daughter) comes unglued when her former husband is awarded custody. At forty-something, she is bewilderingly on her own, bereft of friends and accomplishments. As far as she is concerned, after twenty years of marriage she has nothing to show for her life.

In summary, one might say that while Robert is on top of the world, Sarah's has self-destructed; but that represents a superficial analysis of their situation. To a deeper reading, Robert and Sarah figure closely related states of personal crisis. Sarah's deeper problem is summarized by the fact that when she loses her husband and daughter, she feels that she has and is nothing. She defines herself so completely in terms of her relations with others that she has no "I" distinct from the identities they grant her. She is a lot like Mabel. She needs others to be herself; yet, in another sense, she has no self even when she is with others, since she only echoes their responses to her, their opinions of her. As her dreams and fantasies demonstrate, Sarah exists even in her own imagination of herself only insofar as her image is reflected off of others. *Minnie and Moskowitz* used film clips to show us how we can lose ourselves to various forms of cultural processing; *Love Streams* uses "clips" of Sarah's fantasy life to demonstrate that the problem is not with Hollywood, but with us. The point, *pace* Godard, is that films are only a symptom, not a cause; the movies don't create our problems, and they can't solve them. We get into trouble because of our need for love and approval. Sarah, Mabel, and Cosmo show that we can lose track of who we are even if Bogart and Bergman had never existed.

In a promiscuity of love, Sarah gives herself away, energetically dispersing herself in attempts to be what others want her to be. She tries so hard to please others that she loses track of who she really is and what she really wants or needs. (At a moment of crisis late in the film, she significantly confesses: "I don't know who I am.") She needs others to validate her existence, to tell her who she is. That is why, faced with the disintegration of her marriage and her relationship with her daughter, she flails out at anyone and everyone in sight to whip up instant, new self-defining relationships: at first attempting to reestablish the old connections with her daughter and former husband; failing at that, attempting to conjure magical new intimacies out of thin air with everyone she meets.

No matter how different he seems on the surface, Robert figures a related crisis of identity. While Sarah gives herself away, he hides himself away. While she plunges into groups and crowds in an attempt to find herself, to lay claim to some self that she feels is lacking when she is on her own, he withdraws from groups in a felt need to protect some central part of himself from predation and visibility. The specific form Robert's flight from emotional exposure takes is a withdrawal behind a wall of witty one-liners and endearing winks and nods. As the punning resonances of his last name suggest, Robert specializes in harmonizing harmonies. He is a charmer, a smiling master of public and private ceremonies who turns his life into a series of crowd-pleasing performances. Yet, insofar as he is never "in" any of the roles he plays, Robert's oh-so-dapperly costumed presence is a de facto absence. The more affably present Robert is in a group, the more emotionally missing in action he actually is. Conspicuous visibility is the ultimate cloak of darkness – as is the case also with Cosmo and his strippers, who are most completely hidden within their roles at the moments that they seem most revealed.[6]

Having failed disastrously in his previous relationships, Harmon runs away from any involvement that requires more than style, wit, and the sexual good manners of a one-night stand – the etiquette of the eighties for someone who has confused "the *Playboy* Philosophy" with a philosophy of life. Harmon sleeps with women, but two at a time if possible, and the younger and more in awe of him they are, the better for him to maintain his critical distance. The one sort of closeness he does pursue – which takes the form of a quest for a woman's "secret" – is a travesty of authentic intimacy. It is closer to being something gleaned from *How to Pick Up Girls* than an opportunity for two people to open themselves to one another.

Cassavetes makes a viewer appreciate that even when Robert thinks he is baring his soul to a woman and probing the secrets of her life, he is actually only shuffling through crowd-pleasing formulas in order not to have to risk the emotional demands of conducting a two-way conversation with anyone. Even in his most intimate relationships with women he only cycles through singles' bar pickup routines and canned one-liners.[7] Harmon is so boyishly charming that it is almost impossible to dislike him; but it becomes increasingly clear in the first hour or so that charm, never sufficient as an end in itself in any case, is his way of holding emotional commitments and vulnerabilities at arm's length.

If Sarah is related to Mabel and Gloria, Robert is Cosmo with an Ivy League degree. Cosmo used his nightclub to hide from life; Harmon uses his mansion and his role as a "writer." All the while that he acts open and candid he emotionally shuts himself off from everyone around him. Though he thinks nothing of asking others to bare their souls to him, Harmon never directly reveals anything about himself and his feelings to others. It is significant that, again like Cosmo, Robert's most complex and revealing expressions of himself occur not in the actions or words he presents to his various audiences, but in a private, secret grammar of nervous tics and pauses, eccentric gestures, jerky movements, silent body language, and protracted, unspoken interior monologues.

As exemplified by the scene in which he interviews Joannie, or when he makes a research trip to a gay bar, Robert wants his "raw" experience only when it is stylishly served up under glass with all the trimmings but no real substance. It is not accidental that most of both Cosmo's and Robert's scenes consist of various instances of costuming and packaging the self, physically, emotionally, and theatrically. As the filmmaker described him in an interview: "With no family, no roots, all he has to hold him together is style. Style is all a guy like this ends up depending on." Like Cosmo (and like some film critics), Robert thinks that visual style can replace emotional content. Though Robert is physically uncomfortable in the gay nightclub, Cassavetes makes us realize that he is really imaginatively at home there insofar as it is a realm of masquerade and theater.[8]

In his expressive disillusionment, he has turned all of life into a cynical "game." He believes in nothing and no one, only in playing the game to his advantage. Like the formalist critic who reduces films to contentless "intertextual relations" and "diegetic strategies" (or the Hollywood producer or pop culture analyst who treats works of art as permutations of high-concept formulas), Robert has learned the superficial lessons of deconstruction: that emotions are just words, that love is a game adults play, that truth doesn't exist, and that (as Cassavetes once tersely summarized this attitude) "everything is horseshit." Even his art is insincere. Robert is a novelist who, in his own cynical and jaded formulation, "writes down all the pain and makes money out of it."[9]

If one needed conclusive evidence to confirm Robert and Sarah's mutual inadequacies in the mind of this family filmmaker, it would be the disarray of the communities of intimacy and caring around each of them. They are both cut off from families, feverishly attempting to build substitute families of ersatz relationships, yet failing even at that. The family with which Sarah would forcibly reunite herself (her daughter and divorced husband) doesn't want her, and indeed exists as a family only in her soap-opera imagination of it; and the "family" of pets that she brings to Robert's house is no family at all. In any case, Robert, on his part, doesn't need her animals because he already has his own family of pets long before Sarah shows up. The surrogate mothers and imitation daughters and wives (made up mainly of teenage groupies) Robert gathers around himself to replace the biological families he has repudiated is only another kind of petting zoo. For Robert, women function less as equals than as cuddly "chickies" (to hug and keep him warm), hookers (with whom he can use money and power to control the limits of his involvement), and housekeepers (to clean up the physical and emotional messes he makes of his affairs). As far as being a real father to Albie goes, Robert is too much of a little boy himself to function as a parent.

With two exceptions, there are no truly mature, loving relationships between adults and children in all of *Love Streams*. The interchanges between Susan and her child, and between the Las Vegas chambermaid and Albie, are the only examples of genuine intimacy and caring between an adult and a child in the entire movie. It is significant that neither Robert nor Sarah is present at either moment.

Love Streams is a summarizing work in Cassavetes' oeuvre, and putting it in its proper context requires a few observations about the meaning of his career. All of his work is premised upon the vexed relation of the individual imagination to the practical forms of expression available to it. Faced with a problematic, painful, or difficult act of translation from impulses to expressions, Cassavetes' characters develop various strategies of response.

Some of them, especially the male characters, attempt to finesse the whole problem. They attempt to avoid the pain and difficulty of this challenging process by "canning" their identities, expressions, behavior, and relationships. *Shadows*'s Bennie, *Faces*'s businessmen and suburban housewives, *Husbands*'s Archie, *Minnie and Moskowitz*'s Morgan, Jim, and Zelmo, *Bookie*'s Cosmo, *Opening Night*'s Sarah Goode, and *Love Streams*'s Robert all try to "package" the self into a fixed expressive routine. They close down their definitions of themselves and shut off their sensitivities. They prefer predictability to exploration, and safety to growth, even if it means shutting out the whole world and closing their emotions off from everyone in it.

Robert is the culmination of this tendency. It's been said that from Shakespeare to Beckett the greatest artists really create only one work and a small group of characters over and over again, and it might be said of Cassavetes as well. Even if he wasn't aware of it, his imagination was clearly possessed by a few pet themes and metaphors that pop up throughout the films with the obsessiveness and consistency of the images in a recurring dream. Almost every aspect of Robert's personality and behavior can be found in an earlier film. His champagne, tuxedos, and crystal goblets echo Cosmo's boutonniered nattiness, his limousines, corsages, and Dom Perignon, as well as the tuxedos the dapper Americans wear in *Husbands*. Moreover, the way characters in all three films "script" their actions and use theatrical costumes and props to prop up the wounded, vulnerable self, to stage-manage change and danger, is really only an upscale variation on the way Bennie uses his leather jacket, sunglasses, and beat-generation gestures in *Shadows*. Robert's pursuit of one-night stands is related both to Bennie's cruising for pickups and to the "momentary relationships" *Faces*'s businessmen and *Husbands*'s husbands quest after. Even Robert's fist fights have their parallels in earlier films: They are expressively equivalent to Bennie's, McCarthy's, Zelmo's, and Jim's forms of interaction.

As different as these various behaviors might seem, costuming the self, cruising for girls, and getting into fist fights are all ways of keeping one's identity and relationships in the realm of the predictable, the patterned, and the superficial. They are ways of avoiding genuine self-exposure, self-revision, or self-examination. Whether you fight with someone, sleep with them in a one-night quickie, or retreat into a theatrical role, you won't have to open yourself to them in genuine intimacy or risk letting them discover who you really are. You (and they) can play out a well-defined part in a fixed script. You will never have to take off your mask, your makeup, or your character. You will never have to break your pattern and improvise a truly creative response to life.

Silence and stillness are other ways Cassavetes' characters insulate themselves from the perils of emotional exploration. At moments in *Love Streams*, Robert resembles no one so much as Bennie, Maria Forst, Harry, Minnie Moore, Cosmo Vitelli, or Dorothy Victor – sitting off to the side of a group, cocooned in a blanket of silence, taking refuge in a state of self-imposed exile. Fleeing from the dangers of sexual and emotional warfare, he and each of these others withdraw into a Switzerland of the imagination, a neutral ice kingdom where they make no alliances, ask no one for help, and provide none to anyone. While Cassavetes asks them to unbutton their identities and open themselves up to uncontrolled, unformulated experience, these characters limit what they are willing to allow themselves to feel or know. Feeling betrayed or compromised by the systems of expression around them, they drop out of the game. They are American skeptics with a long and venerable heritage in American film, painting, and literature.[10]

Contrasted with this group of characters in terrified or bewildered flight from vulnerability, erecting walls around themselves in self-defense against the dangers of self-disclosure, is a group of predominantly female characters in many of the same films: *Shadows*'s Lelia, *Faces*'s Florence and Jeannie Rapp, *A Woman Under the Influence*'s Mabel, *Opening Night*'s Myrtle, and Sarah Lawson in *Love Streams*. (The half-out-of-control Harry in *Husbands* is a male relation to them, but one who doesn't go quite as far as they do.) What differentiates them from the other group is that, in various ways and to various degrees, they live an adventure of ontological openness, breaking away from the formulated self, leaving fixed roles, identities, and styles of expression behind.[11]

Opening up one's identity so radically involves a complex double movement that blurs the edges of the self and the boundaries between self and other. On the one hand, these characters aspire to become perfectly expressive (proliferating themselves outward away from any limiting unitary self in waves of passion and imagination); on the other, they aspire to become perfectly responsive (incorporating others' needs and feelings in their performances). In both respects, they move the self beyond individual selfhood, merging themselves with others and merging others with themselves. They knock down the walls of the self and make their identities fluidly responsive to ebbs and flows of energies, both those that originate inside themselves and those outside. The self becomes only a kind of permeable membrane through which impulses pass in both directions. Endlessly offering and receiving intimacies, it shows itself capable of energetically reforming itself in multiple, shifting identities. To change the metaphor, the self becomes an open-ended conduit. It is no longer a package of attributes, but a line of fluid communication back and forth, in and out.

However, open-ended selfhood creates problems of its own, which is why some of these figures – Lelia, Jeannie, and Florence, for example – ultimately withdraw from the dangers of radical openness. They daringly open themselves up at moments, but then step back from the abyss that looms in front of them in fear of losing control of themselves. Only Mabel, Myrtle, and Sarah Lawson truly embrace the adventure of ontological open-endedness and fully face the dangers of such a state. In opening up the self so tenderly to influences from without and within, these characters risk losing track of who they are and what they want. In allowing the currents of the universe to flow so freely through them, they flirt with allowing others to dictate their definitions of themselves. Their state is as risky as it is stimulating. These characters gain a self at the risk of giving it up. Self-annihilation and self-realization blur together. Mabel, Myrtle, and Sarah walk an ontological tightrope between self-creation and self-destruction.

The deepest lesson of Cassavetes' work is that the creativity of these characters is absolutely inseparable from the almost unending pain they are subjected to and the misunderstanding they meet with. Their susceptibility to breakdown is inextricably intertwined with their capacity for creative responsiveness. The emotional vulnerability and ontological fragility are precisely what make them so gloriously responsive, sensitive, and creative. Mabel, Myrtle, and Sarah direct our gaze at the streaming boundary where the compositions and decompositions of our imaginative lives meet – where our strength is our weakness, where our emotional vulnerabilities and imaginative susceptibilities are transmuted into performative power.

There is one final, small group of characters in Cassavetes' work for which I haven't yet accounted: *Faces*'s Chet, *Husbands*'s Gus, and *Minnie and Moskowitz*'s Seymour. In their expressive experimentation and self-exposure they resemble the preceding group, yet they are not radically open (which is to say, out of control) in the way Louise, Lelia, Jeannie, Florence, Mabel, Myrtle, and Sarah intermittently are. Their self-awareness about their iconoclasm and the world's resistance to it allows the three earlier characters to take one step backward from the less self-conscious exposure of the three late characters; Chet, Gus, and Seymour are in control of their openness as Mabel, Myrtle, and Sarah Lawson generally are not. They use it rather than being used by it. The performances they give are exciting and eccentric but not crazy. Seymour Moskowitz, for example, is delightfully zany, but he isn't in danger the way Mabel is. He can be theoretical about his nuttiness (as she can't be), because it is always to some extent under his control. He rides it; it doesn't ride him.

It's fair to wonder where Cassavetes stands in this gallery of creations. In obvious ways, he has something in common with the final group insofar as his very ability to create these different figures demonstrates that he is not unselfconsciously captive to these stances. As an artist, Cassavetes is emphatically *not* careening out of control in the way Mabel, Myrtle, or Sarah Lawson are. He is artistically in control of his effects, similar to the way in which Moskowitz, Chet, or Gus are in control of their social effects. So in a sense, if we look for Cassavetes in his work, we might be said to

Playing games with your identity: Cassavetes momentarily becomes a gun-moll as he shows Gena Rowlands how to fight for her life in *Gloria*.

find him more in the two male characters played by Seymour Cassel and the one played by himself than in the three female characters played by Gena Rowlands.

All that seems beyond argument, yet it would be inappropriate to have that be the final word on the subject, not only because Mabel, Myrtle, and Sarah Lawson are far more profound creations than Gus, Chet, and Moskowitz, but also, and more important, because the states of ontological anxiety and expressive extremity of Rowlands's characters clearly seem to come from a deeper place in Cassavetes' soul than do the more controlled expressions of the three male characters – just as Cleopatra, Hamlet, or Lear clearly take us deeper into Shakespeare's mind than imaginatively related figures like Falstaff, Prince Hal, or Bottom. Moskowitz is entertaining, but he's really not very deep. Even within his own film, Minnie might be said to take us into deeper imaginative water. In *Faces*, Chet is expressively daring and wonderful, but Richard and Maria (and even, arguably, Florence) are more complex and profound imaginative creations. The unmistakable conclusion is that it was the desperate, the out-of-control, half-crazy characters (and not the merely zany ones like Moskowitz or the poised and in-control ones like Chet) that were closest to Cassavetes' heart and that take us most profoundly into his consciousness. In short, if we seek to find the deepest soul of the artist in his art, it seems clear that we should begin by looking at Mabel, Myrtle, and Sarah.

Or perhaps the best way to think of Cassavetes as an artist is as unstably alternating between the qualities of the two groups of figures. At times, he obviously was able to attain the diacritical perspective and poise of Moskowitz and Chet; at other times he was just as obviously as "crazily" exposed and passionately out of control as Sarah, Myrtle, or Mabel. Complicating the question is the insistence of a number of the filmmaker's closest friends and colleagues that as far as they could tell, Cassavetes felt none of Mabel's, Myrtle's, or Sarah's insecurities, vulnerabilities, or pain, and had nothing in common with them. As an example, when I suggested even the slightest connection between Cassavetes and his glorious, tortured protagonists to Al Ruban, he angrily rejected the idea. In Ruban's personal assessment, Cassavetes was made of brass. He never exposed himself or made himself vulnerable to being hurt. He was completely indifferent to criticism. He never doubted himself, and never wanted or needed others' approval. In Ruban's words: "John was *never* depressed, sad, or discouraged. He just didn't care what anyone else thought, and never let *anything* get to him. To say anything else is a slander on his life." My own personal impression of him (admittedly based on much more limited contact) was different. But putting aside personal impressions, on the basis of the films themselves, it seems inconceivable to me that there were not powerful imaginative and emotional connections between Cassavetes and these figures – as inconceivable as that the creator of Cleopatra, Hamlet, and Lear never personally felt any of their midnight despairs, vulnerabilities, self-doubts, and pains. However, given the vehemence of Ruban's and others' denials, the question of precisely where Cassavetes is in this gallery of potential self-portraits must remain unanswered.

One undeniable fact is Cassavetes' clear inability to put these characters behind him or get them out of his system. Whether figured slightly more superficially in early works or more profoundly in the later ones, characters unstably teetering on the tightrope between self-creation and self-destruction haunted Cassavetes' imagination. These characters are all masters and mistresses of mercuriality, but their creator clearly outdid even his own creations in his capacities of imaginative shape shifting, insofar as he not only imagined each figure's cinematic transformations within one film, but then went on to reimagine new possibilities in the next. As many of the photographs in this book document, not only in the scripting, but in the blocking, re-hearsing, and shooting of these films, Cassavetes momentarily *became* Lelia, Florence, Jeannie, Chet, Moskowitz, Mabel, Myrtle, Gloria, Sarah, and his other characters. His face, gestures, and movements were theirs. He played their parts and did their voices, and, like the consummate actor he was, he momentarily became the role he played and the voice he did. Like Mabel, he turned himself into an open-ended conduit for imaginative possibilities. He expanded his self in exactly the same way his most extraordinary heroines do, but even more freely. He completely inhabited each of his characters in each film, but then had the amazing luxury to "be" the next group of figures in the next film. That makes his the most astonishingly open-ended imag-inative identity of them all.

Even more than that, the filmmaking process was a way to build a com-munity that would support his imaginative transformations, an imaginative community he could actually live in for the duration of the film (something Mabel attempts to do, but fails at, in the spaghetti breakfast and other gatherings). That is to say, making the movie was a way for Cassavetes not only to play games with his identity, to express his wildest feelings, and to experiment with improvised, spur-of-the-moment relationships, but also to do it in a world that would not undermine the effort, but sustain it.

I emphasize the social dimensions of the filmmaking process because the fact that Cassavetes' acts of improvisation take place in a social context cuts both ways. As I just noted, in some respects the society nurtures and sustains the performances; in other respects, needless to say, it stringently limits and constrains them. The artistic performance is staged within very definite limits and resistances. Cassavetes' acts of making himself up as he goes along are severely limited by a variety of formal constraints: the dra-matic requirements of the scene, the capabilities of his actors, the technical limits of the shoot. He can play with his identity and expressions, but he can't merely play with them (just as a writer or any other artist can't). As *Minnie and Moskowitz* demonstrates, the free movements of the artist are staged within very definite limits, and in fact the constraint is what makes the partial freedom of the performance both possible and inspiring. There is never even a possibility of absolutely free improvisation in Cassavetes' work. Mabel Longhetti, Cosmo Vitelli, Myrtle Gordon, and Gloria Swenson each are asked to do their best with definitely limited freedom.

As these photographs demonstrate, that freedom consists of a moment-by-moment series of decisions. It is never a matter of pushing preselected buttons or mechanically blocking out foregone conclusions. As Cassavetes makes a film, he is exploring and experimenting with unresolved possibilities

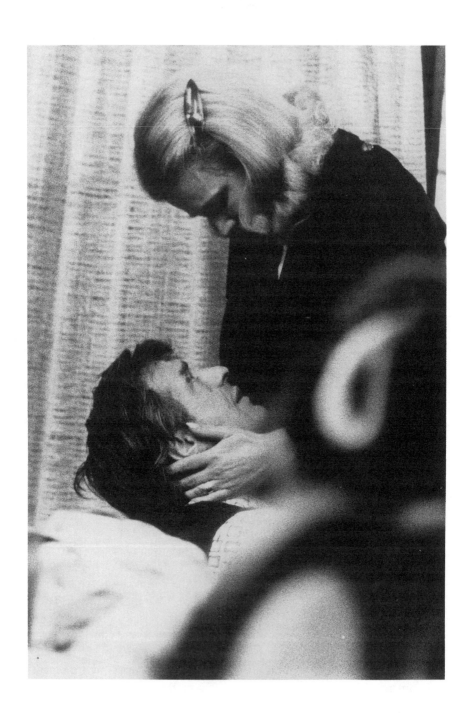

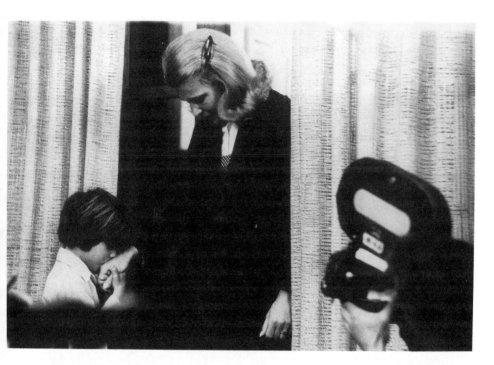

Open-ended selfhood, being anyone and everyone by turns, imaginatively inhabiting all of the roles through profound acts of empathy: (*facing*) Cassavetes becomes Angelo Longhetti greeting Mabel on her return from the hospital while Maria sits and watches in the right foreground; (*above*) Matthew Laborteaux plays the role while Cassavetes photographs it.

in himself. As he blocks out a scene, he is discovering its possibilities in his process of moving through it. As he acts out a character, he discovers things about himself and the character as he plays it.

The consequence is that Cassavetes has an entirely different relationship to his material than a director like Hitchcock, Kubrick, De Palma, or Altman. Since in some sense the characters are all versions of himself, he can't get far enough outside them and their situations to judge them, analyze them, or editorialize about them. He can't be intellectually superior to something he's so close to, to impulses that are in fact his own. Tendentiousness is impossible. Olympian stances are inconceivable.

In various small and large ways, the photographs demonstrate that far from being dominant and controlling, Cassavetes' performance as a director resembled the performances of his greatest characters in being intimate, involved, responsive, and loving. Shooting a scene was not a matter of sitting in judgment of someone, but of establishing or deepening an emotional relationship with them, of learning things about them, of getting partially inside them and seeing from their point of view. That's what was going on when Cassavetes touched or leaned against actors (particularly the children) as he filmed. Rather than holding himself above his characters, he lowered himself to their physical, optical, and imaginative angle of vision and feeling: lying down on the rug with Gena Rowlands, kneeling down to make himself the children's height as he shoots in the bed of the truck. The smile of delight present on his face as he looks through the viewfinder in more than one photograph shows how thoroughly he is living through the shot and with the character, participating in the event, not standing outside of it.

But we don't really need the photographs to see these things. Five minutes viewing *Shadows* or *A Woman Under the Influence* suffices for the style to make the same points. The camera work is not magisterial and aloof, but familiar and involved. The photography and editing are comically tolerant of even the strangest characters' eccentricities. Even if we can't see Cassavetes smiling behind the camera, we can see the photography and editing patiently smiling at characters' foibles. That nonjudgmental quality was probably at least partly one of things that made audiences so uncomfortable. It is always easier to judge. Not judging means you have to have a more complex, more personal, less simply defined relationship to what you see. As Cassavetes himself put it, "People prefer distance." It is far easier and more comfortable to stand in judgment than to enter into a more intimate relationship with a character or a situation.

The only problem with calling this stance a nonjudgmental one is that it characterizes Cassavetes' imaginative relationship to his actors and characters too weakly. As the leaning, touching, kneeling, squatting, and smiling suggest, what was going on was a powerful state of empathy. Cassavetes was feeling *with* these characters and *for* them. Empathy is different from not judging because it completely changes the terms of a relationship from an intellectual basis to an emotional one. Cassavetes' relationship to these characters was not merely the negative one of not judging them; it was the strongly positive one of loving them. The ground of Cassavetes' relationship to his actors and characters was through accesses of inward sympathy and bonds of love. It is not accidental that it is the same as the way figures like Mabel, Myrtle, and Sarah relate to others within their films. The films tell us both in their narratives and their production process that it is only in empathically opening ourselves to others' feelings that we can break out of the prison of formulas and abstractions that separates us from experience. The intellect at its most sublime cannot accomplish what the feelings can, even at their crudest. Letting go of old ideas or opening ourselves to new ideas is not enough; it is only in opening ourselves emotionally to new feelings that we can most profoundly enlarge our identities.

Such openness to others' lives and feelings is only available if one is willing momentarily to abandon oneself, one's memories, one's ideas, one's preconceived notions. Like Florence, Mabel, or Sarah Lawson in their states of abandonment, we must be brave enough to relax control and let something other than our minds dictate our actions. This is in fact how Cassavetes once, only half-facetiously, explained his own function on the set:

> A lot of people know what they are doing. I don't know until the next day. If our films are supposed to be something like life is – some vague thing that life has that films can contain – how can you know what's happening [in advance]? Unless you have such a prescribed life that you're bored with it. . . . Even if you read a script, you don't know how somebody's going to interpret it. I'm not in that much control over the films we make. I'd like to think I am, like anybody else. I'll take credit for it, sure. But I really have no idea from one scene to the next what *it's* going to do. I feel this enormous sense of panic, of letting go.

As much of my argument has been devoted to demonstrating, this is the world Cassavetes' viewers and characters also inhabit – a world in which we must "let go" and let "it" take over for us. We must dare to leave the guidance of the intellect behind, and accept the movements of emotion. Cassavetes is perfectly aware that the inevitable result will be a "sense of panic," but that it is only in plunging into our places of not-knowing that our emotions can teach us anything.

The process of expanding oneself through inward emotional sympathies can never end. That is why the final word about Cassavetes' process of allowing himself to be inhabited by these alien identities is that there can be no final word, no final identity for oneself, no final act of sympathetic imagination with a final character. Cassavetes clearly couldn't get to the end of the process. He couldn't stop his own empathic movements beyond the last empathic movement. He kept writing new scripts until the day he died, and in film after film he clearly couldn't stop feeling new things. He kept wondering about the same characters in slightly different situations over and over again – imagining them in slightly different forms, tinkering with them, exploring their degree of self-awareness and control over their creativity. No more than a viewer can, can he make up his mind about whether the ideal they figure is liberated or irresponsible, inspiring or frightening, joyous or doomed. In fact, by turns he shows it to be all of these things. Is it really better to be open in the way they are? Is the psychic and social cost too high? Uncertainty, however, is not a negative state. In fact, Cassavetes' irresolution about these figures indicates that he and they share a deep similarity in this respect as well as in many others. They too are unable to make up their minds about themselves. He and they live an adventure of staying uncertain, unformulated, and unresolved about one's own identity, ideas, and feelings.

Notwithstanding some of the differences I have pointed out between their work, Emerson remains a seminal guide to the imaginative territory Cassavetes mapped. The following passage in "Circles" almost perfectly describes the expressive situation embodied by Robert and Sarah. Emerson knew that even as we may hope to be "settled" and may devote most of our lives to trying futilely to anchor ourselves in one thing or another (fame, power, money, sex, family, or romance), as Robert and Sarah do, the only real hope for us is to stay frighteningly, courageously, endlessly in motion:

> Why should we import rags and relics into the new hour? In nature, there is no sleep, no pause, no preservation, but all things renew, germinate, and spring. Nature abhors the old, and old age seems the only disease; all others run into this one.... They are all forms of old age; they are rest, conservatism, inertia, not newness, not the way onward. We grizzle every day. I see no need of it.... This old age need not to creep on a human mind. In nature every moment is new; the past is always swallowed and forgotten; the coming only is sacred. Nothing is secure but life, transition, the energizing spirit. No love can be bound by oath or covenant to secure it against a higher love. No truth so sublime, but it may be trivial tomorrow in the light of new thoughts. People wish to be settled; only as far as they are unsettled is there any hope for them.[12]

Yet even if they are describing the same general imaginative predicament, this passage points up yet one more difference between Emerson's and Cassavetes' work. Cassavetes and his greatest characters completely lack the rhetorical poise and meditative perspective that Emerson displays. No matter how radical his insights or how potentially disturbing his conclusions, Emerson's tones are calm and ruminative. By contrast, Cassavetes, his characters, and his films are walking, talking states of uncertainty, agitation, and unsettlement (though admittedly figures like Cosmo and Robert attempt to hide their confusion even from themselves). Emerson imaginatively rises above the disturbance he describes; Cassavetes and his characters plummet headlong into an abyss of confusions and uncertainties. His characters show us what expressive crisis looks like not when summoned to the sessions of sweet, silent thought, but as enacted in the lurching imbalances of incompletely understood events. The expressive problems they live are frightening and disorienting – to them, to a viewer, and to Cassavetes himself – in a way that Emerson's merely theoretical formulations almost never are to him or to his reader.

In a similar vein, although the title of *Love Streams* makes it clear that Cassavetes would have agreed with the epigraph to this chapter from Emerson about the "streamingness" of life and beauty, Emerson's metaphors are too gradual, too innocuous, too insipid by half to capture the feeling of these films. Cassavetes imagines a world not of gentle "flowing" but of violent wrenching and off-balance lurching. That is why, in Cassavetes' work, the "incessant movement and progression of experience" finds its images not in "the annual wave of vegetation" or "the action and reaction of nature," as Emerson would have it, but in the battering Jim administers to Minnie, in Chet's run across the roof in *Faces*, or in the fights Robert gets into in *Love Streams*. Whereas Emerson gently refers us to the "circulation of the blood," Cassavetes' understanding of love's streaming takes the form of hot-blooded arguments and bloody beatings.

As this book has argued, the genius of Cassavetes' work is that the states of disruption and disorientation in the films are not merely attributed to the characters but are participated in by Cassavetes himself. Cassavetes' cinematic style is as agitated and unsettled as the personal expressive styles of his major characters. He is not somewhere outside of the work, above the characters, coolly commenting (and assuredly not at the sardonic or parodic remove of Hitchcock, De Palma, Altman, or Lynch with respect to their characters and situations). Cassavetes' characters' uncertainties are his own. He wrestles with many of the same confusions of feeling that they do. Like them, he explores possibilities and discovers things as he goes along. Like them, he has experiences by the bushel and learns from them step by step, day by day.

If there were any lingering doubt about it, the production process of *Love Streams* stands as conclusive evidence that Cassavetes did indeed use filmmaking as a genuine process of exploration. The filmmaker insisted in interviews that he made the film to try to understand Robert and Sarah, and that he, in fact, kept changing his mind about them throughout the process, from the initial revisions of the script to the very end of postproduction. Concerning Robert in particular (the character Cassavetes played), various members of the crew recall the filmmaker repeatedly asking them questions about him – why he treated people the way he did, what his problems were, whether he would ever be any different, whether there was anything about him worth saving. (The way this typically occurred on the set was that after filming a scene in which Robert appeared, Cassavetes would ask a crew member if the scene had changed his understanding of Robert, made him seem less or more likable, or revealed something new about him.) These were genuinely open-ended discussions in which Cassavetes frequently admitted that he himself didn't quite understand why Robert had said or done a particular thing. As further proof that the open-mindedness wasn't feigned, about two-thirds of the way through the shooting schedule (which was done in continuity), he abandoned the script and wrote an entirely new conclusion because he ceased to believe Robert and Sarah would do what the original script had called for them to do.[13]

One needn't have gone onto the set to observe Cassavetes thinking through his text, however. His directorial open-mindedness about the experiences he was filming is written into *Love Streams* – in the way characters are freed from fixed identities or abstract systems of relationship, in the unpredictability of scenes' development, in the tentativeness and reticence of the film's metaphors, and in the way its tones work not to dictate particular responses, but rather to entertain possibilities. Instead of facilitating and accelerating a viewer's judgmental process, scenes complicate and delay judgments, forestalling resolutions and clarifications and suspending us among possibilities. Tonally, intellectually, emotionally, and metaphorically, Cassavetes keeps viewers slightly in the dark in the service of eliciting from them the same sort of exploratory stance that he himself adopted.

William James is the great philosophical theorist of this state of affairs. His posthumously published *Some Problems of Philosophy* devotes many pages to arguing in favor of what he calls "keeping the doors and windows open" on experience. Change the reference points from philosophy to film in the following passage (from the chapter "Percept and Concept – Some Corollaries"), and one has a pretty fair summary of the differences between Cassavetes' work (which corresponds to what James calls "empiricism") and the work of Hitchcock and Welles, and the expressive tradition they define (which corresponds with what James calls "rationalism"):

Rationalistic philosophy has always aspired to a rounded-in view of the whole of things, a closed system of kinds, from which the notion

Asking questions, wondering about a life during the process of filming: Cassavetes talking with Gena Rowlands about her role between setups in *Love Streams*.

of essential novelty being possible is ruled out in advance. For empiricism, on the other hand, reality cannot be thus confined by a conceptual ring-fence. It overflows, exceeds, and alters. It may turn into novelties, and can be known adequately only by following its singularities from moment to moment as our experience grows. Empiricist philosophy thus renounces the pretension to an all-inclusive vision.... It stays inside the flux of life expectantly, recording facts, not formulating laws, and never pretending that man's relation to the totality of things as a philosopher is essentially different from his relation to the parts of things as a daily patient or agent in the practical current of events. Philosophy, like life, must keep its doors and windows open.[14]

Although "keeping doors and windows open" is a spatial metaphor, James intends it to have temporal consequences. If "we stay inside the flux of life expectantly, recording facts, not formulating laws," knowledge is no longer something eternal, universal, and transcendent, but occurs in and through time. In a world in which "reality . . . overflows, exceeds, and alters . . . [experience] can be known adequately only by following its singularities from moment to moment." Where "novelties" replace consistencies, we are forced to stay open to shifts of tone and meaning. We must assume a newly nimble temporal relationship to an experience that is always only partial and provisional, and that continuously grows.

As much as James's was a philosophy of the wrecking ball, knocking down the "rationalist" structures that systematized the life out of life, Cassavetes assaults characters' and viewers' designs for living in order to allow real living to begin. His goal is to move viewers and characters into James's brave new world of intellectual, emotional, and psychological "expectancy." Needless to say, he was under no illusions about the resistance the effort would meet with. He knew that every fiber of our being fights against this new way of knowing and living, especially when it becomes painful or difficult. In James's metaphor, we crave "laws" to release us from the effort of dealing with "facts." Like James, Cassavetes wants to teach us to think *in* space and time, but he knows that that is the most difficult way of thinking. The films document how difficult. They show us how we flee from genuine openness. When faced with anguish, some of us (like Robert and Cosmo) attempt to withdraw into a Xanadu of the imagination. Confronted with confusion about what we are and want, others of us (like Sarah and Mabel) attempt to turn over our identities to others and allow ourselves to be defined by people around us, rather than trusting ourselves with ourselves.

Cassavetes made assaultive films because he understood that a shock to our systems is often the only way to force us out of them. Pain, disruption, and disturbance are necessary for growth. We only begin to learn when our comfortable designs for living (and understanding) are broken up. *Husbands*'s boy-men begin to grow up only when their closest friend dies. Maria's belated insight into her own situation in *Faces* is purchased at the almost unendurable price of Richard's request for a divorce. Myrtle Gordon begins her journey of self-discovery in *Opening Night* only when an adoring fan is killed in front of her. Gloria only begins to learn something about being a woman when little Phil messes up her life. Cosmo's education starts only after gangsters visit his club. *Love Streams* similarly begins with a pair of upheavals. In the first thirty minutes, Cassavetes tears up the separate deals Robert and Sarah have each cut with life. He breaks up Sarah's marriage and family and throws her out of her own house; concurrently, in a parallel plot, he has Robert's hilltop hideaway invaded.

Robert's universe of style is invaded by three women and a child. Each threatens him with the sort of uncomfortable intimacy and personal involvement his life has been designed to shut out. (It takes four, because his Teflon surface is so slick that only the final visitor actually manages to reach him.) The first is a singer named Susan, whom Robert meets in a bar. She offers him the challenge of an uncontrolled relationship of the sort from which his whole life is a terrified flight. Robert withstands Susan's threat with his unflappable charm and aplomb. In a scene in which she comes to his house almost to plead to be let into his life, he holds her at arm's length with one final, cute gesture and wink.[15]

Robert's next two visitors are a former wife, Agnes, and the son he had with her, Albie. Robert apparently hasn't seen either of them since the boy was born. Albie stays with him a few days over a long weekend, but again, without going into detail, just as it appears that the boy (and, to a lesser extent, the wife) may find a way into his heart, Robert manages a last-minute defense against them. In a climactic scene (which was modeled on a comparable moment in Capra's *Meet John Doe*), Robert puts himself on ice under glass one more time to escape from his own biography. The encroaching confusions of history and memory are successfully contained.

However, the fourth ship-wrecked intruder to wash ashore on Robert's island kingdom is another matter. Sarah unexpectedly arrives at his house with nowhere else to go. It is impossible for Robert to close the door on her, literally or emotionally, the way he does with the others; both of their lives are profoundly affected by their coming together.

Although they are both moved away from positions of safety and comfort and into situations of danger and possibility, they move in the opposite direction from each other. Because Robert has renounced his past, he is asked to meet up with it again. Because Sarah is trapped in her past, she is asked to shake loose from it. Robert has to admit ties to family and friends, claims of others, and emotional responsibilities. Sarah has to break free, to extricate herself from an overelaborate sense of duty and responsibility. She needs to release herself from her former relationship with her husband and daughter. In a series of clumsy, half-crazy, half-comic, yet inspiringly brave and eccentric movements forward through space, she launches herself on a perilous voyage of discovery away from the safe harbor of family, relatives, and friends (which is why she eventually leaves Robert's house).

As in all of Cassavetes' films, however, the mere events are really much less important to the overall effect of *Love Streams* than how we encounter them. That Robert and Sarah are asked to move in opposite directions should indicate that Cassavetes is not urging any particular course of action. That is to say, to him, the outcome of a movement is less important than the process of movement itself. Any destination, any position (including any abstract or thematic position the film urges on us) is a dead end if it inhibits future movements away from it. All of Cassavetes' work is designed to bring us to an awareness of the "streamingness" of life and to teach us how to swim with it rather than attempt to stop its motion. While the meanings in 2001 or *Citizen Kane* are truly written in stone, Cassavetes' meanings stream, as he argues all life does; the task for both viewers and characters is to learn how to live in this watery world.

As much as the plot of *Love Streams* forces Robert and Sarah out of their places of comfort and away from their customary patterns of response, the style forces us out of ours. The destabilizations of a series of downright disorienting stylistic experiences induce a state of expectant uncertainty in the viewer. The audience is propelled along with Robert and Sarah down a cognitive and emotional Open Road. In the service of that process, Cassavetes deliberately denies us most of the ordinary forms of comprehensibility that other films rely on to guide our progress and control our understanding. That is obvious even while the titles are still being presented. While a conventional film would devote its first minutes to establishing as much as possible about what we are seeing and where we are headed, Cassavetes deliberately gets us a little lost, throwing even the most attentive viewer off guard and off course.

The opening scene begins literally in midbreath, plunging the viewer in midsentence into the middle of a heated argument between a man, a woman, and a child about six years old. There is a complete failure to establish where we are, who the characters are, what the argument is about, or where the scene is going. It's not just that we don't have names to put with faces. We don't even have vague identities or relationships to connect the figures. The only thing we can safely conclude is that we are watching a squabble between a husband and wife (with their little girl in the husband's arms). That's not much to go on, but it's better than nothing.

The problem is that we're mistaken. Cassavetes deliberately miscues us.[16] The man, woman, and child aren't a family. This isn't the woman and child's house. The man, Robert, is not married to the woman, nor married at all, in fact. The woman is his secretary, René, and the little girl the man holds, Charlene, is not his child, but hers. We don't figure any of that out until later on, however, long after the scene is over. Furthermore, even when we have pieced together these facts, names, and places, deeper mysteries remain. We never do figure out what the argument was about. Even more important, the further we go, the less clear we are about what Robert's actual relation to René and Charlene is. As I have said, at first we think René is his wife; fifteen or twenty minutes into the film, we conclude that she is his secretary. Sometime midway through, we begin to entertain the possibility that she is more than a secretary; perhaps she is another of Robert's many lovers or former lovers. That makes us wonder whether Charlene is only her daughter or is Robert's too. Maybe the group we saw in the first scene *was* a kind of family, after all. We have come full circle only to end up back where we started – not knowing very much at all. But, by this film's standards, that's the right place to be. Cassavetes would always rather leave us wondering than knowing.[17]

If we think we're lost now, however, wait until the next two sequences. (We're still only a minute or so into the movie.) We watch Robert talking to a number of different women (two are in the driveway, one is in the kitchen, and two are in the bathroom shower together), still with no idea of who they are or what's going on. The shower scene is particularly weird in that the two naked, giggling girls show utterly no embarrassment about Robert coming into the bathroom while they are showering. The kitchen scene is strange in terms of the particular take used. Robert walks into the kitchen and begins to say a few words to an unidentified young woman sitting at the table, but is unable to finish the conversation because he goes into an obviously unscripted coughing fit in midsentence. As if his goal were deliberately to mess up a moment that even momentarily began to verge on incipient intelligibility, Cassavetes chose this "bad take" for his final edit.

In the third scene (we're now two or three minutes into the movie), we watch in mystification while Robert conducts an unexplained tape-recorded "interview" with a girl named Joannie while a group of other young women snicker, watch, and drink cocktails. Neither the reason for the interview, the identity of Joannie, nor the presence of the others is explained. (As if things weren't strange enough, Cassavetes springs the sound and picture relatively free from each other during this scene, so that while we hear Robert talk with Joannie, we are left watching the reactions of the other girls, who seem almost as puzzled about what is going on as we are. Judged by the standards of conventional editing practice, the camera is looking in the wrong place, showing us the wrong people, explaining nothing.)

I've pointed out some of the same techniques in earlier films: the veilings of characters' identities to forestall reductive understandings; the miscuing about the "family" to put us on the qui vive; the keeping us in the dark about where we are to force us to open our eyes wider. But even in *Minnie and Moskowitz* these effects were never so kaleidoscopically compressed and rapidly deployed. Of course, one way to understand the whole sequence is as an act of bravura. The sequence is deliberately outrageous, puckish, provocative, masterful, and perverse, a display of wit and power. Cassavetes is teasing us, flaunting his ability to leave even the most alert viewer in his dust. But there is much more to it than sassiness.

Since the experience keeps sloshing out of the conceptual containers with which we would scoop it up and hold it, Cassavetes puts the viewer in the position William James described in the previous quotation: "stay[ing] in the flux of life expectantly [–and, I would add, humbly–], recording facts, not formulating laws." We watch unfinished stories and incomplete inter-actions as we piece things together, revising our interpretations as we go along. For the next two and a half hours we will have to learn to navigate these crazily shifting currents without a chart or compass to steer by.

To adapt another of William James's slippery metaphors (this time from "A World of Pure Experience"), Cassavetes compels the viewer to live "upon the front edge of an advancing wave-crest."[8] We must feel our way from person to person, fact to fact, functioning in a state of perpetual activity, openness, exposure, and vulnerability, energetically engaged in making something out of each moment without being able to predict the outcome.

This is, however, to couch the effect of *Love Streams*'s style too negatively. It does not merely deny us fixed positions, delay conclusions, and confuse certainties. It also opens entirely new imaginative possibilities. It creates what James calls "novelties." It makes possibility possible. The brief scene about halfway through the movie in which Sarah calls her former husband, Jack, on the phone, can stand as a summary of what this means in action. By this point, Sarah and Jack have been divorced and Jack has gotten custody of their daughter. Sarah has gone to Europe alone and returned, then un-expectedly dropped in on Robert, as I have mentioned. But however many months have gone by since she and Jack separated, she has not been able to sever her attachment to him. She still imagines that a reconciliation is possible. Late one night she calls him in desperation from Robert's house. The conversation begins as follows:

SARAH: Hello, Jack.
JACK: [*with great urgency*] Sarah!...I *need* you....I know none of this doesn't make any sense, but this house is very empty without you.
SARAH: [*playfully, yet passionately*] Hey, I *love* you, you dumbo-head!

That's only a few seconds into the call, and it's impossible to capture the tones on the printed page, but suffice it to say that the effect is electrifying. Sarah has made a series of calls to Jack prior to this one but gotten nowhere in any of them. This time, completely unexpectedly, it suddenly appears that a reconciliation is about to take place. As he talks to Sarah, Jack sits alone in the kitchen stirring instant coffee. It's clear that he genuinely needs and misses Sarah. His voice is sincerely tender and more than slightly weary. The rallying, playful tone of Sarah's response to him shows that she has come to the same conclusion we have. Her fondest dream has come true. The only hitch is that this is what follows:

JACK: [*reprimanding her*] We're *divorced*, Sarah. That part of our life is over.... I'm just saying it's tough to bring up a kid alone. I know that it doesn't make any sense – but that's what *you* should be doing.... Goodbye, Sarah.

Jack's tone now seems stern and distant. We are forced to reverse everything we just concluded. Indeed, precisely because we thought a reconciliation was in the offing, Jack's upbraiding of Sarah at this instant makes his estrangement from her seem even greater than it was before.

Why did we (and she) fall for it? The superficial reason is that it represents a wish-fulfillment. The deeper reason is that Cassavetes has created a narrative world where almost anything is possible, even such a sudden and unexplained reversal of feeling. As other events demonstrate, every relationship in the film is open to revision. Jack's previous rejection of Sarah does not necessarily determine his future reactions to her. The past does not determine the future. Cassavetes springs his cinematic world free from narrative determinism. We can't tell where we are headed from minute to minute. Any scene can lead anywhere. In *this* film, Jack and Sarah *could* suddenly make up. That is one of the things it means to say that possibilities of Jamesian novelty materialize throughout *Love Streams*.

What makes the experience even more open-ended is that one never knows when an important moment or interaction is about to occur. As both this conversation and the first scene of *Love Streams* illustrate, scenes don't gradually build up to climaxes. Cassavetes' scenes can begin with the climax – in the height of an argument or the middle of an apparent reconciliation. Something important can happen at any time.

Climactic events, crucial emotional disclosures, or important personal intimacies can occur not only at any time in a scene, but also between any two people in any situation. That is to say, scenes, characters, and interactions are not regimented into predictable hierarchies of importance. Although the telephone-conversation scene involves two important characters who share an important past relationship, many of the most memorable moments in *Love Streams* feature interactions between Sarah and characters who, at least in another movie, would be mere walk-ons. Consider Sarah's scenes in the bowling alley and the two train stations. In another film such scenes would be merely expository, clueing a viewer in to where Sarah is, or marking time before the next interaction with an important character. In Cassavetes, however, "supporting" characters don't necessarily stay supporting, and "transitional" settings, events, interactions are never predictably transitional in function. There's no telling what will happen to anyone at any time or place. (As an example of this, Sarah meets the man of her dreams at a bowling alley.)

One reason we can be sure that Cassavetes endorses Sarah's personal style (and does not regard her as being merely crazy, as Robert does), is that in scenes like the one in the bowling alley, and the ones with the railroad porters, his narrative style is similar to her social style. That is to say, her personal emotional openness to possibility overlaps with and ultimately becomes indistinguishable from his narrative openness to possibility. Sarah's bet-everything-on-love pitch of desperation makes unexpected and unconventional possibilities of intimacy and personal relationship everywhere she goes (even in her dealings with a baggage porter, the manager of a bowling alley, or a bowler in an adjacent lane) in exactly the same way that his narrative does. Cassavetes does the same thing in his scripting and directing that Sarah does in her life: He cares about those who don't even deserve to be cared for. He honors the most marginal figures. He humanizes and respects even the lowliest of them – the waitresses, the bank clerks, the baggage porters, and the bowling-alley managers of life.[19]

I want to discuss three other scenes to illustrate some of the other ways Cassavetes keeps his meanings on the move. The first involves Robert and two hookers in a car; the second features Robert and Sarah talking together late one night in Robert's kitchen; the third depicts Robert first dancing with Sarah, then walking her up to bed. None of them runs more than a few minutes of screen time, and all of them involve fairly cramped blockings of characters and spatially limited settings. I emphasize brevity of the scenes and the spatial confinements of the staging because an important part of the meaning of these moments is that imaginative movements are possible in most spatially and temporally constricted encounters. Especially the second and third demonstrate that the emotional squalors and grandeurs in Cassavetes' work are unrelated to the world's conceptions of space and time. For Cassavetes, the sublime is not somewhere off in the distance, nor does it take horizons and vistas to evoke (as in much American painting and film); it is figured by two faces, by one pair of eyes looking at another.

The first scene involves Robert's return from a night out with two Las Vegas hookers. Their car pulls up in front of his hotel with him and the girls jammed together in the front seat. All three are laughing hysterically, wriggling together, their bodies intertwined. It goes on just long enough to bait us into laughing along with them, but we no sooner do than Cassavetes yanks us up short. The moment suddenly turns somber and slightly surreal as Robert sits up to make out checks to the girls and asks them to spell their names. A few seconds later, the mood shifts again to the slightly pathetic when he makes an offhand comment about going back to see his son. (He has disgracefully left Albie alone in the hotel room.) Only seconds later, the mood changes once more as the girls, checks now in hand, suddenly become all business. Their laughter gives way to sounds of weariness. They are obviously tired of the long night they spent together, and even more tired of Robert. In a tone that is not entirely playful, one of the girls pronounces: "Go," and nudges him out of the car with her hips. The bubble of fantasy has burst and we (and he) are suddenly back in a world where you can buy sex but not love, and a neglected child waits upstairs.

It's vintage Cassavetes. Though it runs only a couple minutes of screen time and is limited to the four or five feet of space in the front seat of a car, there are enough imaginative and emotional shifts and swerves for an entire movie. What starts out as giggles and fun turns sad beyond words just seconds after the audience has gotten up its courage to laugh along with the characters. Like the writhing bodies themselves, the scene slips and slides and wiggles away from five, six, or more successive positions in a matter of minutes. As with all of Cassavetes' work, what makes the scene such a challenging viewing experience is that the more agile we are at keeping up with tones and meanings, the more we have to keep up. The more we can see, the more there is to see. The faster we can move, the faster the scene moves (which is why viewers who find Cassavetes "slow" are only proclaiming themselves slow learners).

The hooker scene exemplifies temporal movement and tonal instability. The next two scenes I want to describe cultivate a form of fluidity and uncertainty that is even more difficult to characterize. Not only do the meanings and relationships in these scenes keep slipping away from any generalization we make about them, but at any one time they just slightly elude formulation. At any one instant it is extremely difficult to say what the tones or meanings are. Cassavetes pitches them at the precise points categorical understandings break down.

After Sarah's escapade at the bowling alley, Cassavetes brings her and Robert together in the kitchen for a conversation. The scene marks a very special moment for both of them. Sarah, in her joyful abandonment to the first blush of new love (she has fallen in love with a man named Ken whom she met bowling), seems momentarily freed from the fetters of her past. Robert too has himself perhaps been brought to a recognition of his need for others by this point in the film. As they sit at the kitchen table talking together, Sarah opens up emotionally to Robert, and it seems that, inspired by her unguardedness (and as a consequence of his disastrous trip to Las Vegas, the beating he has received, the pleas of Albie's mother, and the chilly reception at Susan's when he blithely assumed she would still be carrying a torch for him), Robert may actually be opening up to her.

In short, given Sarah's and Robert's mutual problems and estrangement from one another up to this point, the kitchen scene represents a moment of truly extraordinary and absolutely unexpected emotional intimacy between them. What makes it most interesting, however, is that we can't quite bring it – or its two characters – into focus. We can't really know exactly what Sarah and Robert feel, or make up our minds how we should feel about them. Even as we crave some sort of clarification (and as the scene seems to dangle the possibility of an opening to intimacy before our eyes), Cassavetes ensures that we can't really know if anything actually has changed between them.

On her part, Sarah talks with a degree of wit, lucidity, and humorous self-deprecation that we haven't seen before. She speaks philosophically about love and art, and alludes to one of her father's favorite bits of advice (that no life is ever too messed up or too far gone to be saved), clearly including both herself and Robert under the optimistic generalization.[20] She talks about her dreams, desires, and goals in life. She reflects on the emptiness and loneliness of Robert's life and speaks of her desire to fill it. Yet Cassavetes refuses to allow things to get too simple or too clear. Even as Sarah seems far wiser, more considerate, and less absorbed in her own problems than we've ever seen her, she is obviously not quite "cured." She is still more than a little dotty (as when she says she is going to "buy [Robert] a baby"), and she appears to be just as obsessive about her family and her attempt to get them to love her as she has ever been. In short, Sarah is suspended between brilliance and daffiness. Furthermore, there's the whole issue of what we make of Sarah's so suddenly falling in love. Can anything that has bloomed so rapidly be trusted to last? Does it matter if it lasts? Is this a love that points a way out of Sarah's problems of dependency, or only one more manifestation of them?

Robert's performance too is pitched at a similar point of remaining just slightly beyond clarification. Is he emotionally opening up to Sarah (which, if true, would mark the first time in the film he does make himself vulnerable to another human being), or are we (and Sarah) just imagining it, hoping too hard for it? Cassavetes makes these questions even less resolvable than they might ordinarily be by placing Robert behind a wall so that we can't see his face during the entire scene.[21]

The consequence is an extraordinarily suspended moment of imaginative possibility. It suddenly seems as if there just might be some common ground Robert and Sarah share. It seems as if everything could change, as if Sarah's father may have been right, and that "for every problem there is an answer." I emphasize the subjunctiveness of the preceding, because the wonder of the scene is that it is suspended among possibilities without declaring, resolving, or deciding any of them. As Sarah puts on the teakettle or talks about her father's advice, or when Robert reaches across the table and briefly takes her hand, truly extraordinary possibilities of intimacy and emotional expressiveness materialize, but they remain in the realm of possibility.

As it turns out, nothing comes of any of it. The grand imaginative possibilities turn out to have been only imaginative, which is to say that though they are brought into existence by Cassavetes' style (and possibly exist in one or both characters' consciousnesses), they cannot actually be lived. Robert remains guarded and distant. He unclasps Sarah's hand and makes another of his cute finger gestures (with which the film has made us so impatient by this point). We reluctantly realize that he has not made the emotional movement toward her that we imagined. On her part, after waxing so poetic, Sarah abruptly truncates her meditation, says she's changed her mind about having tea, gets up, and wearily trundles off to bed. (The emotional ebb and flow of the scene is summarized by her typically Cassavetean action–reversed action with the teakettle first on and then off.) By the end of the scene, every possibility it conjured into existence seems to have evaporated; but one doesn't want to attach too much importance to the end of the scene. In another respect it doesn't matter that nothing came of any of it, since Cassavetes is far less interested in outcomes than processes. The imaginative closing down at the end doesn't erase or invalidate the opening up that preceded it. The scene entertains possibilities that are cherished even if they cannot be realized in actual forms of practical expression and relationship. In fact, they are cherished all the more because they are *not* able to be lived.

The third and most complex example of imaginative liquidity and suspension – for both viewers of *Love Streams* and characters in it – occurs about ten minutes before the kitchen scene. It is also only a few minutes long, and, since it is largely silent, it demonstrates that the ebb and flow of imaginative possibilities in Cassavetes' work doesn't take words to be expressed. The moment is dramatized almost entirely through a pantomime of bodily gestures and movements exchanged between Robert and Sarah.

There are two sections to the scene: In the first, Robert is in the far left background of the shot swaying to the strains of a Mildred Bailey song on his Wurlitzer when Sarah comes into the room in the near right foreground. He silently gestures toward her and she slowly walks toward him and the jukebox. With delicate swayings of their bodies, they hesitantly respond to each other's movements, delicately synchronize their rhythms, and briefly dance together. However, the shared moment no sooner gets started than Cassavetes makes us realize that it is already long over. Sarah casually mentions that Susan called while Robert was out. Robert suddenly stops dancing, draws away, and goes to the phone to call Susan. In its ebb and flow of imaginative relationship, the scene resembles the kitchen moment, only it all takes place not only wordlessly, but infinitely faster. A series of imaginative transactions pass before our eyes at the speed of light. In a matter of seconds, opportunities of relationship have been born, have developed, and have decayed.

The second part of the scene, consisting of the two minutes or so that follow, presents an even more complex and intricate minuet of imaginative openings and closings than does the jukebox moment. Only seconds after their abortive dance of shared intimacy, in his haste to get to Susan's house, Robert tries to trundle Sarah off to bed (so that she will be off his hands and he can go tomcatting). They walk through the house together, but she resists his suggestion and politely protests that she is not sleepy. Then, as he continues almost forcibly to usher her upstairs, she suddenly changes her mind and declares her intention to go to bed after all. In an extraordinary silent sequence on the steps that ends the moment, Robert begins to follow her upstairs, then turns to go downstairs, then changes his mind, too, and follows her upstairs into her bedroom. The awkward sequence of movements and countermovements exchanged between Robert and Sarah as they walk to the stairs and then up them – unsynchronized, conflicting actions and reactions of mind even more than of body – are all the more striking following so closely on the heels of the tender but fleeting pas de deux they danced in front of the jukebox.

Both parts of the sequence are as alluring as they are mysterious. What passes between Robert and Sarah in the jukebox part of the scene? Why does Robert break off his dance with Sarah so rudely? Why does Sarah initially resist going to bed, then suddenly change her mind on the steps? Why does Robert decide to go back upstairs after her, after initially turning to go downstairs? What is either of them thinking?

The dance in front of the jukebox in particular illustrates another aspect of Cassavetes' work: the vulnerability of the beauties – both those in life and those in art. This moment is one of the most gorgeously lit and framed scenes in *Love Streams*, but one of the things that makes the elegances in Cassavetes' work so precious is that they are so rare. There are far more moments that resemble the harshness of the daylight and the rust and peeling paint of the car in the hooker scene than the elegant atmospherics of this moment. Cassavetes' elegances of lighting, framing, and scoring are deliberately intermittent. He avoids the sorts of systematic visual and acoustic gorgeousness (elegant photography, artful framings, and stylish musical orchestrations) that suffuse arty movies from *Citizen Kane* to *Manhattan* because, in his view of it, experience essentially resists elegant imaginative arrangements (as *The Killing of a Chinese Bookie* demonstrated in other ways). The very rare "beauty shots" that do occur in his work – of Minnie's bedroom, of Minnie and Seymour in the *2001* sequence, of Nick and Mabel in bed after making love, of Robert and Sarah dancing in the illumination of the jukebox in this instance – declare their own fragility because they never last for more than a few seconds. The beauties are momentary and fugitive. As even the doomed Cosmo proved, elegance takes continuous work to maintain. Our attainments of order are always on the verge of loss or corruption, which is in fact what makes them so valuable. Our compositions – emotional, social, and aesthetic – are continuously decomposing. In these films, ever-encroaching forces of disorder threaten our least achievements of order. Possibilities of intimacy and relationship must be made over and over again against the pressure of time and events working to unmake or degrade them. Laughter no sooner begins than it turns hollow, as in the scene with the hookers. A hand-clasp between a man and a woman over a kitchen table endures only a few seconds before the man withdraws his hand, or the woman changes her mind. A dancing scene that works up to a delicate act of partnering disintegrates only seconds later into the brusque rudeness of "can we walk and talk?"

Cassavetes' world asks a lot, both of his characters and his viewers. Since viewers are put through the same experience of flowingness as are the characters, it's as demanding for us to make sense of as it is for them to live in. In a world in which meaning is continuously decaying, a viewer has to work to keep up with it, just as the characters have to work to remake it. While we want rest, Cassavetes asks unceasing effort. While we want anchorage, Cassavetes forces us to live on turbulent, shifting seas.

That suggests what is most profoundly wrong with both Robert and Sarah. In their different ways, they each want to stand outside of the flow of their own film's scenes. They each want something solid and unmovable to lean on. They want to anchor their identities and relationships (for Robert, in charm, fame, sexual power, and money; for Sarah, in family, motherhood, marriage, and love). Cassavetes believes that is a futile and doomed effort, which is why he puts their lives in flux. He shows them and us that they and all of their relationships stream. They (and we) must learn to live within the current of these ebbings and flowings.

Offbeat humor is another way Cassavetes liquefies his meanings and lubricates his characters' relationships. The weird comedy of Sarah's hearing-room colloquies (comedy bordering on pathos), like the intermittent farcicality of her scenes with the baggage porters and the manager of the bowling alley, suspend the viewer in a state of cognitive and emotional irresolution. What in the world are we to make of her performances? How are we supposed to feel? We don't know whether to laugh or cry. Sarah's "I Love Lucy" daffiness prevents us from judging her harshly. It melts the congealings of morality. We are too boggled and bemused by the bizarreness of some of her words and actions to judge her at all. (The semicomedy of many of Mabel's scenes in *A Woman Under the Influence* functioned similarly.) Cassavetes once said that he preferred comedy to straight drama because there was "more possibility" in it, and *Love Streams* shows how comedy can allow characters and viewers to remain open to almost anything.

It is entirely appropriate that the final hour of *Love Streams* leaves us with more questions than answers about Sarah and Robert:

Does Sarah get anywhere in the course of the film? Does she conquer her obsession with being loved? Is she only in love with love? How are we to feel about her decision to go off with Ken – a man she met at a bowling alley, a man she hardly knows, a Ken? What is going to happen a day, a week, or a month later? Is she brave or foolhardy?

To what extent does Robert really open up in the kitchen scene? When he dances with Sarah? When he dances with Margarita? Does he grow emotionally or learn anything in the entire movie? When he proposes that Sarah remain with him (rather than going off to spend the night with Ken), does it represent a real emotional opening on his part, or is it only one more charming gesture? (Or worse yet, one more example of his immaturity: a proposal that he and she flee even further from experience into a state of emotional, and perhaps physical, incest?)[22] Is Robert's relationship with Jim the dog a step forward or back in his emotional development? What does the dog-man hallucination mean anyway? What does his final wave mean?

The questions have no answers because Cassavetes breaks his characters free from the sorts of summarization upon which they are premised. They make us wonder why we assume that characters and situations in a work of art will yield themselves up to the sort of thumbnail leitmotifs and black–white, good–bad judgments that none of us would ever feel to be adequate to understand our own lives. It is telling that Cassavetes was unhappy when the ending of a trial assembly of the film played more clearly and decisively for a preview audience (so that when Robert proposed that Sarah stay with him, the audience clapped and cheered his obvious change of heart and profession of need for her). Ted Allan, the film's cowriter, was present at the screening and told me he was mystified by Cassavetes' negative reaction, since the response seemed to guarantee that the film would be a commercial success: Cassavetes had finally made a movie audiences could cheer the ending of. But Cassavetes did not want to let the audience off the hook with an easy emotional clarification and release. After the screening, he recut the ending to make the moment much more muted, and to make it harder to read Robert. Audiences of the present edit do not cheer him.

Cassavetes refused to meet the viewer more than halfway. He would not cut his sense of truth to fit the prefabricated emotional and intellectual patterns even the best-intentioned members of his audience brought with them into the movie theater. At the end of the film, when ninety-nine viewers out of a hundred crave a little simple emotion to carry away with them, Cassavetes stands by scenes, characters, and relationships that won't provide condensed meanings. In a culture addicted to easy listening and "lite" viewing, he deliberately made it more than a little hard to read his scenes and characters. Cassavetes refuses to tame the uncertainties of life. He leaves us wonderfully uncertain and suspended. He returns us to the ambiguities and unclarities of lived experience. We can't ultimately "figure out" Robert and Sarah or their film. No more than any of the previous works does *Love Streams* pose easy questions and provide comfortable answers. It leaves us with perplexities, contradictory feelings, and doubts. Cassavetes gives us a form of art that does not attempt to offer clarities and resolutions, but rather tensions and unresolved mysteries. Most films offer clarifications of life. They hand out little fictions to live by, or at least to momentarily displace the confusions associated with the experiences we have outside of the movie theater. Cassavetes goes in the opposite direction. He strips away fictions. He denies us intellectual distance on experience. He forces us into our places of discomfort. He offers a difficult form of art (though it might also be called an invigorating one). As everything I have been arguing should suggest, the emotional irresolution of these scenes is not something to be gotten beyond, but to be lived into. Cassavetes knows not only that growth is painful, but also that growth comes only from pain. Rather than trying to allay our fears and doubts, he forces us into them. In having our easy solutions frustrated, we may come to learn hard truths.

This book has argued that Cassavetes' films mean in an entirely different way than do those of Welles, Hitchcock, or Kubrick. Cassavetes gives us flowingness where they offer stasis, irresolution where they offer conclusion and uncertainty where they provide definitiveness. He gives us meanings that are tentative, plural, and provisional. They melt before our eyes. They relentlessly decompose their own compositions.

That is not to put the difference strongly enough, however. In some respects, it is clear that Cassavetes wants his films to resist interpretation altogether. As I argued in my discussion of *Minnie and Moskowitz*, meaning itself is a limitation beyond which viewers and characters must move. There are wonderful unresolved moments near the end of *Love Streams* after Robert throws Dr. Williams out of the house and begins caring for Sarah himself, when it is impossible to know whether Sarah's state of exposure, desperation, and vulnerability has reached and moved Robert or not. As in the course of any emotional upheaval, it is probably impossible for Robert himself to know what he feels and believes at this moment. Especially in some of the spooky storm scenes, there are magical, Hawthornean moments of imaginative suspension in which Cassavetes orchestrates experiences too deep to be understood the way experiences in Hitchcock or Welles can be.

Perhaps that's a misleading way of formulating the situation, however, since, as I've pointed out throughout the argument, Cassavetes' enemy is not other films' ways of structuring knowledge. His reediting of the ending of *Love Streams* demonstrates that his effort is ultimately pitched against the emerging structurings of his own work. The hooker scene, the kitchen scene, and the jukebox and stairs scenes demonstrate that he fights against the ways narrative inevitably organizes the disorganized, clarifies the mysterious, and stabilizes the fluxional. He struggles against the tendency of his own scenes to clear up things that he wants vague. He resists his own films' tendency to resolve possibilities that he wants to keep open.

As I pointed out in my discussions of *Shadows* and *Faces*, Cassavetes' characters and scenes are endowed with the capacity to move out from under the structurings his own narratives impart to them. Robert is no different in this respect than Lelia, Forst, McCarthy, Moskowitz, or Mabel. As I've already indicated, he is presented in terms of a fairly small number of recurring visual images. His positioning behind walls and around corners, his tuxedo "costuming," his use of his crystal goblet "props," and his clinical "tape recorder interview" approach to personal interaction all function to characterize him and his relationships with others. They might be said to summarize Robert if it were not that each of the scenes involving him (including each of the ones I have mentioned) shows him moving out from under the understandings his own film's images propose. That is to say, the particular details of his performance repeatedly contradict the general metaphors by which it is characterized. His second-by-second expressions of himself (which can be fleetingly considerate, loving, mysterious, funny, and caring) contradict the abstract understandings. He is too interesting, too human to be understood schematically. In effect, the abstractions are present only to provide Robert with a structure to leave behind. He isn't entirely consistent and comprehensible – which is to say he is a little unpredictable. As doomed as Robert may seem to be, Cassavetes' style tells us that his life is still open to possibility.

Near the end of *Love Streams*, Sarah has a dream. In it, she imagines a stunning reunion with her husband and daughter in a grand operatic and balletic wedding ceremony. Her dream represents a glorious ideal of full expression. It imagines a world in which she and everyone around her can live "love's dreams" (to allude to the pun in the film's title) of perfect relationship and complete expression. Insofar as it is staged as a dream sequence, a pure expression of consciousness, however, Cassavetes is proclaiming its limitations. As we saw with the negative example of Cosmo's dreams of beauty, Cassavetes values dreams only insofar as they form the basis for an act of translation into lived expressions and relationships. Sarah's imperative, and her film's, is that she must wake from her dream and engage herself with a world of expressive mediation, frustration, and muddlement. As her dangerous movement out into the storm in the final scene tells us, we must "turn our faces toward sensation" (in James's terms), and live our dreams in actions and events that have none of the clarity and glamour of our ideals.

All of Cassavetes' work might be said to explore what is lost and what is gained in that attempt. Chet, Jeannie, Moskowitz, Mabel, and Myrtle pose the same questions that Sarah does: Can we find a home within which we may live our ideals of free expression? Is the creative imagination isolated and alone? Do our imaginations enrich our lives or only estrange us from others? Can there be a society within which we can express our finest and freest impulses? The films are undeluded about all that is unavoidably lost in the translation of our dreams of freedom and free expression into the limiting expressive realities of life, yet they never give up on the attempt.

Even if they are dubious about the attainment of the goal, Cassavetes' process-centered works are wildly hopeful about the process. That is what makes them feel so strangely uplifting, notwithstanding the suffering they chronicle. No matter the outcome, the attempt is of inestimable value. Indeed, it is almost as if suffering were necessary for something valuable to be created. Sarah has to be moved out of her places of comfort in order to learn anything. She has to be shunted aside, first by Jack and then by Robert, for her to become brave enough to leave behind the false shelter each offers. Perhaps even Robert gains something through the pain of Sarah's departure. In this respect, Cassavetes resembles one of the filmmakers he most admired: Carl Dreyer. For both, spiritual growth is not opposed to suffering, but is made possible by it. Only in being tested by fire can we truly be saved. For Dreyer's Jeanne, Herlofs Marte, Anne, Johannes, Mikkel, Morten, Gabriel, and Gertrud, as for Cassavetes' Lelia, Maria, Minnie, Mabel, Myrtle, and Sarah, the pain is the growth.

The pain isn't depressing because no matter what pressures they are subjected to, characters like Jeannie, Chet, Moskowitz, Mabel, Myrtle, and Sarah are strong enough to take it and still hold onto their visions of possibility. Even the most doomed of Cassavetes' major figures, walking wounded like Robert, Cosmo, and Richard and Maria Forst, don't give up. Their energy is sufficient to the challenges they face. They never (in William James's formulation) "collapse into masses of plaintiveness and fear."[23] They don't abandon their dreams of love or their visions of self-expression no matter how absurd or impossible they seem. The energy of even the craziest and most damned of Cassavetes' figures in the face of overwhelming opposition is far more inspiring than the easy victories of Hollywood heroes. That, finally, is the deepest connection between these characters and their creator, and is why his works deserve a permanent place in any future history of the great American expressive experiment.

Epilogue
The Religion of Doing

I am tiring myself and you, I know, by vainly seeking to describe by concepts and words what I say at the same time exceeds either conceptualization or verbalization. As long as one continues *talking*, intellectualism remains in undisturbed possession of the field. The return to life cannot come about by talking. It is an *act*; to make you return to life, I must set an example for your invitation, I must deafen you to talk, or to the importance of talk, by showing you...that the concepts we talk with are made for purposes of *practice* and not for purposes of insight. Or I must *point*, point to the mere *that* of life, and you by inner sympathy must fill out the *what* for yourselves. ...I say no more: I must leave life to teach the lesson.   – William James[1]

My life? It's not very exciting. The excitement is the work. I live through my films. They are my life.   – John Cassavetes

There is a final reason that none of Cassavetes' films was considered for admission into the artistic canon during his lifetime: The American critical tradition is premised upon a conception of artistic expression entirely different from that to which he subscribed. Almost without exception, American film critics take for granted that art is essentially a Faustian enterprise – a display of power, control, and understanding. In a word, their conception of artistic performance is virtuosic. They prize mastery, arrangement, and prowess. They assume that a work's greatness is traceable to its ability to limit, shape, and organize what the viewer sees, hears, knows, and feels in each shot. Leaf through the pages of film texts as different from one another as Louis Giannetti's *Understanding Movies*, David Bordwell's *Film Art*, and Bruce Kawin's *How Movies Work* (texts largely given over, not surprisingly, to the films of avowed masters of visual and acoustic arrangement in the service of cognitive and emotional control – filmmakers like Eisenstein, Lang, Sternberg, Hitchcock, Welles, Minnelli, Kubrick, and Lynch) and what you will find is an implicit equation of virtuosity and greatness that extends to every aspect of a film's creation: from the writer's ability to create "revelatory" dialogue; to the director's, cameraman's, and lighting supervisor's ability to use lighting, framing, camera angles, and movements to manipulate what the viewer knows and feels; to the editor's and musical supervisor's ability to orchestrate the pacing and dramatic intensity of events down to the last beat. Control and mastery are the goals.

An only slightly debased manifestation of the same set of aesthetic assumptions in journalistic reviewing is the elevation of smartness, cleverness, wit, or stylishness to the status of artistic virtues. They're the workingman's version of what I am calling virtuosity. Once one buys into this value system it's not hard to see why *Citizen Kane*, *Psycho*, *Blood Simple*, *Blue Velvet*, *Manhattan*, and *Dressed to Kill* are treated as artistic masterworks. They *are* smart, witty, clever, and stylish – to a fault. They dazzlingly deploy and play with the conventions and history of cinematic expression.

It is not accidental that there is usually no higher accomplishment within these works than for the most important characters to be witty, clever, stylish, or wised-up in the same way the director of the film shows himself to be. Welles wants his protagonists to have the same kind of personal stylistic panache he displays as a director. The Coens' figures get into trouble precisely to the extent that they are not as wised-up to the rules of the game and as cynically manipulative of them as their creators. A Hitchcock character who is not as clinically detached from an event as he is, who is emotionally vulnerable, open, and unguarded, is definitely going to be in trouble. Even in Woody Allen's work, verbal precocity, cultural literateness, and intellectual acumen are almost always the supreme virtues available to the protagonist.[2]

As this suggests, filmmaking within the virtuoso tradition is essentially a celebration of knowing. These films create worlds in which everyone and everything of importance can be understood, and is understood. Characters are presented and scenes are arranged in certain shorthand ways to facilitate understanding – to eliminate mysteries and uncertainties. (Of course, in certain cases, as with thrillers or mystery films, temporarily keeping us in the dark may serve the narrative purpose of creating an even greater desire for the ultimate explanation, which will always be fulfilled.) The screenwriters, actors, crew, director, and the viewers all participate in a community of psychological, emotional, and intellectual knowing. A large part of the critical and commercial appeal of such works is precisely that they allow the viewer and reviewer to feel that they are part of this cult of complete and perfect knowledge. The central narrative project of these works involves moving from being "out" to being "in," from confusion to clarity, from doubt to certainty.

No set of values could be more opposed to Cassavetes' beliefs about either the process of living or the function of art. Making a film was for him not a display of power and mastery, but rather an act of humility. It did not involve virtuosic arrangement and masterful organization, but patient exploration and tentative discovery. As he himself often said, for his actors, his crew, his viewers, and himself, it was a matter of asking questions to which you didn't know the answers and holding yourself tenderly open, ready to come across new questions at any moment. The work that resulted was an admission of what you didn't know and might never be able to understand. It was not about moving from confusion to clarity – for the actor, the director, or the viewer. Getting lost was the goal – being forced to break your old habits and understandings, giving up your old forms of complacency. The way to wisdom was through not-knowing. The master plot of Cassavetes' work – for himself, his actors, his characters, and his viewers – is an antivirtuosic one: to move out of positions of power and control and into places of fear and uncertainty. That is why the narratives themselves are almost always about going out of control. To allow yourself to let go, to lose control, was part of learning anything. Everything else was what Cassavetes called just doing tricks and playing games with expression. They might be charming, dazzling, entertaining tricks and games (like Robert Harmon's in *Love Streams*), but they are not forms of discovery. Like a bad artist, Harmon pushes preselected buttons; he does not really explore. Cassavetes presents realities too wonderful and too elusive to be served up on a platter according to a prearranged menu. He presents experiences too complex to be reduced to expressive formulas. The result is an art of genuine discoveries.

What is wrong with knowingness is that it removes us from the stimulating turmoil of experience. It separates the individual from the scrambling confusion of living because it figures a set of understandings worked out in advance of the event. For Cassavetes, thought was not something that was done separate from, or that allowed you to rise above, the turbulence of experience, but rather was the process of hacking a path through an experience as it happens. Another way of putting that is to say that, for Cassavetes, filmmaking was not about life, not something that followed the living or analyzed the living; it *was* the living. The styles of Hitchcock, Welles, De Palma, Kubrick, and Lynch tell us that they use film to present

A noncontemplative form of art in which thinking is doing: plunging into an experience in order to learn about it. Working out the scene in which Harry

(Ben Gazzara) humiliates his wife (Meta Shaw) in *Husbands*. Mike Chapman photographs it.

ideas and feelings that they have already worked out. They did their living and thinking, and when they reached a certain point of clarity and resolution, they summarized it in their work. They used the filmmaking process (every stage of it, from scripting to postproduction) to paint by numbers they had determined before they ever studied the dailies. That is not what filmmaking was for Cassavetes. Every dialogue passage, every camera movement or refocusing, every cut tells us that making a film was a way of exploring possibility, of wondering about life, and of reevaluating it, not of reflecting on it from a distance.

Rather than art being a mirror held up to nature that gives back a pale, partial, or distorted reflection of life, in this vision of it, art becomes life itself – life lived at its most intense, interesting, and engaged. It is not in the least a sacrosanct realm set apart from life, with different rules or materials. Henry James and Balzac never lived more excitingly and alertly than when they sat in a room writing, and Cassavetes never lived more sensitively and passionately than when he was making his movies. As he rewrote his scripts, darted about on his sets blocking out actions, or compared trial assemblies in the movieola, he was having experiences with the highest degree of complexity that he could ever attain. In the filmmaking, he launched himself on an adventure of discovery more thrilling, forward-moving, and excitingly exploratory than even those experienced by the characters within the films.

This is thought at its fastest and most acute (and as my comparisons have been meant to suggest, thought fully as profound and complex as Emerson's and William James's philosophical writing), but we need a new definition to do it justice. Living in the shadow of Plato, all of our thinking about thinking is tainted with a contemplative bias. Thought is something that we do when we're not living. It is an intermission from responding to events. It happens in our heads, not in our bodies. It is theoretical and intellectual, not lived and felt. It is rigorous, systematic, and consistent, not playful, experimental, or revisionary. It is conceptual and mental, not active and practical. Our thinking about art is similarly biased – favoring the distancing effects of contemplation over the involvements of action, the stabilities of explanation over the turbulence of experience, and the essences of epistemology over the flowing movements of history. Cassavetes reversed these valuations and practiced a different kind of thought – thought in motion, something that might aptly be called thinking on your feet (and in your body). This is thought not as a contemplative withdrawal from action and event, but as an immersion in them. This is thought not as something static and detached from experience, but as engaged and on the move. This is

Thinking on your feet *in* a film: Gloria and Phil on the run in *Gloria*, improvising a continuously shifting and creative trajectory of response by leaving system, planning, and predictability behind.

thought not as a time-out from the pressures and limitations of life, but as a path of performance through life. This is thought unsupported by (and unfettered by) system and theory and regularity; thought as a state of abandonment to the pursuit of an impulse and the inevitable revision of the course that follows. This is thought not abstracted out of the world, but plunging into it and living in the senses. This is thinking in space, time, and the body.

Among the lively arts, perhaps only in film could such a form of thinking seem unusual or bizarre. It is accepted without question in dance, music, and drama. George Balanchine described it in an interview in terms of his choreographic process:

> [When I'm making a dance, I may] feel something can be done, but if I don't try it out, then I can never do it. You can't sit down and think about dancing, you have to get up and dance. You take people and move them and see if their movements correspond to the music.[3]

When Charlie Parker and Dizzy Gillespie were jamming together, they were thinking this way – not deliberating in advance of the act, not reflecting

Thinking on your feet and in your body, making meanings in space and time. Utterly focused and intensely living in the present moment, Cassavetes works out the blocking and gestures for the sequence leading up to Mabel's suicide attempt and the sequence immediately following it near the end of *A Woman Under the Influence*. Note the script-continuity girl, Elaine Goren, taking notes in the background (*facing, lower right*), and Falk's and Rowlands's well-thumbed copies of the script just put down on the sofa.

on it from a distance, not meditatively rising above the pressures of the performance – but thinking in action. Their thought was the activity of negotiating both sensory and theoretical pressures and constraints, of performing with them and against them, and of shaping a continuously adjusted path of advance along them. In this non-Platonic model, the engagements of action replace the disengagements of contemplation as a way of moving through life.

I hope that this description of Cassavetes' thought process doesn't sound merely poetic. Anyone present on the sets while his films were being made actually witnessed the thinking process I am describing. The filmmaker himself mimed the faces, played the actions, and walked through the blockings in the process of exploring the imaginative possibilities in a scene. He concretely created his own and his characters' destinies in space and time,

step by step, minute by minute. Things were understood not by sitting back and mulling something over, but by stepping into a situation and working through and with it. Given the way the films were created, it is not surprising that the same process of thinking on your feet is the model for all of the important acts of thought that occur within them. Watch Chet, Myrtle, and Gloria – and Mabel and Sarah, above all – in performance and you come close to seeing Cassavetes creating the performances. They are all thinking in and through action, thinking in space and time. They are thinking in their senses and bodies. While other films offer us the luxuries of disembodied visions, contemplative stances, renunciations of action, and various other turns out of the world of practical events and expressions, Cassavetes, like Mabel and Sarah Lawson, shows us possibilities of mastery by involvement. He and they show us what we stand to gain by plunging in over our heads, if we are brave or foolhardy enough to jump out of our seats and run to embrace the world (as Mabel and Sarah repeatedly do).

In these creative circumstances, the nature of meaning itself changes. Whereas the Faustian filmmaker sets out to display an intellectual and emotional mastery of experience, to follow a plan of action, to bend experience to make a series of predetermined "points," in Cassavetes' vision of art, there is no argument, meaning, or point to prove. There is only exploring and moving on, with no end to the process of experiencing, and no goal to reach. That is why he was indifferent to the films as finished products. As he often said, the films didn't matter. What mattered was the doing, the learning, the scrambling, the growing, the discoveries along the way. The work itself (as a series of characters, blockings, camera angles, and editorial choices) was only the tracks left behind as the artist moved through a set of challenging, stimulating experiences. It was the historical record of a series of choices. What this entire book has been devoted to demonstrating is that, to the most alert viewing, that is what the films become again – not bodies of codified knowledge, not a series of views, messages, or statements about experience, but examples of the experiences themselves.

This is film not as *about* thought, or as documenting the conclusions thought has arrived at, but as an act of thought in itself – as a great jazz or dance performance is an act of thought. And like a lucky recording of one of Louis Armstrong's or Charlie Parker's more exultant solos, the film stands not as a statement *about* something, but as a moving illustration of thought in action – thought at its most brilliant and exciting, happening in the present tense. The films are captured records of courses of events – experiences of living intensely, responding rapidly, and feeling your way in the dark. They are enactments of what it is like to live at the highest pitch of awareness, at a level of engagement and responsiveness that few people ever reach in their lives. To a viewer agile enough to keep up with their twists and turns, their energetic swerves, they become inspiring examples of some of the most exciting, demanding paths that can be taken through experience. It's as if Cassavetes hacked his way through a jungle of experiences and we were left studying the moving record of the trail his movements left behind. That is to say, the films are records of movements. They don't yield up meaning as a product, but provide inspiring examples of the energy, intelligence, and emotional agility it takes to have experiences of the most meaningful sort.

Cassavetes' supreme accomplishment is that as a viewer watches the films he actively participates in the same process of exploring, learning, wondering, and changing his mind that the filmmaker did in making them. If we are nimble and strong enough, we move through these experiences the way we move through life at our best. The films themselves are the closest thing to life lived at its most intense; they allow us the experience of fresh, growing, changing experiences. That is why, in the end, we remember them only to be able to forget them. We go to them only to leave them behind by moving beyond them in our own experiences. They bring us back to life.

"I can understand that certain people would like a more conventional form, so that they can borrow it, much like the gangster picture.... You can 'read' it, because it's something you know already. But if you deal with a scene [in an unconventional way], it's very hard for people to get with the film because of their expectations. Once it gets going, they think 'Okay, now let's get going.' It may be going [already], however, in some area they're not aware of.... Other films depend on shorthand, a shorthand for living. You recognize certain incidents and you go with them. People prefer that you condense; they find it quite natural for life to be condensed in films. They like it 'canned.' It's easy for them. They prefer that because they can catch onto the meanings and keep ahead of the movie. But that's boring. I won't make shorthand films. In my films there's a competition with the audience to keep ahead of them. I want to break their patterns. I want to shake them up and get them out of those quick, manufactured truths."

Notes

Introduction: Thinking in Space, Time, and the Body

1. William James, *Writings, 1902–1910* (New York: Library of America, 1987), pp. 762–3.

2. Jonathan Kozol, *The Night Is Dark and I Am Far from Home* (New York: Simon and Schuster, 1990), p. 200.

3. John Simon's dismissal of Cassavetes' oeuvre appeared in *Esquire*, April 1975, p. 54; Stanley Kauffmann's appeared in *The New Republic*, December 28, 1974, p. 20. However, under the principle that any review is better than none, Cassavetes' reception by academic critics might be said to have been even worse than his treatment by journalists: He was as ignored as if he had never lived. The two major American academic film journals, *Wide Angle* and *Cinema Journal*, failed to include a single essay about him during his lifetime, and the complete works of David Bordwell, to cite one representative example, never mention his name.

4. Quotations from and stories about John Cassavetes, Peter Falk, Gena Rowlands, Ben Gazzara, and Al Ruban, and information about the making of the films, come from a variety of published and unpublished sources. Where a quotation or story originated in a previously printed source, the location is cited; otherwise, as in this case, the reader may assume that it comes from the author's informal conversations, taped interviews, and written correspondence with the filmmaker and many of the individuals who knew and worked with him. (For the names of those spoken with, beyond the filmmaker himself, see my acknowledgments.)

For the interested reader, I would note that the largest single collection of Cassavetes' own statements about his life and work (including much previously unpublished material gathered together and published for the first time) is in a French-language book edited by the present author: *John Cassavetes: Autoportraits* (Paris: Editions de l'Etoile/Cahiers du cinéma, 1992). It is indicative of the scholarly and popular indifference to Cassavetes' work in the United States, that, at least as of the time this is written, no American publisher has shown interest in publishing a comparable English-language volume.

5. Marshall McLuhan, *Understanding Media* (New York: McGraw-Hill, 1964), p. 239.

6. I would emphasize that, although for the sake of clarity I couch the argument in terms of Cassavetes' uniqueness, I do not mean to give the impression that his work stands alone. Many other American independent filmmakers (including Robert Kramer, Jim Jarmusch, Charles Burnett, Barbara Loden, Paul Morrissey, and Sara Driver, within the feature tradition, as well as host of documentary filmmakers) are doing things quite similar to Cassavetes.

And, although I only allude to it several times in a few later chapters, outside of the American tradition, Cassavetes' work has important similarities with the work of several European filmmakers, particularly that of Jean Renoir, several of the Italian neorealists (Rossellini and De Sica in particular, for whom Cassavetes frequently expressed his fondness), and certain neo-Renoirian filmmakers like Claude Sautet.

7. Even on the basis of this thumbnail sketch, it should be clear that cinematic essentialism is basically an extension of nineteenth-century Romantic and melodramatic understandings of expression. In the most extreme cinematic cases (which are affiliated with Gothic forms of expression), these depths may be mysterious or hidden or hard to get to, and access to them may be withheld by the artist until the last possible moment, but the principle is the same. When Welles uses Kane's lost childhood as a principle of explanation for much of his later behavior in *Citizen Kane* or when Hitchcock uses Norman Bates's mother complex to account for his behavior in *Psycho*, and both filmmakers conceal the "deep" explanations for their characters' behaviors as long as possible from the viewer, they are simply using a more exaggerated, but not fundamentally different version of the essentializing convention.

I would note that the most detailed argument about the "antiessentialism" of Cassavetes' work is presented in my essays on *Opening Night* and *The Killing of a Chinese Bookie*, in the "Special Issue: John Cassavetes" of *Post Script* (East Texas State University), 11, no. 2 (Winter 1992), 65–90.

8. For a more detailed analysis of this stylistic pattern (which I there call "the meditative shift"), see my *American Vision: The Films of Frank Capra* (Cambridge University Press, 1986), pp. 159–68, 235–40, 433–45.

9. William James, *Writings, 1902–1910*, p. 602.

10. There are a few exceptions to this generalization in Cassavetes' work, but fortunately very few. In fact, the few false moments in his films seem to me to be the occasions in which he attempts to summarize a feeling or a mood in a visual or acoustic effect in the way Welles or Hitchcock do. The yelling back and forth between Richard in the bedroom and Jeannie in the kitchen in *Faces* is an example of what I have in mind. The shouting is clearly meant to symbolize the characters' "noncommunication" with each other. Similarly, the tear that runs down Jeannie's cheek a moment later is meant to tell us something once and for all, outside of the contingencies and entailments of spatial and temporal expression, and independent of her acting. In an earlier scene, the kick-lighting on Jeannie's face when she throws Freddie out and stands opposite Richard represents another expressively unearned moment in which Cassavetes attempts to use visual stylistics to create feelings not expressively enacted by his characters. These moments ring false, and stick out from the rest of *Faces* because they are so different expressively.

11. The substitution of feeling for action is quite thoroughgoing. The airport scene

in *Casablanca* not only implicitly tells us that Rick and Ilsa's states of feeling for each other are more important narratively than their acting on those feelings, but, even more astonishingly, that their states of feeling are more important than Victor Lazlo's present or future actions to save the world.

12. This should suggest the chasm that looms between the work of Cassavetes and that of Woody Allen (with whom he is frequently compared). Allen's work embraces the contemplative-meditative-quietistic turn, relentlessly cultivating states of enriched feeling and thought as substitutes for action and social expression, while Cassavetes' utterly rejects it. For more on the meditative impulse (and what I there call the "slack Romanticism" of Allen's work, see my "Modernism for the Millions: The Films of Woody Allen," *Alaska Quarterly Review*, 8, no. 1–2 (Fall–Winter 1989), 139–69.

13. Ralph Waldo Emerson, *Essays and Lectures* (New York: Library of America, 1983), p. 26. Cassavetes' connection with Emerson, James, and Dewey is a topic that will take this entire book to develop. My general argument is that Cassavetes' work demonstrates what a "pragmatic aesthetic" looks like. His work attempts to bring us to our senses and return us to the world in many of the same ways Emerson, James, and Dewey theorize about. In fact, in several places, I suggest that Cassavetes' work, in the concreteness of its recognition of bodily and sensory reality, is more radical than their theorizing. Needless to say, I am not suggesting that Cassavetes had read Emerson, James, and Dewey. The connection between their work and his is much deeper and more extensive than could have come about through mere acquaintance with their ideas. Merely being "influenced by" them could never have created an artistic style this complex and profound.

14. In *Faces*, the characters' expressions are especially unreliable because of the kinds of figures from which they originate. Most of the main characters are salesmen, professional self-promoters, or semiprofessional con men. What we know about Richard, Freddie, McCarthy, Jackson, and Chet can never be disentangled from their own self-serving motives.

15. I have omitted one other common form of relationship as irrelevant to the present discussion: the romantic blending or blurring of characters' identities that occurs at moments in films like *Casablanca, It Happened One Night, Intermezzo,* and *Now, Voyager.* Although it doesn't represent the competitive defending of individual positions, it is interesting that even in this model of interaction there is not a genuine opening of one character's identity to another's. In place of the sort of robust social interaction between equals that occurs in Cassavetes' work, there is only the absorption of one identity into another.

16. For more on this subject, see the opening pages of my memorial essay on Cassavetes' life and work: "The Adventure of Insecurity," *Kenyon Review*, 13, no. 2 (Spring 1991), 102–21.

1. Selves in the Making: Shadows

1. D. H. Lawrence, "A Propos of *Lady Chatterley's Lover*," *Phoenix II* (New York: Viking, 1968), p. 493; "Morality and the Novel," *Phoenix* (New York: Viking, 1964), p. 529.

2. Henry James, *The Portrait of a Lady*, chapter 19, in *Henry James: Novels, 1881–1886* (New York: Library of America, 1985), p. 398.

3. "The *Playboy* Interview: John Cassavetes," *Playboy* 18 (July 1971), 70.

4. This is, incidentally, why the experience of "otherness" (which I take to be the laudable goal of the multicultural movement) can be just as available in the works of certain "dead white males" as in the works of artists from a minority background, and frequently more available. What many multiculturalists overlook in their attacks on the canon of European and American high art is that the supreme works of genius in the Western tradition are, in the defamiliarizations and dislocations of their styles, often more hospitable to minority sentiments than works with explicitly minority-oriented themes and characters. From Chaucer's poetry and Shakespeare's plays, to Henry James's novels and Sargent's paintings, the most stylistically ambitious works within the Western tradition cherish and bring back to consciousness lost, forgotten, and unexamined impulses within all of us. These works call us to an awareness of the minority *within*. The presence of racially- or sexually-based characters, settings, and references is no guarantee of minority imaginative content, in this sense, and is in fact irrelevant to it. That is why Spike Lee's films can be judged to be far more mainstream, middle-class, middlebrow, and "Hollywood" in their point of view than those of Cassavetes. While Lee merely recycles standard Hollywood melodramatic formulas and clichés, the stylistic experiences of Cassavetes' work provide the viewer with the opportunity to participate imaginatively in truly alien and unconventional forms of knowledge. The presence of minority characters is not what is revolutionary about *Shadows* (or *Killer of Sheep*); the style is. Cassavetes' style represents a breakthrough into a new way of knowing and feeling, something that the presence of no number of minority characters or politically correct themes guarantees the other sort of film.

For another perspective on the role of style in film, see my interview, "Ray Carney's Rules of the Game," *Visions Magazine* (Boston Center for the Arts), no. 10 (Summer 1993), 10–15; 48–9.

5. As proof that the racial dimension of *Shadows* could be taken away without really changing the film, Cassavetes in effect remade the movie with all white principals in 1961 as *Too Late Blues*. In that film, "Ghost" Wakefield, a white musician, negotiates the same expressive snares and traps as do Ben and Hugh.

A flat-minded emphasis on the racial angle of *Shadows* creates interpretive Catch-22s. David James's *Allegories of Cinema* (Princeton, N.J.: Princeton University Press, 1989) sets up a damned-if-you-do, damned-if-you-don't scenario by assuming that *Shadows*'s subject is race relations and then proceeding to condemn Cassavetes for not dealing with the subject directly enough. Perhaps what makes the racial side of *Shadows* so misleading is that Cassavetes is among the most color-blind of filmmakers. This is true not only of *Shadows*, but of his five other works that feature nonwhite characters: *Too Late Blues*, *Husbands*, *A Woman Under the Influence*, *The Killing of a Chinese Bookie*, and *Love Streams*. In recent American film, only the work of Charles Burnett seems equally free from racial stereotyping. While, for example, in Spike Lee's work, a person's race is the most important fact about him, in Cassavetes and Burnett we are all absolutely equal under the skin. For more on James's more or less wholesale misreading of Cassavetes' work, see my review of his book in *American Studies* (Lawrence, Kansas: University of Kansas), 32, no. 1

(Spring 1991), 123–4, and my "Looking without Seeing," *Partisan Review*, 58, no. 4 (Fall 1991), 717–23.

6. All of which should suggest the difference between the work of Cassavetes and not only that of Frank, but of Andy Warhol, Laurie Anderson, David Byrne, John Waters, and David Lynch as well. Lelia shows that as early as 1957 Cassavetes saw postmodernism coming but certainly wasn't rushing to embrace it. (Gloria, Cassavetes' shape-shifting mistress of mercuriality in his 1980 *Gloria*, explores the ethical consequences of being a postmodern personality in even more detail.)

7. As an example, consult David James's *Allegories of Cinema* again, in which this pronouncement occurs: "It is difficult to know whether Ben Carruthers's parody of the James Dean hipster is a function of the actor or the role" – however archly phrased, the context revealing that Professor James clearly intends it to be a limiting judgment on both the actor and his director. I leave undecided whether the actors are choosing to give us slightly bad acting, or are simply *being* slightly bad. In the case of *Shadows*, since we lack extended examples of the actors' performances in other roles, the question is historically undecidable. *Husbands*, on the other hand, stands as clear evidence that Cassavetes was capable of eliciting moments of deliberate "bad acting" (which is of course really great acting) from actors of superb training and ability.

I would also note that although the conflation of the expressive realms (the expressive limits of the performer and the expressive limits of the character he or she plays) is rare in American film, it is routine in works of dance. Choreographers like George Balanchine and Paul Taylor almost always retain and use particular dancers' expressive "limitations" within their performances. Of course, in another sense, what I am calling "limitations" are not limitations at all, but profound strengths. That is what Cassavetes meant when he said: "I try to have the actors not be better than they are. Only in that way can they really say something and reveal themselves."

8. Emerson, *Essays and Lectures*, pp. 57–8.

9. If the difference in the two forms of expression isn't obvious, let me count some of the ways Cassavetes presents the "how do I love thee" moment. In *Shadows*: Tony's remark to Lelia ("I like you"); and Davey's to Lelia ("It's you I like"). In *Husbands*: Gus's comments to Mary in their final conversation ("I'm nuts about you.... I l[ove you]"). In *Minnie and Moskowitz*: Jim's to Minnie ("I love you"); Zelmo's to Minnie ("I just wanted to take you out, show you a little love and understanding"). In *Opening Night*: Manny's to Myrtle ("I love you.... you're the only one I love"). Declared or enacted loving or liking figures everything but the direct and transparent expression of a simple, essential state of loving or liking. In short, *Shadows* is not *Casablanca*.

10. This is repeated in the difference between Chayefsky's *The Bachelor Party* and Cassavetes' *Husbands* – two other apparently similar films with entirely different attitudes toward self-expression. (For the record, *Husbands* is far more indebted to Rogosin's *On the Bowery* and Lumet's *Bye Bye Braverman* than to Chayefsky's work, notwithstanding the plot similarities between Cassavetes and Chayefsky.)

11. When Lelia keeps Davey waiting prior to their date, it becomes impossible to say where her playful teasing of him ends and her genuine insecurity begins. It is probably impossible for her to say, either. When the salesmen in *Faces* carry on in

front of the call girls they pick up, their performance is so theatrical we can't tell what their real feelings are, or even if it means anything to talk about real feelings underneath the performed ones. The connection between surface expressions and feelings becomes even less obvious in the later work. In *A Woman Under the Influence* Mabel seems always to be somewhere just beyond the roles she is playing, never really "in" any of them. In *The Killing of a Chinese Bookie* and *Opening Night*, even though the two main characters are almost never offstage or off-screen, for long periods they seem invisible and inscrutable. Not only can't we tell where they are behind the roles they play, but we can't even tell if there is anyone there at all, anything other than the performance. Virtually everything presented to view is "an act" – a series of stances, gestures, and speeches scripted and edited for public consumption. When *Opening Night*'s Myrtle Gordon "faints" during a play rehearsal, or *Love Streams*'s Sarah Lawson collapses on the floor in the courthouse, either moment is at least potentially as much an act as a faint – an act that cannot be disentangled from a faint even by the character.

12. Henry James, *The Europeans*, chapter 4, in *Novels, 1871–1880* (New York: Library of America, 1983), p. 921.

13. Ibid., chapter 10, p. 1000.

14. Ibid., chapter 4, p. 920.

15. For somewhat more on "scene making" in general, and on the complex ontological status of Sargent's and James's posers, see my *American Vision: The Films of Frank Capra* (Cambridge University Press, 1986), pp. 55–60.

16. Henry James, *The Portrait of a Lady*, chapter 19, in *Henry James: Novels, 1881–1886*, p. 397.

17. Emerson, *Essays and Lectures*, p. 412.

18. I am of course speaking of popular-culture studies as presently constituted as a field of study in American universities. It would be possible to imagine an entirely different and more complex study of popular culture; however, as it now exists, the field is interested in, and its methods of analysis are capable of, dealing with only the lowest and least complex forms of expression – television, Hollywood movies, and popular music. It simply cannot handle the complexities of genuine artistic expression.

The field is also founded on a conceptual fallacy: that just because certain forms of entertainment are broadcast widely in a technological culture, they mirror the complexities of the imaginative or material life of its people. That simply isn't true, at least not in contemporary America. In short, there is virtually no relationship between the actual popular culture on the streets and in our homes, and what passes for the objects of "pop culture" in the university curriculum. Why should there be? The objects studied are not really forms of popular culture at all, since they are neither a creation of the common person, nor a true expression of his or her feelings and beliefs. In fact, works like "The Cosby Show," *Star Wars*, beer commercials, and Madonna's videos are even more the creation of cultural elites and an expression of parochial special interests than Cassavetes' films are, and they bear even less relationship to the way the man or woman on the street really lives and feels than his films do.

Actual popular feelings and practices in America (and in any imaginable culture) are infinitely more complex and nuanced than television, music, and the movies depict, and only college professors seem to make the mistake of confusing one thing with the other. By misdirecting its attention in this way, away from the complex and authentic forms of popular culture that actually exist in the form of families, jobs, and living conditions, and toward the most banal forms of mass marketing, popular-culture studies make the simpleminded reductiveness of its own analyses possible. If some future, but as yet unrealized, form of popular-culture studies actually shifted its attention away from junky movies and music, and to the authentic manifestations of American popular culture – the American family, American dating practices, the American workplace, etc. – and developed methods nimble and flexible enough to deal with those things as they really exist in all of their complexity, that form of popular-culture studies would not necessarily be unable to deal with the semantic slipperiness of Cassavetes' work.

19. Other moments in which one hears the filmmaker more or less directly speak through a character include Burt Lancaster's remark that "We ought to be treating the parents, not the kids" in A Child Is Waiting; Seymour Cassel's "mechanical men" speech near the end of Faces; Cosmo's "I'm amazing," and Gena Rowlands's comment that "for every problem there is an answer" in Love Streams.

20. Husbands is an exception to this generalization. Almost as if Cassavetes needed relief from the unremitting horrors of Faces, he hearkens back to the lighter tone and mood of Shadows. But with that exception, I would note that even his "lightest" subsequent works, Minnie and Moskowitz and Gloria, border on being paranoid visions. A Woman Under the Influence, Opening Night, and The Killing of a Chinese Bookie more than border on it.

2. Noncontemplative Art: Faces

1. The quotation from John Cassavetes is compiled from several different sources. The first section, before the ellipsis, is from Gautan Dasgupta, "A Director of Influence," Film (England), May 1975, p. 6; the second excerpt is from Jonas Mekas, "Movie Journal," Village Voice, Dec. 23, 1971, p. 64; the third excerpt is from John Cassavetes, Faces (New York: New American Library, 1970), pp. 8–9. The first sentence of the second paragraph is from The Film Director as Superstar, Joseph Gelmis, ed. (New York: Doubleday, 1970), p. 78. The rest of the paragraph is from André Labarthe, "A Way of Life: An Interview with John Cassavetes," Evergreen, March 1969, p. 47.

2. Love Streams is an even more extreme example of Cassavetes' antiestablishing technique: The true relationship of the two main characters – arguably the most important single fact about them – is suppressed until the movie is about two-thirds over. This aspect of his work, which constitutes some of its most carefully crafted effects, unfortunately only provided ammunition for reviewers to argue that it proved how disorganized his scripting and how sloppy his editing was. A comparison of Cassavetes' shooting scripts with the final films refutes the charge that such effects were the result of cinematic inadvertence or self-indulgence. The lacunas and ellipses in his work either were scripted into them (e.g., the zany jumps between scenes in Minnie and Moskowitz) or were introduced during the editing process, when interstitial explanatory footage was deliberately omitted from the assembly. In no case are the narrative gaps the consequence of failing to have sufficient coverage of a

scene or due to improvisatory deviations from the script. Far from Cassavetes being casual or slipshod in his methods, all of the evidence is that he deliberately worked to "mess up" overly neat sequences, frequently by removing explanatory material that was already there. Cassavetes rearranged (or dropped) shot footage in order to avoid explaining too much, pinning down characters' intentions, or revealing details of their relationships too early in a film. He felt that such information would inhibit his viewers from being as interpretively open and active as he wanted them to be.

3. The first paragraph is from "The Pragmatist Account of Truth and Its Misunderstanders," James, *Writings, 1902–1910*, p. 929; the second and third are from "Bergson and His Critique of Intellectualism," pp. 745–7.

4. Several scenes in *Husbands* similarly use drunkenness to justify their characters' intensity, but by the time Cassavetes made *Minnie and Moskowitz* and *A Woman Under the Influence* he simply dispensed with the pretext and began with the state of full expression. Cassavetes' two most explicit dream films, *Gloria* and *The Killing of a Chinese Bookie*, are only the most extreme examples of the way in which, as in a dream, narrative events function as externalizations of states of internal eventfulness. All of his films are dream films to this extent: They are attempts to give full expression to unusually intense states of feeling.

5. *Opening Night* takes the fallacies of identification as its explicit subject. It is about an actress named Myrtle Gordon; the narrative concerns three characters' acts of identification and the problems they create for the characters who indulge in them. Two of Myrtle's fans, Nancy Stein and Dorothy Victor, identify with the fictional characters she plays on stage, and more or less live their lives through them. The third act of identification in the film is Myrtle's own. She profoundly identifies with Nancy Stein (whose life represents an ideal of emotional openness and sexual desirability in Myrtle's mind) and attempts to live her life through Nancy.

What tells us that Cassavetes saw identification as a limiting stance is that he embeds these acts of identification in a cinematic narrative that repeatedly points out their inadequacy. While Nancy Stein, Dorothy Victor, and Myrtle herself, in effect, attempt to focus the narrative and reduce it to one point of view, Cassavetes repeatedly disperses it into a series of views beyond their own. The most obvious way he does this is by simply presenting three different acts of identification in one movie, so that the viewer can't wholeheartedly enter into ("identify with") any one of them. More complexly, however, in the course of *Opening Night* he makes the viewer skeptical of *all* merely personal views. Whereas Myrtle, Nancy, and Dorothy attempt to reduce the film and everything that happens in it to an expression of a personal perspective (their own situation conflated with that of the fantasy figure through which they imaginatively live), Cassavetes' cinematic style spins the actual narrative away from the control or knowledge of any one individual. At every point in the narrative that each of the three characters attempts to reduce experience to a private imaginative relationship, Cassavetes shows the viewer that her act of identification leaves out important sides of the story. While identification simplifies, he complicates.

The fallacies of the identification process in *Opening Night* become a shorthand way of indicating how we imaginatively falsify experience when we see it only through one set of eyes. The film's imaginative multiplicity relentlessly criticizes every form of single-mindedness. The consequence is a dazzling (and sometimes dizzying) "perspectivism" in which Cassavetes continuously circulates the viewer through irreconcilable views of the same experience.

The cultivation of multiple-mindedness extends to the smallest details of the film. The shots of groups pick up one individual's face after another and emphasize how many different personal points of view there are in even the simplest gatherings of people. No matter how minor a character, he or she is given at least a momentary "voice" in the film. In many of the scenes in the theater, Cassavetes' camera will uncannily ignore a major character and unexpectedly linger on one of the supporting characters – a stagehand, Myrtle's dresser, or the stage manager – in order to give each of them his due. In the midst of one of the most emotional moments in the film (the scene in which Myrtle fails to show up for the New York opening night and the director is running to a telephone to speak with her after she calls in at the last minute) one astonishing shot concludes by letting the emotional action (the director's dash for the phone) pass through and out of the shot, which remains bizarrely paused on a stagehand sitting off to the side, emotionally uninvolved, amused by the crisislike atmosphere. Cassavetes forces us to acknowledge the stage-hand's truth too. He audaciously yanks us outside the hyped-up emotionalism and forces us to recognize that even while Myrtle is having a nervous breakdown and a production is being put in jeopardy, others are ignoring or laughing at the whole thing. *Opening Night* flickers with weird glimpses of other lives, other ways of living.

Although this film is Cassavetes' most elaborate experiment in multiple-mindedness, to some extent all of his work does the same thing, with the partial exceptions of *A Woman Under the Influence* and *Gloria*. One might speculate that the commercial success of both works was in fact due to their being the most conventional of Cassavetes' films in terms of allowing fairly uninterrupted identi-fication with one central figure, and maintaining more or less one personal point of view on the events (with some exceptions).

6. William James, *Writings, 1902–1910*, pp. 874–5.

7. If it weren't already clear, *Faces*'s style demonstrates the deep connection be-tween the James who wrote "On a Certain Blindness in Human Beings," on the one hand, and the James of *The Meaning of Truth* and *A Pluralistic Universe*, on the other. James's respect for different personal points of view is completely of a piece with the perspectivism of his philosophical stance. His metaphysical pluralism is an extension into the realm of the intellect of his democratic eclecticism in life.

8. To avoid confusion, let me emphasize that although the conventional view of *Citizen Kane* is that it is doing this, it is in fact not happening. Providing a series of partial narrations is entirely different from providing a partial view with no narrator. The very fact that we can say that each of Welles's storytellers may be personally biased in one way or another is an indication that if personal bias were filtered out, a correct or ideal view could emerge. Cassavetes simply doesn't believe this is possible. All views, even personally unbiased ones, even nonpersonal ones, are partial and incomplete. Cassavetes is far more philosophically skeptical than Welles.

9. William James, *Writings, 1902–1910*, p. 1160.

10. The world would be a boring place if our words did mean the same thing: I

had no sooner written the preceding paragraph than I noticed the UPS truck coming up my street. Because an important overnight package was scheduled to arrive, I trotted to the front door and greeted the delivery man as he was on his way up the front steps, but before he had a chance to ring the bell. I explained why I had beaten him to the door by enthusiastically declaring, "I knew you were coming." He replied by muttering something about "the noisiness of that damn engine." It was truly something out of a Cassavetes movie. Where either or both of us expected a meeting of minds (and where the delivery man left perhaps still thinking one had taken place), the brief interchange revealed no shared perspective, but the discovery (for me at least) that I was as much trapped in a box as he was. My eagerness to get the package was ultimately as alien to him as his day-to-day engine troubles were to me. Abyss had greeted abyss.

11. As an illustration of how one way of thinking can be preferred over others, notice the extent to which the major characters in Woody Allen's *Manhattan* and *Annie Hall* sound like little Woodies, even to the point that gender differences are erased, the women sounding as much like chips off the fatherly block as the men. The vocal homogenization in Allen's work implicitly tells us that a "best" or "correct" imaginative stance exists that a character must live up to. In fact, to the extent that Allen's characters haven't mastered their creator's forms of wry meditativeness, self-deprecating humor, witty weltschmerz, and comical cynicism, they are judged to be intellectually and emotionally inadequate. Allen's films are less dramas (in which different points of view are genuinely respected and honored), than acts of ventriloquy, in which one voice speaks through everyone and everything. There is only one point of view in Allen's work: the director's.

While I am on the subject of Allen's work, I would note in passing that the level of abstraction in Allen's approach to his characters and his material goes hand in glove with the level of abstraction in the content of the characters' conversations and the tones of their voices. That is to say, the absence of individual voices in Allen's work is actually only a symptom of a larger failure of contact with the specifics of sensory and emotional experience. His films are essentially works of abstraction, abstracted from the felt textures of life in several different ways: They compare abstract imaginative stances; do it from an abstracted perspective; and cultivate states of abstraction in their viewers. They are allegories peopled with characters who are depersonalized spokesmen for abstract imaginative positions. For somewhat more on this subject, see my previously cited essay: "Modernism for the Millions: The Films of Woody Allen" and *Post Script*, pp. 38–9.

12. It was ironic that during Cassavetes' lifetime, these aspects of his dialogue passages were written off by his reviewers as a side effect of the filmmaker's alleged improvisational methods. The actors were apparently making up their lines and not doing a very good job of it. In fact, not only was the loopiness and elision scripted, but a comparison of successive drafts of Cassavetes' scripts reveals that he usually moved from neatness to clutter in his revisions. He messed up previously clear conversations with side issues, worked against an overly logical presentation of an argument, and muddled the clarity of ideas with confusions of feeling.

13. The confusingly elliptical, convoluted inarticulateness of the main characters in *Husbands* is another example of how Cassavetes holds his characters beyond reductive understanding and their situations beyond simplifying definition. Cassavetes

gives us unsettled consciousnesses which cannot be understood in terms of specific problems or solutions. There is an anecdote related to this issue concerning a comment Cassavetes made to Ben Gazzara during the shooting of *Husbands*. Gazzara was genuinely bewildered by the inarticulateness of the character he played, and asked Cassavetes why his character couldn't simply say what his problem or need was at some point in the movie. Cassavetes' answer was that if such articulateness were possible they wouldn't need to make a feature film in the first place. The actors and actions could be eliminated, and *Husbands* could be done with a voice-over narration.

14. For a literary analogue to what Cassavetes does dramatically, one might compare similar imaginative expansions and contractions of characters' identities in Hawthorne's "The Canterbury Pilgrims" or "The Ambitious Guest," or in Henry James's *What Maisie Knew* or *The Spoils of Poynton*. James and Hawthorne depend on a reader's ability to pursue imaginative flutterings in their prose, energetic verbal pulsings that won't quite resolve or formulate themselves. Cassavetes similarly depends on his viewers' ability to suspend themselves amid the unresolved vocal and facial twitchings in his actors. In either case, what is explored is the ability of a character to elude reductive definitions of character. Whether in prose or in pictures, the effect is as challenging to describe as it is exhilarating to experience. I'd emphasize that most of the fluxions in Cassavetes' scenes are expressed not in characters' words and actions, but, much more subtly, in their changing facial expressions, gestures, and vocal intonations. Looking ahead to the time Cassavetes' work becomes widely available for viewing on videotape, I'd anticipate that much of the effect will be lost when the films are viewed on a small screen. There is no substitute for 35mm projection on a theatrical screen, especially with works that ask us to enter into the process of watching and listening so intensely.

15. "John Cassavetes Goes for the Edge," in Grover Lewis, *Academy All the Way* (San Francisco: Straight Arrow Books, 1974), p. 115.

16. William James, *Writings, 1902–1910*, p. 600.

17. Emerson, *Essays and Lectures*, p. 404.

18. Ibid.

19. Ibid., p. 119.

20. Bruce Henstell, ed. *Dialogue on Film #4: John Cassavetes and Peter Falk* (Beverly Hills, Calif.: American Film Institute, 1972), p. 13.

21. Henstell, *Dialogue on Film #4*, p. 12.

3. *Beating the System:* Minnie and Moskowitz

1. The first paragraph is from "Circles" in Emerson, *Essays and Lectures*, pp. 404–5; the second is from "Fate," pp. 953 and 964.

2. I would note that a sexual bias is implicit in the screwball form insofar as the woman is almost always asked to change more than the man. *Minnie and Moskowitz* participates in that aspect of the form as well. Cassavetes asks Minnie to meet Seymour more than halfway. More of the drama involves her moving toward his position than his moving toward hers. At the same time, the film isn't entirely a one-way street. Seymour is asked to break his patterns too, and to come at least part of the way toward her. He has obviously spent his life as a carefree, footloose,

no-strings-attached Romeo, and must prove his ability to be emotionally committed to one person. He must show that he is willing to settle down and have a family.

3. This is true not only of the character, Seymour Moskowitz, but of the actor, Seymour Cassel, who played him, and is one of the reasons Universal wanted Cassavetes to replace Cassel with Jack Nicholson as the lead in the film. Nicholson is rakish, dashing, and exciting in the conventional Hollywood way. Cassavetes realized that casting him as Moskowitz would have undermined the critique of Hollywood values that the character was designed to figure.

4. This suddenly changes in the final scene of the film, at which point Cassavetes moves his characters into a "green world" in a fairy-tale coda. As in so much other American art, at the end of *Minnie and Moskowitz*, Cassavetes creates a dream world, a community of imagination, when he can't find a way to bring one into existence in reality.

5. The passage is from the final version of the shooting script, dated 3/23/71 on its title page. (The movie Minnie and Florence attend was originally planned to be *Algiers*, hence the references to Charles Boyer.) The written passage differs slightly from Gena Rowlands's filmed performance, but I am quoting it, rather than the actual film, in order to give a concrete illustration of how closely Cassavetes' actors adhered to the script in their performances. (The ellipses do not indicate missing matter, but are in the script itself.)

6. This earlier version of the script was published by Black Sparrow Press in 1973 in a limited, numbered edition signed by the director and cast.

7. Emerson, *Essays and Lectures*, p. 462.

8. This is equally true of *The Killing of a Chinese Bookie*, in which Cassavetes idiosyncratically appropriates and redeploys characters and images from Sternberg's *The Blue Angel* (with an occasional tip of his hat toward Welles's *Citizen Kane*). As if to show that acts of troping may be directed toward oneself as well, in his final film, *Love Streams*, Cassavetes plays with and against characters and images from his own previous work.

9. Emerson, *Essays and Lectures*, pp. 403 and 409.

10. Ibid., p. 476.

11. Ibid., p. 954.

12. For more on this topic I would refer the reader to my "The Adventure of Insecurity: The Films of John Cassavetes," *Kenyon Review*, 13, no. 2 (Spring 1991), 111–13.

13. I would note that the gymnastic energy and quickness of Cassavetes' performance as a director distinguishes it from the cooler, more meditative and intellectual play of European filmmakers like Godard, Rivette, or Resnais. Cassavetes' movements are not cerebral or deliberative but as athletic, quick, intuitive, and action-oriented as Charlie Parker's playing or Jackson Pollock's painting. Godard and the others call us out of the world of events into a realm of meditation and contemplation. Like Pollock and Parker, Cassavetes calls upon us to turn our thoughts into actions. Furthermore, unlike the work of most European artists and critics, Cassavetes' "critique" or "deconstruction" of cinematic forms is not negative or nihilistic. His performance is exultant. It is an affirmation of power. To the extent that we can bend these forms, we are strong, not weak. His characters display the same off-balance balance that the filmmaker does. Cassavetes is not nostalgic for a time when

the forms with which he performs could merely be accepted; he does not see their fragmentation or destruction as a loss, or as placing a limitation on our present expressive possibilities. This seems to me to be where Kouvaros and Zwierzynski go wrong in their otherwise admirable essay on Cassavetes' work: "Blow to the Heart: Cassavetes' *Love Streams*," *Post Script*, 11, no. 2 (Winter 1992), 27–36.

14. William James, *Writings, 1902–1910*, p. 1313.

15. Emerson, "Self-Reliance," *Essays and Lectures*, p. 261.

16. Ibid., p. 265.

17. Ibid., p. 271.

18. As a sidelight I'd mention that, like many accomplished actors, Cassavetes was a talented mimic. In a conversation he would occasionally throw off voices, faces, and gestures to the point that you couldn't quite tell where "he" was underneath it all. As one of his closest friends put it: "I never knew what he really thought. He was always 'on,' at least a little bit."

19. I have brought together three separate statements by the filmmaker. The first three sentences were said to Grover Lewis in "John Cassavetes Goes for the Edge," p. 116; the sentence between the ellipses was said to Dolores Barclay in *The Los Angeles Times*, July 8, 1980, part 6, p. 4; following the second ellipsis, the final sentence was published by Jonas Mekas in "Movie Journal," *Village Voice*, December 23, 1971, p. 63.

4. An Artist of the Ordinary: A Woman Under the Influence

1. Lawrence, "Why the Novel Matters," *Phoenix*, p. 534.

2. Walt Whitman, "Democratic Vistas," in *Whitman: Poetry and Prose* (New York: Library of America, 1982), pp. 929, 931, and 936.

3. Cassavetes acknowledged in an interview that when he shopped for locations, he considered and rejected more ethnically realistic ones than the house and location he finally chose: "We looked at maybe 150 houses. It was really hard to find one within our budget. Some of the houses had plastic on the furniture, plastic on the walls. And most of the money went into electric appliances. That's a very real thing. But we didn't want it." Judith McNally, "*A Woman Under the Influence*," *Filmmaker's Newsletter*, January 1975, p. 26.

4. Henry James, *The Portrait of a Lady*, chapter 19, in *Novels, 1881–1886* (New York: Library of America, 1985), p. 398.

5. See the various discussions in my *American Vision: The Films of Frank Capra* (Cambridge University Press, 1986).

6. Stanislavski gave license for this understanding of the Method in his best-known text, the one used by Lee Strasberg as a kind of bible, *An Actor Prepares*. I quote from the 1932 Hapgood translation, the edition used by the first generation of teachers and trainees at the Actors Studio:

> Of significance to us is the reality of the inner life of a human spirit in a part, and a belief in that reality. We are not concerned with the actual naturalistic existence of what surrounds us on the stage, the reality of the material world! This is of use to us only insofar as it supplies a general background for our feelings. (p. 122)

7. Many of Cassavetes' central characters clearly function as alter egos for the filmmaker. In fact, in response to an earlier book I wrote about his work, he said, "The thing that interested me most was that you found me in the films." Cassavetes naturally imagined ordinary experience in dramatic metaphors. He thought of people as being actor-directors of their everyday lives. The metaphor of the main character as an actor-director runs through most of his work, and is more than implicit in the two films Cassavetes made immediately following this one: *The Killing of a Chinese Bookie* and *Opening Night*. I discuss this aspect of his work in more detail in my essays on *Woman Under the Influence* and *The Killing of a Chinese Bookie* in *Post Script*, 11, no. 2 (Winter 1992), 58–77.

There is further circumstantial evidence that Nick and Mabel are alter egos for the director–actor pair of Cassavetes and Rowlands. Cassavetes and Rowlands frequently presided over meals for the cast and crew of their films very similar to the meal of spaghetti that Nick and Mabel supervise in the movie. According to Sam Shaw and Peter Falk, between takes of *A Woman Under the Influence*, the cast and crew ate spaghetti with Cassavetes and Rowlands at the same table at which Nick and Mabel and their construction worker friends eat in the movie. As Falk jokingly explained: "A lot of spaghetti got eaten.... You never knew when the camera might be going."

This is the place to mention that another moment in *A Woman Under the Influence* overlaps with the film's real-life process of creation. Mabel's brief scene with Eddie in the kitchen in which she yells at him for tracking up the floor playfully alludes to frequent occurrences on the set during the shooting. The set decorator, Cassavetes' cousin Phedon Papamichael, was notorious for his fussiness about keeping the set clean and frequently berated the cast and crew for tracking up the floor or messing up the house.

8. On the subject of Cassavetes' directing strategies, and specifically his technique of shooting an actor when he might be unaware the camera was running, Peter Falk only half-facetiously described his experience in *Woman* (in a continuation of his remarks from the previous note): "You never knew when the camera might be going. [Laughing] And it was never: 'Stop. Cut. Start again.' [John] would walk in the middle of a scene and talk; [and though you didn't realize it,] the camera kept going. So I never knew what the hell he was doing. [Laughs] But he ultimately made me, and I think, every actor less self-conscious, less aware of the camera than anybody I've ever worked with."

On Leola Harlow's experience in *Husbands*, see my essay on the film in *Post Script*, 11, no. 2 (Winter 1992), 48.

9. Joseph Gelmis, "John Cassavetes," in *The Film Director as Superstar* (New York: Doubleday, 1970), p. 83.

10. The possibilities of intimacy that Mabel makes around her dining room table or in her backyard, and that Cassavetes made on his set, *Love Streams*'s Sarah Lawson will attempt in public settings. She bares her soul and offers an instant, intimate relationship with complete strangers – with occasionally comic consequences, as in the scenes with the two train station baggage porters, or with the manager of a bowling alley.

11. Number 451: *The Complete Poems of Emily Dickinson*, Thomas Johnson, ed. (Boston: Little, Brown, 1960), pp. 216–17.

12. As I have pointed out, Cassavetes employed comparable moments of deliberately bad acting in some of Lelia's, Ben's, and Tony's scenes in *Shadows*. Her melodramatics and their unmotivated slouches, jaw tightening, mumbling, and beat taking were attempts to make rhetoric substitute for truth. In the two films following this one, *The Killing of a Chinese Bookie* and *Opening Night*, Cosmo Vitelli's three successive curtain-closing speeches, and many of Sarah Goode's scenes, are textbook examples of using acting not to dig down to emotional truth, but to cover it up and deny its existence.

13. John Dewey, *Art as Experience* (New York: Putnam, 1934), p. 3.

14. Ibid., p. 3.

15. Ibid., p. 9.

16. Ibid., p. 6.

17. John Dewey, *Experience and Nature* (La Salle, Illinois: Open Court, 1925), pp. 288–90.

18. Dewey, *Art as Experience*, p. 19.

19. Emerson, *Essays and Lectures*, p. 492.

20. What made Cassavetes' movies harder to interpret was that they didn't do the viewers' or the critics' work for them. The films to which they were accustomed declared their own meanings; they told the critic what to know and how to feel at every moment. They made things easy. Their allegorical, metaphoric, symbolic truths made meaning simple, abstract, and clear. Cassavetes didn't. He didn't believe in the possibility of easy, abstract, excerptable forms of meaning.

21. Another perspective on the subject of bodily knowledge is presented in my *Speaking the Language of Desire* (Cambridge University Press, 1989), pp. 147–52, and in my *American Vision*, pp. 311–23.

22. Emerson, *Essays and Lectures*, p. 414. I would note that similar moments of abandon are expressed by Florence in *Faces* and by Sarah in *Love Streams* – most thrillingly when she throws herself into Ken's arms and kisses him.

23. It is possible that Cassavetes was inspired to experiment with these sorts of tonal swerves by his friendship with Edward McSorley, a novelist to whom Sam Shaw introduced him at the start of his career. McSorley's writing is characterized by extreme tonal oscillations. If such an influence existed, the student outdid the teacher: Even McSorley never blended the comic and tragic as seamlessly and delicately as Cassavetes does in this film.

24. Lawrence, "The Novel," in *Phoenix II*, p. 418.

25. "Who's Crazy Now? [John Cassavetes] Interview with Marjorie Rosen," in *MS Magazine*, February 1975, 34.

26. This layering is entirely different in effect from the kind of visual layering Bazin describes in Wyler's work, and different also from that in the work of Welles or Altman. It does not function tendentiously and intellectually (as theirs does), but rather suggests the impossibility of reducing experience to a series of abstract "points." Wyler's, Welles's, and Altman's layerings are acts of analysis and simplification; Cassavetes' are acts of complication.

27. It is central to Cassavetes' conception of her that Mabel is a "theatrical artist" of family life. Cassavetes was repeatedly attracted to the depiction of "theatrical" figures – ranging from onstage pros like Hughie, Cosmo, and Myrtle, to offstage practitioners of amateur theatricals like Ben, Lelia, Gus, Mabel, Gloria, and Sarah

– because such figures free themselves from the constraints of any one identity by making themselves capable of many. Like the most interesting figures in *Shadows* and *Faces*, Mabel is endowed with a capacity to cut against her own tones and stances that implicitly equates her performative powers with the writing-directing-editing powers of her creator. Her capacity to create and revise herself as she goes along is as great as Cassavetes' own capacity to revise her. Yet, at the same time, as Lelia, Gloria, Mabel, and Sarah Lawson show, Cassavetes knew that living the theatrical ideal of plasticity was much harder than merely writing, acting, and directing it on stage or film.

28. *Ralph Waldo Emerson*, Richard Poirier, ed. (New York: Oxford University Press, 1990), p. 471.

29. Cosmo Vitelli, the principal character in the film following this one, goes even farther in the direction of giving himself away than Mabel does. He devotes himself so completely to fulfilling others' dreams and ideals that he gives up his own. He makes himself so responsive to and responsible for others, that he forgets his responsibilities to himself. I go into more depth about this side of the film in my essay in the previously cited "Special Issue: John Cassavetes," *Post Script*, pp. 65–77.

30. In recent interviews, Peter Falk has said he felt that if Nick truly loved Mabel and had told her so, many of her problems would have been alleviated; but this understates the complexity of her situation. In any case, telling her he loves her is strictly a verbal, mental approach to Mabel's problem, when all of *Woman* is designed to tell us that meaning has its source in much deeper places than our minds and our words. Meaning must be enacted and embodied to count for anything in Cassavetes' work, and if Nick does anything, he has to find a way to show love, not just say it. Even that, however, would not change Mabel's fate materially. She is what she is, independently of others' expressions or wishes, just as Myrtle Gordon or Sarah Lawson are. She is free and independent (even in her tragedy), not a victim of anyone else's actions.

31. *Shadows*'s Lelia and *Too Late Blues*'s "Ghost" Wakefield figure this same state of turning themselves into missing persons. In *The Killing of a Chinese Bookie*, *Opening Night*, and *Gloria*, Cassavetes' respective masters and mistresses of ventriloquy – Cosmo Vitelli, Myrtle Gordon, and Gloria Swenson – carry the expressive crisis beyond the point of crisis. They become invisible in their own work. (For literary examples of comparable ontological crises, compare James's *The Princess Casamassima* and *The Spoils of Poynton*. Hyacinth Robinson and Fleda Vletch are distant cousins to Cassavetes' Mabel, Myrtle, and Sarah.)

5. The Path of Greatest Resistance: The Killing of a Chinese Bookie

1. D. H. Lawrence, *D. H. Lawrence and Italy* (New York: Viking Press, 1972), p. 107 (*Etruscan Places*: "Volterra"); and *The Symbolic Meaning: The Uncollected Versions of "Studies in Classic American Literature,"* Armin Arnold, ed. (Fontwell, Arundel, England: Centaur Press, 1962), p. 236.

2. The thriller genre in general, and the works of the master of cinematic control and emotional manipulation in particular, are diametrically opposed to those of Cassavetes. While his films are celebrations of an adventure of discovery for both their characters and their creator, Hitchcock's are machines for the working out of mechanical systems of determinism, predestination, and control.

3. It seems clear to me that the greatest artists have understood this model of creation all along, but critics have been slow to grasp its lessons. In this sense, "improvisation" is not an avant-garde concept, but is the way *all* great art is made. Its meanings are discovered in the work of doing. Certainly this is the way all writing is accomplished.

4. One can't help feeling that it is only because film criticism is in its adolescence that Welles's rhetorical hand waving – his narrative hocus-pocus, stylistic blue smoke and mirrors – can pass for artistic complexity. It's kitsch-modernism – modernism for the multitudes who would never put up with the real thing in D. H. Lawrence or William Faulkner. In terms of the depth of its mysteries, *Citizen Kane* is closer to *The Adventures of Sherlock Holmes* than to *The Sound and the Fury*. A similar point might be made about the oft-praised "bravura" passages in Hitchcock's work.

5. Henstell, ed., *Dialogue on Film #4*, pp. 6–7.

6. Unfortunately, even much criticism of avant-garde and independent film suffers from the same limitations. Rather than talking about a text's relationship to life, it discusses its relationship to other texts. Texts have only a diacritical purpose. You would think from the work of David James, for example, that independent film's most important function and meaning is to criticize mainstream film. One work chases the tail of another so closely that noncinematic experience never breaks through the hermeneutic circle. In this intertextual orgy of recycling, stupid, messy, wonderful life never gets in the way. Perhaps that helps explain why Cassavetes' work was ignored by so-called advanced American film criticism for three decades, notwithstanding that he was America's most advanced filmmaker.

7. There are autobiographical dimensions to Cosmo. One of them is that around the time he made *Bookie*, the filmmaker himself frequently talked about establishing a community to support independent filmmaking and dramatic production that would have had rough parallels with Cosmo's repertory theater company. He never did it, and the so-called farm never got beyond the talking stage (although twice in the subsequent years, in 1979 and again in 1987, he briefly organized his own Los Angeles–based repertory theater company.) On the other side of the issue, the thrust of my argument is that the differences between Cosmo and Cassavetes are far more important than the similarities.

8. Cosmo's club is decidedly old-fashioned compared with the massage parlors that have dominated the strip for the past two decades. As a sidelight, it is worth mentioning that Cassavetes had a personal interest in burlesque as an art form. He was introduced to it by his longtime friend and sometimes producer, Sam Shaw, in New York in the 1950s, during the final decade or so before changes in American culture forced burlesque houses out of business, and during the last years of the careers of many of the legendary performers. In this respect, Cosmo's story is an homage to Cassavetes' own youthful experiences. On the subject of nudity in art, the filmmaker once told me: "Bodies are not interesting; it's our imaginations that make them interesting." Cosmo's life and work are dedicated to the same belief.

9. Charles Hartman, *Jazz Text: Voice and Improvisation in Poetry, Jazz, and Song* (Princeton, N.J.: Princeton University Press, 1991), p. 82.

10. Compare the moments in *A Woman Under the Influence* when the car stalls, the

beer fizzes, the water spills, or the telephone cord gets tangled; or, near the end of *Husbands*, notice Mary's slip on the sidewalk. Consider, in addition, the moment in *Love Streams* in which the door of the hearing room momentarily sticks when Sarah Lawson tries to open it, or the moment a few scenes later when Robert Harmon takes a misstep around a cab in his driveway. At the very beginning of the same film, notice Robert's blowing his line when he has a brief coughing fit; or, later on, note the ash on his lapel when he is standing in front of a Vegas casino. Are these moments mere accidents or errors? Many of them clearly are not. For example, a careful viewing of *Woman* reveals that the car stalling didn't occur at all as a real event, but was added as a sound effect in postproduction. In *Husbands*, Cassavetes oiled the sidewalk. Is even a genuine accident still an accident if the filmmaker deliberately includes it in his film? Is it accidental that one of the most important events in *Love Streams*, Sarah's meeting of her future lover, is made possible because her finger accidentally sticks in a bowling ball? The frictional accident redeems her life.

I would also note that one of the most remarkable aspects of the more than thirty plays and screenplays the director left behind at his death is the sensory descriptions they contain. Unlike most other screenplays, they are virtually novelistic in their inclusion of the oddball details of life – detailed physical descriptions of indoor and outdoor locations; of how characters walk, talk, and dress; of their facial and bodily expressions. Nothing is merely generally or abstractly presented. Cassavetes' embrace of the life of the senses, his gusto for the physical, is as obvious in his writing as it is in his filmmaking.

11. *The American Film Institute Seminar with John Cassavetes*, December 18, 1973 (Los Angeles: American Film Institute, 1978), p. 28.

12. It is telling that when Al Ruban tried to sell Cassavetes on the idea of making *Husbands*'s three main characters more likeable, and proposed doing an edit that would keep the audience "with them," for example by downplaying or eliminating the vomiting scene, the filmmaker rejected the idea out of hand. According to Ruban, Cassavetes wasn't even interested in discussing it, let alone seeing a trial assembly.

13. This frictional sense of life energizes all of Cassavetes' work, even his comedies. In *Minnie and Moskowitz*, when Seymour pulls into a parking space, there is a spate of horn honking between his pickup and a car about who will occupy the space. A little later, Minnie goes into an ice-cream parlor and gets into a misunderstanding with a waitress about placing her order. A minute later, phoning Seymour and proposing that he join her there, she gets into a tiff with him.

14. Emerson, *Essays and Lectures*, p. 1075.

15. Ralph Waldo Emerson, *Natural History of Intellect and Other Papers* (Boston: Houghton Mifflin, 1893), p. 40.

16. William James, *Writings, 1902–1910*, 929.

17. Henry James, "The New Novel," *Literary Criticism: American and English* (New York: Library of America, 1984), p. 147.

18. William James, *The Principles of Psychology* (Cambridge, Massachusetts: Harvard University Press, 1983), p. 246.

19. William James, *Writings, 1902–1910*, p. 609.

20. William James, excerpts from two letters: to Walter Taylor Marvin, June 6, 1905 (before the ellipsis), and to George Fredrick Stout, October 17, 1905 (after the ellipsis). See Fredrick Scott (ed.), *William James: Selected Unpublished Corre-*

spondence, 1885–1910 (Columbus: Ohio State University Press, 1986), pp. 376–7 and 386.

21. William James, "Pragmatism and Humanism," *Writings, 1902–1910* (New York: Library of America, 1987), pp. 601–2.

22. This is the mistake Kouvaros and Zwierzynski make in their essay on *Love Streams* in *Post Script*. What would a criticism look like that accepted this doctrine and broke away from the quest for essences, or the nostalgic lament of the absence of them? What such a work of art would look like, Cassavetes shows us. He points the way beyond the nostalgia of deconstructionist analyses.

23. William James, *Writings, 1902–1910*, pp. 1175 and 1181.

24. Ibid., p. 741.

25. I'm reminded of a student's response to my observation that *Bookie*'s plot does not proceed from A to Z in a linked chain of causality. He topped it by arguing that nothing in the movie went even from A to B without a disruption, an interruption, or the possibility of an interpretive mistake – not even something as simple and apparently instantaneous as a blowout.

Given Cassavetes' candid acknowledgment of how much he learned from the neorealists (De Sica and Rossellini in particular), it is fair to notice a connection between the narrative organization of their works and the structure of his. Whereas Hollywood narrative depends on the linear presentation of a series of linked narrative causes and effects, the neorealist style cultivated narrative digressions, interruptions, pauses, shifting and uncertain focuses of attention within a fill-lighted frame. Films like *The Bicycle Thief* and *Voyage in Italy* rejected straight lines of development – both spatially and causally – to pursue narrative curlicues, geographical excursuses, glimpses of this and that, and leisurely spatial and temporal detours down side alleys and passageways. Especially in the early work of De Sica and Rossellini, narrative was freed from the determinism of plot and the tendentiousness of intentionality in ways very similar to Cassavetes'. The viewer was ushered into a world of casual relations, stimulating indeterminacies, mysteries, and loose-fitting connections. A realm of interpretive pluralism, openness, and possibility was brought into existence that is very similar to Cassavetes'.

Even Cosmo's being yanked out of his car on the way to the hit, and his ending up on foot, has a parallel in these two films. De Sica takes away Antonio's bicycle and forces him to walk the streets in order to make possible a more eccentric, more impulsive path of discovery than a vehicle would allow. Rossellini slows down the movement of Ingrid Bergman's car with herds of animals and crowds of people (and slows down the forward movement of his narrative), then eventually forces her out of it (thus arresting narrative eventfulness altogether) so that a more intimate and eccentric relationship with her surroundings becomes possible. Though it is only a punning coincidence, William James captures the essence of all three filmmakers' acts of narrative retardation with his praise of "ambulatory" knowledge over "saltatory."

26. A distinguished film critic called me up a few weeks after I wrote this passage to say that he had just seen the *The Killing of a Chinese Bookie* for the first time. He said that though he found the film interesting, there was a problem with the screening he had attended: The projectionist had mixed up some of the reels and left out at least one of them. He then cited the "missing" climax of this scene as proof of the missing reel, and some of the other weird jumps and elisions I have mentioned as evidence of transposed reels. I tell the story to emphasize that even someone familiar with every cinematic trick in the book couldn't believe his eyes when faced with the obliquity of Cassavetes' presentation.

There is another kind of murkiness that also deserves to be mentioned. Cassavetes presents three moments of deliberate acoustic ambiguity: Early in the film a group of teenagers drive by Cosmo's club and shout out something that just eludes comprehensibility ("your mother's [father's?] dead"); during the murder, the godfather says something to Cosmo that we can't quite make out ("I'm so ... "); and in his conversation with Cosmo in the warehouse, Flo says something that trails off into inaudibility ("What the whole world needs is a ... "). All three encounters are presented as "quasi-revelatory" or summarizing moments, but the point of this anti-essentialist film, is that even in revelatory moments nothing is revealed. (Compare Cosmo's cryptic references to "rivers" for a similar effect.)

27. Some examples from the first half of the movie: Cosmo's brief pause on the steps of Rachel's house as he drops her off after their night at the casino; the beat he takes prior to getting up and going outside when the boy who parks cars calls him out to meet the Mob; the beat Gazzara inserts in his performance in the front seat of the gangsters' car before he tears up "the markers"; the beat he takes as he gets out of the gangsters' car; the beat he takes on the street in front of Betty's house after the shooting.

28. When I watch Cosmo (or Gazzara) taking a beat, I can't help being reminded of something the filmmaker said about Martin Sheen's performance in *Apocalypse Now*. We both agreed that Coppola's film was poorly written and pretty dreadful overall, but then Cassavetes made a remark the first part of which surprised me, and the second part of which puzzled me. He said that an actor can save even the most doomed script (that was surprising but understandable), and went on to add that "if Sheen had only put in some delays" he might have been able to make something of his role. The use of the word "delays" and its application to Sheen's performance baffled me at the time, but after watching Gazzara/Cosmo in this parable about the power of the actor to resist the all-but-inexorable plots of life and art, I finally understood what he was getting at. An actor's ability to delay can allow him to stand out from even the most Wagnerian schemes of oppression.

29. Cassavetes acknowledges the filmmaking process in many of his works: the notorious microphone boom at the end of *Husbands*; the edit of two takes of the same scene back to back in Jim's "I've got to go" scene in *Minnie and Moskowitz*; the visibility of lighting tripods in many of the shots inside the club in *Bookie*; a shot of a camera crane in the blowout scene.

30. As an indication that Cassavetes was fully conscious of and in control of these meanings, at one point in the long print of *Bookie* he has Cosmo's disembodied, tape-recorded voice playing over the loudspeakers of his club while Cosmo is doing something else. (One of Cassavetes' favorite movies, Capra's *Meet John Doe*, has a similar scene which may well have inspired this one.) Cosmo has to explain to a customer how he can be standing in one place and seem to be speaking from another. The point is to remind a viewer that Cosmo's theatrical project is essentially one of depersonalization and disembodiment, even as Cassavetes' cinematic agenda is one of repersonalization and reembodiment. In this respect, as in every other as well,

Cosmo contrasts with Mabel. He erases his identity and anonymizes himself in the roles he plays; she personalizes even the most apparently impersonal events (like asking the time of passersby). Mabel anticipates *Love Streams*'s Sarah Lawson in this respect, while Cosmo foreshadows Robert Harmon.

31. Many of these characters are closely related in Cassavetes' mind. *Shadows*'s Ben might be Cosmo as a young man. And Cosmo's quest for "comfortableness" is repeated in Robert Harmon's similar attempt in *Love Streams*. Cosmo's Stern-bergian retreat into the artistic world of his club is strictly comparable to Harmon's Gatsby-like retreat into the world of thirties jukebox jazz.

32. One of the most revealing (and ironic) lines in *Husbands* occurs just prior to the final visit Gus and Archie make to Harry, when the two men turn to each other and vow to "be cool." Cassavetes' comment about the countess is contained in Henstell, ed., *Dialogue on Film #4*, p. 12.

33. Quoted by Patricia Bosworth, "Cassavetes: Why Do Marriages Go Sour?" *New York Times*, December 1, 1968, section D, p. 15.

34. The parallel with Cassavetes' career as a maker of "risky" films is obvious. For the record, Cassavetes was personally fond of betting, gambling, and games of chance.

35. William James, *Writings, 1902–1910*, pp. 940–1.

36. For more in this vein, see my comments on the fiftieth anniversary of *Citizen Kane*'s release in David Sterritt, "Orson Welles and 'Rosebud' Ride Again," *The Christian Science Monitor*, April 30, 1991, p. 13.

37. The concept of returning the repressed to consciousness (or, in the metaphor of this film and the following one, letting the audience see what goes on behind the velvet curtain) is important. All of Cassavetes' films have this dimension, from *Shadows*'s "backstage" view of artistic compromises and humiliations, to *Husbands*'s showing its playboy characters vomiting after a night on the town, to *A Woman Under the Influence*'s bringing babies, in-laws, and sexual infidelity into the enchanted realm of romance.

6. *Compositions and Decompositions:* Love Streams

1. "Beauty," in *The Conduct of Life*, printed in Emerson, *Essays and Lectures*, pp. 1104–5.

2. D. H. Lawrence, from "Art and Morality" and "Why the Novel Matters," *Phoenix*, pp. 525 and 536.

3. *Big Trouble*, which bears Cassavetes' name in its credits as director, is not actually his work. My "Note on *Big Trouble*," *Film Comment* (May–June 1989), 49, briefly explains the checkered history of the film's production and Cassavetes' merely honorific involvement in it. In a conversation with me near the end of his life, the filmmaker expressed his dismay that "people not only would think I made *Big Trouble*, but that it was my final film."

4. That Robert and Sarah are in many respects the same figure viewed twice is also suggested by the visual comparisons that run through the film. Scene after scene involving Robert echoes physical blockings, camera movements, and images from scenes involving Sarah. For example, notice how Robert's pursuit of Albie in his

car repeats Sarah's pursuit of Jack and Debbie in her "Lovemobile"; or the way several scenes compare and contrast how different characters bend over Sarah and Robert when they are down on the ground or floor.

5. There is circumstantial evidence to suggest that the character of Harmon was loosely modeled on Frank Sinatra or Leonard Bernstein.

6. Jon Voight played the Harmon character in the stage version of the script, and emphasized the radical insincerity of Robert's character more obviously than Cassavetes does. Cassavetes told me he actually preferred Voight's performance to his own, which he called "the saddest thing I've ever done." Voight made Harmon manic, comic, ebullient; Cassavetes makes him lugubrious and withdrawn. For slightly more on the stage origins of the film, see my essay, "Love's Dreams: *Love Streams* and the Films of John Cassavetes," *Persistence of Vision*, 6 (Summer 1988), 41–66.

7. As I observed in a previous chapter, a character's conscious intentions count for nothing in Cassavetes' work. Robert is not trying to be superficial, insincere, or hypocritical; he just *is* those things. It would be truer to say that Robert is unaware of, and does not understand, his own intentions. (It may sound paradoxical to talk about intentions of which a character is unaware, but it is the greatness of Cassavetes' work to make the concept perfectly clear. Intention is less a verbalizable explanation of one's behavior than a habitual pattern of response.) The behavior in these films is generated from a place deeper than a character's professed intentions can reach or his consciousness can know. The tape-recorder interview scene brilliantly shows us that even as Robert genuinely wants to probe Joannie's secrets, he is actually building a wall around himself that prevents her or anyone else from getting within ten miles of him emotionally. The scene with Susan at the door in another example: Robert is the last one to be able to understand what an absolute kiss-off his wink and wave are. As the filmmaker said to me once: "Nobody's a phony the way they are in the movies. People believe the things they do, no matter how horrible or unkind. Even when they are hurting themselves and others, they *think* they are doing the right thing." Robert is one of those people, but so are we all.

8. *Love Streams*'s gay nightclub is more than a witty inversion of *Bookie*'s realm of strident heterosexuality. It is Cassavetes' declaration of the similarity of the two fantasy islands of desexualized illusionism, escapism, and visionary disembodiment. (As a sidelight on this aspect of the movie, it seems clear to me that certain aspects of *Love Streams*'s script, which was based on a Ted Allan play, but which was completely rewritten by the filmmaker in the late 1970s and early 1980s, are indebted to incidental scenes, characters, and events in Richard Benner's 1977 *Outrageous!*, a film that Cassavetes knew and admired.)

9. This is a veiled reference to Pauline Kael's venomous characterizations of Cassavetes' own *Faces*, *Husbands*, and *A Woman Under the Influence*. Kael, relentlessly hostile to Cassavetes' work, repeatedly implied that the filmmaker himself was only doing this – exploiting depictions of pain and suffering – for box-office bucks. In a career of being consistently wrong about most things, there is no filmmaker about whom Kael was more wrong.

10. For literary analogues in the work of Poe, Stevens, Nabokov, Barth, and Coover, and cinematic analogues in the work of Capra, see my discussions in *American Vision*, pp. 159–70, 198–201, and 291–98.

11. Like Sarah, many of these characters begin their films resembling the other group of characters – attempting to close up shop on their identities and to get their acts down pat in one way or another. However, what makes them different from the others is that these characters show themselves capable of changing, of breaking their own patterns, of becoming improvisers of their identities. In their different ways, in the course of their films they open themselves up. (Lelia succeeds in doing so only in the final seconds of her final scene.) It is as if Cassavetes regarded these characters' initial extroverted involvement with others as being less dooming than the other characters' introverted withdrawal. He is telling us that while the expressive disengagement of a Cosmo or Harmon is a spiritual dead end, there is always possibility of growth and change in Lelia's, Mabel's, Myrtle's, or Sarah's spirited engagement with others, however dangerous or painful it may also be.

Another way to understand this difference is to say that, for reasons this book has been devoted to explaining, in Cassavetes, action is always preferable to contemplation. Robert's relationship to experience, like Cosmo's or Ben's, is fundamentally contemplative; Lelia's, Mabel's, and Sarah's is stimulatingly active. As far as the filmmaker is concerned, in activity there is possibility, in intellectualism none.

12. Emerson, *Essays and Lectures*, pp. 412–13.

13. In addition to an account by Cassavetes, I am indebted to Larry Shaw, Sam Shaw, and Michael Ventura for information about the production process of *Love Streams*.

14. William James, *Writings, 1902–1910*, pp. 1033–4.

15. Cassavetes enlisted Peter Bogdanovich to rehearse and direct this particular scene, the only moment in *Love Streams* in which the filmmaker turned over the directorial duties to someone else. Bogdanovich also makes a cameo appearance at the end of *Opening Night* as a fawning, insincere fan. In both scenes Cassavetes was pointedly using Bogdanovich to make a point about the hollowness of charm.

16. Compare the two railroad station scenes for an equally blatant miscuing (built around a misleading match cut of a chain-link fence). What Cassavetes does geographically in those scenes, he does imaginatively and emotionally in all of his important scenes: He puts the viewer cognitively in motion along with the characters.

17. I would emphasize again that these uncertainties (or any of the others I will describe) are not the result of inadvertence or sloppiness. The shooting script of *Love Streams* reveals that Cassavetes deliberately created the disorienting effect of this scene in the editing process by transposing it from its original scripted position later in the film to its current position at the beginning. (For the record, the screenplay, marked "copyright 1982" on its title page, begins with the arrival of Albie and Agnes at Robert's house, which is itself rapidly followed by the arrival of Sarah. The argument between Robert and René was scripted to occur at a later point in the movie.)

This sort of editorial juggling was fairly standard operating procedure for Cassavetes. After taking great pains to film as much as possible in continuity, during the editing process, the filmmaker wouldn't hesitate to abandon continuity in order to free his scenes from having too apparent a direction. He wanted to deny the viewer a narrative road map through challenging terrain. *Shadows, Faces,* and this film all begin with sequences that were originally scripted and shot to occur in the middle of the works.

18. William James, *Writings, 1902–1910*, p. 1172.

19. This reverence for all of God's creatures is even more obvious in the written texts of his plays and films. Cassavetes lovingly describes even the most minor figure with great care and affection. Even the most flawed figure is never treated dismissively. This marks a decisive difference from superficially similar moments in Robert Altman's work. Sarah's innocence and unguardedness are not sneered at or patronized the way the Shelly Duvall character is in Altman's *Three Women*, or the character of Griffin Bell's idealistic assistant is in *The Player*. Altman's work appears to be narratively "open" in ways that might be confused with Cassavetes', but the difference is that Altman's openness is merely visual and acoustic, while Cassavetes' is psychological and emotional. That is to say, while Altman shows us a lot, he is emotionally guarded, extremely judgmental about what it means, and closed-minded about how we are to use it. Cassavetes is the opposite: He is extraordinarily tolerant of different points of view, generously appreciative of different ways of living, and nonjudgmental about any of it. Cassavetes' cinematic openness is Renoirian. Rather than making editorial points about his characters in Altman's way, he genuinely appreciates them in Renoir's. The simplest way to see this is to notice the difference in the kinds of characters the two filmmakers imagine. In his cynicism and negativism, Altman simply can't imagine or believe in characters who have a vision equal to or superior to his own; his characters are victims, dupes, or self-deceiving frauds. Cassavetes, in his kindness and generosity, almost always images his central figures to be at least as loving, brave, tolerant, and aware as his own cinematic style is. Mabel and Sarah are as sensitive and perceptive as their creator.

20. As he acknowledged in an interview, this is in fact something Cassavetes' own father used to say, and something that the filmmaker believed. But then, his films tell us this over and over again, even if he hadn't said so directly. (For what it is worth, this is the place to mention that Cassavetes told me that this scene was his personal favorite in the film.)

21. This shot has certain superficial resemblances with placements of characters behind walls in both *Rosemary's Baby* (where Ruth Gordon makes a phone call partially occluded by a doorway) and *Rear Window* (in which our view of Jimmy Stewart making a phone call is similarly blocked). However, the effect is much less emotionally evocative and imaginatively mysterious in Polanski and Hitchcock than in Cassavetes. In Polanski in particular, the veiling reads merely as cleverness and trickery, an effect Cassavetes' antivirtuosic cinema avoids.

22. As an indication that the incestuous overtones of Robert and Sarah's relationship are not a figment of a viewer's overactive imagination, I would mention that Robert and Sarah had an explicitly incestuous relationship in the original Ted Allan stage play on which the film was based. Incest suits them thematically insofar as, for the romantically shell-shocked (which both are), it is the most protected form of love. For the gun-shy lover, incest is the ultimate in safe sex – whereas Cassavetes is obviously a proponent of unsafe.

23. William James, *The Principles of Psychology*, p. 1181.

1. William James, "The Continuity of Experience," *A Pluralistic Universe* in *Writings, 1902–1910*, pp. 762–3.

2. I don't want to leave the impression that there are no exceptions to this cinema of virtuosity other than Cassavetes. Elaine May, Barbara Loden, Sara Driver, Jim Jarmusch, Su Friedrich, Robert Kramer, and Paul Morrissey come to mind as equally pursuing a non-Faustian aesthetic, in their very different ways. (The fact that four out of my seven counterexamples are women seems not unimportant. The cinema of virtuosity is largely a *cinéma du papa*.)

3. George Balanchine, interviewed by Johathan Cott, *Voices and Visions* (New York: Doubleday, 1987), p. 90.

Bibliography

Benedetto, Lucio. "Forging an Original Response: A Review of Cassavetes Criticism in English," *Post Script* (Commerce: East Texas State University) "Special Issue: John Cassavetes," 11, no. 2 (Winter 1992). 101–11.

Benson, Sheila. "Cassavetes: Man Behind the Myths," *Los Angeles Times*, March 16, 1991, Section F, pp. 16–17.

Carney, Ray. "*A Woman Under the Influence*," *Magill's Survey of Cinema – Second Series* vol. 6 (Pasadena, Calif.: Salem Press, 1981), pp. 2711–14.

"*Minnie and Moskowitz*," *Magill's Survey of Cinema – Second Series* vol. 4 (Pasadena, Calif.: Salem Press, 1981), pp. 1594–7.

American Dreaming: The Films of John Cassavetes and the American Experience (Berkeley and Los Angeles: University of California Press, 1985).

"*Love Streams*," *Magill's Cinema Annual – 1985* (Pasadena, Calif.: Salem Press, 1985), pp. 293–302.

"*Mikey and Nicky*," *Magill's Cinema Annual – 1985* (Pasadena, Calif.: Salem Press, 1985), pp. 576–80.

American Vision: The Films of Frank Capra (Cambridge University Press, 1986).

"*The Killing of a Chinese Bookie*," *Magill's Cinema Annual – 1987* (Pasadena, Calif.: Salem Press, 1987), pp. 549–57.

"Love's Dreams: *Love Streams* and the Films of John Cassavetes," *Persistence of Vision* (City University of New York), no. 6 (Summer 1988), 41–66.

"*Gloria*," *Magill's Cinema Annual – 1988* (Pasadena, Calif.: Salem Press, 1988), pp. 458–62.

Speaking the Language of Desire: The Films of Carl Dreyer (Cambridge University Press, 1989).

"Complex Characters," "Unfinished Business," and "A Note on *Big Trouble*," *Film Comment* 25 (May–June 1989), 30–3 and 48–9.

"The Energizing Spirit," *Harvard Film Archive Bulletin* (September–October 1989), 4.

"Modernism for the Millions: The Films of Woody Allen," *Alaska Quarterly Review* 8, no. 1–2 (Fall–Winter 1989).

The Films of John Cassavetes (Souvenir Program) and program notes for twelve films distributed at the fifteen sites of the United States tour of the complete films of John Cassavetes, curated by the Walker Art Center (Minneapolis) and the Pacific Film Archive (Berkeley, Calif.), September 1989–September 1990.

"Waking Up in the Dark: Learning from John Cassavetes," Program essay for the 1989 United States Film Festival, Sundance Institute, Park City, Utah, January 1989; reprinted in *Alaska Quarterly Review* 8, no. 3–4 (Spring–Summer 1990), 123–33.

Review of *Allegories of Cinema, American Studies* (Lawrence: University of Kansas), 32, no. 1 (Spring 1991), 123–4.

"The Adventure of Insecurity: The Films of John Cassavetes," *Kenyon Review* 13, no. 2 (Spring 1991), 102–21.

"Looking without Seeing," *Partisan Review* 58, no. 4 (Fall 1991), 717–23.

"A Polemical Introduction: The Road Not Taken," and "Seven Program Notes from the American Tour of the Complete Films: *Faces, Husbands, Minnie and Moskowitz, A Woman Under the Influence, The Killing of a Chinese Bookie, Opening Night,* and *Love Streams,*" *Post Script* (Commerce: East Texas State University) "Special Issue: John Cassavetes," 11, no. 2 (Winter 1992), 1–12 and 37–100.

"Prophet Without Honor," *Boston Phoenix*, February 28, 1992, Section 3, p. 6.

"Cassavetes on Cassavetes," *Visions Magazine* (Boston Center for the Arts) no. 7 (Summer 1992), 22–9.

John Cassavetes: Autoportraits (Paris: Editions de l'Etoile/Cahiers du Cinéma, 1992).

"John Cassavetes: Allegro con Brio," in *The Greek Influence on World Cinema*, John Pyros, ed., the program of the Greek-American Film Festival (Tarpon Springs, Fla.: February 1993).

"Ray Carney's Rules of the Game," *Visions Magazine* (Boston Center for the Arts) no. 10 (Summer 1993), 10–15 and 48–9.

Learning from John Cassavetes (Carbondale: Southern Illinois University Press, 1994).

Cassavetes, John. "Cassavetes: Why Do Marriages Go Sour?" (interview with Patricia Bosworth), *New York Times*, December 1, 1968, section D, p. 15.

Faces (New York: New American Library, 1970).

"The Playboy Interview," *Playboy* 18 (July 1971), 68–75.

Dialogue of Film #4: John Cassavetes and Peter Falk, Bruce Henstell, ed. (Beverly Hills, Calif.: American Film Institute, 1972).

"A Woman Under the Influence," interview by Judith NcNally, *Filmmaker's Newsletter*, January 1975, 26.

The American Film Institute Seminar with John Cassavetes, December 18, 1973 (Los Angeles: American Film Institute, 1978).

Minnie and Moskowitz (Los Angeles: Black Sparrow Press, 1973).

"Who's Crazy Now? Interview with Marjorie Rosen," *MS Magazine*, February 1975, 32–35.

"Interview by Dolores Barclay," *Los Angeles Times*, July 8, 1980, part 4, p. 4.

Cott, Jonathan. "Interview with George Balanchine," *Voices and Visions* (New York: Doubleday, 1987).

Dewey, John. *Experience and Nature* (La Salle, Illinois: Open Court, 1925).

Art as Experience (New York: Putnam, 1934).

Dickinson, Emily. *The Complete Poems*, Thomas Johnson, ed. (Boston: Little, Brown, 1960).

Emerson, Ralph Waldo. *Natural History of Intellect and Other Papers* (Boston: Houghton Mifflin 1893).

Essays and Lectures (New York: Library of America, 1983).

Ralph Waldo Emerson, Richard Poirier, ed. (New York: Oxford University Press, 1990).

Gavron, Laurence, and Denis Lenoir. *John Cassavetes* (Paris: Rivages, 1986).

Gelmis, Joseph. "John Cassavetes," in *The Film Director as Superstar* (New York: Doubleday, 1970).

Hartman, Charles. *Jazz Text: Voice and Improvisation in Poetry, Jazz, and Song* (Princeton, N.J.: Princeton University Press, 1991).

James, David. *Allegories of Cinema.* (Princeton, N.J.: Princeton University Press, 1989).

James, Henry. *Literary Criticism: American and English* (New York: Library of America, 1984).

Novels, 1871–1880 (New York: Library of America, 1983).

Novels, 1881–1886 (New York: Library of America, 1985).

James, William. *The Principles of Psychology* (Cambridge, Mass.: Harvard University Press, 1985).

William James: Selected Unpublished Correspondence, 1885–1910, Fredrick Scott, ed. (Columbus: Ohio State University Press, 1986).

Writings 1902–1910 (New York: Library of America, 1987).

Writings 1878–1899 (New York: Library of America, 1992).

Jousse, Thierry. *John Cassavetes* (Paris: Cahiers du Cinéma/Editions de l'Etoile, 1989).

Katzman, Lisa. "*Opening Night*: Moment by Moment," *Film Comment* 25 (May–June 1989), 34–9.

"John Cassavetes and *Opening Night*," *New York Times*, May 12, 1991, section 2, pp. 11–12.

Kozol, Jonathan. *The Night Is Dark and I Am Far from Home* (New York: Simon & Schuster, 1990).

Kouvaros, George, and Janice Zwierzynski. "Blow to the Heart: Cassavetes' *Love Streams*," *Post Script* (Commerce: East Texas State University) "Special Issue: John Cassavetes," 11, no. 2 (Winter 1992), 27–36.

Labarthe, André. "A Way of Life: An Interview with John Cassavetes,"*Evergreen*, March 1969, 47.

Lawrence, D. H. *Phoenix* (New York: Viking, 1964).

Phoenix II (New York: Viking, 1968).

D. H. Lawrence and Italy (New York: Viking, 1972).

The Symbolic Meaning: The Uncollected Versions of "Studies in Classic American Literature, Armin Arnold, ed. (Fontwell, Arundel, England: Centaur Press, 1962).

Lewis, Grover. "John Cassavetes Goes for the Edge," in *Academy All the Way* (San Francisco: Straight Arrow Books, 1974).

McLuhan, Marshall. *Understanding Media* (New York: McGraw-Hill, 1964).

Mekas, Jonas. "Movie Journal," *Village Voice*, December 23, 1971, p. 63.

Riley, Christina. "Cassavetes Remembered: Interview with Ray Carney," *UCLA Film Archive Newsletter*, February–March 1990, pp. 4–5.

Stanislavski, Constantin. *An Actor Prepares*, Elizabeth Hapgood, trans. (New York: Theater Arts, 1932).

Sterritt, David. "Orson Welles and 'Rosebud' Ride Again," *Christian Science Monitor*, April 30, 1991, p. 13.

"Fresh Look at Cassavetes' Career," *Christian Science Monitor*, November 3, 1992, p. 11.

Viera, Maria. "Script, Performance, Style, and Improvisation," *Journal of Film and Video* 42 (Fall 1990), 34–40.

"Cassavetes' Working Methods," *Post Script* (Commerce: East Texas State University) "Special Issue: John Cassavetes," 11, no. 2 (Winter 1992), 13–19.

Whitman, Walt. *Whitman: Poetry and Prose* (New York: Library of America, 1982).

Zucker, Carole. "The Illusion of the Ordinary: *Husbands*," *Post Script* (Commerce: East Texas State University) "Special Issue: John Cassavetes," 11, no. 2 (Winter 1992), 20–6.

"It's never as clear as it is in the movies. People don't know what they are doing most of the time, myself included. They don't know what they want or feel. It's only in the movies that they know what their problems are and have game plans for dealing with them.... Film is an investigation of our lives. What we are. What our responsibilities in life are – if any. What we are looking for. Why would I want to make a movie about something I already understand?"

Filmography

Shadows (filmed 1957–9; released 1959)
Screenplay: John Cassavetes
Photography: John Cassavetes, Erich Kollmar
Editors: John Cassavetes, Maurice McEndree
Producers: Maurice McEndree and Nikos Papatakis
Cast: Ben Carruthers (Ben), Lelia Goldoni (Lelia), Hugh Hurd (Hugh), Anthony Ray (Tony), David Pokitillow (David), Rupert Crosse (Rupert), Davey Jones (Davey)
Running time: 87 minutes
Availability: video – Buena Vista (Disney); film – Castle Hill (New York)

Too Late Blues (filmed 1961; released 1962)
Screenplay: John Cassavetes and Richard Carr
Photography: Lionel Lindon
Editor: Frank Bracht
Producer: John Cassavetes
Cast: Bobby Darin (John "Ghost" Wakefield), Stella Stevens (Jess Polanski), Everett Chambers (Benny Flowers), Nick Dennis (Nick), Rupert Crosse (Baby Jackson), Val Avery (Frielobe)
Running time: 103 minutes
Availability: video – Paramount; film – Paramount

A Child Is Waiting (filmed 1962; released 1963)
Screenplay: Abby Mann
Photography: Joseph LaShelle
Editor: Gene Fowler, Jr.
Producer: Stanley Kramer
Cast: Burt Lancaster (Dr. Matthew Clark), Judy Garland (Jean Hansen), Gena Rowlands (Sophie Widdicombe), Steven Hill (Ted Widdicombe), Bruce Ritchey (Reuben Widdicombe), Gloria McGehee (Mattie)
Running time: 102 minutes
Availability: video – MGM/UA; film – United Artists

Faces (filmed 1965; released 1968)
Screenplay: John Cassavetes
Photography: John Cassavetes, Al Ruban, George Sims
Editors: John Cassavetes, Al Ruban, Maurice McEndree
Producers: John Cassavetes, Maurice McEndree
Cast: John Marley (Richard Forst), Gena Rowlands (Jeannie Rapp), Lynn Carlin (Maria Forst), Seymour Cassel (Chet), Fred Draper (Freddie), Val Avery (Jim McCarthy), Dorothy Gulliver (Florence)
Running time: 129 minutes
Availability: video – Buena Vista (Disney); film – Castle Hill (New York)

Husbands (filmed 1969; released 1970)
Screenplay: John Cassavetes
Photography: John Cassavetes, Victor Kemper, Mike Chapman
Editors: John Cassavetes, Peter Tanner
Producers: Al Ruban, Sam Shaw
Cast: Ben Gazzara (Harry), Peter Falk (Archie), John Cassavetes (Gus), Jenny Runacre (Mary Tynan), Jenny Lee Wright (Pearl Billingham), Noelle Kao (Julie), Leola Harlow (Leona)
Running time: 140 minutes
Availability: video – none; film – Columbia/Films Incorporated/Kit Parker

Minnie and Moskowitz (filmed 1971; released 1971)
Screenplay: John Cassavetes
Photography: John Cassavetes, Alric Edens, Arthur J. Ornitz, Michael Margulies
Editors: John Cassavetes, Robert Heffernan
Producer: Al Ruban
Cast: Gena Rowlands (Minnie Moore), Seymour Cassel (Seymour Moskowitz), Val Avery (Zelmo Swift), John Cassavetes (Jim), Elsie Ames (Florence), Tim Carey (Morgan Morgan)
Running time: 115 minutes
Availability: video – none; film – Universal

A Woman Under the Influence (filmed 1972; released 1974)
Screenplay: John Cassavetes
Photography: John Cassavetes, Caleb Deschanel, Tim Ferris
Editors: John Cassavetes, Tom Cornwell
Producer: Sam Shaw
Cast: Gena Rowlands (Mabel Longhetti), Peter Falk (Nick Longhetti), Katherine Cassavetes (Mama Longhetti), Lady Rowlands (Mabel's mother), O. G. Dunn (Garson Cross), Eddie Shaw (Doctor Zepp), Mario Gallo (Harold Jensen)
Running time: 147 minutes
Availability: video – Buena Vista (Disney); film – Castle Hill (New York)

The Killing of a Chinese Bookie (filmed 1976; released 1976 and again in 1978, in a completely reedited print; both versions are of equal interest)
Screenplay: John Cassavetes

314

Photography: John Cassavetes, Frederick Elmes (uncredited, due to union restrictions)
Editor: John Cassavetes
Producer: Al Ruban
Cast: Ben Gazzara (Cosmo Vitelli), Azizi Johari (Rachel), Meade Roberts (Mr. Sophistication), David Rowlands (Lamarr, the chauffeur), Marty Reitz (Al Ruban), Tim Carey (the white-gloved gangster), Virginia Carrington (Betty), Alice Freeland (Sherry), Donna Gordon (Margo)
Running time: 135 minutes (1976); 108 minutes (1978)
Availability: video – Buena Vista (Disney); film – Castle Hill (New York)

Opening Night (filmed 1977; released 1978 and withdrawn; re-released 1991)
Screenplay: John Cassavetes
Photography: John Cassavetes, Al Ruban
Editors: John Cassavetes, Tom Cornwell
Producer: Al Ruban
Cast: Gena Rowlands (Myrtle Gordon), John Cassavetes (Maurice), Ben Gazzara (Manny Victor), Joan Blondell (Sarah Goode), Zohra Lampert (Dorothy Victor), Paul Stewart (David Samuels), Laura Johnson (Nancy Stein)
Running time: 144 minutes
Availability: video – Buena Vista (Disney); film – Castle Hill (New York)

Gloria (filmed 1980; released 1980)
Screenplay: John Cassavetes
Photography: Fred Schuler, John Cassavetes
Editors: John Cassavetes, George Villasenor
Producers: John Cassavetes, Sam Shaw
Cast: Gena Rowlands (Gloria), John Adames (Phil Dawn), Julie Carmen (Jeri Dawn), Buck Henry (Jack Dawn), Janet Rubin (female cabbie), Basilio Franchina (Tony Tanzini), Asa Adil Qawee (East 104th Street cabbie)
Running time: 110 minutes
Availability: video – Columbia; film – Columbia/Kit Parker

Love Streams (filmed 1983; released 1984)
Screenplay: John Cassavetes, Ted Allan
Photography: John Cassavetes, Al Ruban
Editors: John Cassavetes, George Villasenor
Producers: Manahem Golan and Yoram Globus
Cast: Gena Rowlands (Sarah Lawson), John Cassavetes (Robert Harmon), Diahnne Abbott (Susan), Seymour Cassel (Jack Lawson), Margaret Abbot (Margarita), Jakob Shaw (Albie Swanson), Joan Foley (Judge Dunbar), Risa Martha Blewitt (Debbie Lawson), Doe Avedon (Mrs. Kiner)
Running time: 141 minutes
Availability: video – released in a limited edition by MGM/UA in 1987, currently out of stock and unavailable; film – MGM Classics/Swank

Life is a series of surprises and would not be worth the taking or the keeping if it were not.... Onward and ever onward. The coming only is sacred.... Nothing is secure but life, transition, the energizing spirit....

No wonder the children love masks and costumes, and play horse, play soldier, play school, play bear, and delight in theatricals. The children have only the instinct of the universe, in which becoming somewhat else is the perpetual game of nature, and death the penalty of standing still. 'Tis not less in thought. I cannot conceive any good in a thought which confines and stagnates. The universe exists only in transit, or we behold it shooting the gulf from the past to the future. Transition is the attitude of power.... The truest state of mind rested in is false....

Heroism made easy is that for which people are always seeking to find some recipe. But God saith, It shall not be. Heroism means difficulty.... Court defeat, mortification, and disgrace.... Every soul must go over the whole ground.... Be a football to time and chance, the more kicks the better.... Man was made for conflict, not for rest. Routine, the rut, is the path of indolence, of cows, of sluggish animal life....

Genius is not a lazy angel contemplating itself and things. It is insatiable for expression. Thought must take the stupendous step of passing into realization. A master can formulate his thought.　　　　　 – R.W. Emerson

Index

abandonment, 113, 171, 248–9, 277,
  297n22
acting, as a source of meaning, 12, 14–15,
  17–18, 100–4, 165–6; see also bad
  acting; bodies; Method acting
Actors Studio, 148
agitation, stylistic, 188–90, 227–34, 244–5,
  246–7, 250–1
Algiers (Cromwell), 118, 294n5
Allan, Ted, 267, 304n8, 306n22
Allen, Woody, 57, 97, 98, 111, 171, 209,
  213, 265, 272, 285n12, 292n11
alter egos, characters as stand-ins for the
  filmmaker, 111–12, 136, 150–9, 194–
  5, 227, 230–4, 243–5, 289n19, 296n7,
  299nn7,8
Altman, Robert, 59, 111, 112, 140–1, 226,
  247, 251, 297n26, 306n19
American film criticism, limitations of, 66,
  123, 192–3, 197, 206, 231, 238, 272–
  3; see also critical reception; ideological
  analysis
Anatomy of a Murder (Preminger),
  146
Anderson, Laurie, 287n6
Aristotelianism, 71, 72, 183
Armstrong, Louis, 280
art and life, overlap of, 45–6, 56–7, 104–5,
  134, 150–8, 162–5, 229, 231–2, 276,
  288n11, 316; see also theatricality
Astor, Mary, 119, 121, 140
avant-garde film, 38, 134, 299n6
Avery, Val, 55, 107, 132, 152, 191

bad acting, as an expressive device, 44–6,
  158–9, 232, 287n7, 297n12
Balanchine, George, 158, 188, 193, 277,
  287n7

Bazin, André, 90, 297n26
Beckett, Samuel, 240
Beethoven, Ludwig von, 194
Bergman, Ingrid, 4, 7, 13, 236, 301n25
Bergson, Henri, 81–2
Big Trouble (Bergman), 303n3
Blade Runner (Scott), 6
"blueprint" model of creation, 46–7, 187–
  9, 193–4
Bob Roberts (Robbins), 14, 146
bodies, expressive effects of, 13–17, 65–6,
  84, 164–72, 199–202, 275–80; see also
  acting; physicality
Bogart, Humphrey, 4, 7, 13, 118–21, 123,
  128, 140, 148, 228, 236
Bogdanovich, Peter, 305n15
Bonnie and Clyde (Penn), 115
Bordwell, David, 84, 192, 197, 271,
  283n3
Brando, Marlon, 29, 44, 46, 133, 148
Brooks, Peter, 148
burlesque, 299n8
Burnett, Charles, 284n6, 285n5, 286nn4,5
Byrne, David, 287n6

Canby, Vincent, 20, 53, 120
Capra, Frank, 77, 123, 146, 304n10
  It Happened One Night, 115, 285n15
  It's a Wonderful Life, 120
  Meet John Doe, 255, 302n30
  Mr. Deeds Goes to Town, 115
  Mr. Smith Goes to Washington, 208
Carey, Tim, 132, 191
Carlin, Lynn, 75, 84
Carnell, Cliff, 69, 175
Carruthers, Ben, 46, 67, 69, 287n7
Cassavetes, Katherine, 31
Cassel, Seymour, 75, 84, 107, 132, 137,

148, 158, 191, 224, 243, 280, 289n19, 294n3
character, limitations of, 54–6, 62, 99–100, 130–1, 297n27
Chayefsky, Paddy, 51
  The Bachelor Party, 287n10
  Marty, 51
Chekhov, Anton, 99
Child Is Waiting, A (Cassavetes), 28, 74, 289n19, 313
Clift, Montgomery, 29, 44, 147, 148
Coen, Joel and Ethan, 9, 14, 18, 20, 189, 190, 272
  Blood Simple, 6, 14, 88, 190, 272
Coleridge, Samuel Taylor, 229
contemplative stances, rejection of, 16, 163, 212–13, 274–7, 305n11
Coppola, Francis, 9, 77, 88, 302n28
  Apocalypse Now, 6, 14, 36, 302n28
  The Godfather, 144, 206
Crawford, Joan, 148, 208
critical reception, of Cassavetes' work, 1–2, 14, 20, 27–8, 35, 41, 45, 52–3, 63, 70, 82–3, 87–8, 98, 116–17, 119, 133–4, 152, 154, 162, 164–6, 168, 171, 182, 184–8, 194, 202, 210, 217, 220, 223, 227, 233, 238, 283nn3,4, 289n2, 292n12, 297n20, 299nn3,4, 299n6, 304n9; *see also* American film criticism; Bordwell, David; difficulty, of Cassavetes' work; ideological analysis
Crying Game, The (Jordan), 48
Curtiz, Michael, 6, 7, 121
  Casablanca, 4, 6–7, 13, 15, 17, 18, 118–21, 123, 125, 166, 203, 208–9, 285nn11,15, 287n9

Davis, Bette, 148, 208
Dean, James, 29, 44–7, 133, 139, 147, 148, 287n7
deconstruction, Cassavetes' critique of, 63, 103, 301n22
delaying tactics, in Cassavetes' work, 217–19, 222–4, 302n28
De Palma, Brian, 9, 77, 88, 189, 190, 247, 251, 272, 273–6
  Dressed to Kill, 190, 272
  The Fury, 27
Derrida, Jacques, 177; *see also* deconstruction
De Sica, Vittorio, 12, 90, 203–6, 284n6, 301n25
  The Bicycle Thief, 203–5, 301n25
Dewey, John, 95, 162–4, 197, 285n13
Dickinson, Emily, 159
differences, vocal, 93, 208–12

difficulty
  in Cassavetes' work, *see* work, effort
  of Cassavetes' work, 123–4, 138, 224–5, 256–68, 273–4; *see also* critical reception
Dirty Dozen, The (Aldrich), 27
Disney, Walt, 196–7, 202, 229
Draper, Fred, 15, 107, 152
Dreyer, Carl-Theodor, 270
Driver, Sara, 284n6, 307n2

Eakins, Thomas, 146, 188
eccentricity, 56, 65–7, 102–3, 130–1, 173–6, 206–8
Eisenstein, Sergei, 14
Emerson, Ralph, Waldo, 17, 55, 58, 71, 83, 91, 93, 100, 107–10, 114, 122–4, 127, 130, 133–4, 141, 164, 171, 173–4, 177, 179, 182, 199, 211, 213, 235, 250–1, 276, 285n13, 316
Engel, Morris, 90
establishing technique, abrogation of, 19, 78–81, 124–7, 256, 289n2, 305nn16,17
excess, 56, 83, 130, 134, 242–4
expressive gap, 50–3

Faces (Cassavetes), 10–13, 15, 18, 20–1, 25, 28, 32, 45, 49, 55, 71, 73, 74–114, 131, 134-7, 139–40, 143, 146, 156, 158, 162, 170–1, 178–80, 185, 189–90, 209–11, 226–8, 239–45, 249, 251, 254, 268–70, 277, 280, 284n10, 285n14, 287n11, 289n19, 297n22, 304n9, 305n17, 314
Falk, Peter, 138–9, 144, 148, 153, 157, 166, 174, 180, 191, 192, 278, 283n4, 296nn7,8, 298n29
Farber, Manny, 192
Faulkner, William, 146, 147, 299n4
film noir, 215, 223, 225
Flaubert, Gustav, 162, 164, 188
Foucault, Michel, 103
Frank, Robert, 38, 287n6
  Pull My Daisy, 38
friction, 202–12, 299n10, 300n13
Friedrich, Su, 307n2
Frost, Robert, 58, 72, 136, 188

gambling, 228, 303n34
Gazzara, Ben, 148, 166, 191, 192, 227, 275, 283n4, 293n13, 302nn27,28
Giannetti, Louis, 27
Gillespie, Dizzy, 193, 277
Gloria (Cassavetes), 21, 28, 32, 49, 53, 71, 87, 98, 114, 143, 150, 210, 238, 243,

245, 254, 277, 287n6, 290n4, 291n5, 297n27, 298n31, 315
Godard, Jean-Luc, 226, 236, 294n13
Goldoni, Lelia, 35, 67; *see also Shadows*
Goren, Elaine, 153, 278
Griffith, D. W., 77
Grodin, Charles, 148

Harlow, Leola, 153, 296n8
Hartman, Charles, 197
Harwood, Bo, 28, 31, 173, 180
Hawthorne, Nathaniel, 146, 268, 293n14
Hedren, Tippi, 101
Herrmann, Bernard, 15
history, as brought into existence within Cassavetes' style, 139–41, 144, 211-12
Hitchcock, Alfred, 4, 6, 7, 9, 13–15, 17, 20, 22–4, 36, 51–2, 54–5, 57, 69, 77, 86, 88–9, 93, 95, 97, 100–3, 171–2, 187–90, 203–5, 212, 247, 251, 268, 272–6, 284n10, 299nn2,4, 306n21
  The Birds, 101
  North by Northwest, 4, 6, 7, 9, 20, 22–3, 54, 89, 97, 203, 209
  Psycho, 4, 6, 7–8, 9, 15, 17, 22–3, 54, 63, 77, 88–9, 101–3, 165, 168, 190, 203–5, 272, 284n7
  Rear Window, 6, 7, 9, 14-15, 22, 89, 101–2, 203, 306n21
  Strangers on a Train, 4, 20, 22, 55
  Vertigo, 4, 6, 7, 9, 16, 22–3, 36, 55, 89, 101, 172, 203
Holiday, Billie, 46
Homer, Winslow, 146
Hopper, Edward, 146
Humoresque (Negulesco), 208
Husbands (Cassavetes), 21, 28, 30, 45, 52, 87, 114, 133, 137, 139–40, 152, 153, 162, 166–7, 170, 172, 185, 192, 205, 209, 228, 239–43, 254, 286n5, 287nn7,9,10, 289n20, 290n4, 292n13, 296n8, 297n27, 300nn10,12, 302n29, 303nn32,37, 304n9, 314

identification, indifference to, 86–8, 208–9, 290n5
ideological analysis, limitations of, 63, 66, 139–41, 144, 182, 192, 214–15; *see also* American film criticism; critical reception; deconstruction
Imitation of Life (Sirk), 48
improvisation
  in the repudiated version of *Shadows*, 26
  as a technique of discovery, 187–95, 245–8, 251–4, 299n3
  see also jazz aesthetics; working methods

Intermezzo (Ratoff), 285n15
Ivory, James, 213

Jaglom, Henry, 213
James, David, 299n6
  Allegories of Cinema, 286n5, 287n7
James, Henry, 27, 53–5, 57, 73, 129, 135, 144–7, 177, 182, 214, 271, 276, 286n4, 288n15, 293n14, 298n31
James, William, 1, 11, 16, 21, 48, 61, 81–2, 88-90, 96, 98, 103, 107, 108, 129, 130, 149, 176, 211, 213–15, 219–21, 229, 233, 252–4, 258–9, 269–71, 276, 285n13, 291n7, 301n25
Jarmusch, Jim, 284n6, 307n2
jazz aesthetics, in Cassavetes' work, 52, 62, 68, 84, 86, 128; *see also* Gillespie, Dizzy; Parker, Charlie

Kael, Pauline, 20, 45, 53, 82, 238, 304n9
Kateb, George, 150
Kauffmann, Stanley, 2, 20, 144
Kawin, Bruce, 271
Kazan, Elia
  East of Eden, 147, 148
  On the Waterfront, 147-8
  Wild River, 147
Keats, John, 177, 235
Killers, The (Siegel), 29
Killing of a Chinese Bookie, The (Cassavetes), 1, 19, 21, 28, 30, 32, 49, 53, 57, 79–80, 87, 98, 108, 117, 137, 139, 147, 149–50, 158, 162–3, 170–1, 179, 184–234, 236–9, 245, 254, 265, 269–70, 286n5, 288n11, 290n4, 294n8, 296n7, 297n12, 298nn29,31, 304n8, 305n11, 314–5
Kozol, Jonathan, 1
Kramer, Robert, 284n6, 307n2
Kramer, Stanley, 74, 75, 115
Kubrick, Stanley, 9, 14, 15, 18, 20, 51, 69, 88, 128, 168, 172, 203, 247, 268, 272, 273–6
  Dr. Strangelove, 203
  The Shining, 203
  2001, 6, 14, 15, 18, 63, 88, 103, 121–4, 127–8, 140, 165–6, 168, 172, 188, 203, 256, 265
Kuleshov, Lev, 14, 101

Lancaster, Burt, 289n19
Lang, Fritz, 14
Lawrence, D. H., 27, 72, 86, 143, 174–5, 184, 235, 299n4
Lee, Spike, 286nn4,5
Loden, Barbara, 147, 284n6, 307n2
Love Streams (Cassavetes), 21, 28, 32, 49,

53, 56–7, 79–80, 83, 87, 98, 114, 117,
131, 134, 136, 139, 147, 152, 162,
170, 179, 181, 186, 189–90, 196, 198,
208–10, 228–9, 235–70, 273, 277–80,
286n5, 288n11, 289nn19,2, 294n8,
296n10, 297nn22,27, 298nn29,31,
300n10, 301n22, 303nn30,31, 315
Lumet, Sydney, 144
  Bye Bye Braverman, 287n10
Lynch, David, 9, 14, 18, 20, 213, 251,
273–6, 287n6
  Blue Velvet, 6, 88, 272
  Twin Peaks, 15

McLuhan, Marshall, 2
McSorley, Edward, 297n23
Malick, Terrence, 14
Malkovich, John, 148
Maltese Falcon, The (Huston), 119, 120–1
Mankiewicz, Herman, 188
Mann, Delbert, 90
marginality, 32–4, 148–50
masks, 36–8, 49
May, Elaine, 147, 174, 307n2
Mazursky, Paul, 140, 144
  Tempest, 27
Mekas, Jonas, 38, 184
Melville, Herman, 117
mess, clutter, noise in Cassavetes' work, 16,
205–8, 232–3, 290n2
Method acting, 44–5, 50, 59, 71, 132–3,
147–9, 159, 295n6; *see also*
Stanislavski, Constantin
Minnie and Moskowitz (Cassavetes), 18, 21,
28, 32, 55–6, 80, 83, 87, 112–43, 155,
171, 174, 178–9, 183, 185, 211, 215,
227–9, 236, 239–40, 242–5, 251, 257,
265, 268, 269–70, 289n2, 290n4,
300n13, 302n29, 314
Moore, Marianne, 115
moral categories, inadequacy of, 50–1
Morrissey, Paul, 284n6, 307n2
MTV, 196, 200, 202, 230
multiculturalism, shortcomings of, 286n4
mystery and uncertainty, in Cassavetes'
work, 187–9, 293, 224–7; *see also*
establishing technique; vagueness

Nabokov, Vladimir, 198, 304n10
Newhart, Bob, 218
Nicholson, Jack, 94, 112, 133, 294n3
Now, Voyager (Rapper), 208, 285n15

Opening Night (Cassavetes), 1, 20–1, 28,
30, 36, 49, 53, 57, 79, 87, 131, 139,
159, 170, 179, 186, 190, 198, 205,
208, 226, 228, 231–2, 239, 240–5,
248, 254, 269–70, 277, 287n9,
288n11, 290n5, 296n7, 297nn12,27,
298nn30,31, 305nn11,15, 315
Outrageous! (Benner), 304n8
overlap of art and life, *see* art and life

Papamichael, Phedon, 296n7
paranoia, 73
Parker, Charlie, 46, 47, 68, 84, 193, 277,
280, 294n13
Pater, Walter, 231
pattern breaking, 59–62, 69–70, 114–15,
127–8, 133, 240, 254, 282
Perkins, Anthony, 101, 102, 103
perspectivism, 86–93, 189, 210–12, 290n5,
291n10
physicality, 166, 172–3, 201–5, 275–80;
see also bodies
Picasso, Pablo, 184, 188
Platonism, 81–2, 163, 188, 204, 212, 276,
277–8
Poe, Edgar Allan, 146, 304n10
point-of-view editing convention, 8–9, 15–
16, 77–8, 89
Poirier, Richard, x, 56
Polanski, Roman, 27, 158, 306n21
Pollack, Sydney, 144
  Tootsie, 146
Pollock, Jackson, 65, 231, 294n13
popular culture studies, fallacy of, 63,
288n18
postmodernism, 40, 200, 202, 287n6
Pound, Ezra, 164
Proust, Marcel, 162
Putnam, David, 140
puzzle-solving experience, 67–8, 190–1; *see
also* difficulty, of Cassavetes' work

race, indifference to in Cassavetes' work,
35, 286n5
Rappaport, Mark, 147
Ray, Nicholas, 123, 150
  Rebel Without a Cause, 45, 47, 120, 147,
148, 150
Ray, Tony, 43–5; *see also Shadows*
Renoir, Jean, 12, 93–4, 111, 206, 226,
284n6, 306n19
Ritt, Martin, 29, 144, 146
  Crime in the Streets, 29
  Norma Rae, 146
Rivette, Jacques, 226, 294n13
Roberts, Meade, 30, 191
Rockwell, Norman, 126
Rogosin, Lionel, 90
  On the Bowery, 287n10
Rossellini, Roberto, 90, 284n6, 301n25
  Voyage In Italy, 301n25

Rowlands, Gena, 75, 138, 144, 148, 150,
154, 157, 171, 175, 195, 227, 235,
243, 247, 253, 279, 283n4, 289n19,
294n5, 296n7; see also specific films
Ruban, Al, 75, 76, 137, 191, 223, 244,
283n4, 300n12

Sargent, John Singer, 53, 54, 57, 146, 182,
188, 286n4, 288n15
Sarris, Andrew, 192
Sautet, Claude, 284n6
Schrader, Paul, 140, 144
Scorsese, Martin, 77
Taxi Driver, 25
screwball comedy, 115–16, 293n2
sensory particularity, see physicality
selfhood, open and closed, 20–5, 54–6,
131–2, 176–83
Shadows (Cassavetes), 11–2, 20–1, 25, 27–
73, 75, 83, 87, 95, 104–8, 114, 116–
17, 131–4, 137, 139–40, 146–7, 170,
184, 196, 199, 226–7 239–42, 245–8,
268, 270, 297nn12,27, 298n31,
303nn31,37, 305nn11,17, 313
Shakespeare, William, 73, 83, 99, 113, 135,
182–3, 198, 240, 243–4, 255, 286n4
Shaw, Eddie, 31
Shaw, Jakob, 152
Shaw, Larry, ix, 305n13
Shaw, Meta, 275
Shaw, Sam, ix, 28, 296n7, 297n23, 299n8,
305n13
Sheen, Martin, 302n28
Shelly, Percy Bysshe, 95
Shepherd, Jean, 29, 32
Simon, John, 2, 20, 45, 53
Simon, Neil, 97, 98, 171, 209
"small feelings," 33–4, 61, 148–50
Some Like It Hot (Wilder), 208
Spielberg, Steven, 14, 188, 189, 197, 230
Stanislavski, Constantin, 295n6
An Actor Prepares, 132, 295n6
see also Method acting
Stevens, George, A Place in the Sun, 147,
148
Stevens, Wallace, 196
Stewart, Jimmy, 13, 101, 148
Stone, Oliver, 140
Strasberg, Lee, 132–3, 295n6
Streep, Meryl, 94, 133
Sturges, Preston, 127

Taylor, Paul, 287n7
Tennyson, Alfred Lord, 231
theatricality, as a form of freedom, 50–7,
98–100, 103–5, 150–8, 162–5, 226–8,
297n27, 316; see also art and life

theory, Cassavetes' resistance to, 214–15
Three Plays of Love and Hate (Cassavetes),
1
Tocqueville, Alexis de, 93
Too Late Blues (Cassavetes), 28, 55, 74,
114, 139, 147, 200, 228, 286n5,
298n31, 313

Universal Studios, 115, 294n3

vagueness, 215–16; see also mystery and
uncertainty
veiling, 36, 47–8, 70, 79–80, 124–7, 256–
7; see also establishing technique
Ventura, Michael, 305n13
voice, see differences, vocal
Voight, Jon, 148, 304n6
Von Sternberg, Josef, 14, 17, 51, 88,
155, 197, 198, 199, 229, 233, 272,
303n31
The Blue Angel, 88, 197, 294n8
The Saga of Anatahan, 6, 198
Von Stroheim, Erich, 155

Wagner, Richard, 302n28
Warhol, Andy, 287n6
Welles, Orson, 6, 9, 11–15, 17, 19, 23–4,
36, 51–2, 88, 100, 102, 171–2, 188–
90, 197, 203, 212, 229–31, 233, 268,
272–6, 284n10, 291n8, 297n26
Citizen Kane, 5–6, 9–15, 19, 23–4, 63,
66, 88, 102–3, 132, 165–6, 168, 172,
188, 190, 197, 203, 208, 229–31, 233,
254, 256, 265, 272, 284n7, 291n8,
294n8, 299n4
The Trial, 6, 11, 12, 36, 102
Wexler, Haskell, 76
Whitman, Walt, 91, 143, 162, 164, 177,
256
Woman Under the Influence, A
(Cassavetes), 21, 28, 30, 32, 36, 41,
45, 49–50, 53, 56–7, 80, 83, 94, 105,
131, 133, 134, 141–83, 185–6, 189–
90, 198, 200, 202, 206, 209–11, 226,
228, 236, 238, 241–9, 254, 265–6,
268–70, 277–9, 280, 286n5, 288n11,
290n4, 291n5, 299n10, 303nn30,37,
304n9, 305n11, 306n19, 314
Woolf, Virginia, 162, 231
work, effort, difficulty in Cassavetes' films,
210–14, 220, 228–9, 316
working methods, Cassavetes', 137, 150–8,
160–1, 187–8, 191–4, 245–9, 251–3,
271–81, 289, 290n2, 292n12, 296n8,
305n17

drawing on the personalities of his actors, 56–60, 132, 191–2, 287n7
photographs of, 30–1, 34, 39, 49, 69, 149, 153, 157, 160–1, 167, 169, 173, 180–1, 195, 203, 217, 225, 243, 246–7, 253, 274–5, 278–9, 312, 316

writing, shooting, and editing process, 119, 136–8, 187–8, 193–4
Wyler, William, 297n26
The Best Years of Our Lives, 146

Yeats, William Butler, 113, 230